CHRISTOLOGY, CONTROVERSY AND COMMUNITY

New Testament Essays in Honour of David R. Catchpole

EDITED BY

DAVID G. HORRELL

AND

CHRISTOPHER M. TUCKETT

TUTA SUB AEGIDE PALLAS · 1683 ·

BRILL
LEIDEN · BOSTON · KÖLN
2000

This book is printed on acid-free paper.

Library of Congress Cataloging-in-Publication Data

Christology, controversy, and community : New Testament essays in honour of David R. Catchpole / edited by David G. Horrell and Christopher M. Tuckett.
    p.   cm. — (Supplements to Novum Testamentum, ISSN 0167-9732 ; v. 99)
    Includes bibliographical references and indexes.
    ISBN 9004116796 (alk. paper)
    1. Catchpole, David R. 2. Jesus Christ—Person and offices—History of doctrines—Early church, ca. 30-600. 3. Jesus Christ—Person and offices—Biblical teaching. 4. Community—Biblical teaching. 5. Bible. N.T.—Criticism, interpretation, etc. I. Catchpole, David R. II. Horrell, David G. III. Tuckett, C.M. (Christopher Mark) IV. Series.

BT198.C445 2000
225.6—dc21
                                                                    00-044441
                                                                    CIP

Die Deutsche Bibliothek – CIP-Einheitsaufnahme

Christology, controversy and community : New Testament essays in honour of David R. Catchpole / ed. by David G. Horrell and Christopher M. Tuckett. – Leiden ; Boston; Köln : Brill, 2000
    (Supplements to Novum testamentum ; Vol. 99)
    ISBN 90–04–11679–6

ISSN   0167-9732
ISBN   90 04 116796

CHRISTOLOGY, CONTROVERSY AND COMMUNITY

SUPPLEMENTS TO
NOVUM TESTAMENTUM

VOLUME XCIX

TUTA SUB AEGIDE PALLAS · 1683 ·

Professor David Catchpole

CONTENTS

PREFACE

When we heard that David Catchpole planned to retire from his position as the St Luke's Foundation Professor of Theological Studies we immediately began to plan a *Festschrift* for him. Many of his colleagues in the field were more than willing to join in this venture to honour David—a warm tribute in itself to his qualities as scholar, teacher, administrator and friend. Others would have liked to contribute but were prevented by various circumstances from doing so. From any would-be contributors whom we have inadvertently overlooked, we ask forgiveness.

Right from the start we were clear that we wanted to give contributors the opportunity to write on a subject of their choice that would reflect their own research interests and approaches. We therefore hit upon a broad theme—or collection of themes—which would provide some coherence to the volume without unduly constraining the contributors. The essays therefore range across a wide diversity of topics and methods yet with some common threads running between them. Many of them explore the evidence, nature and consequences relating to various kinds of christological claim, whether by the historical Jesus, or in the Q tradition, in John, Paul, or the synoptics. Many of the essays, of course, interact directly with David Catchpole's own work, sometimes in agreement and support, sometimes critically. Many of them make fresh contributions to important debates, or develop new perspectives on New Testament texts. We trust that David Catchpole will enjoy these essays, and enjoy engaging with them, and that other New Testament scholars will find the collection worthy of their attention. We offer them to David as a token of esteem and affection—and look forward to hearing his (no doubt penetrating and perceptive) reactions to them.

Abbreviations throughout the volume follow the *JBL* conventions. Finally, David Horrell would like to thank Sally O'Shea, of the Department of Theology at Exeter, for her wisdom and help in regard to this project.

The Editors

CONTRIBUTORS

STEPHEN C. BARTON is Senior Lecturer in New Testament Studies, University of Durham

PEDER BORGEN is Emeritus Professor of New Testament, University of Trondheim

RICHARD A. BURRIDGE is Dean of King's College London

JAMES D.G. DUNN is Lightfoot Professor of Divinity, University of Durham

E. EARLE ELLIS is Emeritus Research Professor of Theology and Scholar in Residence, Southwestern Baptist Theological Seminary, Fort Worth, Texas

BIRGER GERHARDSSON is Emeritus Professor of Exegetical Theology, University of Lund

MICHAEL D. GOULDER is Emeritus Professor of Biblical Studies, University of Birmingham

MORNA D. HOOKER is Emerita Lady Margaret's Professor of Divinity, University of Cambridge, and an Emerita Fellow of Robinson College, Cambridge.

DAVID G. HORRELL is Lecturer in New Testament Studies, University of Exeter

MARINUS DE JONGE is Emeritus Professor of New Testament and Early Christian Literature, University of Leiden

JOHN S. KLOPPENBORG VERBIN is Professor of New Testament, University of St Michael's College, Toronto

ROBERT MORGAN is Reader in New Testament Theology, University of Oxford

JOHN PAINTER is Professor of Theology, St Mark's National Theological Centre, Charles Sturt University, Canberra

RONALD A. PIPER is Professor of Christian Origins and Principal of St Mary's College, University of St Andrews

PETER RICHARDSON is Professor Emeritus, University College and the Centre for the Study of Religion, University of Toronto

CHRISTOPHER ROWLAND is Dean Ireland's Professor of the Exegesis of Holy Scripture, University of Oxford

GRAHAM N. STANTON is Lady Margaret's Professor of Divinity, University of Cambridge

CHRISTOPHER M. TUCKETT is University Lecturer in New Testament Studies, University of Oxford

N.T. WRIGHT is Canon Theologian of Westminster Abbey, London

DAVID CATCHPOLE: A PROFILE

Graham N. Stanton

David Catchpole began New Testament research at Pembroke College, Cambridge in 1963 with an extremely impressive academic track record from The Queen's College, Oxford: double first class honours in Mathematics, followed by first class honours in Theology. At Pembroke he was following in the footsteps of another distinguished mathematician turned New Testament scholar, C.K. Barrett. When I first met David he was starting his third year of research under the late Dr Ernst Bammel. I was immediately impressed by his gentle manner and his sharp mind, and grateful for the warm welcome and assistance he gave to a naïve New Zealander starting out on the long lonely road which faces every newcomer to research in the humanities.

At first I was unaware that mathematics was David's first love. Eventually I realised that his training as a mathematician partly accounted for his mastery of the complexities of source criticism and of traditio-historical criticism of the synoptic gospels, and his uncanny ability to judge angles and distances on the croquet pitch. David was a model researcher: disciplined, well-organised, and ready to follow the evidence wherever it led.

David's Ph.D. thesis, "The Trial of Jesus in Jewish Historiography" was examined by the late Josef Blinzler, internationally renowned for his own work on this most difficult and sensitive of topics. The announcement that Josef Blinzler was to be one of the examiners of David's thesis sparked off tremors of anxiety among his fellow New Testament researchers. If Cambridge was willing to engage this great scholar as an external examiner, who would be called upon to examine our own much more modest efforts?

David took up his first teaching post at Clifton Theological College, Bristol while completing the final stages of his Ph.D. thesis. His three years there helping to prepare students for ministry were fulfilling. It is perhaps significant that in the final years of his career David has returned to church-related teaching responsibilities at Sarum College, Salisbury. David's teaching and research have never been divorced from the on-going life of the church.

David revised and extended considerably his Ph.D. thesis before
publishing it. The first two sentences of the Introduction succinctly
set out the scope of the published version. "This book is an attempt
to survey and analyse the distinctive views of Jewish scholars who
have written about the Trial of Jesus during the last two hundred
years. It also represents an effort to examine some of the many historical problems surrounding that trial" (p. xi). A thorough discussion of one of those two topics would have been a formidable
challenge for a young scholar, but to tackle both, and to show their
inter-relationship was an astonishing feat. It is hard to think of a
published version of a Ph.D. thesis which is as learned and which
discusses so many complex issues. This book is still well worth con-
sulting on a wide range of topics: for example, Jesus and the law,
Jesus and the zealots, the identity of the arrest party, the origin and
historical value of Luke 22:54–71, the relation of Jesus' trial to
Mishnaic legal procedures, and the question of Jewish freedom not
only to pass but also to execute death sentences.

Very few major studies of the trial of Jesus have appeared since
David's book. That this is in part a reflection of the quality of his
work is confirmed by the fact that David's *magnum opus* is cited regularly in articles on the topics with which it deals. The warm welcome given to David's book led rapidly to an invitation to write the
article on the trial of Jesus in the Supplementary Volume to the
Interpreter's Dictionary of the Bible (1976).

David has mentioned to me in conversation more than once that
he would now want to modify some of the arguments of his first
book. One would be surprised if further study and reflection had
not led to re-appraisal of certain points. Nonetheless, on re-reading
David's book I am impressed even more strongly by the sharpness
of its arguments and by its sensitivity to hermeneutical issues. Again
and again David shows that even the most rigorous historical critical
exegesis cannot be carried out in a vacuum: both Jewish and Christian
scholars work with history on their backs.

After three years at Bristol, David was appointed to a lectureship
in the Department of Religious Studies at the University of Lancaster.
Unlike most departments and faculties of Theology in British Universities, Lancaster offered courses in Christianity on an equal footing
with courses in other religions. David rapidly made his mark in a setting very different from Clifton Theological College. At the same time
he continued to take in-service training courses and study days for

Anglican clergy and laity over a wide area in the northwest of England, and to serve as a Reader (lay-preacher) in the Church of England.

David even found time to serve as the treasurer of the local tennis club. The Catchpole family must have been an impressive sight on the tennis court as they regularly played doubles as a family unit. According to David, his wife Ann (a very able tennis player) and his two daughters Helen and Kate all took pains not to expose his limitations as a tennis player! During the Lancaster years both David and Ann were heavily involved with the work of the local Samaritans, a highly respected charity which offers support to those engulfed by dark depression and contemplating suicide. In due course Ann became a qualified social worker, a career she has followed with distinction for many years.

During his time at Lancaster (1969–1984) David published several articles related to his work on the trial of Jesus, but then turned his attention to quite different issues. The Bibliography included at the end of this profile provides full details of his major publications. Several of David's articles from the late 1970s made a strong impact on scholarship. I shall refer briefly to three to which I have returned time and again. No doubt other specialists will have their own 'favourite' Catchpole articles.

The issues relating to the Apostolic Decree are as complex as those surrounding the trial of Jesus. David's important article on the Apostolic Decree (1977) shows the same rigour and skills so evident in his work on the trial. He argues that the issues at stake in the so-called incident at Antioch (Gal 2:11–14) are none other than the demands of the Decree: the emissaries who came from James to Antioch brought the Decree. "Far from being a gesture of conciliation, it was by intention and effect a move back from those ideas of Church and gospel which had been accepted at the conference as the basis of Gentile Christianity" (p. 443). Paul resisted, but he lost.

David's article on the parable of the sheep and the goats (Matt 25:31–46) is equally impressive. In this lengthy wide-ranging study David shows his formidable traditio-historical skills. He argues that the primary version of Matthew's discourse is closely related to the tradition underlying Mark 9:33–41. The discourse voices demand rather than consolation, just as Jesus had done in the background of Mark 9:37a, 41. My own copy of this article is heavily annotated: there are more indications of approval than of doubt! This study certainly deserves to be more widely known.

David's better-known study of the so-called triumphal entry (1984) dates from this period in his career, though its publication was long-delayed. I have often urged my students to study this article closely, for it raises major questions of method and sets out conclusions that invite further discussion. David argues that the "triumphal" entry and the Temple cleansing traditions have been welded together into a single whole under the combined influence of an already existing Jewish pattern and a post-Easter christological conviction. "In the Temple incident Jesus is seen as what he was before Easter, the prophet of the near kingdom. In the 'triumphal' entry Jesus is seen as what he later became, after Easter, the Davidic Messiah" (p. 334).

In 1977 David was appointed Assistant Secretary of Studiorum Novi Testamenti Societas (SNTS), the international learned society in his field. He held this post for five years, before serving for a further five years as Secretary. These major administrative responsibilities were carried out with universally admired efficiency—and with diplomatic skills when necessary. David was not one of the more talkative members of the Society's committee, but when he did contribute to discussion his views were always treated with the greatest respect. While holding these two posts David worked closely with many leading New Testament scholars from around the world. Several became close friends, most welcome visitors to David's Department for lectures and seminars, and in due course contributors to this volume!

In 1984 David took up his appointment to the Chair of Theological Studies and a year later the Headship of the Department at Exeter. This was a challenge few others would have been prepared to tackle. The Department at Exeter was very different from Lancaster: its courses were more traditional, and as a small department it was struggling to attract able students. Professorial Chairs in UK Universities are normally tenable until retirement, but the Chair at Exeter was supported by a trust fund and was tenable for only seven years in the first instance. On hearing the news of David's appointment his friends were delighted that his scholarly abilities and qualities of leadership had been recognized by the University of Exeter. However, we were somewhat anxious about the unusual limitation of the appointment to seven years. What would happen if the St Luke's Trust were to decide after seven years that there were other priorities for its funds, or that David was not the right person for the post? David made his mark so quickly and to such good effect that there was never the remotest possibility that his appointment would not be renewed.

David enjoyed the strong support of senior members in the University. At the time of David's appointment, Professor Ronald Atkinson, Head of the Department of Philosophy, was not at all certain that the small Department of Theology could survive, but was delighted when events proved him wrong. "What most impressed me as I came to know David were: the outstanding amiability and considerateness he showed to *everyone* he came into contact with; his complete integrity and conscientiousness; and his real effectiveness. Deservedly, he won the confidence of the then new Vice Chancellor, David Harrison."

Sir David Harrison gave David and the Department the strong support that was sorely needed. He writes as follows: "David was a very fine Head of Department. Had he not arrived when he did, I doubt whether Theological Studies would have survived. He was immensely hard-working, as was perhaps inevitable in a Department with few staff; the Departmental 'ship' was a happy one in my observation." Sir David also notes that David was a substantial contributor to teaching programmes in Continuing Education in the South West, which involved a considerable amount of travelling to support part-time students. "Altogether he was a splendid colleague and friend."

David developed close links with the Cathedral in Exeter and led a number of study days in the Chapter House. The former Dean, the Very Reverend Richard Eyre became a good friend. He notes that David made an enormously effective contribution in the diocese of Exeter through the course, "Theology Quest and Questions" for which David has lectured in various centres. "He laboured gigantically to bring the fruits of academic theology to the Church at large, and was profoundly respected as a superb teacher in that context. He really set people on fire for the New Testament."

David's colleagues at Exeter are equally fulsome in their appreciation of his gifts and leadership. They all stress his enormous contribution to every aspect of the Department as its Head, his skills as a teacher, and above all his commitment to his students. As an administrator, he was remarkably efficient and well-organised, blessed with a clarity of thought and sharpness of mind that enabled him to see the pros and cons of possible decisions, and to anticipate and evaluate the consequences. A colleague recalls that David was not afraid to delegate. "He expected us all to pull our weight and fulfil our responsibilities, but he himself carried a good deal of the day-to-day administration that enabled our Department to function smoothly. I am sure that some of my research time (and leisure time!) was, in effect, bought for me by the weekends David spent writing letters, minutes, prospectuses, course documents and so on."

Not all leading scholars are also gifted teachers. David has always had the happy knack of being able to inspire students from a wide variety of backgrounds. One of his students remarked recently that David was so brilliant it was a shame a few Bishops in the Church of England weren't more like him! A colleague enjoyed team teaching with him, but found that it was like being cross-examined in court by a leading lawyer; his summing up was invariably a masterly performance.

As a supervisor of research students David was a model, combining an ability to lead and guide with a sensitivity to stand back and let his students explore their own (sometimes slightly crazy) ideas. Drafts of work were read with meticulous care and annotated in minute detail in David's distinctive handwriting. The only slightly unnerving experience was to be gently encouraged by David to explore one topic, and after giving him a rather amateurish effort discover that he himself had already written a definitive study on the topic, but with typical modesty had failed to mention it!

What most impressed David's colleagues over many years was his commitment to his colleagues and his students, and his keen interest in their well-being. David's trade-mark was an open office door. By leaving his office door open whenever he was not occupied with someone, he made it clear that he was available to all. Hence he always seemed to know most about the particular difficulties or circumstances any colleague or student was facing.

David gave himself unstintingly to his Department, which certainly flourished under his leadership. It is one of the very few Departments of Theology or Religious Studies in the UK to grow numerically in recent decades, both in terms of staff and of student numbers. This achievement must have brought great satisfaction to David, though with characteristic modesty he rarely spoke about it.

Very occasionally colleagues would be surprised to discover that David had slipped away from the office to watch a cricket match. Cricket has been a long-standing interest shared with his wife Ann.

Sometimes David watches cricket with a friend or colleague. Conversation flows freely, for cricket allows plenty of time for relaxed discussion of traditio-historical problems.

Some of David's friends have wondered from time to time whether he might have written more major books had he not given priority to his varied teaching and administrative duties. This may be so. On the other hand, there's more on every page that David writes than in many an article or chapter written by others. As the Bibliography at the end of this profile confirms, there has been a steady stream of publications over the years. We can look forward to another major book, *Resurrection People: Studies in the Resurrection Narratives of the Gospels*, which will be published at about the same time at this *Festschrift*. This book is a much-expanded version of lectures given in Salisbury Cathedral in April and May 2000. It will contain the fruits of David's fascination over many years with the resurrection traditions in the Gospels, and with Resurrection theology. The chapters I have been privileged to read in advance show David's customary skill in disentangling layers of tradition, but more importantly, his own deep commitment to resurrection faith.

Resurrection People will complement David's other recent major book, *The Quest for Q* (1993) which is now cited regularly and discussed appreciatively by specialists on Q. *The Quest for Q* is the outcome of David's intense study of Q traditions over a long period. There is no doubt that it will stand the test of time, and be recognized as one of the most outstanding studies of Q in the twentieth century.

The opening 60 page chapter "Did Q Exist?" is a detailed exposition of two of the most compelling arguments for the existence of Q. David discusses briefly some general issues which have been prominent in recent discussion before mounting his own formidable defence of the Q hypothesis. No fewer than 16 directly related Matthew/Luke traditions are discussed in detail in order to show that where there is verbal variation, Luke has frequently preserved the original form. Once this is accepted, the proposal that Luke has used Matthew, and that Q did not therefore exist, is undermined.

A second argument is mounted in discussion of the same 16 passages: there is "some sort of space" between the theology of Q and the theology of Matthew. Hence a huge question mark is placed against the claim by Michael Goulder and others that Q and Matthew are source-critically indistinguishable because they are theologically indistinguishable.

The remaining chapters of the book examine meticulously many of the most important Q traditions. As always, David is courteous to those with whom he disagrees, but these chapters offer far more than a dialogue with the plethora of recent studies of Q, for they plough their own distinctive furrow through the complex issues involved. In some respects, David's views are unusual and challenge more "conventional" and/or fashionable theories on Q. For David, Q is known to Mark, its outlook is fundamentally determined by eschatological rather than sapiential categories. Q represents a Jewish Christian community anxious above all to retain its place within the broader Jewish community; and the much discussed possible "Cynic" outlook of Q is barely mentioned. Whatever one may think of individual parts of the package, the case is invariably argued with sustained and detailed study of the phenomena of the text. There is no doubt that David's arguments will have to be taken seriously long after the dust has settled on some current debates.

David's publications are notable for their careful attention to detail and their rigorous pursuit of the logic of the argument wherever it leads. In particular, they are characterised by a thorough-going commitment to traditio-historical analysis of the New Testament writings. While appreciative of synchronic or more "narrative" approaches, David has always maintained that a careful appreciation of the history and development of texts is crucial to their sensitive exegesis.

David's outstanding leadership of the Department at Exeter over a 12 year period from 1985 to 1997 has led to a lively, flourishing Department which enjoys a high reputation all over the UK. David continues to teach part-time at Exeter, alongside his teaching duties at Sarum College, Salisbury. This combination of University and church-related teaching has been a hall-mark of David's whole career. His friends hope that now that he has relinquished major administrative duties, he will have more time for research and writing—and for cricket!

MAJOR PUBLICATIONS OF DAVID CATCHPOLE

"The Problem of the Historicity of the Sanhedrin Trial", *The Trial of Jesus* FS C.F.D. Moule (ed. E. Bammel, London: SCM 1970) 47–65.

"The Answer of Jesus to Caiaphas (Matthew XXVI.64)", *NTS* 17 (1971) 223–6.

The Trial of Jesus. A Study in the Gospels and Jewish Historiography from 1770 to the Present Day. Studia Post-Biblica XVIII (Leiden: Brill, 1971) xiii + 324 pp.

"The Synoptic Divorce Material as a Traditio-historical Problem", *BJRL* 57 (1974) 92–127.

"The Trial of Jesus", *Interpreter's Dictionary of the Bible. Supplementary Volume* (Nashville TS: Abingdon, 1976) 917–9.

"Tradition History", *New Testament Interpretation*, ed. I.H. Marshall (Exeter: Paternoster, 1977) 165–80.

"The Fearful Silence of the Women at the Tomb. A Study in Markan Theology", *Journal of Theology for Southern Africa* 18 (1977) 3–10.

"The Son of Man's Search for Faith (Luke XVIII.8b)", *NovT* 19 (1977) 81–104.

"Paul, James and the Apostolic Decree", *NTS* 23 (1977) 428–44.

"John the Baptist, Jesus and the Parable of the Tares", *SJT* 31 (1978) 557–70.

"On Doing Violence to the Kingdom", *Journal of Theology for Southern Africa* 25 (1978) 50–61.

"The Poor on Earth and the Son of Man in Heaven. A Study of Matthew XXV. 31–46", *BJRL* 61 (1979) 355–97.

"The Sermon on the Mount in Today's World", *Theologia Evangelica* 14 (1981) 4–11.

"The Angelic Son of Man in Luke XII 8", *NovT* 24 (1982) 255–65.

"The ravens, the lilies and the Q hypothesis. A form-critical perspective on the source-critical problem", in A. Fuchs, ed., *Studien zum Neuen Testament und seiner Umwelt* 6–7 (1981–2) 77–87.

"Q and 'The Friend at Midnight' (Luke 11.5–8/9)", *JTS* 34 (1983) 407–24.

"Reproof and Reconciliation in the Q Community. A Study in the Tradition History of Mt 18, 15–17.21–2/Lk 17,3–4" in *Studien zum Neuen Testament und seiner Umwelt* 8 (1983) 79–90.

"The 'triumphal' Entry", *Jesus and the Politics of his Day*, ed. E. Bammel and C.F.D. Moule (Cambridge: CUP, 1984) 319–34.

"Jesus and the Community of Israel—the Inaugural Discourse in Q", *BJRL* 68 (1986) 296–316.

"The Law and the Prophets in Q", *Tradition and Interpretation in the New Testament* FS E.E. Ellis (ed. G.F. Hawthorne and O. Betz; Grand Rapids, Michigan: Eerdmans, 1987) 95–109.

"Q, Prayer and the Kingdom. A Rejoinder", *JTS* 40 (1989) 377–88.

"Beatitudes", *A Dictionary of Biblical Interpretation* (ed. R.J. Coggins and J.L. Houlden; London: SCM, 1990) 79–82.

"Temple Traditions in Q", *Templum Amicitiae. Essays on the Second Temple presented to E. Bammel* (ed. W. Horbury; Sheffield: Sheffield Academic Press, 1991) 305–29.

"Ein Schaf, eine Drachme und ein Israelit. Die Botschaft Jesu in Q", *Die Freude an Gott—unsere Kraft.* FS O. Knoch (ed. J.J. Degenhardt; Stuttgart: Katholisches Bibelwerk, 1991) 89–101.

"The Mission Charge in Q", *Early Christianity, Q and Jesus* (ed. J. Kloppenborg; Semeia 55; Atlanta: Scholars, 1992) 147–74.

"The Beginning of Q: A Proposal", *NTS* 38 (1992) 205–21.

"The Centurion's Faith and its Function in Q", *The Four Gospels 1992.* FS F. Neirynck (ed. F. Van Segbroeck *et al.*; Leuven: University Press, 1992) 517–40.

"The Question of Q", *Sewanee Theological Review* 36 (1992) 33–44.

"The Anointed One in Nazareth", *From Jesus to John. Essays on Jesus and New Testament Christology in Honour of Marinus de Jonge* (ed. M.C. de Boer; Sheffield: JSOT, 1993) 231–51.

The Quest for Q (Edinburgh: T&T Clark, 1993) xv + 344 pp.

"Mark", *Early Christian Thought in its Jewish Context.* FS M.D. Hooker (ed. J.M.G. Barclay and J.P.M. Sweet; Cambridge: CUP, 1996) 70–83.

"Q" in J.W. Bowker ed., *Oxford Companion to World Religions* (Oxford: OUP, 1997) 782.

"Form, Source and Redaction Criticism of the New Testament" in S.E. Porter, ed., *Handbook to Exegesis of the New Testament* (NTTS; Leiden: Brill, 1997) 167–88.

"The Beloved Disciple and Nathanael", in C. Fletcher-Louis and C.C. Rowland, eds., *Understanding, Studying and Reading. Essays in Honour of John Ashton* (Sheffield: Sheffield Academic Press, 1998) 69–92.

"The Role of the Historical Jesus in Jewish-Christian Dialogue" in Dan Cohn-Sherbok, ed., *The Future of Jewish-Christian Dialogue.* Toronto Studies in Theology 80 (Lampeter: Edwin Mellen, 1999) 183–216.

Resurrection People: Studies in the Resurrection Narratives of the Gospels (London: Darton Longman & Todd, 2000).

"ARE YOU THE MESSIAH?":
IS THE CRUX OF MARK 14.61-62 RESOLVABLE?

James D.G. Dunn

1. *Introduction*

By common consent, Mark 14:61–62 is one of the most important texts in the Gospels, particularly in any quest for Jesus' self-understanding and for the historical circumstances of Jesus' death. In it Jesus is asked by the High Priest whether he is "the Messiah, the Son of God". Jesus answers in the affirmative and then makes a prediction regarding the Son of Man sitting on God's right and coming on the clouds. The High Priest responds by charging him with blasphemy. In this one text, therefore, we find no less than three of the most important christological titles being used. Jesus seems to accept two of them (Messiah, Son of God), and a very plausible interpretation of the third (Son of Man) is that Jesus was also speaking of himself. Moreover, we have clearly indicated the reason why Jesus was rejected by the priestly authorities and why he was then handed over to the Roman authorities for execution. If all, or any, of this is historically accurate, or close to the events which led up to Jesus' execution, the consequences for Christian understanding of Jesus and of the reasons for his death are tremendous. If, alternatively, this is much elaborated or even wholly created tradition, then much as it tells us about early Christian belief regarding Jesus and the cause of his death, its value in answering important questions like, Who did Jesus think he was?, and Why was he executed?, becomes highly dubious if not worthless.

These of course are issues which David Catchpole addressed in his early studies,[1] which stimulated my own early interest in them.

---

[1] D.R. Catchpole, "'You have heard His Blasphemy'", *Tyndale House Bulletin* 16 (1965) 10–18; also "The Answer of Jesus to Caiaphas (Matt 26.64)", *NTS* 17 (1970–71) 213–26; "The Problem of the Historicity of the Sanhedrin Trial", in *The Trial of Jesus: Cambridge Studies in Honour of C.F.D. Moule* (ed. E. Bammel; SBT, 2nd series 13; London: SCM, 1970) 47–65; *The Trial of Jesus* (Studia Post-Biblica 18; Leiden: Brill, 1971).

Since then, much water has flowed under the Cambridge bridges
which we regularly traversed in each other's company back in the
'60s. And in the meantime the issues have been debated endlessly
and seem to have become ever more complex. The prospect of entering into the complexities of that debate in a single essay to any good
effect would seem to be bleak. Fortunately, however, scholarship at
the turn of the millennium has the benefit of Raymond Brown's
magnificent survey and ground-clearing *magnum opus*.[2] So comprehensive, magisterial and measured is it (as with all Brown's work)
that it raises the opposite question: whether there is anything more
needing to be said. Nevertheless, in my own judgment, less well
honed in this area of NT studies I freely admit, there do seem to
be two aspects in particular on which more can usefully be said,
and on these I will focus this essay: the High Priest's question as
the very understandable outcome of a particular line of questioning;
and the possible significance of merkabah mystical practice for understanding Jesus' answer and the ensuing verdict of blasphemy.

For convenience I will provide here both the Nestle-Aland Greek
text and the NRSV translation of Mark 14:55–64:

55 οἱ δὲ ἀρχιερεῖς καὶ ὅλον τὸ συνέδριον ἐζήτουν κατὰ τοῦ Ἰησοῦ μαρτυρίαν
εἰς τὸ θανατῶσαι αὐτόν, καὶ οὐχ ηὕρισκον· 56 πολλοὶ γὰρ ἐψευδομαρτύρουν
κατ᾽ αὐτοῦ, καὶ ἴσαι αἱ μαρτυρίαι οὐκ ἦσαν. 57 καί τινες ἀναστάντες ἐψευδομαρτύρουν κατ᾽ αὐτοῦ λέγοντες 58 ὅτι Ἡμεῖς ἠκούσαμεν αὐτοῦ λέγοντος
ὅτι Ἐγὼ καταλύσω τὸν ναὸν τοῦτον τὸν χειροποίητον καὶ διὰ τριῶν ἡμερῶν
ἄλλον ἀχειροποίητον οἰκοδομήσω. 59 καὶ οὐδὲ οὕτως ἴση ἦν ἡ μαρτυρία
αὐτῶν. 60 καὶ ἀναστὰς ὁ ἀρχιερεὺς εἰς μέσον ἐπηρώτησεν τὸν Ἰησοῦν λέγων,
Οὐκ ἀποκρίνῃ οὐδὲν τί οὗτοί σου καταμαρτυροῦσιν; 61 ὁ δὲ ἐσιώπα καὶ
οὐκ ἀπεκρίνατο οὐδέν. πάλιν ὁ ἀρχιερεὺς ἐπηρώτα αὐτὸν καὶ λέγει αὐτῷ, Σὺ
εἶ ὁ Χριστὸς ὁ υἱὸς τοῦ εὐλογητοῦ; 62 ὁ δὲ Ἰησοῦς εἶπεν, Ἐγώ εἰμι, καὶ
ὄψεσθε τὸν υἱὸν τοῦ ἀνθρώπου ἐκ δεξιῶν καθήμενον τῆς δυνάμεως καὶ
ἐρχόμενον μετὰ τῶν νεφελῶν τοῦ οὐρανοῦ. 63 ὁ δὲ ἀρ	ιερεὺς διαρρήξας τοὺς
χιτῶνας αὐτοῦ λέγει, Τί ἔτι χρείαν ἔχομεν μαρτύρων; 64 ἠκούσατε τῆς
βλασφημίας· τί ὑμῖν φαίνεται; οἱ δὲ πάντες κατέκριναν αὐτὸν ἔνοχον εἶναι
θανάτου.

55 Now the chief priests and the whole council were looking for testimony against Jesus to put him to death; but they found none. 56
For many gave false testimony against him, and their testimony did
not agree. 57 Some stood up and gave false testimony against him,

---

[2] R.E. Brown, *The Death of the Messiah: From Gethsemane to the Grave. A Commentary
on the Passion Narratives in the Four Gospels* (2 vols; New York: Doubleday, 1994).

saying, 58 "We heard him say, 'I will destroy this temple that is made with hands, and in three days I will build another, not made with hands'". 59 But even on this point their testimony did not agree. 60 Then the high priest stood up before them and asked Jesus, "Have you no answer? What is it that they testify against you?" 61 But he was silent and did not answer. Again the high priest asked him, "Are you the Messiah, the Son of the Blessed One?" 62 Jesus said, "I am; and 'you will see the Son of Man seated at the right hand of the Power', and 'coming with the clouds of heaven'". 63 Then the high priest tore his clothes and said, "Why do we still need witnesses? 64 You have heard his blasphemy! What is your decision?" All of them condemned him as deserving death.

2. *The Charge against Jesus*

We need not become involved in the old question of whether Mark 14:55–64 is the account of a proper trial before a properly convened body properly described as "the Sanhedrin". All that the account itself indicates is a hearing before an *ad hoc* council convened by Caiaphas to advise him.[3] To pursue questions of legality is therefore largely a waste of time, with so many probable anachronisms in play as to render the question itself almost meaningless. This is not to deny that some sort of legal process took place. The fact that Jesus was "handed over" is well rooted in the tradition. It is true that the term has been characteristically elaborated in terms of Judas as the "betrayer",[4] and theologised in terms of Jesus being "handed over" for our sins/us.[5] But the more basic technical sense of "handed over into the custody of" is still evident,[6] including the semitic construction, "delivered into the hand(s) of".[7] So there is a strong likelihood that behind Mark 14:55–64 lies the historical fact that Jesus was "handed over" to the Roman authorities as the outcome of a hearing before an *ad hoc* council convened by the High Priest Caiaphas.

---

[3] See particularly E.P. Sanders, *Judaism Practice and Belief 63 BCE–66 CE* (London: SCM/Philadelphia: TPI, 1992) 475–90; "The trial of Jesus agrees very well with his (Josephus') stories of how things happened" (p. 487).

[4] Mark 3:19/Matt 10:4/Luke 6:16; Mark 14:10–11, 18, 21, 42, 44/Matt 26:15–16, 21, 23, 24–25, 46, 48/Luke 22:4, 6, 21–22; Matt 27:3–4; Luke 22:48; 24:20.

[5] Rom 4:25; 8:32; Gal 2:20; Eph 5:2, 25.

[6] Mark 10:33/Matt 20:19/Luke 18:32; Mark 15:1, 10/Matt 27:2, 18; Mark 15:15/Matt 27:26/Luke 23:25; Matt 26:2; Luke 20:20; John 18:30, 35; Acts 3:13; cf. 1 Cor 11:23.

[7] Mark 9:31/Matt 17:22/Luke 9:44; Mark 14:41/Matt 26:45; Luke 24:7.

As to the account itself, there can be little doubt that Mark 14:55–59 is at best a partisan account of what happened. It is certainly likely that the first followers of Jesus were curious about what had transpired before Caiaphas's council. Some information may have been gleaned from one or two of those present—whether from attendants, or guards, or even a member of the council, and whether by direct information or through the popular account circulated in the market place and Temple courts is of less moment. But the record of the testimony against Jesus as "*false* testimony" (14:56–57, 59) is certainly a Christian slant on the proceedings.

This point is all the more significant, since the accusation against Jesus—that he had been heard to say, "I will destroy this temple (καταλύσω τὸν ναὸν τοῦτον) that is made with hands, and in three days I will build another, not made with hands"—has a substantial degree of plausibility. Jesus is recalled elsewhere as predicting the destruction of the Temple (Mark 13:2/Matt 24:2/Luke 21:6), a possibility which no one with any political sensitivity could easily discount.[8] And the tradition that Jesus was remembered as saying something about both its destruction and its restoration has surprisingly strong roots. Not only does the saying appear as the accusation against Jesus in the hearing before Caiaphas (Mark 14:58/Matt 26:61), to be echoed by the crowd later (Mark 15:29/Matt 27:39–40). But it also appears on Jesus' own lips in John 2:19: "Destroy this temple (λύσατε τὸν ναὸν τοῦτον) and in three days I will raise it up". And in Acts 6:14 it reappears in the testimony brought against Stephen: "We have heard him say that this man Jesus of Nazareth will destroy this place (καταλύσει τὸν τόπον τοῦτον) and will change the customs that Moses handed to us".

On the basis of this evidence, it has to be judged likely both that Jesus did in fact say something about the destruction of the Temple, and that reports of this saying constituted the principal and most effective testimony against him at the hearing before Caiaphas. That other testimony was offered is indicated by Mark and Matthew (Mark 14:55–56/Matt 26:59–60), but no indication is given of what it amounted to. And all the testimony against Jesus, including the testimony on his Temple saying, is branded by Mark and Matthew as

---

[8] C.A. Evans summarizes the various premonitions and prophecies of the destruction of the Temple in "Jesus and Predictions of the Destruction of the Herodian Temple", *Jesus and his Contemporaries: Comparative Studies* (Leiden: Brill, 1995) 367–80.

"false". Yet the fact that John had no hesitation in attributing more or less the same saying to Jesus himself (John 2:19) confirms the less explicit testimony of Mark 13:2, that Jesus did indeed say something politically sensitive about the Temple. Luke's omission of the whole sequence may indicate no more than another example of him wishing to delay important sayings and developments till his second volume.[9]

There could be several reasons why the first followers of Jesus regarded the testimony at the hearing as "false", including the form of wording used. (1) Matthew omits the very Greek antithesis χειρο-ποίητον/ἀχειροποίητον which thereby probably indicates Matthew's awareness that the antithesis had been added by Mark.[10] It is true that Stephen in his own critique of the Temple echoes the same anti-thesis (Acts 7:48), but that probably confirms the likelihood that in both cases the tradition of Jesus was being transposed into Hellenistic Jewish categories.[11] (2) Did Jesus claim that he himself would destroy the Temple (ἐγὼ καταλύσω)? The Acts 6:14 version also attributes the destruction to Jesus himself. But John 2:19 implies a destruction for which Jesus had no responsibility. (3) Was it the second half of the saying which proved embarrassing for Jesus' first followers? John may also indicate some embarrassment at this point, in that he imme-diately interprets the whole saying as a reference to Jesus' own body: "he was speaking of the temple of his body" (John 2:21). And in Acts 6:14 the second half of the saying has become, ". . . and will change the customs that Moses handed on to us". Consequently the reference to "three days" has also disappeared, though it should not be assumed at once that the time reference in the Markan version (διὰ τριῶν ἡμερῶν) is derived from the tradition of the empty tomb and first resurrection appearances, since it may constitute an impre-cise interval (as we would say, in two or three days, or even in a few days);[12] Matthew evidently felt it necessary to correct the simi-larly imprecise timing in the three passion predictions (μετὰ τρεῖς

---

[9] Cf. particularly Mark 7 with Acts 10; also Mark 6:17–29 with Acts 24:24–26, and Mark 4:12 with Acts 28:25–27.

[10] See further my "Matthew's Awareness of Markan Redaction", in *The Four Gospels 1992*, FS F. Neirynck (ed. F. Van Segbroeck et al.; Leuven: Leuven University & Peeters, 1992) 1349–59.

[11] Similarly Brown, *Death*, 439; though O. Betz, "Probleme des Prozesses Jesu", *ANRW* II.25.1, notes that ἀχειροποίητος is Aramaic (p. 631 n. 184) and draws atten-tion particularly to 4Q174/4QFlor 1:2–3, 6 (pp. 631–2).

[12] See e.g. C.F.D. Moule, *An Idiom-Book of New Testament Greek* (Cambridge: CUP, ²1959) 56.

ἡμέρας) to accord with the tradition of Jesus' resurrection "on the third day" (τῇ τρίτῃ ἡμέρῃ). Particularly interesting is the fact that none of those who deal with the tradition take the opportunity to refer Jesus' words to an alternative temple community, even though there was a precedent at Qumran (cf. 1QS 9:6; CD 3:12–4:12; 4QFlor 1:1–7), and even though there are some hints that the earliest Christian community regarded itself as the temple of God built upon important "pillars", or within which important "pillars" were incorporated (Gal 2:9; Rev 3:12).[13]

All this suggests that the first followers of Jesus felt it necessary to blunt what they regarded as an unacceptable interpretation by his unidentified accusers of a saying about the Temple which Jesus was widely remembered as actually articulating.[14]

This conclusion also accords well with other indications that it was primarily, if not exclusively the priestly party which took against Jesus and sought to have him removed.[15] And it also ties in well with the tradition usually known as "the cleansing of the Temple" (Mark 11:15–19). There is a wide consensus that Jesus did indeed engage in a symbolic act in the Temple, an act which could hardly have been understood by the priestly authorities as other than critical of the Temple in its present form or operation.[16] Here we need to bear in mind that the Temple was the principal focus for economic and political power as well as for religious power. An act seen as critically or prophetically subversive of the priestly power, upon which Israel's stability under Roman rule was thought to depend, would provide sufficient excuse for a policy of *real politique* to dictate Jesus' removal from the scene. Whether Jesus' saying about the Temple was uttered by him on that occasion (as in John 2) or not, it seems to have provided the excuse needed.

---

[13] J.D.G. Dunn, *The Partings of the Ways between Christianity and Judaism* (London: SCM/Philadelphia: TPI, 1991) 60. If some sort of reconstitution of Israel was at all in view, then Hos 6:2 could have supplied the three day reference.

[14] See further the full discussion in Brown, *Death*, 444–60.

[15] "Chief priests" (ἀρχιερεῖς) dominate the passion narrative; "Pharisees" hardly appear (details in Dunn, *Partings*, 51).

[16] In the debate about the significance of Jesus' act occasioned by E.P. Sanders, *Jesus and Judaism* (London: SCM, 1985) 61–71, see particularly R. Bauckham, "Jesus' Demonstration in the Temple", in *Law and Religion: Essays on the Place of the Law in Israel and Early Christianity* (ed. B. Lindars; Cambridge: James Clarke, 1988) 72–89; and C.A. Evans, "Jesus' Action in the Temple: Cleansing or Portent of Destruction?", *CBQ* 51 (1989) 237–70, reprinted in *Jesus and his Contemporaries: Comparative Studies* (Leiden: Brill, 1995) 319–44.

3. *The High Priest's Question*

The charge against Jesus was that he said he would both destroy the Temple and build it again "in three days". Whether this is an accurate report of something Jesus actually said, or was a tendentiously hostile interpretation of a less controversial saying, either way, the important point in the Markan/Matthean accounts is that the saying in the form reported (true or false) provides the occasion for the High Priest's questioning: "Have you no answer? What is it that they testify against you?" Jesus' refusal to answer then provokes the follow-up question, "Are you the Messiah, the Son of the Blessed One?" The implication is that having failed to entice Jesus to respond to the charge with an open question, Caiaphas then challenged Jesus with (one of) the obvious corollary/(ies) which followed from the charge. But what is the logic which links charge and corollary? Why should talk of destroying and building the Temple lead to the thought of Messiah and divine sonship? The issue is rarely posed, commentators usually being content to pass from verse to verse without examining the connection of thought.

An answer, however, has long been available in the Dead Sea Scrolls. One of the most fascinating of the fragmentary scrolls published early on was 4QFlorilegium (4Q174/4QFlor), what appears to be a collection of Hebrew Bible texts interpreted eschatologically and messianically, to give substance to the community's own eschatological expectations. Only one column has been sufficiently preserved to provide a coherent text. The first half of that column is in effect an exposition of 2 Sam 7:10–14, integrated with other texts, including Exod 15:17–18, and the column ends with what may have been the beginning of a linked exposition of Ps 2.

The relevance to our present inquiry is twofold. (1) 2 Sam 7:12–14 is interpreted messianically. The text is first quoted: "The Lord declares to you that he will build you a House. I will raise up your seed after you. I will establish the throne of his kingdom [for ever]. [I will be] his father and he shall be my son" (2 Sam 7:12–14). Then, in accordance with the normal Qumran *pesher* style, the text is interpreted: "He is the 'Branch of David' who shall arise with the Interpreter of the law [to rule] in Zion [at the end] of time".[17] Of

---

[17] For convenience I follow Vermes' translation, with the modification of indicating

particular interest here is the readiness to link together the concepts of son of David (the promise of 2 Sam 7:14 had its immediate reference to Solomon) and son of God ("I will be his father and he shall be my son"). The point would be strengthened if indeed the scroll proceeded to interpret Ps 2 in similar vein, since Ps 2 is widely recognized as an enthronement psalm, and includes Yahweh's affirmation to the new Davidic king: "You are my son; today I have begotten you" (2:7). Even if we can have no assurance on this last possibility, the point remains that Qumran had already by the time of Jesus linked the ideas of royal/Davidic messiahship and divine sonship.

(2) The 2 Sam 7:12–14 sequence also clearly established in the mind of the writer a connection between the building of the eschatological temple and this expected messianic figure. The preserved column 1 begins by citing 2 Sam 7:10, and interprets it thus: "This is the House which [he will build for them in the] last days, as it is written in the book of Moses, 'In the sanctuary which thy hands have established, O Lord, the Lord shall reign for ever and ever'" (Exod 15:17–18). Linked with the exposition of 2 Sam 7:12–14 a few lines later, the expectation seems to be clear: that the Davidic Messiah would fulfil the ancient promise to David and build the eschatological temple. The further publications of 11QTemple and several fragments describing the new Jerusalem (particularly 4Q554–555 and 5Q15) confirm the community's fascination with the prospect of a re-established Temple in the last days.

Otto Betz was the first to draw on 4QFlorilegium and to observe that it provided the explanatory link between Mark 14:58 and Mark 14:61.[18] Somewhat surprisingly, his essay attracted little attention. Even Raymond Brown does not refer to it in his exhaustive treatment of the passage,[19] possibly because he himself does not pursue the question of the linkage of thought between 14:58 and 14:61. But Betz's observation remains important: the Qumran treatment of 2 Sam. 7:12–14 indicates a very plausible explanation of why the charge

---

that the "Branch of David" was obviously a reference to (quotation of) the familiar and well established messianic expectation based on Isa 11:1 (Jer 23:5; 33:15; 4Q174/4QFlor 1:11; 4Q252/4QpGen[a] 5:3–4/Frag. 2:3–4).

[18] O. Betz, "Die Frage nach dem messianischen Bewusstsein Jesu", *NovT* 6 (1963) 24–37; also "Probleme", 625–8, 633–4.

[19] Though he does refer in his bibliography to Betz's "Probleme des Prozesses Jesu", *ANRW* II.25.1 (1982) 565–647.

that Jesus had claimed to build another Temple might well prompt the High Priest to ask his question, "Are you the Messiah, the Son of the Blessed?" The Qumran beliefs regarding the Temple would hardly be unknown to the Temple authorities.[20] And it would not be necessary for any particular link between Jesus and Qumran to have been in mind. All that would be necessary was the recognition that a claim had been imputed to Jesus which was probably eschatological in character and therefore echoed the sort of claim being made at Qumran. A natural question in follow up would be, "If you are claiming to build the eschatological Temple, are you therefore claiming to be the Davidic Messiah and son of God (in the terms provided by 2 Sam 7:12–14)?"[21]

Brown has pointed out that the phrase used in Mark 14:61, "the son of the Blessed" (ὁ υἱὸς τοῦ εὐλογητοῦ) is without precedent at the time of Jesus.[22] But since, in terms of the implied issue, the time of Jesus is not very different from the time of Mark, or from the time of the earlier shaping of the passion narrative into this form, the force of Brown's point may be weaker than at first appears. Whoever put the tradition into this form assumed that this was an appropriate phrase to attribute to the High Priest. If it was deemed so in the Diaspora of the 40s and 50s it may not be so far from the mark in the Jerusalem of the 30s. Here we have to be alert to the illogicality which historical critical analysis sometimes finds itself in, by asserting that a new development in form or concept cannot be recognized unless there is a precedent! How then, methodologically, can one recognize the historically new or unprecedented? In every developing tradition (whether the tradition of God-talk in Judaism or the Jesus-tradition) there are times when traditional forms are reformulated in a different (new) way or when those outside the tradition express it in (new) ways that the insiders might not (at first) recognize. The historical critical resolution of the phrase "the son of the Blessed" may therefore be the conclusion, "First time so formulated", rather than, "Historically without precedent and therefore anachronistic or simply inaccurate".

---

[20] The Damascus Document seems to envisage (Essene) communities more widely scattered through Israel and governed by judges (CD 9–14), but no doubt in communication with Qumran.

[21] Cf. also Zech 6:12–13—"the man whose name is the Branch . . . shall build the Temple of the Lord . . . and shall sit and rule upon his throne".

[22] Brown, *Death*, 469–70.

The more precise issue is whether the High Priest could/would have used such a phrase or not. But one could equally observe that to speak of God as "the Blessed" has no precedent within early Christian usage either, even though both traditions are familiar with benedictions uttered in praise of God.[23] Consequently, on the available evidence, it is just as difficult to see this as a Christian formulation as it is to see it as a Jewish-Christian formulation of the 50s or 60s as it is to see it as a High Priestly formulation of the 30s.[24] The resulting uncertainties and obscurities are therefore probably insufficient to call in question the conclusion which was emerging above: that the charge against Jesus of willing the destruction and (re)building of the Temple provoked the understandable question whether Jesus was also claiming to be Messiah and God's son (in terms of the expectations based on 2 Sam 7:14).

It is also worth noting that this is the only issue of substance which is reported in regard to the hearing before the council. We have already noted that other charges are left vague and unspecific (Mark 14:55–56). What we have, in fact, is at best a brief extract of what presumably was a much lengthier process. Presumably, also, whatever else was said, this (14:58–61) was the crucial and/or climactic phase. It was just this central and (in the event) decisive issue which we could expect to be reported (however unofficially) to and among Jesus' intimates[25] or to and through the market-place rumour mill. Despite the obvious difficulties for a historical judgment on this point, therefore, including the question of sources and their reliability, the plausibility of the sequence of such a charge prompting such a question remains surprisingly strong. Even in the absence of any better data we may be confident that Mark's account gives a fair impression of the climax to the hearing before Caiaphas's council.

---

[23] E.g. Gen 14:20; 1 Sam 25:32; Ps 41:13; in NT—Luke 1:68; Rom 1:25; 9:5; 2 Cor 1:3; 11:31; Eph 1:3; 1 Pet 1:3.

[24] C.A. Evans, "In What Sense 'Blasphemy'? Jesus before Caiaphas in Mark 14:61–64", *Jesus and his Contemporaries: Comparative Studies* (Leiden: Brill, 1995), argues that "the Blessed" is a forerunner of the later, expanded rabbinic expression, "the Holy One blessed be He" (p. 422).

[25] The tradition that Peter (and another disciple—John 18:15–16) was/(were) close at hand during the hearing is also strongly attested (all four Gospels).

4. *Jesus' Reply*

Mark gives Jesus' reply to the High Priest's question as follows: "I am; and 'you will see the Son of Man seated at the right hand of the Power', and 'coming with the clouds of heaven'"—ἐγώ εἰμι, καὶ ὄψεσθε τὸν υἱὸν τοῦ ἀνθρώπου ἐκ δεξιῶν καθήμενον τῆς δυνάμεως καὶ ἐρχόμενον μετὰ τῶν νεφελῶν τοῦ οὐρανοῦ. (Mark 14:62). NRSV puts quotation marks round two of the clauses in Jesus' answer, no doubt on the assumption that the text is quoting or at least deliberately echoing two passages of scripture. The first is Daniel's vision in Dan 7:13, "I saw one like a son of man coming with the clouds of heaven"—ἰδοὺ μετὰ τῶν νεφελῶν τοῦ οὐρανοῦ ὡς υἱὸς ἀνθρώπου ἐρχόμενος ἦν. The second is Ps 110:1 (LXX 109:1), "The Lord says to my lord, 'Sit at my right hand . . .'"—εἶπεν ὁ κύριος τῷ κυρίῳ μου κάθου ἐκ δεξιῶν μου.

Here too the problems go well beyond the scope of a single essay. For our purposes it is necessary to comment briefly on only six of them. (1) How should the ἐγὼ εἰμι be understood? (2) Whether Jesus could/would have used the phrase τὸν υἱὸν τοῦ ἀνθρώπου of his expectations for himself. (3) Similarly, could/would Jesus have drawn on Ps 110:1 to articulate his expectations? (4) Where did the reference to God as "the Power" (τῆς δυνάμεως) come from? (5) Why the sequence of "sitting" followed by "coming"? And (6) what does the ὄψεσθε signify?

(1) Mark's ἐγὼ εἰμι is singular in the replies offered by Jesus to the question of the High Priest and to the corresponding question of Pilate in the following Roman trial. In Matthew the reply to the High Priest is σὺ εἶπας (Matt 26:64), and in Luke it appears as ὑμεῖς λέγετε ὅτι ἐγὼ εἰμι (Luke 22:70). In the Roman trial Pilate's equivalent question is, "Are you the king of the Jews?" (Mark 15:2/Matt 27:11/Luke 23:3). In all three cases Jesus replies σὺ λέγεις. The predominant view in the Synoptics, therefore, is that Jesus gave an ambivalent answer, "You say so", meaning in effect, "That is your way of putting it". Mark's variation may be most simply explained by the fact that Mark did not wish to portray Jesus as seeming to dispute or even refuse the status of Messiah.[26] In so doing, Mark

---

[26] Some mss add "You say that" (συ ειπας οτι) a curious mixture of Matt 26:64 and Luke 22:70. It is just possible that they preserve the original text written by Mark: which scribe would change the positively confident "I am" for the much

would be responding to the tradition he received, in the same way
that Matthew responded to the equivalent ambivalence of Mark's
account of Jesus' response to Peter's confession that Jesus was Messiah
(cf. Matt 16:16–20 with Mark 8:29–30). In the event, however, the
more ambivalent replies ring more true to a situation where Jesus
probably did not wish to be identified with the popular expectation
of a royal Messiah as a military leader.[27] In other words, the ambivalence of Jesus' answer to both questions could be paraphrased as "It
depends what you mean by the term".

It also has to be remembered that when the first Christians went
on to confess Jesus as Messiah it was with a significance drawn from
his suffering and death, as illuminated by scriptures not previously
regarded as messianic.[28] That however would not have been the
High Priest's concept of the royal Messiah, and if it is indeed the
case that he put such a question to Jesus, a more ambivalent answer
is probably what we should have expected.

However, the issue is relatively unimportant, since clearly the
emphasis in Mark's account falls on the rest of Jesus' answer.

(2) In order to avoid becoming trapped in the Saragosa Sea of
the complex "Son of Man" issues, the question here can be reduced
to the following: Is it likely or unlikely that Jesus could have drawn
upon Daniel's vision to speak of his own expectations? Certainly it
must be judged highly probable that Jesus did in fact use the Aramaic
phrase *bar °nasa*; the entirely consistent Gospels tradition of a phrase
used exclusively by Jesus and hardly picked up anywhere else only
makes sense if it was a remembered characteristic of Jesus' own
speech.[29] And if he did so use the phrase, it would be hardly a great
innovation for him at some point to link his own speech usage with
the particular reference in Dan 7:13. Here the same point made
above (§3) about the illogicality of historical critical analysis also has
bearing: in this case in terms of a critical unwillingness to recognize

more ambivalent "You say that I am"? On the evidence, however, it must be judged
more probable that the weakly attested ms tradition is the result of conforming
Mark to the dominant tradition.
    [27] See further my "Messianic Ideas and their Influence on the Jesus of History",
in *The Messiah: Developments in Earliest Judaism and Christianity* (ed. J.H. Charlesworth;
Minneapolis: Fortress, 1992) 365–81.
    [28] E.g. Luke 24:25–27, 44–46; Acts 8:30–35; 17:3, 11; 1 Cor 15:3; 1 Pet 1:11.
    [29] The statistics remain compelling: the phrase occurs 86 times in the NT, 69 in
the Synoptics and 13 in John. Of the remaining four, three are OT quotations and
non-titular (Heb 2:6; Rev 1:13; 14:14), and only one clearly titular (Acts 7:56).

any innovation on the part of one (Jesus) to whom the Jesus tradition attributes considerable innovation in exposition of scripture (e.g. Mark 11:24–27; Matt 5:38–42).

A similar point can be made about Jesus' expectation for himself. Historical criticism finds itself, understandably, dubious about the historical value of any tradition which sounds like an early Christian confession of faith. More or less since the Enlightenment, the rule has been that the presence of dogma indicates the later perspective of Christian faith—again understandably, since the 19th century quest of the historical Jesus was so much dominated by the desire to "liberate" the real (historical) Jesus from the distorting and obscuring layers of later theology. But Jesus as "the Son of Man" hardly appears as a Christian dogma, outside Jesus' own use of the phrase "son of man" in the Gospels.[30] A more rational explanation, as Albert Schweitzer pointed out, in response to William Wrede's discovery of the "dogma" of the "messianic secret" as the shaping force of Mark's Gospel, is that any dogma at this point was the dogma of Jesus himself.[31]

Here we should draw in the acute observation of Eduard Schweizer:

> If Jesus did foresee suffering and rejection for himself and his disciples, then, of course, he saw it not as catastrophe but as a gateway to the glory of the coming kingdom. If he did call himself the Son of Man and connected the title (*sic*) with his lowly state on earth as well as the glory to come, then he must have expected something like his exaltation to the glory of God.[32]

Leaving aside Schweizer's own interpretation of Jesus' usage of the "son of man" phrase, the main observation is sound. Given the proverbial fate of prophets and of his immediate predecessor (John the Baptist), Jesus can hardly have ignored the likelihood that he would meet a similar fate. In which case, Schweizer is right: Jesus would not have thought of such an outcome as catastrophe and failure; in line with the tradition of the suffering righteous,[33] he would have expected vindication following such suffering and death.

---

[30] Only Acts 7:56 really counts; and that can hardly be counted as typical within earliest Christianity.

[31] A. Schweitzer, *The Quest of the Historical Jesus* (London: Black, 1910) 386, 390; in response to W. Wrede, *The Messianic Secret* (Cambridge: James Clarke, 1971).

[32] E. Schweizer, *Lordship and Discipleship* (London: SCM, 1960) 36.

[33] See further E. Schweizer, *Erniedrigung und Erhöhung bei Jesus und seinen Nachfolgern* (Zürich: Zwingli, ²1962) §§2–3; G.W.E. Nickelsburg, *Resurrection, Immortality and Eternal*

The fact is that the Dan 7:13–14 vision was a high point in the tradition of the suffering righteous and their vindication. If Jesus was indeed arraigned before Caiaphas's council, then any previous thought that he might escape death (cf. Mark 14:33–36) would have soon disappeared. In these circumstances Daniel's vision of one like a son of man exalted in heaven and interpreted in reference to the "saints of the Most High" in their vindication after terrible suffering (Dan 7:17–18, 21–27), would have provided a powerful solace and assurance for Jesus. We need not attempt to resolve the tricky question as to whether Jesus referred in this phrase ("the son of man") to himself or to another.[34] The text remains open on this issue. What the text does imply is that Jesus drew on this text to express his confidence that God would not abandon him and would vindicate him following the suffering and death which must have been looming ever more likely by the minute.

(3) The case of Ps 110:1 is more tricky, since the evidence runs in a direction quite opposite to that concerning the Son of Man. On the one hand, it is clear that Ps 110:1 was much used within early Christian reflection to make sense of what had happened to Jesus.[35] On the other hand, the indication that earlier in his ministry Jesus took Ps 110:1 as some kind of self-reference is about as isolated within the Synoptic tradition (Mark 12:36 pars) as Acts 7:56 is within early (post-Easter) Christology. The predominant opinion among scholars, therefore, is to follow Norman Perrin's argument that Mark 14:62 is a Christian "pesher" (interpretation), the result of early Christian reflection on the death and resurrection of Jesus, drawing on Dan 7:13 and Ps 110:1.[36] The question would then be whether the probable post-Easter origin for the Ps 110:1 allusion necessarily implies that the whole formulation is post-Easter, or whether the saying could be explained along the lines of the Ps 110:1

Life in Intertestamental Judaism (Harvard Theological Studies 26; 1972), particularly ch. 2.

[34] The two chief options respectively canvassed by English- and German-speaking scholarship through the 20th century.

[35] Acts 2:34–35; Rom 8:34; 1 Cor 15:25; Eph 1:20; Col 3:1; Heb 1:3, 13; 8:1; 10:12–13; 12:2; 1 Pet 3:22.

[36] N. Perrin, "Mark 14:62: The End Product of a Christian Pesher Tradition?", *NTS* 12 (1965–66) 150–5, reprinted in *A Modern Pilgrimage in New Testament Christology* (Philadelphia: Fortress, 1974) 10–18. Perrin also argued that the ὄψεσθε of the Markan/Matthean form of the tradition was derived from Zech 12:10.

allusion being inserted into a report which derived originally from a remembrance of something said by Jesus himself.

(4) Where did the reference to God as "the Power" (τῆς δυνάμεως) come from? Here the case is similar to that concerning "the Blessed" in 14:61. Brown similarly notes that the absolute use of "the Power" in the Mark/Matthew version has no true contemporary parallel.[37] But as with God as "the Blessed", so here with God as "the Power", it is necessary to point out that the lack of parallel includes the rest of earliest Christian writing: "the Power" is neither a Jewish nor a Christian way of speaking about God. Where then does the phrase come from? The same considerations apply as in regard to the High Priest's question. Mark 14:62/Matt 26:64 themselves constitute evidence for this way of speaking about God within the first century CE. Someone within the eastern seaboard of the Mediterranean first spoke of God as "the Power", and already within forty years of Jesus' death at the latest. How did it get into the text here? No answer is wholly satisfactory. But they boil down to three options: either it is a Philonic-type Christian innovation put into the tradition at this point for some unknown reason, or an early rabbinic formulation taken over by early Christian tradents, or it was indeed an innovative formulation used by Jesus himself on the basis of the common recognition that power was a primary attribute of God. On the evidence available, there is little to choose between these options.

That the phrase appears as part of the allusion to Ps 110:1 complicates the issue. It could have been suggested by the double reference to God's power in the next two verses of the Psalm (LXX).[38] But the evidence referred to under (3) suggests that the whole allusion was early Christian in origin. So possibly that tips the case in favour of the view that the reference to God as "the Power" was itself part of the early Jewish-Christian shaping of the tradition—though the question, "Why was it so shaped?" remains as puzzling as the question, "Would/could Jesus have so spoken of God?"

(5) The sequence of "sitting" followed by "coming" is also a puzzle. The more natural sequence, one would think, is the reverse: the Son

---

[37] Brown, *Death*, 496; Evans, "In What Sense?", 422, provides parallels in later rabbinic usage.

[38] "The Lord sends forth your mighty sceptre (ῥάβδον δυνάμεώς σου); LXX is quite different for verse 3 (μετὰ σοῦ ἡ ἀρχὴ ἐν ἡμέρᾳ τῆς δυνάμεώς σου . . .) (Ps 110:2–3/LXX 109:2–3).

of Man comes on the clouds (to God) and then sits on his right.
This is certainly the picture implied by Daniel's own vision: coming
to the Ancient of Days, presented to him, and given dominion, glory
and kingship (Dan 7:13–14). And it was how the vision was subsequently interpreted within Judaism.[39] Indeed, the logic of the double vision of Dan 7:9–10 and 13–14 is that the man-like figure was
given the other throne beside the Ancient One (7:9 speaks of plural
"thrones").[40] The text of Mark 14:62/Matt 26:64, however, seems
to envisage an enthronement of the Son of Man (à la Ps 110:1), followed by his coming with the clouds. It is hard to escape the inference that what was in view in this form of the tradition was the
coming *again* of Jesus *to earth*, rather than to heaven.[41] Since Jesus'
coming again/parousia was an early Christian expectation,[42] though
probably drawing on Jesus tradition,[43] the obvious inference is that
the Mark 14:62 demonstrates early Christian influence.[44]

Taken together with (3) and (4) the most obvious solution would
appear to be that the Ps 110:1 allusion has been inserted into an
older tradition which spoke only of the Son of Man coming on the
clouds, that is to God. An interesting alternative is provided by Luke,
whose version has only the Son of Man (à la Dan 7:13) sitting on
the right hand of the Power of God (à la Ps 110:1), without any
mention of coming on clouds. Is this evidence of an independent
source for Luke,[45] a source without the problems just discussed (4
and 5), or evidence that Luke (or his source) was aware of the problems posed by the Markan version?[46] Either way, the problem of Ps

---

[39] Daniel's vision is taken up in *1 Enoch* 46:1–6 and 4 Ezra 13:1–4 and interpreted in the following chapters/verses in terms of judgment, though the imagery
is more complex.
[40] According to rabbinic tradition, rabbi Akiba speculated that the occupant of
the second throne was the Messiah (*b. Hag.* 14a; *b. Sanh.* 38b).
[41] Cf. Mark 13:26/Matt 24:30–31/Luke 21:27; Matt 25:31.
[42] 1 Cor 15:23; 1 Thess 2:19; 3:13; 4:15; 5:23; 2 Thess 2:1, 8; Jas 5:7–8; 1 John
2:28.
[43] Cf. the several parables in Mark 13:34–36 and Matt 24:42–25:30.
[44] Evans, however, argues that if the throne was conceived as the *chariot* throne
(see below §5), then the "coming" could indeed follow the "sitting", since the chariot throne was moving; he also notes that Dan 7 and Ps 110:1 are combined in
the Midrash on Ps 2:9 in that sequence ("In What Sense?", 419–20). However, he
produces no parallel to the idea of the chariot throne "coming with the clouds".
[45] An issue closely discussed by Catchpole in his *Trial*.
[46] But the concept of "sitting on the right of the power of God" is as problematic as the concept of God as "the Power".

110:1 (3) remains: on these issues Luke provides no surer way into what Jesus may have said at the hearing before Caiaphas than the Markan/Matthean version.

(6) Why the ὄψεσθε? Perrin explained its presence here as a pesher using Zech 12:10 and Dan 7:13, then conflated with Ps 110:1. Zech 12:10, ". . . when they look on the one whom they have pierced, they shall mourn for him . . ." (LXX—ἐπιβλέψονται πρός με ἀνθ᾽ ὧν κατωρχήσαντο καὶ κόψονται ἐπ᾽ αὐτὸν κοπετὸν), was almost certainly a factor in earliest Christian reflection regarding Jesus' death: it is cited in John 19:37 and used in combination with Dan 7:13 in Rev 1:7, in the way that Perrin suggested.[47] Whether the single word, ὄψεσθε, in the Markan/Matthean (not Lukan) version of Jesus' words is sufficient to demonstrate the allusion to Zech 12:10 is less clear, but Perrin's thesis is certainly plausible. Even so, the form of the tradition at this point required it to be formulated as a second person address ("you will see"), rather than Zech 12:10's "they shall see".

So the question still stands: to what "seeing" does the saying refer? John 19:37 refers it simply to the witnessing of the crucifixion itself. But Rev 1:7 seems to envisage a universal epiphany of Christ's coming in eschatological glory and final judgment. Mark 14:62 is much more in tune with the latter. Is this, then, another indication of Christian formulation of an expectation developed in connection with the hope of Jesus' parousia? Or would a thesis that Jesus himself could have said something in this vein therefore imply that Jesus expected not just vindication following death, but a public vindication, his own epiphany in heavenly glory? That would certainly go beyond a hope built primarily on Dan 7:13 itself. But it would have the support of Mark 13:26—"They will see the Son of Man coming in clouds . . ." (ὄψονται τὸν υἱὸν τοῦ ἀνθρώπου ἐρχόμενον ἐν νεφέλαις). The historical critical choice, therefore, is: to conclude either that Jesus was remembered as speaking of the son of man coming in clouds as a visible event, seen by those on earth; or that the ὄψεσθε is a further post-Easter reformulation of an original expectation framed solely in terms of Dan 7:13. And the overall conclusion has to be much the same: either that the saying as a whole attests an expectation of visible vindication beyond anything else within the Jesus

---

[47] John 19:37 and Rev 1:7 show that the form of Zech 12:10 (Greek) known in earliest Christian circles used the uncompounded ὄψονται; the further use of κόψονται in Rev 1:7 puts the reference to Zech 12:10 beyond dispute.

tradition; or that an expectation of vindication expressed in terms of Dan 7:13 was elaborated at a very early stage of Christian tradition by adding allusions to Ps 110:1 and Zech 12:10, thus transforming the hope of vindication into one also of parousia. If the final issue is the plausibility of (an) unofficial report(s) of Jesus responding to the High Priest in some terms expressing his hope in God, the latter alternative, with its single allusion to Dan 7:13, would seem to be stronger than the former, with its complex allusion to three different scriptures.

5. *The Verdict of Blasphemy*

According to Mark 14:63–64, Jesus' reply provokes the High Priest to find Jesus guilty of blasphemy, and therefore deserving of death: "Then the high priest tore his clothes and said, 'Why do we still need witnesses? You have heard his blasphemy! What is your decision?' All of them condemned him as deserving death" (ὁ δὲ ἀρχιερεὺς διαρρήξας τοὺς χιτῶνας αὐτοῦ λέγει, Τί ἔτι χρείαν ἔχομεν μαρτύρων; ἠκούσατε τῆς βλασφημίας· τί ὑμῖν φαίνεται; οἱ πάντες κατέκριναν αὐτὸν ἔνοχον εἶναι θανάτου). This has created puzzlement similar to that caused by talk of God as "the Blessed" and "the Power". For on a strict definition of "blasphemy" it is very doubtful whether there is any blasphemous content, even in the full answer of Mark 14:62. "Blasphemy" strictly speaking referred only to naming the name of Yahweh (Lev 24:16 LXX; *m. Sanh.* 7:5), and even "Son of the Blessed" does not fall under that definition.[48] How, then, could the High Priest have condemned Jesus for blasphemy?

Once again, however, the same point has to be pressed. Whether it was in the 30s, or in the 50s or 60s, someone believed that what Jesus (is reported to have) said would have been counted as blasphemy by the High Priest of the time. This must indicate either a Christian misunderstanding of what was quite a technical matter of Jewish law, or that Christian belief regarding Jesus soon became so unacceptable to Jewish belief in God that it was counted blasphemous in at least some Jewish quarters, or that Jesus' own hope of vindication (§4) was regarded as sufficiently threatening to traditional

---

[48] See Brown, *Death*, 521–22; *pace* J. Marcus, "Mark 14:61: 'Are You the Messiah-Son-of-God?'", *NovT* 31 (1989) 125–41.

understanding of God's purpose for Israel that it could be condemned as "blasphemous". Bound up with these options, of course, is the further question of whether the term "blasphemy" could/would only have been used in a strictly legal sense, or could/would have been used in a looser sense (of any serious threat to a Israel's conviction regarding Israel's God), or whether a rhetorical/exaggerated/polemical/politically-motivated-and-theologically-tendentious usage would have been recognized/acceptable within the Israel of Jesus' day.[49]

This is where the possible influence of merkabah mysticism at some stage of the traditioning process becomes relevant. We know that a mystical practice based on meditation on the great chariot (merkabah) chapter of Ezek 1 was already being practised in the Israel of Jesus' day. There are already hints to that effect in Sir 49:8 and *1 Enoch* 14:18–20. The Qumran Songs of the Sabbath Sacrifice imply something to the same effect being practised in the worship of Qumran. Paul himself may have been a practitioner of such mysticism (2 Cor 12:2–4).[50] The great rabbi Yohannan ben Zakkai, founder of the rabbinic school at Yavneh following the disaster of 70, is also attested to have been a practitioner (*t. Hag.* 2:1). In all cases the aim was to experience the reality of heaven and the presence of God immediately, the Jewish equivalent of the later Christian desire for "the vision of God".

Most interesting of all is the rabbinic tradition that four practitioners early in the second century shared a mystical experience in which they entered paradise (*t. Hag.* 2:3–4; cf. 2 Cor 12:2–4). One of them was rabbi Akiba, and it is likely that his reported speculation about the occupant of the other throne (of Dan 7:9) had the same mystical or speculative root.[51] Another was Elisha ben Abuyah, who is reported to have been so overwhelmed by the vision of a glorious being other than God, that he cried out, "There are indeed two powers in heaven". For this, Elisha is condemned in rabbinic tradition as the arch-heretic, because he denied the Jewish axiom of the unity/oneness of God (*b. Hag.* 15a; *3 Enoch* 16).

Some scholars have recently drawn attention to this tradition and

---

[49] See again Brown, *Death*, 522–6; also Evans, "In What Sense?", 409–11.
[50] J.W. Bowker, "'Merkabah' Visions and the Visions of Paul", *JSS* 16 (1971) 157–73. See also A.F. Segal, *Paul the Convert: The Apostolate and Apostasy of Saul the Pharisee* (New Haven: Yale University Press, 1990).
[51] See above n. 10.

asked whether it provides an explanation for the High Priest's charge of blasphemy.[52] It is true that the term "blasphemy" does not occur in connection with Elisha. But it would not take much loosening of the definition of "blasphemy" for the term to be regarded as wholly appropriate to Elisha's case. The issue would then be whether Jesus' reply could/would have been regarded as in effect a claim to the other throne in heaven, and therefore as some kind of threat to the divine majesty, and therefore as "blasphemous" in a looser sense of the term. Certainly that seems to be the logic of the sequence in Mark 14:62–64; the tradition assumed that Jesus' reply would/could have been regarded as blasphemous by the High Priest of the day.

Here the same sort of questions arise as with the earlier verses. Was it only the later Christian claims for Jesus which would have triggered such a response by the Jewish authorities at the time the tradition was first formulated in these terms? Or could Jesus' own hope of vindication, expressed by reference to Dan 7:13, have been sufficient to trigger such a condemnation? The problem with the former alternative is, once again, that the situation in late Second Temple Judaism was, so far as we can tell, little different between the 30s and the 60s. We have a surprising lack of indication that the Christian claims for Jesus as exalted created any problems for Jewish monotheism in that period. The law was a problem. A crucified Messiah was a problem (1 Cor 1:23). But belief in an exalted Christ and Lord could evidently be expressed in terms consistent with Jewish monotheism (as in 1 Cor 8:6) so as to create no problem.[53] The point is this: according to the available evidence, Jesus' reply as formulated in Mark 14:62 was little more likely to provoke the condemnation of "blasphemy" at the time when the Markan tradition received its enduring form, than was a reply by Jesus formulated in terms of Dan 7:13 in his own time.

[52] J. Schaberg, "Mark 14:62: Early Christian Merkabah Imagery?", in *Apocalyptic and the New Testament*, J.L. Martyn FS, ed. J. Marcus & M.L. Soards (JSNTSup 24; Sheffield: JSOT, 1989) 69–94; Evans, "In What Sense?", 419–21; and particularly D.L. Bock, "Key Jewish Texts on Blasphemy and Exaltation and the Jewish Examination of Jesus", *SBL Seminar Papers 1997* (Atlanta: Scholars, 1997) 115–60; idem, *Blasphemy and Exaltation in Judaism and the Final Examination of Jesus* (WUNT 2.106; Tübingen: Mohr-Siebeck, 1998).

[53] See further my "How Controversial was Paul's Christology?", in *From Jesus to John: New Testament Christologies in Current Perspective*, FS M. de Jonge (ed. M.C. de Boer; Sheffield: JSOT, 1993) 148–67; reprinted in my *The Christ and the Spirit: Vol. 1. Christology* (Grand Rapids: Eerdmans, 1998) 212–28.

In addition, we have to consider the political situation at this final stage of Jesus' career. There is little doubt that Jesus was executed by the Roman authorities as a messianic pretender. The *titulus* on the cross ("The King of the Jews"—Mark 15:26/Matt 27:37)[54] is hardly a Christian formulation, and would still less have been approved by the Jewish authorities. Nevertheless, the implication that Jesus was denounced to the Roman governor in these terms is very strong. At the same time, it should be appreciated that for the Jewish authorities, the question of Jesus' messiahship was in fact a less serious issue. Moreover, for them to denounce to Pilate one who was a credible claimant to royal messianic status would even have been dangerous for themselves, in terms of the support they might expect from their fellow Jews. In which case, if the priestly authorities were determined to rid themselves of Jesus, for whatever real reason, the easiest way to do that was to denounce him to Pilate as a threat to the political stability of the province: a pretender to royal power (Messiah, in Jewish terms) was the obvious category to use.[55] But for "home" consumption, to present Jesus as a threat to Israel's fundamental beliefs about God would serve much more effectively to ensure the support of the crowd.

In other words, *real politique* cynicism was probably evident at every stage of Jesus' downfall. It was important that the High Priest could report to Pilate a proven charge that Jesus laid claim to royal messiahship. But it was equally important that the High Priest was able to defend his council's action to his own people as finding Jesus' claims for himself a threat to Israel's foundational belief in God. From which it follows, of course, that reports of what happened before the council may have been deliberately spread around Jerusalem to ensure the people's support for the action. Finally, the notice over the cross ("The King of the Jews") was probably Pilate's own cynical attempt in turn to "rub the High Priest's nose" in his own political deviousness.

---

[54] The variations in Luke 23:28 and John 19:19 are insignificant.
[55] Does Luke 23:2 simply spell out what was implicit but obvious in Mark's account?

6. *Conclusion*

Where then does all this leave us in historical terms? On the basis of the above analysis, the most likely reconstruction of the scene reported in Mark 14:55–64 would include the following. (1) A Jesus who said something about destroying and building again the Temple. Whatever he said, it evidently was taken as a threat to the power of the Temple authorities, not least in the light of his symbolically acted-out criticism of the present Temple. The saying provided the occasion for his denunciation before a quasi-legal council convened by the High Priest, Caiaphas. (2) A question/charge put to Jesus by the High Priest, as the direct corollary to a claim about rebuilding the Temple: "Are you the (royal) Messiah, son of God/the Blessed?" The corollary was clear enough; so, apart from an outright denial by Jesus, whatever he said in response would provide sufficient grounds for him to be "handed over" to the Roman authorities as a political threat to the stability of Roman rule. (3) An answer by Jesus in which he appears to have expressed his confidence that, whatever was to happen to him following the council hearing, he would be vindicated by God, as the "one like a son of man" (the saints of the Most High) was/were vindicated in Daniel's vision. (4) A condemnation by the High Priest which used Jesus' reply as an excuse to brand him as not just a threat to Roman rule, but, more seriously, as a threat to Judaism's core belief in the God of Israel as one and alone God. In short, there is a good deal more to be said for the historical value of the tradition on which Mark drew in his narrative 14:55–64 than is usually recognized within critical scholarship. That this conclusion accords as closely as it does with David Catchpole's own early conclusions is an added and delightful bonus.

IS THERE A NEW PARADIGM?

John S. Kloppenborg Verbin

One of the persistent criticisms of the current state of Synoptic scholarship by both William Farmer and Michael Goulder is that the
fundamental issue of the Synoptic Problem is often treated as if H.J.
Holtzmann or B.H. Streeter had solved it definitively. The criticism
is perhaps most justified when applied to scholarship in Germany,
where the Two Document hypothesis (2DH) or minor variations of
it are still overwhelmingly accepted and correspondingly little discussion of other options occurs.[1] In both North America and the
United Kingdom, however, the criticism is less than fair: In North
America there has been a lively debate of the Griesbach (or Two

---

[1] See, however, the detailed account of the current state of synoptic problem
scholarship by W. Schmithals, *Einleitung in die drei ersten Evangelien* (Berlin: de Gruyter,
1985) 44–233. There has been an active discussion by German and Swiss scholars
of the "minor agreements" (G. Strecker, ed., *Minor Agreements: Symposium Göttingen
1991* [GTA 50; Göttingen: Vandenhoeck & Ruprecht, 1993]) and various modifications
of the 2DH, including: (a) subsidiary influence of Matthew upon Luke, without
eliminating the need for Q (R. Morgenthaler, *Statistische Synopse* [Zürich and Stuttgart:
Gotthelf, 1971] 303–5); (b) the positing of a deutero-Markus in order to account
for certain minor agreements (A. Fuchs, "Die Behandlung der Mt/Lk Überein-
stimmungen gegen Mk durch S. McLoughlin und ihre Bedeutung für die synop-
tische Frage: Probleme der Forschung", *SNTU/A* 3 (1978) 24–57; "Das Elend mit
der Zweiquellentheorie: Eine Auseinandersetzung mit zwei neuern Dissertationen
zum Thema der minor agreements", *SNTU/A* 18 (1993) 183–243; "Zum Umfang
von Q: Anfragen an eine neue Arbeit zur Logienquelle", *SNTU/A* 21 (1996) 188–210;
H. Aichinger, "Quellenkritische Untersuchung der Perikope vom Ährenraufen am
Sabbat Mk 2,23–28 par Mt 12,1–8 par Lk 6,1–5", *SNTU/A* 1 [1976] 110–53;
C. Niemand, *Studien zu den Minor Agreements der synoptischen Verklärungsperikopen* [EHS.T
352; Frankfurt, Bern and New York: Lang, 1989]; A. Ennulat, *Die "Minor Agreements":
Untersuchung zu einer offenen Frage des synoptischen Problems* [WUNT 2/62; Tübingen:
J.C.B. Mohr [Paul Siebeck], 1994]); and (c) the positing of recensions of Q
(D. Kosch, "Q: Rekonstruktion und Interpretation: Eine methonkritische Hinfüh-
rung mit einem Exkurs zur Q-Vorlage des Lk", *FZPT* 36 [1989] 409–25).
The most serious recent dissent from the Two Document hypothesis is offered
by H.-H. Stoldt (*Geschichte und Kritik der Markus-hypothese* [Göttingen: Vandenhoeck &
Ruprecht, 1977; ²1986]), who favours the Griesbach hypothesis. E. Linnemann's
Gibt es ein synoptisches Problem? (Nürnberg: VTR, ³1998 [¹1991]) is an attack on synoptic scholarship in general, but one that suffers from an unfortunate lack of acquain-
tance with much of the relevant literature (see my review in *Critical Reviews in Religion
1993* [Atlanta: Scholars, 1993] 262–4).

Gospel) hypothesis.[2] And in the United Kingdom, C.M. Tuckett has offered a detailed analysis and critique of the Griesbach hypothesis,[3] and Farrer's thesis of Markan priority coupled with Lukan dependence on Matthew[4] has elicited learned replies from D.R. Catchpole, F.G. Downing, and C.M. Tuckett.[5]

The work of David Catchpole on Q has proved important not only for the host of insights into the construction and thought of Q,

---

[2] A large number of publications have issued from the research team assembled by Farmer, most recently, A.J. McNicol, *Beyond the Q Impasse—Luke's Use of Matthew: A Demonstration by the Research Team of the International Institute for Gospel Studies* (with D.L. Dungan, and D.B. Peabody; Valley Forge, Pa.: Trinity Press International, 1996). See the review by R.A. Derrenbacker, "The Relationship among the Gospels Reconsidered", *Toronto Journal of Theology* 14 (1998) 83–8. For earlier engagements with the Two Gospel hypothesis, see C.H. Talbert, and E.V. McKnight, "Can the Griesbach Hypothesis be Falsified?" *JBL* 91 (1972) 338–68, with a reply by G.W. Buchanan, "Has the Griesbach Hypothesis Been Falsified?", *JBL* 93 (1974) 550–72; S.E. Johnson, *The Griesbach Hypothesis and Redaction Criticism* (SBLMS 41; Atlanta: Scholars, 1991); R.H. Stein, *The Synoptic Problem: An Introduction* (Grand Rapids, Mich.: Baker 1987); J.S. Kloppenborg, "The Theological Stakes in the Synoptic Problem", in *The Four Gospels 1992: Festschrift Frans Neirynck* (ed. F. Van Segbroeck et al.; BETL 100; Leuven: Leuven University and Peeters, 1992) 93–120; M.E. Boring, "The Synoptic Problem, 'Minor' Agreements, and the Beelzebul Pericope", *The Four Gospels 1992*, 587–619; R.H. Gundry, "Matthean Foreign Bodies in Agreements of Luke with Matthew against Mark: Evidence that Luke used Matthew", in *The Four Gospels 1992*, 1467–95; D.S. New, *Old Testament Quotations in the Synoptic Gospels and the Two-Document Hypothesis* (SCS 37; Atlanta: Scholars, 1993).

[3] C.M. Tuckett, *The Revival of the Griesbach Hypothesis: An Analysis and Appraisal* (SNTSMS 44; Cambridge and New York: CUP, 1983); idem, "The Griesbach Hypothesis in the 19th Century", *JSNT* 3 (1979) 29–60; idem, *Q and the History of Early Christianity: Studies on Q* (Edinburgh: T. & T. Clark; Peabody, Ma.: Hendrickson, 1996) 11–16. See also P.M. Head, *Christology and the Synoptic Problem: An Assessment of One Argument for Markan Priority* (SNTSMS 94; Cambridge and New York: CUP, 1997).

[4] A.M. Farrer, "On Dispensing with Q", in *Studies in the Gospels in Memory of R.H. Lightfoot* (ed. D.E. Nineham; Oxford: Basil Blackwell, 1955) 57–88; repr. in *The Two-Source Hypothesis: A Critical Appraisal* (ed. A.J. Bellinzoni; Macon, Ga.: Mercer University, 1985) 321–56. Farrer's thesis has been defended and elaborated by M.D. Goulder, *Midrash and Lection in Matthew* (London: SPCK, 1974); idem, *Luke: A New Paradigm* (JSNTSup 20; 2 vols. Sheffield: JSOT, 1989); idem, "On Putting Q to the Test", *NTS* 24 (1978) 218–34; idem, "A House Built on Sand", in *Alternative Approaches to New Testament Study* (ed. A.E. Harvey; London: SPCK, 1985) 1–24; idem, "Luke's Knowledge of Matthew", in *Minor Agreements* [n. 2], 143–60; idem, "Is Q a Juggernaut?" *JBL* 115 (1996) 667–81; idem, "Self-Contradiction in the IQP", *JBL* 118 (1999) 506–17.

[5] D.R. Catchpole, *The Quest for Q* (Edinburgh: T. & T. Clark, 1993), esp. pp. 1–59; F.G. Downing, "Towards the Rehabilitation of Q", *NTS* 11 (1965) 170–81; idem, "A Paradigm Perplex: Luke, Matthew and Mark", *NTS* 38 (1992) 15–36; C.M. Tuckett, "On the Relationship between Matthew and Luke", *NTS* 30 (1984) 130–42; *Q and the History of Early Christianity* [n. 3], 16–31.

but for the constant attention he pays to the basic issue of the Synoptic Problem. His main dialogue partner is Goulder, for Catchpole rightly recognizes that if it could be shown in a systematic fashion that Luke could be derived from Matthew (and Mark), Q would become a superfluous supposition.[6] Hence, Catchpole's essay "Did Q Exist?"[7] just as systematically shows that at numerous points it is difficult to derive Luke's directly text from Matthew, for Matthew contains elements that one would otherwise expect Luke to have taken over had he seen Matthew.

In this essay, I should like to offer a different sort of reflection on the synoptic problem, not pursuing the painstaking work of Catchpole in defending the independence of Matthew and Luke, but raising a more theoretical question of what it is that synoptic theories are designed to accomplish, taking as a point of departure the main British challenge to the 2DH, Michael Goulder's "New Paradigm."

Goulder calls his proposal "a new paradigm", expressly invoking a term popularized by Thomas Kuhn in *The Structure of Scientific Revolutions* (1962, 1970).[8] In this critical reflection, I would like to ask three questions: First, what does Goulder mean by "paradigm"? Second, is Goulder's "paradigm" new? And third, does Goulder's thesis offer a compelling critique of the Two Document Hypothesis?

Goulder on Paradigms

Ever since the publication of Kuhn's volume, the term "paradigm" has become rather a buzzword among theological writers. A quick consultation of the ATLA database shows that the word appears in the titles and abstracts of one thousand monographs and articles published since 1980, almost 1200 since 1970. Though a handful of

---

[6] The key term here is "systematic", since as Catchpole notes with T.A. Friedrichsen ("The Matthew-Luke Agreements Against Mark: A Survey of Recent Studies: 1974–1989", in *L'évangile de Luc: Problèmes littéraires et théologiques. Mémorial Lucien Cerfaux* [revised and enlarged edition, ed. F. Neirynck; BETL 32; Leuven: Peeters, 1989] 335–392, esp. p. 391), the demonstration that (e.g.) the minor agreements betray Luke's dependence on Matthew would not by itself foreclose the possibility that Matthew and Luke used another source alongside Mark for the double tradition in general.

[7] Catchpole, "Did Q Exist?", *The Quest for Q*, 1–59.

[8] T.S. Kuhn, *The Structure of Scientific Revolutions* (International Encyclopedia of Unified Science, Foundations of the Unity of Science 2/2; Chicago: University of Chicago, 1962; 2nd enlarged edition, 1970). All references are to the 1970 edition.

these discuss the paradigms in the Greek and Hebrew verbal sys-
tems, many others implicitly or explicitly invoke Kuhn by announc-
ing "shifting", "new" and "emerging" paradigms.

Some of these usages are—no doubt rhetorical—attempts to lend
some unearned legitimacy to novel theses by claiming that they are
part of "new" or "emerging" paradigms. The rhetorical appeal of
the term is obvious. No one, after all, would want to be associated
with the old and dying view that combustion and rusting involves
the release of phlogiston when Lavoisier's new paradigm of oxidation,
reduction, and acidity is on the horizon. Nevertheless, it should be remembered that for Kuhn, a "paradigm" is not merely an idea or a
theory, but an *achievement* involving theories and practices (new ways
of approaching the phenomena and new equipment), and promot-
ing a new research program (naturally suggesting new puzzles as well
as new solutions).[9] New paradigms, moreover, are more easily recognized with hindsight than at the moment of their birth,[10] precisely
because it takes some time for the paradigm to take hold in theory,
in practices, and in the discursive modes adopted by practitioners.

Hence, advertisements of the birth of new paradigms (and the
death of old ones) are always likely to be a bit premature. To be
fair to Goulder, however, his rehabilitation of Farrer's theory, even
if it has not attracted a large group of practitioners,[11] has been articulated over the course of twenty-five years and has achieved a practical embodiment in two significant commentaries, one on Matthew
and another on Luke. It is not clear to me, nevertheless, that Goulder's
theory has done what Kuhnian paradigms ought to do, namely to
suggest a new set of problems to be solved. And as I shall suggest
below, Goulder's theory involves no substantially new practices or
tools: Goulder remains a redaction critic, and a fine one at that,

---

[9] See C. Strug, "Kuhn's Paradigm Thesis: A Two-edged Sword for the Philosophy
of Religion", *Religious Studies* 20 (1984) 269–79, esp. 270.

[10] As Kuhn notes, it is sometimes even difficult to identify the point at which a
paradigm-shifting discovery occurs, as in the case of the discovery of oxygen in the
1770s. See *Structure*, 53–6.

[11] See, e.g., H.B. Green, "The Credibility of Luke's Transformation of Matthew",
in *Synoptic Studies: The Ampleforth Conferences of 1982 and 1983* (ed. C.M. Tuckett;
JSNTSup 7; Sheffield, JSOT, 1984) 131–55; idem, "Matthew 12.22–50 and Parallels:
An Alternative to Matthaean Conflation", *Synoptic Studies*, 157–76; E.P. Sanders and
M. Davies, *Studying the Synoptic Gospels* (London: SCM; Philadelphia: Trinity Press
International, 1989); M.S. Goodacre, *Goulder and the Gospels: An Examination of a New
Paradigm* (JSNTSup 133; Sheffield: JSOT, 1996).

employing the standard tools of the trade in a relatively conventional manner.

Falsifiability: Goulder's Popperian View

In order to probe more deeply into what Goulder means by "paradigm", it is useful to scrutinize the opening paragraphs of *Luke: A New Paradigm*. There he refers both to Popper[12] and to Kuhn, arguing (with Popper) that knowledge progresses by conjectures, which are then subjected to deductive testing that attempts to refute them. For Popper, conjectures that survive are not thereby shown to be certainly true or even as probably correct, but they do appear to us to be better approximations of the truth than competing conjectures which fail deductive testing.[13] Falsifiability—the susceptibility of an hypothesis to refutation by means of empirical observations—is for Popper what sets scientific conjectures apart from non-scientific ones.[14]

Goulder describes the Two Document hypothesis as a "paradigm" or "complex of hypotheses" that includes a conjectured sayings source Q and the hypothesis of the independence of Matthew and Luke. Since on most accounts Q's contents did not include material parallel to the Markan passion narrative,[15] the 2DH implies that while in Mark 1–13 there might be Matthew-Luke agreements against Mark that result from their incorporation of Q into the Markan

---

[12] K. Popper, *The Logic of Scientific Discovery*, revised ed. (London: Hutchinson, 1968; first English edition, 1959); idem, *Conjectures and Refutations: The Growth of Scientific Knowledge* (London: Routledge and Kegan Paul, 1963).

[13] Popper, *Conjectures*, vii; *Logic*, 32–33.

[14] This is Popper's criterion of demarcation between scientific and non-scientific (and metaphysical) statements. "I proposed . . . that *refutability or falsifiability* of a theoretical system should be taken as the criterion of demarcation. According to this view, which I still uphold, a system is to be considered as scientific only if it makes assertions which may clash with observations; and a system is, in fact, tested by attempts to produce such clashes, that is to say by attempts to refute it. Thus testability is the same as refutability, and can therefore likewise be taken as a criterion of demarcation" (*Conjectures*, 256, emphasis original).

[15] Goulder's statement is much stronger: "Now Q is *defined* as a body of sayings material and some narrative, beginning from the preaching of John and ending before the Passion. . . ." [*Luke: A New Paradigm*, 6, emphasis added] and "there is no Q in the Passion story *ex hypothesi*." This appears to be an effort to make the refutation of the supposition of Q analytic—by defining terms in such a way that simple understanding of the terms renders hypotheses using those terms true or false on the basis of grammar—rather than *a posteriori*. But Q in fact is only "defined" as the non-Markan source of Matthew and Luke. It *turns out* not to have Passion sayings, but this is not part of the definition of Q.

framework, there should be no significant agreements of Matthew and Luke against Mark in the passion narrative. This is a simple deductive test, and one which, apparently, the 2DH fails: there is at least one significant minor agreement, Matt 26:67–68/Luke 22:63–64 against Mark 14:65.[16]

I will return to the issue of the minor agreements later, but for the moment it is important to observe that Goulder's understanding of a "paradigm" corresponds to Popper's idea of the "problem-situation" or "framework" into which the scientist fits her own work.[17] For Popper, the scientist works within a definite theoretical framework; but he emphasizes that "at any moment" the scientist can challenge and break out of that framework.[18] But Popper in fact rejects Kuhn's model of a single dominant, controlling paradigm. On the contrary, multiple competing theories exist at any given time; they are generally commensurable; and, if scientific, they are falsifiable. For Popper, science progresses in a continuous process of conjectures and refutations, with multiple conjectures vying for dominance.

This erodes Kuhn's distinction between "normal" and "extraordinary" science, between those phases of scientific research generally informed by one broad conceptual paradigm, related practices, and commending a certain research program, on the one hand, and on the other, transitional periods when a prevailing paradigm has become problematized due to a critical mass of uncooperative data and anomalous observations, which eventually lead to its displacement by a new paradigm. Popper in fact understands Kuhn's term "normal science" in a pejorative sense, connoting the activity of the "non-revolutionary" and "not-too-critical professional", "the science student who accepts the ruling dogma of the day".[19]

---

[16] See below, n. 37.

[17] K. Popper, "Normal Science and its Dangers", in *Criticism and the Growth of Knowledge* (ed. I. Lakatos, and A. Musgrave, Proceedings of the International Colloquium in the Philosophy of Science 4; Cambridge: CUP, 1970) 51–58, esp. p. 51.

[18] Popper, "Normal Science", 56.

[19] Popper, "Normal Science", 52. Similarly, *Logic*, 50: "A system such as classical mechanics may be 'scientific' to any degree you like; but those who uphold it dogmatically—believing, perhaps, that it is their business to defend such a successful system against criticism as long as it is not *conclusively disproved*—are adopting the very reverse of that critical attitude which in my view is the proper one for the scientist. In point of fact, no conclusive disproof of a theory can ever be produced; for it is always possible to say that the experimental results are not reliable, or that the discrepancies which are asserted to exist between the experimental results and the theory are only apparent and that they will disappear with the advance of our

Ironically, "paradigm" for Goulder has a Popperian ring, despite the fact that the title of his Luke book advertises a new paradigm. To be sure, Goulder takes from Kuhn the idea that dominant paradigms often accommodate anomalies by making *ad hoc* adjustments. But while Kuhn takes such adaptations to be a standard and necessary part of normal science,[20] Goulder sees the attempts of the 2DH to accommodate anomalies by adjusting the theory—positing other intermediate documents, or oral tradition, or textual corruption—as leading to an "elastic", unfalsifiable, and therefore unscientific hypothesis. He observes, moreover, that paradigms resist displacement because researchers have invested careers in research programs informed by those paradigms. For Goulder, as for Popper, paradigms *ought* to be susceptible to deductive testing that could well lead to their immediate collapse. The fact that they do not collapse is a symptom of the dangers of "normal science".[21] Thus he bemoans the fact that generations of graduate students will imbibe and later perpetuate a paradigm which, he thinks, is logically indefensible.[22] Throughout

---

understanding. . . . If you insist on strict proof (or strict disproof) in the empirical sciences, you will never benefit from experience, and never learn from it how wrong you are."

[20] T.S. Kuhn, "Logic of Discovery or Psychology of Research?", in *Criticism and the Growth of Knowledge* (ed. I. Lakatos, and A. Musgrave; Proceedings of the International Colloquium in the Philosophy of Science 4; Cambridge: CUP, 1970), 1–23, esp. 13: "It is important, furthermore, that this should be so, for it is often by challenging observations or adjusting theories that scientific knowledge grows. Challenges and adjustments are a standard part of normal research in empirical science, and adjustments, at least, play a dominant role in informal mathematics as well". Contrast Popper's statement in *Logic* (42): "For it is always possible to find some way of evading falsification, for example by introducing *ad hoc* an auxiliary hypothesis, or by changing *ad hoc* a definition. It is even possible without logical inconsistency to adopt the position of simply refusing to acknowledge any falsifying experience whatsoever. Admittedly, scientists do not usually proceed in this way, but logically such procedure is possible; and this fact, it might be claimed, makes the logical value of my proposed criterion of demarcation dubious, to say the least."

[21] Popper, "Normal Science", 52–53. Goulder (*Luke*, 4) asserts that Kuhn's use of "normal science" is pejorative, but this seems to be a case of reading Kuhn *via* Popper. Kuhn (*Structure*, 65) in fact sees "normal science" not as antithetical to extraordinary science, but as embodying the practices that lead to its own displacement. "By ensuring that the paradigm will not be too easily surrendered, resistance guarantees that scientists will not be lightly distracted and that the anomalies that lead to paradigm change will penetrate existing knowledge to the core. The very fact that a significant scientific novelty so often emerges simultaneously from several laboratories in an index both to the strongly traditional nature of normal science and to the completeness with which that traditional pursuit prepares the way for its own change."

[22] Goulder, "Juggernaut" [n. 4], esp. p. 668.

his introduction to *Luke: A New Paradigm*, he refers to adherents of the 2DH with the apparently pejorative term, "paradigmers".

Kuhn's reply to Popper is that paradigms, precisely because of their complexity, can seldom be cast in a form that is susceptible to the sort of refutations that Popper (or Goulder) seeks. Tolerance to anomalies is not a special characteristic of paradigms that are about to collapse, or of paradigms that irrationally resist falsification; it is a mark of all paradigms. For example, Schrödinger wave mechanics and his wave equation produce coherent results for electrons travelling much below the speed of light; but at higher velocities, and for other particles travelling near light-speed, Schrödinger's equation does not work. The equation produces coherent results for electrons in the hydrogen atom, but not for more complex atomic structures. But these are not sufficient grounds to abandon the equation. It is for reasons such as this that paradigms in Kuhn's sense do not collapse when faced with bits of anomalous data. An old paradigm is declared invalid only when anomalies have accumulated to the extent that the paradigm cannot bear their weight *and* when a new candidate is there to take its place. The choice to abandon one is simultaneously a choice to embrace another.[23]

Goulder's Popperian perspective on the issue of the falsification of scientific hypotheses and his Popperian sense of paradigms helps to account for the strategy he adopts in criticizing the 2DH: he proposes simple deductive tests—principally, the presence of minor agreements and the presence of "Matthaean" vocabulary in Luke—with the expectation that such tests should refute the theory, leaving place for his own. This is also why he prefers the position of the so-called "hard-liners", Neirynck and Tuckett, who respond to the issue of the minor agreements by suggesting either coincidental redaction by Matthew and Luke, or textual corruption.[24] This is in contrast to the "soft-liners", who appeal to multiple recensions of Mark, the interference of oral tradition, or intermediate gospels. The "hardline" position, because it requires Neirynck and Tuckett to be able

---

[23] Kuhn, *Structure*, 77.
[24] On the notorious minor agreement at Mark 14:65, see C.M. Tuckett, "On the Relationship between Matthew and Luke" [n. 5], 136–37 and F. Neirynck, "ΤΙΣ ΕΣΤΙΝ Ο ΠΑΙΣΑΣ ΣΕ?; Mt 26,68/Lk 22,64 (diff. Mk 14,65)", *ETL* 63 (1987) 5–47; repr. with an additional note in *Evangelica II: 1982–1991 Collected Essays* (ed. F. Van Segbroeck; BETL 99; Leuven: Leuven University and Peeters, 1991) 94–138.

to supply plausible redaction critical reasons for a coincidental agreement in altering Mark, or to point to an early and reliable manuscript that eliminates the minor agreement, is, Goulder believes, easily falsifiable. Thus while he invokes Kuhn, the key issue for Goulder is falsification. The existence of a "paradigm" only accounts for the resistance encountered by new proposals. It is a term connoting institutional inertia.[25]

I wish to suggest that there are two reasons why Goulder's criticism of the 2DH has not proved effective and his own theory has not been embraced—a fact conceded by Goulder himself. First is that Goulder's Popperian view of falsification is not shared by most of those he criticizes. The 2DH is believed to be able to accommodate anomalies, just as Kuhn's paradigms routinely both produce and accommodate anomalies in the course of the puzzle-solving of normal science. The 2DH is not perceived as imperiled by the problem of the minor agreements and it provides a generally coherent account of a host of synoptic data. Simply put, the 2DH is still an effective hypothesis.

The second reason is that Goulder's thesis produces its own puzzles having to do with Luke's editorial procedures that Goulder has not sufficiently addressed. I will return to some of these later, but for the moment I would like to comment on falsification and the 2DH.

Are Synoptic Theories Falsifiable?

When it was first formulated, the 2DH—or at least, the supposition of (Ur-)Markan priority and the existence of a sayings source—was advertised as incorrigible, beyond falsification. Albert Schweitzer, Holtzmann's erstwhile student at Strasbourg, is a good example of such rhetorical bravado: "The [Markan] hypothesis has a literary existence, indeed it is carried out by Holtzmann to such a degree of demonstration that it can no longer be called a mere hypothesis".[26] A half-century later Marxsen echoed this:

---

[25] Goulder ("Juggernaut", 668–69) ventures that modern support for the 2DH is due to a combination of inertia, personal attachments, lack of academic integrity in admitting "that [proponents] have been wrong for years" and the daunting mass of scholarly literature on the topic that few can read or master. Missing from Goulder's list is the possibility that some embrace the 2DH on the basis of a careful examination of synoptic data and the explanations that best account for those data.

[26] A. Schweitzer, *The Quest of the Historical Jesus* (New York: Macmillan, 1910, repr. 1968) 202.

> This Two-Sources theory [sic] has been so widely accepted by schol-
> ars that one feels inclined to abandon the term "theory" (in the sense
> of "hypothesis"). We can in fact regard it as an assured finding—but
> we must bear in mind that there are inevitable uncertainties as far as
> the extent and form of Q and the special material are concerned.[27]

This is a grave logical mistake that has now been exposed, thanks
in part to the efforts of Chapman, Butler, Farmer and Goulder.
Happily, it is difficult to find such inflated rhetorical claims made
by contemporary adherents of the Two Document hypothesis. The
2DH is an hypothesis. Deductive testing might refute an hypothesis,
but it can never prove one or establish it as a fact.

Ironically, perhaps, proponents of other hypotheses have sometimes succumbed to the temptation of similar rhetoric. For example,
in the defence of the Two Gospel hypothesis (2GH) offered by
McNicol and his colleagues, McNicol repeatedly describes data in
Luke (either the sequence of Lukan materials or certain phrases or
words) as *evidence* of Luke's direct use of Matthew.[28] It is not evidence or proof; rather, it is *data* for which the 2GH may offer a
plausible accounting, but for which the 2GH is not the *only* plausible accounting. A yet more blatant example of rhetorical overstate-
ment is Farrer's assertion:

> The Q hypothesis is a hypothesis, that is its weakness. To be rid of
> it we have no need of a contrary hypothesis, we merely have to make
> St. Luke's use of St. Matthew intelligible; and to understand what
> St. Luke made of St. Matthew we need no more than to consider
> what St. Luke made of his own book. Now St. Luke's book is not a
> hypothetical entity. Here is a copy of it on my desk.[29]

---

[27] W. Marxsen, *Introduction to the New Testament: An Approach to Its Problems* (Philadelphia: Fortress, 1968) 118. Similarly, W.G. Kümmel (*Introduction to the New Testament*,
revised English edition [Nashville: Abingdon, 1975] 64) asserted that Luke's direct
dependence on Matthew was "completely inconceivable" ("völlig undenkbar"), while
citing as proponents of this view Rengstorff, Schlatter, Ropes, Butler, Farrer, Turner,
Farmer, Argyle, Simpson, Wilkens, and Sanders.

[28] McNicol, *Beyond the Q Impasse* [n. 2], 18 (sequential parallels between Luke
3:1–10:22, divided into five sections, and the sequence of Matt 3:1–18:5); 23 (agreements of Luke 4:31–32; 7:1 with Matt 7:28–29); 24 (Luke's use of the "Matthaean"
absolute genitive + ἰδού, Luke's use of a participial form of προσέρχομαι to introduce a finite verb [23:52], and Luke's use of σκανδαλίζειν). In the summary
(318–19), McNicol claims that this data can *only* be explained on the 2GH, even
though other explanations are not entertained.

[29] Farrer, "On Dispensing with Q", in *The Two-Source Hypothesis: A Critical Appraisal*
[n. 4], 333.

This is a sleight of hand. Luke indeed "existed" on Farrer's desk, though Farrer did not seem to appreciate the fact that the Greek text that lay on his desk was itself the *reconstruction* of text critics such as Tischendorf, Westcott, Hort, and Nestle that was based on *hypotheses* concerning the transmission of the text of Luke. But what did *not* exist on Farrer's desk was Luke's *relationship* to Matthew. *That* was Farrer's hypothesis and that is his "weakness".

Goulder engages in similar rhetorical flourishes when he asserts: "Luke's use of Mark is a fact (or generally accepted as one), while Q is a mere postulate" and further, "Q is now hardly defended in the University of Oxford".[30] Goulder's subordinate clause, "Q is a mere postulate", is perfectly correct: Q is a postulate of the hypothesis that affirms both the priority of Mark to Matthew and Luke and the mutual independence of Matthew and Luke. One may quibble only with Goulder's adjective "mere". Q is not a "mere" postulate; on the contrary, it follows *necessarily* from the two logically prior postulates.[31]

As to Luke's use of Mark being a "fact" or even a "generally accepted fact", neither is the case. The key piece of data from the Synoptic gospels, that Matthew and Luke never agree against Mark in the sequence of triple tradition pericopae,[32] admits (logically speaking) of any explanation that places Mark in a medial position. This includes the 2DH and the Farrer-Goulder hypothesis (FGH). This datum, however, is also explicable, for example, on the Two Gospel hypothesis and Boismard's multi-stage hypothesis, which allows only a mediated relationship between Mark and Luke.[33] Such explanations

---

[30] M.D. Goulder, "Is Q a Juggernaut?", *JBL* 115 (1996) 667–681, here 670, 668. The irony of the latter statement is that by the time the *JBL* article appeared, C.M. Tuckett, one of the ablest defenders of the 2DH, had come to Oxford.

[31] Similarly, C.M. Tuckett, "The Existence of Q", *The Gospel Behind the Gospels: Current Studies on Q* (ed. R.A. Piper; NovTSup 75; Leiden: Brill, 1995) 21 = *Q and the History of Early Christianity* [n. 3], 4, who rightly calls the "Q hypothesis" a "negative theory" insofar as it is predicated on the denial of a direct relationship between Matthew and Luke. Because Q is an integral part of the 2DH, it is infelicitous to speak of "the Q hypothesis" as if it were logically separable from the 2DH.

[32] See E.P. Sanders, "The Argument from Order and the Relationship between Matthew and Luke", *NTS* 15 (1968–1969) 249–261, and the answers by F. Neirynck, "The Argument from Order and St. Luke's Transpositions", *ETL* 49 (1973) 784–815 and R.H. Fuller, "Order in the Synoptic Gospels: A Summary", *SecCent* 6/2 (1987–1988) 107–109.

[33] This is characteristic of all of Boismard's slightly varying solutions. In *Évangile de Marc: sa préhistoire* (Études biblique, nouvelle série 26; Paris: Les Éditions du Cerf,

are hypotheses, not unassailable facts. Moreover, whether Luke used Mark (2DH, FGH) or Mark used Luke (2GH) or both derived from some intermediary (Boismard) cannot conclusively be proved or disproved, since virtually all of the directional indicators are stylistic or theological, and most or all of the arguments are reversible. Luke's use of Mark thus remains an hypothesis—a reasonable and effective hypothesis, in my view—but no volume of scholarly literature in its support (and no voting from Oxford—or Birmingham or Toronto, for that matter) will elevate its ontological status to anything more than that.

The Nature of Synoptic Hypotheses

If we set aside the various rhetorical overstatements, we are still left with the broader conceptual question of the nature and function of competing synoptic hypotheses.

In my view, it is foolish to claim incorrigibility, but equally mistaken to insist on the degree of simplicity that Goulder's requirement of falsifiability implies. In the formulation of hypotheses concerning the synoptic gospels, we are caught between two incompatible constraints: to formulate hypotheses that are as simple and clear as possible and which are generally falsifiable by reference to the array of synoptic data; and to formulate hypotheses that are sufficiently attentive to the complexity of technological and human factors involved in the production and transmission of the gospels to be a near approximation to what might have happened. Moreover, synoptic hypotheses are not *pictures* of what happened; they are only heuristic *tools* that offer convenient lenses through which to view data.

From the point of view of logic, it is desirable to have a simple theory according to which Matthew and Luke used Mark—a supposition common to both the Farrer-Goulder and the Two Document hypotheses. It is, however, most improbable from a historical perspective that Matthew and Luke used the *same* copy of Mark. And given what we know about the early transmission of manuscripts, it

---

1994), Luke and Matthew are dependent on an intermediate version of Mark (Mark[int]), and the final version of Mark is dependent on a Marco-Lukan editor. His 1972 hypothesis lacked Mark's dependence on a "rédacteur marco-lucanien" but affirmed the dependence of Mark and Luke on Mark[int]. See M.-É. Boismard *Synopse des quatre évangiles en français. Tome 2: Commentaire* (preface by P. Benoit; Paris: Les Editions du Cerf, 1972).

is highly unlikely that any two copies of Mark were in every respect identical. After all, none of the early papyri of the gospels is identical with another. Two copies of Mark would at a minimum be subject to copyists' mistakes, and conceivably to more substantial alterations. There is, moreover, no reason to suppose that Matthew's Mark and *our* Mark are identical, or that Luke's Mark was identical with either. The same considerations apply, *mutatis mutandis*, to Q on the 2DH or Matthew and Luke on the 2GH.[34]

Synoptic hypotheses are convenient *simplifications* of what was undoubtedly a much more complex—and unrecoverable—process of composition and transmission. Under such circumstances, it seems perverse to insist on simple pictures that we know *in advance* to be too simple, merely because they are also easily falsifiable, or to bemoan the resort to more ornate solutions on the grounds that certain features of the more ornate hypotheses place them beyond falsification.

The Minor Agreements and the 2DH

As noted above, the agreements of Matthew and Luke against Mark are the key problem for the 2DH. Some proponents of the 2DH accommodate the minor agreements by adjusting the model of the 2DH, suggesting recensions of Mark (*Ur-* or *Deutero-Markus*) which agreed with Matthew and Luke; others account for the minor agreements by the supposition of interference from oral tradition; others still suggest textual (post-Markan) corruption; and a few have posited intermediate gospels. Goulder objects to most of these strategies since they place the hypothesis beyond falsification.

While Goulder's point is well taken, it is also the case that none of the adjustments mentioned above is inherently implausible. First, we know of other literature that existed in multiple recensions: the Greek and Coptic versions of the *Gospel of Thomas*, for example, display significant variations, including abbreviation and contractions of

---

[34] This assertion might appear odd, coming from one of the three editors of *Documenta Q* and the critical edition of Q by the International Q Project. I do not, however, believe that in text-critical labours or in the reconstructive efforts of the IQP it is realistic or theoretically possible to reconstruct *the* original text of a gospel or Q. What is reconstructed is an imaginary point on a continuum of textual and textual transmission. This imaginary point presumably approximates to a near degree a document that once existed; but its primary theoretical function is to account for preceding and subsequent textual history, to the extent that this is known.

sayings, and the relocation of one saying to a new context.[35] Second, as recent studies of ancient literacy have shown, oral performance was involved in literary production at several stages. Composition sometimes involved preliminary drafts, oral recitation before select audiences, and final editing taking into account the audience reaction. Moreover, the difficulties inherent in reading texts written *scripta continua* meant that in the "reading" of a work, the text functioned in a manner more akin to a musical score requiring performance than to a text which was to be recited.[36] This implies that the way a work was heard was a combination of textual and (oral) performative features; or to put it differently, when *we* read ancient texts, we see only part of what was actually heard. We have no way to gauge the conventions that governed its performance or the oral elements that typically formed part of its performance. Finally, the study of early NT papyri shows a remarkably unstable textual situation, with harmonization and parallel influence attested at a very early stage. If such variation is empirically attested in NT manuscripts, it seems perverse to insist on a scenario that forecloses the possibility of transcriptional variations between multiple copies of Mark (or Q).

Given these facts, it makes no sense to insist, as Goulder does, on mathematically simple hypotheses. The imperative of synoptic problem research is not to produce generalizations or schematic models simply so that they achieve a state of maximal falsifiablity; the task of research is to produce models that account for as much of the data as possible. Any one of the adjustments to the 2DH noted above is capable of accommodating the few significant minor agreements—and they are relatively few.[37] If there is a difficulty with the

---

[35] Compare the abbreviation of *P.Oxy.* 655 i 1–17 in *GThom* 36 and the expansion of *P.Oxy.* 654.5–9 in *GThom* 2. The second part of *P.Oxy.* 1.22–30 (= *GThom* 30) is found in Coptic as *GThom* 77.

[36] K. Quinn, "The Poet and his audience in the Augustan Age", *ANRW* 2.30.1 (1982) 75–180, esp. p. 90.

[37] Although raw tabulation of the minor agreements produces seemingly impressive numbers—610 positive and 573 negative agreements by Ennulat's (*Die "Minor Agreements"* [n. 1]) counting—many of these are "agreements" only in the most general sense and hardly imply any collaboration of Matthew and Luke; others are rather easily explained on the basis of Matthaean and Lukan redactional habits. There is a small number of difficult cases: Matt 13:11/Luke 8:10 against Mark 4:11; Matt 9:20/Luke 8:44 (τοῦ κρασπέδου) against Mark 5:27; Matt 9:26/Luke 4:14 (not in the same Markan context); Matt 22:34–40/Luke 10:25–28 (which some have ascribed to Q) against Mark 12:12–34; Matt 26:67–68/Luke 22:63–64 against

2DH, it is not that it cannot give an account of the minor agreements; rather, it is that we do not know which of the several available adjustments is preferable. Nor for that matter is there agreement on the interpretation and implications of Heisenberg's Uncertainty principle—whether the position and velocity of electrons cannot be ascertained simultaneously or whether the electron is a dispersed cloud with which the act of measurement interferes.

This view is bound not to please Goulder but it is a realistic approach under the circumstances. It does render falsification of the 2DH more difficult but not, I think, impossible. The 2DH allows for a coherent accounting of both Matthew's and Luke's editorial practices and although it also generates some anomalies, these are no more serious than those generated on other hypotheses.

Is Goulder's "Paradigm" New?

There is little doubt about the novelty of Goulder's theory of synoptic relationships. While there are some anticipations in the nineteenth century in the work of Karl Credner (1836),[38] and closer comrades in J.H. Ropes (1934)[39] and Morton Enslin (1938),[40] Goulder's theory is far more learned and ambitious than those of his predecessors, for he accounts for most of the non-Markan material in Matthew and Luke as the result of redactional invention by the evangelists.

The Kuhnian question, however, is, "Is this a new *paradigm?*" The answer is, I think, No. A paradigm for Kuhn is significantly larger than a particular theory or hypothesis. A paradigm "stands for the

---

Mark 14:65; Matt 26:75/Luke 22:62 against Mark 14:72; and Matt 28:1/Luke 23:54 (ἐπιφώσκειν) against Mark 16:1. See my review of Ennulat in *Toronto Journal of Theology* 13 (1997) 101–3. The fundamental work on the minor agreements is still F. Neirynck, *The Minor Agreements of Matthew and Luke against Mark: With a cumulative list* (BETL 37; Leuven: Leuven University Press, 1974); see also Neirynck, "The Minor Agreements and the Two-Source Theory", *Evangelica II* [n. 24], 3–42.

[38] K.A. Credner, *Einleitung in das Neue Testament* (Halle: Buchhandlung des Waisenhauses, 1836) 201–5, who posited Luke's dependence on Matthew, and both on an Aramaic proto-Gospel also used by Mark. But Credner also invoked the *logia* source to account for the double tradition.

[39] J.H. Ropes, *The Synoptic Gospels* (Cambridge, Mass.: Harvard University; London: Oxford University, 1934; 2nd impression, with a new preface, London: OUP, 1960) 66–8, 93–4.

[40] M. Enslin, *Christian Beginnings* (New York, Harper & Brothers, 1938) 431–4.

entire constellation of beliefs, values, techniques, and so on shared by the members of a given [research] community". It is "the concrete puzzle-solutions which, employed as models or examples, can replace explicit rules as a basis for the solution of the remaining puzzles of normal science".[41] Moreover, Margaret Masterman observes that in the genealogy of a new paradigm, it is often not the formal theory that comes first, but what she calls a "trick, or an embryonic technique, or picture, and an insight that is applicable to the field".[42] This combination of "trick" and "insight" constitutes the paradigm, which is then worked out in explicit theory and more advanced techniques.

As an example, one might think of advances in quantum mechanics: faced with Compton's evidence that X-rays had particle as well as wave properties, de Broglie's suggested that all matter has both properties. This intuition was tested with defraction devices, which had been employed ever since Augustin-Jean Fresnel's experiments in 1815 that demonstrated wave theory in visible light. But instead of defracting electromagnetic radiation, Davisson and Germer tried electrons and showed in 1927 that they too could be defracted and hence exhibited wave properties. Only later did Schrödinger's wave mechanics provide the mathematical resolution of the two seemingly opposed characteristics of electrons.

The main paradigm shift in the study of the gospels came, not with Goulder or even Holtzmann, but in the late eighteenth century, with Reimarus and Griesbach. Since the time of Tatian, Celsus, and Porphyry, the disagreements among the gospels were well known, but were resolved in two different manners. Augustine, in his *De consensu evangelistarum*, treated differences among the gospels as divergent yet ultimately compatible depictions of Christ, Matthew focussing on royalty, Mark on humanity, Luke on priesthood, and John on divinity. The differences among the gospels could not gainsay the truth of *the* Gospel, the latter understood in Augustine's Platonism as a transcendental idea that was partially and perspectivally embodied

---

[41] Kuhn, "Postscript—1969", in *Structure*, 175. The first sense Kuhn calls "sociological", and the second sense, a "shared example". M. Masterman ("The Nature of a Paradigm", in *Criticism and the Growth of Knowledge* [ed. I. Lakatos, and A. Musgrave, Proceedings of the International Colloquium in the Philosophy of Science 4; Cambridge: CUP, 1970] 59–89, esp. 67) refers to the second as a construct-paradigm.

[42] Masterman, "The Nature of a Paradigm", 69.

in the text of the gospels.[43] Harmonists employed a different strategy. They referred disagreements to the artificially constructed meta-text of the gospel harmony. This practice came under increasing pressure with the advent, in the sixteenth century, of a verbally-based doctrine of inspiration. Andreas Osiander's *Harmonia evangelica* (1537) insisted that even small variations in seemingly parallel accounts were significant, and indicated discrete historical events.[44] Thus he desynchronized pericopae that earlier harmonists had treated as parallel, a policy that produced in his synopsis and those that followed him a string of absurd repetitions. Osiander, for example, had three healings of blind men near Jericho, three centurions' sons healed, three anointings of Jesus, and the Temple cleansed three times.[45]

A new paradigm emerged with an insight concerning the "particularity" or individuality of each gospel. Particularity had been a feature of Osiander's harmony insofar as particularities of the gospels were registered as discrete events in his meta-text. But particularity took on a new significance when Hermann Samuel Reimarus (1778) argued that the contradictions among the gospels implied that their authors had produced inconsistent, indeed fraudulent, accounts of Jesus' career.[46] For Reimarus the gospels were discrete works, not related to some reconciling meta-text. Instead, he viewed the gospels in relation to a plausible historical reconstruction of their referent (Jesus) and their composers (the evangelists).

This turn towards the particularity of the gospels was made possible by a new "device", the three-gospel synopsis, created by J.J.

---

[43] Augustine's Platonism is noted by S. McLoughlin, "An Approach to the Synoptic Problem", S.T.L. thesis, Katholieke Universiteit Leuven, 1963: "Augustine speaks of Mk following Mt, and while in our scientifically-minded age such a suggestion carries causal implications, it is much less certain that it does so for the Platonic-minded Augustine: a second witness, who adds nothing to what the first and principal witness had already said, could well in such a mentality be described as his follower" (28).

[44] A. Osiander, *Harmoniae evangelicae libri quatuor Graece et Latine* (Geneva: Stephani, 1537).

[45] See the discussion of pre-Griesbach synopses in H.K. McArthur, *The Quest through the Centuries: The Search for the Historical Jesus* (Philadelphia: Fortress, 1966) 85–101 and M.H. de Lang, "Gospel Synopses from the 16th to the 18th Centuries and the Rise of Literary Criticism of the Gospels", in *The Synoptic Gospels: Source Criticism and New Literary Criticism* (ed. C. Focant; BETL 110; Leuven: Leuven University and Peeters, 1993) 599–607.

[46] H.S. Reimarus, "Von dem Zwecke Jesu und seiner Jünger", in *Fragmente des Wolfenbüttelschen Ungenannten* (ed. G. Lessing; Berlin: Sander'sche Buchhandlung [Eichhoff], 1778); ET: *Fragments* (ed. C.H. Talbert; Philadelphia: Fortress, 1970).

Griesbach at virtually the same time.[47] The synopsis allowed for the first time a close comparison of agreements and disagreements among the gospels. In retrospect, one might locate a paradigm shift in Griesbach's stated refusal to embrace the harmonist's program of creating a harmonious narrative, for this was impossible *in principle*.[48]

The "trick" of the new paradigm of gospel study is synoptic comparison, made possible first by the critical synopsis, and subsequently by the many tabular comparisons of the sequence of synoptic pericopae and the special and shared vocabulary of the gospels, culminating in sophisticated tools such as Morgenthaler's *Statistische Synopse*, Neirynck's *New Testament Vocabulary*, and the Hoffmann-Hieke-Bauer *Synoptic Concordance*.[49]

The combination of an insight (the historical particularity of the gospels) and a device (the synopsis) constituted a paradigm in which the puzzle-solving of normal "science" could take place. This took the form of a succession of attempts to solve the literary puzzle of the relationship of the Synoptics, first in the rather loose and impressionistic theories of Lessing and Herder, then in the baroque source theories of Eichhorn, then in Saunier and de Wette's popularization of the Griesbach hypothesis, and finally in Holtzmann's rehabilitation of C.H. Weisse's 1838 two-source theory. What is common to these theories, and to the Streeterian Four Source Hypothesis, the Farrer-Goulder hypothesis, and the Two Gospel hypothesis which followed them, is that, as divergent as they may seem, they no longer refer differences to some metanarrative, but understand differences to be the function of the literary, historical, and rhetorical particularity of the gospels themselves.

In the course of two centuries of gospel study many variations of the paradigm have been introduced. Source criticism in the nineteenth

---

[47] The Synopsis originally appeared in 1774 as part of Griesbach's *Libri historici Novi Testamenti graece* (Halle: Curtius, 1774) and was printed separately two years later as *Synopsis Evangeliorvm Matthaei, Marc et Lvcae* (Halle: Curtius, 1776).

[48] J.J. Griesbach, *Synopsis Evangeliorum Matthaei, Marci et Lucae, una cum iis Joannis pericopis; Quae historian passionis et resurrectionis Jesu Christi complectuntur* (2nd ed.; Halle: J.J. Curtius, 1797) v–vi.

[49] R. Morgenthaler, *Statistische Synopse* (Zürich and Stuttgart: Gotthelf, 1971); F. Neirynck and F. Van Segbroeck, *New Testament Vocabulary: A Companion Volume to the Concordance* (BETL 65; Leuven: Peeters and Leuven University, 1984); P. Hoffmann, T. Hieke, and U. Bauer, *Synoptic Concordance: A Greek Concordance to the First Three Gospels in Synoptic Arrangement, Statistically Evaluated* (4 vols.; Berlin and New York: Walter de Gruyter, 1999–).

century seemed to prefer rather strict documentary approaches, not entertaining the possibility of the influence of oral tradition upon the writers. This habit accounts both for the positing of intermediate documents such as *Ur-Markus* to account for slight differences between canonical Mark and the "Mark" which Matthew and Luke seemed to use, and for the scouring of patristic sources for references to possibly important lost documents such as the *Gospel of the Hebrews* or Papias' *Logia*. In the early twentieth century, appeal to the interference of oral tradition became a standard part of many synoptic theories; and by mid-century, the advent of redaction criticism obviated the theoretical need to posit earlier forms of Mark or Matthew, since differences, including additions, deletions, and modifications, could plausibly be referred to the creativity of the evangelists.

In this sense, Goulder's theory is a utilization hypothesis that accounts for the differences between Matthew and Mark, and between Luke and Matthew/Mark, by appealing to a now-standard lexicon of editorial manoeuvers: abbreviation, expansion, transposition, rewriting, and free invention. All of this fits snugly within the prevailing paradigm of synoptic research, despite its nonconformity with the 2DH, the dominant source *theory* (not paradigm) of synoptic relationships.

Genuinely new paradigms might be on the horizon—one thinks of the narrative approaches, which often prescind from diachonic features of composition and focus on the narrative syntax of the gospel text. There may even be a new "device", the gospel parallel, which allows each gospel to be viewed in its narrative integrity rather than cutting the text into source- or form-critical slices.[50] Or again, the turn towards social history has discovered the tool of the Mediterranean anthropologist's field report and has applied some of her conceptual categories to the gospel text. Whether such innovations will turn out to offer a new paradigm may be doubted, however: both synchronic aspects of the gospel text and the constellation of embedded social values have now been subsumed in socio-rhetorical exegesis.[51] In any event, neither narrative approaches nor social-scientific approaches have served to solve the puzzles endemic to the study of the synoptic problem.

---

[50] See R.W. Funk, *New Gospel Parallels: Vol. 1,2: Mark* (revised edition; Foundations & Facets: Reference Series; Sonoma, Calif.: Polebridge, 1990) and Funk's *The Poetics of Biblical Narrative* (Sonoma, Calif.; Polebridge, 1988).

[51] See V.K. Robbins, *The Tapestry of Early Christian Discourse: Rhetoric, Society and Ideology* (London and New York: Routledge, 1996).

Is the 2DH Imperilled?

Goulder's main challenge to the 2DH is threefold:
(1) First, he notes that there is no mention of Q in patristic literature. Of course in the nineteenth century, Schleiermacher, Lachmann, Credner and Weisse supposed that Papias' λόγια referred to Q or something very much like Q. But Goulder is quite right to insist: "Papias is sand".[52] Indeed, Papias is sand, as Lührmann has most recently shown, and as the majority of twentieth century synoptic scholars hold.[53] But it is a misrepresentation to assert that "the Q hypothesis rests in part on a misunderstanding",[54] if what is meant is that the hypothesis rests *logically* on Papias. It does not. A careful reading of Holtzmann shows that, despite the fact that he referred to Q with the siglum Λ (for λόγια), Papias' testimony played no role in the *architecture* of Holtzmann's argument.[55] In the early twentieth century such critics as W.C. Allen, J.A. Robinson, F.C. Burkitt, B.W. Bacon, and J.C. Hawkins rejected the designation "logia" as question-begging.[56] It should be noted that even those who wished to maintain an Aramaic Q based their case not on Papias' dubious statements, but on Wellhausen's theory of translation variants.[57]

That Q is never mentioned in patristic sources is also noted by Goulder as a consideration against its existence. Tuckett's point that other documents of the early Jesus movement have gone missing does not, of course, quite meet Goulder's objection. But it is not far

---

[52] Goulder, *Luke: A New Paradigm*, 33; "Juggernaut", 669.

[53] D. Lührmann, "Q: Sayings of Jesus or Logia?", in *The Gospel Behind the Gospels: Current Studies on Q* (ed. R.A. Piper; NovTSup 75; Leiden, New York and Köln: Brill, 1995) 97–116.

[54] Goulder, "Juggernaut", 669.

[55] H.J. Holtzmann, *Die synoptischen Evangelien: Ihr Ursprung und geschichtlicher Charakter* (Leipzig: Engelmann, 1863). See J.S. Kloppenborg Verbin, *Excavating Q: The History and Setting of the Sayings Gospel* (Minneapolis: Fortress, 2000) chap. 6.

[56] J.A. Robinson, *The Study of the Gospels* (London: Longmans, Green, 1902) 70; W.C. Allen, "Did St Matthew and St Luke use the Logia?", *ExpT* 11 (1899–1900) 424–426, esp. 425; F.C. Burkitt, *The Gospel History and its Transmission* (Edinburgh: T. & T. Clark, 1906) 127, 130; B.W. Bacon, "A Turning Point in Synoptic Criticism", *HTR* 1 (1908) 48–69; J.C. Hawkins, *Horae Synopticae: Contributions to the Study of the Synoptic Problem.* (Oxford: Clarendon, ²1909; repr. 1968) 107.

[57] E.g., J.C. Hawkins, "Probabilities as to the so-called Double Tradition of St. Matthew and St. Luke", in *Oxford Studies in the Synoptic Problem* (ed. W. Sanday; Oxford: Clarendon Press, 1911) 95–140, esp. p. 104; G.D. Castor, *Matthew's Sayings of Jesus: The non-Marcan Common Source of Matthew and Luke* (Chicago: University of Chicago Press, 1918) 17–18.

off. After all, we know of Paul's "tearful letter" to the Corinthians not because it is listed in any patristic source, but merely because of a quite passing comment made by Paul himself. Without this notation, we would have no hint at all of such a letter. Or again: we deduce the existence of a "Two Ways" document, not because it is ever mentioned in a patristic source, but because its existence follows *logically* from an analysis of the possible literary relationships among the *Didache, Barnabas,* and the *Doctrina Apostolorum.*[58] Hence, the non-mention of Q in early Christian sources is neither unparalleled nor, under the circumstances, particularly troubling.

(2) Goulder's second objection has to do with the minor agreements. I have already indicated that these can be accommodated on several "realistic" versions of the 2DH. Of course, they can also be explained on the complex hypotheses of Boismard, or on Robert Gundry's view that Luke had some access to Matthew as well as Q,[59] or on the 2GH or FGH.

(3) Goulder's final and most important argument against the existence of Q has to do with the appearance of allegedly Matthaean vocabulary in Luke or, to put it differently, the allegedly Matthaean character of Q's vocabulary and thought.[60] This is an issue that requires far more space than is available in order to provide a satisfactory reply[61] but David Catchpole's work has contributed to this debate in two important regards.

Catchpole has shown, first, that while some of the vocabulary of Q (or double tradition) appears in Matthew (and hence, on the FGH might be Matthaeanisms in Luke), Matthew has a significant number of phrases and terms in double-tradition contexts to which Luke is favourable. For example, Matthew's extension of the quotation from Deut 8:3 to include the phrase ἀλλ' ἐπὶ παντὶ ῥήματι ἐκπορευομένῳ διὰ στόματος θεοῦ (Matt 4:4) has not been adopted by Luke, in spite of the fact that the "word of God" is an obvious Lukanism.[62] On the 2DH, it was Matthew who added the phrase to Q, not Luke

---

[58] See J.S. Kloppenborg, "The Transformation of Moral Exhortation in *Didache* 1–5", in *The Didache in Context: Essays on its Text, History and Transmission* (ed. C.N. Jefford; NovTSup 77; Leiden: Brill, 1995) 88–109.

[59] Gundry, "Matthean Foreign Bodies" [n. 2].

[60] See Goulder's "Self-Contradiction in the IQP" [n. 4].

[61] R.A. Derrenbacker and I will reply to Goulder's criticism of the IQP in "Self-Contradiction in the IQP?: A Reply to Michael Goulder", *JBL* 119 (2000) forthcoming.

[62] Catchpole, *Quest for Q*, 13.

who deleted it (from Q or Matthew). Similarly, the FGH requires one to assume that Luke omitted Matt 5:5 μακάριοι οἱ πραεῖς, 5:6b καὶ διψῶντες τὴν δικαιοσύνην, 5:7 μακάριοι οἱ ἐλεήμονες, and 5:8 μακάριοι οἱ καθαροὶ τῇ καρδίᾳ, in spite of the fact that Luke shows an interest in righteousness, mercy, meekness, and purity of heart.[63] These and many other observations make difficult Goulder's thesis that Luke used Matthew directly. The 2DH appears to account better for these data.

Second, Catchpole has shown that at several points, Q's perspective differs from Matthew's, something that should not happen if indeed it is the case (as Goulder alleges) that Q is basically Matthaean. But the double tradition, exemplified by Q 6:20b–21; 9:57–60; 10:4–7; 12:22–31; and 16:13, is much more emphatic on extolling and enjoining poverty than is Matthew, who does little or nothing to enhance the theme he inherited from Q and who passes over Mark 12:41–44. Catchpole concludes that although Matthew has taken over a tradition on poverty, he "is clearly happier with piety than with poverty".[64] He observes, moreover, that Q (or the double tradition) shows very little interest in Matthew's concern for the status of the Torah[65] or with Matthew's penchant for connecting miracles with Jesus' Davidic kingship.[66] In other words, Catchpole has pointed to a gap between Q's thought and that of Matthew, a gap that tells against collapsing Q into Matthew.

The force of Catchpole's observation is to undermine the case that Goulder has tried to mount in support of Luke's direct dependence on Matthew and against the need to posit a common source for Matthew and Luke. A full reply to Goulder's 800 pages of *Luke: A New Paradigm* would require a monographic treatment; but Catchpole's limited response is sufficient to underscore the considerable problems with Goulder's own view, and the considerable merits of deriving the common Matthew-Luke material from a common source.

---

[63] Catchpole, *Quest for Q*, 20–21.

[64] Catchpole, *Quest for Q*, 23.

[65] Catchpole, *Quest for Q*, 42. I have argued that Q's interest in the perdurance of the Torah comes late in the editorial history of Q, and in not central to the main thrust of Q's thought: J.S. Kloppenborg, "Nomos and Ethos in Q", in *Gospel Origins and Christian Beginnings: In Honor of James M. Robinson* (ed. J.E. Goehring et al.; Sonoma, CA: Polebridge, 1990) 35–48.

[66] Catchpole, *Quest for Q*, 44–45.

Conclusion

In this paper I have argued, first, that Goulder has adopted a view of paradigms that corresponds more closely to Popper's view of scientific theories than it does to Kuhn's. The significance of this observation lies in the fact that it seems apparent that Goulder's interlocutors do not share his rather strict Popperian view of falsification. Moreover, whatever its applicability to hypotheses in the experimental sciences, Popper's view is inappropriate when it comes to the study of the Synoptic Problem. In place of a schematic and easily falsifiable model of Synoptic interrelationships, I have argued for a historically and technically "realistic" view. To adopt such a view, as I believe that most proponents do, renders ineffective most of the arguments that Goulder mounts against the 2DH.

Second, I have suggested that Goulder's own view is not a paradigm, at least by Kuhn's standards. It fits easily within the broad paradigm of gospels studies that has prevailed since the early 1800s. This paradigm privileges the gospels in their historical, literary, and socio-rhetorical particularity, and seeks to establish a plausible theory of literary dependence. Formally speaking, Goulder's hypothesis is no different from the 2DH, the 2GH, or the several more complex hypotheses that are advocated today although, to be sure, Goulder has several interestingly different emphases in his explanatory theory.

Finally, I have argued the objections that Goulder has raised to the 2DH are not especially threatening and that, on the other hand, there are considerable problems with Goulder's own view. A "realistic" model of the 2DH can accommodate the few problematic minor agreements without collapsing, and the evidence that Goulder adduces of Matthaeanisms in Luke (or Q) at certain points is met by the balancing observation of the *lack* of Matthaeanism in Luke at others, and the non-Matthaean character of the double tradition.

Reflection on Goulder's hypothesis and its reception raises an interesting puzzle. Goulder has not been successful in offering decisive objections to the 2DH,[67] but even if he has not, it is a perfectly

---

[67] Goulder seems to concede this point, though he has varying explanations: In "Farrer on Q" (*Theology* 83 [1980] 194), his explanation is *ad hominem*: "Q is not going to collapse: it has the highest vested interest of any New Testament hypothesis in that virtually ever scholar has written a book assuming its truth". Elsewhere, his explanation has more to do with the nature of refutation: "In matters of this kind we cannot hope for proof. The four hypotheses [2DH, 2GH, FGH, and

rational option to embrace his hypothesis, since it provides a ready solution to the issue of the minor agreements and the allegedly Matthaean vocabulary in Luke. It is possible to account for Lukanisms in Matthew by his notion of "Luke-pleasing" vocabulary. To be sure, there are some serious technical problems involved in rendering his thesis plausible, notably accounting for Luke's almost complete detachment of the double tradition from the context in which he found it in Matthew and his relocation of that material elsewhere, or the puzzle that when faced with material common to Mark and Matthew, Luke never prefers Matthew's sequence over Mark's, and almost never prefers Matthew's wording to Mark.

It might be that resistance to the FGH comes down to the inability of exegetes to imagine such activities on Luke's part. But I doubt it. I think it rather more likely that ideological factors are at play. For much of its history, Q has served as a way to bridge the gap between Matthew and Luke, in the 80s or 90s, and the historical Jesus. Harnack believed Q to be a largely unadulterated collection of Jesus sayings. And despite the fact that most of the technical studies that have appeared on Q since Hoffmann's 1972 *Habilitationsschrift*[68] have tried to treat Q primarily as a document in its own right rather than as a source for the historical Jesus, outside of these specialist circles, Q is still regularly thought to offer immediate or near immediate access to Jesus. Hence John P. Meier quickly dismisses studies that attempt to ascertain a composition history of Q as "hypothetical"—what in New Testament studies do we do that is not hypothetical?—and satisfies himself with the caricature of Q as a "grab bag".[69] This allows him to use Q pretty much as Harnack had done, and to quarry Q for Jesus tradition without having to inquire whether Q's own editorializing and creativity renders those excavations problematic.

Deutero-Markan theories] are in competition with one another in plausibility....
The Two-Source hypothesis starts with the tremendous advantage of having been widely taught as *the* solution for at least fifty years" ("Luke's Knowledge of Matthew" [n. 4], 144–5).

[68] P. Hoffmann, *Studien zur Theologie der Logienquelle* (NTAbh NF 8; Münster: Aschendorff, 1972; ²1975; ³1980).

[69] J.P. Meier, *A Marginal Jew: Rethinking the Historical Jesus. Volume Two: Mentor, Message, and Miracles* (ABRL; New York: Doubleday, 1994) 179–81: Meier's characterization of Q as a "grab bag" without a coherent theology or a supporting "community" allows him to prescind from the literary and historical questions of its origin, tradents, and editorial tendencies, and to use Q simply as a "distinct and valuable source for sayings . . . of Jesus and John".

If theories of the stratification of Q have been regarded as imperiling the quest of the historical Jesus, Goulder's thesis would have a yet more devastating effect. Not only is most of the double tradition treated as the result of Matthaean editorial activity; but the special Lukan material, including the parables of the Man Going Down the Road and the Lost Son, so central to many constructions of the historical Jesus, would dissolve into Luke's exegetical imagination.

An examination of the history of solutions to the Synoptic puzzles can show how rather technical, almost algebraic, solutions to literary puzzles have functioned within broader theological paradigms and have been embraced not so much because they solved literary problems, but because they seemed to provide literary models that cohered with broader ideological interests. This is true of the use of the Griesbach hypothesis by D.F. Strauss and his associates; and it is true of the use of the Markan hypothesis by liberal theology up to Harnack. The 2DH is difficult to displace not only because it still serves as an effective compositional hypothesis and because compelling counter-evidence has not been produced; but it also allows for a relatively fulsome picture of Jesus and seems to lend support to general theological models concerning the gradual development and articulation of christological, eschatological, and ecclesiological doctrines.

In order for the Farrer-Goulder hypothesis to be an effective counterforce to the 2DH, it is necessary to show not only that it solves literary puzzles more effectively than the 2DH, but that it holds the promise of addressing larger theoretical issues raised in the dominant paradigm, such as the relationship of the historical Jesus to the pictures of Jesus in the early Jesus movement, and a comprehensive theory of the creation, use, and transmission of early christian texts. *That* would begin to constitute a "new paradigm".

THE EARTHLY JESUS IN THE SYNOPTIC PARABLES

Birger Gerhardsson

Almost all utterances which the synoptic tradition attributes to Jesus of Nazareth must, with regard to form, be assigned to one and the same Jewish genre: the mashal (Hebrew מָשָׁל, Greek παραβολή). The Jews used that broad term for any text which was brief and formulated in an artistic way; in other respects these texts differ widely from each other. In our modern exposition, we find it worthwhile to divide the synoptic sayings of Jesus into logia and parables—I prefer the designations aphoristic and narrative meshalim—but we must keep in mind that this division is one we make ourselves; it is not articulated in the text material.[1]

The dominical sayings in the synoptic tradition are thus all meshalim, apart from a few occasional statements ("Let us go across to the other side" Mark 4:35) and rejoinders. This ought to mean that their content, too, is homogeneous; they should in principle treat the same themes. But we notice, surprisingly enough, certain differences of content between the aphoristic meshalim and the narrative ones. I intend to discuss one of these differences here. I dedicate this essay to my friend David Catchpole, who is well known among New Testament scholars throughout the world, not only through his fine contributions to biblical scholarship but also through his years of service as an efficient and gracious secretary in the SNTS.

Aphoristic Meshalim about Jesus Himself

One of the two main types of synoptic meshalim, the logia, includes a long series of statements in which Jesus speaks of himself and his ministry. Most important of these are two groups of closely related sayings:

---

[1] See B. Gerhardsson, "The Narrative Meshalim in the Synoptic Gospels: a Comparison With the Narrative Meshalim in the Old Testament", *NTS* 34 (1988) 339–63.

1. Son of Man sayings (utterances containing the designation the
Son of Man, ὁ υἱὸς τοῦ ἀνθρώπου),
2. "I"-sayings (logia in the first person).
Let me comment briefly on these sayings in turn.

1. Regarding the Son of Man sayings, many scholars think that some
of them originally referred to a person other than Jesus, a future
apocalyptic figure. I doubt that. But even if this was the case at the
beginning, it is beyond dispute that these sayings, within the framework of the completed Gospels, always refer to Jesus himself. In my
translation I shall, in order to stress this key aspect of the utterances,
replace the expression "Son of Man" (SM) with "I" (Jesus).[2]

What does the synoptic Jesus say about himself in these sayings?
In terms of content, it is well known that these sayings all fall within
three distinct subject fields, which are never mixed or combined. I
quote here the most important examples. It is not, for my present
purpose, necessary to be exhaustive, or even to account for the vari-
ant readings within the synoptic tradition. A rough result is quite
adequate.

(a) None of the sayings directly concerns the question who Jesus
is. In some of them, however, he comments upon his situation and
position, his powers and tasks at the present time on earth:

Matt 8:20 (Luke 9:58): . . . but I (the SM) have nowhere to lay my
    head
Matt 9:6 (Mark 2:10, Luke 5:24): But so that you may know that
    I (the SM) have authority on earth to forgive sins . . .
Matt 11:19 (Luke 7:34): I (the SM) came eating and drinking . . .
Matt 12:8 (Mark 2:28, Luke 6:5): For I (the SM) am lord of the
    sabbath
Matt 12:32 (Luke 12:10): Whoever speaks a word against me (the
    SM) will be forgiven . . .
Matt 13:37: The one who sows the good seed is me (the SM)
Matt 20:28 (Mark 10:45; cf. Luke 22:27): Just as I (the SM) came
    not to be served but to serve and to give my life a ransom for
    many
Luke 19:10: For I (the SM) came to seek out and to save the lost.

---

[2] Apart from this, I adopt in this essay the translations of *The New Revised Standard
Version*.

These pronouncements thus concern the great authority and power (ἐξουσία) of Jesus (to forgive sins, to heal on the sabbath, etc.), his outreach in Israel, that he sows the good seed, that sin against him will be forgiven, that he came to serve and to seek the lost, that he is homeless; in other words, both his majesty and his humble serving.

(b) In a number of other SM sayings, Jesus anticipates his imminent passion, death, and resurrection:

Matt 12:40 (Luke 11:30): For just as Jonah . . . so for three days and three nights I (the SM) will be in the heart of the earth

Matt 17:9 (Mark 9:9): Tell no one about the vision until after I (the SM) have been raised from the dead

Matt 17:12 (Mark 9:12): . . . So also I (the SM) am about to suffer at their hands

Matt 17:22 (Mark 9:31, Luke 9:44): I (the SM) am going to be betrayed into human hands, and they will kill me, and on the third day I will be raised

Matt 20:18–19 (Mark 10:33–34, Luke 18:31–33): . . . and I (the SM) will be handed over to the chief priests and scribes, and they will condemn me to death; then they will hand me over to the Gentiles to be mocked and flogged and crucified; and on the third day I will be raised

Matt 26:2: You know that after two days the Passover is coming, and I (the SM) will be handed over to be crucified

Matt 26:24 (Mark 14:21, Luke 22:22): I (the SM) go as it is written of me, but woe to that one by whom I (the SM) am betrayed!

Matt 26:45 (Mark 14:41): See, the hour is at hand, and I (the SM) am betrayed into the hands of sinners

Luke 22:48: Judas, is it with a kiss that you are betraying me (the SM)?

Most of these utterances are portentous, preparing the disciples directly and clearly for the Easter events which are about to take place: Jesus will suffer, be crucified and die, but also be raised. One of the sayings, however, merely mentions the resurrection as an important point in time, and one expresses a woe on the traitor.

(c) A third group of SM sayings looks ahead with a somewhat longer perspective. Jesus speaks in them about his future appearance on the clouds, with power and glory, as the final judge:

Matt 10:23: You will not have gone through all the towns of Israel before I (the SM) come

Matt 13:41: I (the SM) shall send my angels, and they will collect out of my kingdom all causes of sin and all evildoers, and they will throw them into the furnace of fire . . .

Matt 16:27 (Mark 8:38, Luke 9:26): For I (the SM) am to come with my angels in the glory of my Father, and then I will repay everyone for what has been done

Matt 16:28 (Mark 9:1, Luke 9:27): Truly I tell you, there are some standing here who will not taste death before they see me (the SM) coming in my kingdom

Matt 19:28 (Luke 22:28–30): Truly I tell you, at the renewal of all things, when I (the SM) am seated on the throne of my glory, you who have followed me will also sit on twelve thrones, judging the twelve tribes of Israel

Matt 24:27 (Luke 17:24): For as the lightning comes from the east and flashes as far as the west, so will be my coming (the coming of the SM)

Matt 24:30 (Mark 13:26, Luke 21:27): Then my sign (the sign of the SM) will appear in heaven, and then all the tribes of the earth will mourn, and they will see me (the SM) coming on the clouds of heaven with power and great glory

Matt 24:37 (Luke 17:26): For as the days of Noah were, so will be my coming (the coming of the SM)

Matt 24:39: . . . so will be my coming (the coming of the SM)

Matt 24:44 (Luke 12:40): Therefore you also must be ready, for I (the SM) am coming at an unexpected hour

Matt 25:31: When I (the SM) come in my glory, and all the angels with me, then I will sit on the throne of my glory

Matt 26:64 (Mark 14:62, Luke 22:69): From now on you will see me (the SM) seated at the right hand of Power and coming on the clouds of heaven

Luke 17:22: The days are coming when you will long to see one of my days (days of the SM), and you will not see it

Luke 17:28–30: Likewise, just as it was in the days of Lot . . . it will be like that on the day when I (the SM) am revealed

Luke 18:8: And yet, when I (the SM) come, will I find faith on earth?

These sayings foretell the parousia and suggest what is then going to happen: Jesus will triumph, in power and glory, assisted by a multitude of angels; righteous and wicked people will be separated and will either inherit the kingdom or be sent to the eternal fire in retribution for their works; the twelve will be given the task of judging Israel; all this will take place soon and will come as a surprise.

I repeat that the three groups of sayings are never mixed or combined. The only exception is the retrospective reference in the saying that those who have followed Jesus will be enthroned at the parousia.

2. Jesus speaks of himself elsewhere in the Gospels as well, most explicitly in the so-called "I"-sayings. Some of these mention the earthly ministry of Jesus or aspects of it. In others, Jesus makes sweeping statements about his position. Most interesting from our point of view are the following logia:

Matt 5:17: Do not think that I have come to abolish the law or the prophets; I have come not to abolish but to fulfil

Matt 9:13 (Mark 2:17, Luke 5:32): For I have come to call not the righteous but sinners

Matt 10:32 (Luke 12:8): Everyone therefore who acknowledges me before others, I also will acknowledge before my Father in heaven. But . . .

Matt 10:34–39 (Luke 12:51–53, 14:26): Do not think that I have come to bring peace to the earth; I have not come to bring peace but a sword. For I have come to set a man against his father, and a daughter against her mother . . .

Matt 11:27 (Luke 10:22): All things have been handed over to me by my Father; and no one knows the Son except the Father, and no one knows the Father except the Son and anyone to whom the Son chooses to reveal him

Matt 12:27–28 (Luke 11:19–20): If I cast out demons by Beelzebul, by whom do your own exorcists cast them out? . . . But if it is by the Spirit of God that I cast out demons, then the kingdom of God has come to you

Matt 15:24: I was sent only to the lost sheep of the house of Israel

Luke 12:49: I came to bring fire to the earth.

In these utterances, Jesus says that the Father has handed over all things to him, that the kingdom of God has come to Israel if he casts out demons with God's spirit (NB that Jesus here teaches about his exorcisms), that he has come to fulfil the law and the prophets, that he was sent to sinners or to the lost sheep of Israel, that his followers must acknowledge him before others, that they must love him more than their own father and mother, and that they must be ready to lose their lives for his sake.

Especially important is of course the solemn declaration of the resurrected Jesus at the end of the Gospel:

Matt 28:18: All authority in heaven and on earth has been given to me.

The aphoristic meshalim I have discussed here all have a declarative character; some of them are almost programmatic statements and manifestos. They are not hints or circumlocutions. Jesus gives simple and explicit information about himself and his aims, even in the midst of his earthly ministry.

We need not here discuss the question to what extent these *aphoristic* meshalim are genuine sayings of Jesus. It seems reasonable as a rough judgment to say that a basic core of them is authentic, while others may have been rephrased or even created in the course of tradition or by the evangelists. And since we can assume that the *narrative* meshalim of the gospels also include both authentic parables and ones formulated within the church after Easter or by the evangelists themselves, we would expect that Jesus plays the same role in the narrative meshalim as he does in the aphoristic ones. Is that the case?

Jesus (the Son of Man/the Son) in the Narrative Meshalim

Jesus' narrative meshalim do not fulfil the function of proclaiming, declaring or defining. They illuminate and illustrate; Jesus resorts to them when he wants to clarify his point more fully.[3] In the discussion that follows, I will, for the sake of simplicity, use the verb "elucidate" in distinction from just "touching upon" or "mentioning". To what extent do the parables deal with Jesus himself? Let me list those of them which are of interest for our question.

---

[3] See Gerhardsson, "If We Do Not Cut the Parables Out of Their Frames", *NTS* 37 (1991) 321–35 (repr. in Gerhardsson, *The Shema in the New Testament. Deut 6:4–5 in Significant Passages* [Lund: Novapress, 1996] 224–38), esp. 325–9.

A. *Matthew: Material*

11:16–19   The Playing Children. This parable is about the way in
which the people of God ignore both God's severe announcement
through John the Baptist and his joyful message through Jesus. Jesus
is mentioned in the interpretation (v. 19); he says that I (the SM)
came, in contrast to the Baptist, "eating and drinking". Thus Jesus'
ministry in Israel is touched upon, as a vibrant activity, in this parable, but it itself is not elucidated; rather it is mentioned in order to
elucidate the disobedience of Israel.

13:1–23   The Sower. The man who sows is possibly thought to
be Jesus, but he is not the object of any interest here. The parable
elucidates the fate of the seed: the sowing is fruitless in three cases
and fruitful in one. No christological interest is reflected, no interest in Jesus himself.

13:24–30, 36–43   The Tares. The farmer who sows good seed
in his field is, according to the recorded interpretation (v. 37), Jesus
(the SM). He is identified as part of the picture but is, in the narrative, just a point of departure, playing only a background role.
The parable deals with the tares in the field and elucidates three
questions: whence they come, why God lets them remain and when
they are going to be cleared away. No christological interest is dis-
cernible, no interest in Jesus.

13:47–50   The Dragnet. The fishermen are not mentioned. The
point is simply that fishing is carried out in two main phases: first
a general collection and then a concluding separation. This is interpreted (vv. 49–50) as referring to a general gathering into the kingdom
of heaven followed by a separation of the wicked from the righteous
at the last judgment. No christological interest is reflected, no interest in Jesus.

18:10–14   The Lost Sheep. The parable elucidates the joy at the
recovery of that which was lost, the joy of the Father in heaven. No
christological interest, no interest in Jesus.

21:33–44   The Wicked Husbandmen. The Matthean version of
this parable is something of an allegory of salvation history. The
owner of the vineyard sends two rounds of messengers (the former
and the latter prophets) and finally his son. When the tenants kill
him as well, it is the last straw; they are rejected. Keeping in mind
that the mashal has in this case undergone a certain amount of alle-
gorization, the thought is presumably that the landowner's son is

Jesus. The son does not, however, play any active role in the narrative; he is just sent by his father and killed by the tenants. The point
is that the insubordinate tenants cannot avoid punishment for their
persistent obstinacy, since they reject and kill even the son. The son
himself is not the object of the narrator's interest.

22:1–10, 11–14 The Great Feast and The Wedding Garment.
A king gives a wedding banquet for his son. The prince does not
play any active role in the parable. He is merely mentioned at the
beginning to indicate what a wonderful invitation the chosen guests
refuse. In the attached parable (vv. 11–14), he is not referred to.
Thus a christological motif is touched upon initially, but it does not
play any role in the course of events.

24:42–44 The Burglar. The parable is interpreted with a statement (v. 44) that Jesus (the SM) will come at a time when he is not
expected. Thus the returning, heavenly Jesus is at the centre of the
parable. The elucidated point is not, however, his person, but the
fact that his parousia will occur unexpectedly.

24:45–51 The Servant in Authority. In this parable the master
has put a servant in charge of his household, to give the other servants their allowance of food at the proper time. The narrative elucidates how the master at his return will reward his servant if he
has done his work but punish him without mercy if he has not. No
interest is devoted to the master himself, only to the actions he will
take. The master is probably Jesus. His severity is underlined.

25:1–13 The Ten Virgins. At the beginning of the mashal, the
bridegroom's coming is expected. In the narrative, he appears after
a delay, welcomes the five virgins who are ready, and takes them
into the wedding banquet. When, later, the remaining five virgins
come after a delay, they are locked out, inexorably. The elucidated
point is the bridegroom's absolute "No!" to those who prepare
themselves too late; he judges them without mercy and condemns
them. The bridegroom is certainly to be identified with the returning Jesus.

25:14–30 The Talents. The basic role in this parable is played
by the master of the slaves: he distributes the tasks among them and
settles accounts with them, rewarding the two who are trustworthy
and punishing the lazy one. The point of the narrative is that unfaith-
fulness in stewardship will be severely punished at the final accounting (the parousia and judgment), while trustworthy stewardship will
be rewarded abundantly. The master of the slaves is certainly Jesus

(the SM). He is characterised, interestingly enough, as a harsh and exacting man.

25:31–46 The Last Judgment. This mashal tells how Jesus (the SM) is going to reward good individuals from all peoples and punish the wicked; the criterion will be whether they have had a heart for fellow humans in need, so acting, in Jesus' terms, as unto him. The meaning is not that Jesus (the SM) declares himself identical with distressed people. Rather the old biblical theme is recalled that help to people in need is counted as done to God. We find no proper christological interest or interest in Jesus in this mashal, but only interest in the last judgment and the criteria that will then be applied.

Commentary

When we ask to what extent Jesus himself or his activity in Israel, from the baptism until the crucifixion, is *elucidated* in the parables in Matthew, the answer is: Not in any one of them. His outreach in Israel is *mentioned* and characterized in the interpretation of the parable of the Playing Children. But what is *elucidated* here, is not the ministry, but simply that this ministry as well as that of the Baptist finds no receptiveness in Israel.

Jesus' preaching and teaching is perhaps the point of departure for the parable of the Sower, but it is not elucidated. The focus is rather on the broad motif that the ongoing preaching of the Word meets with diverse responses.

Jesus' exorcisms and acts of healing are never taken up in the parables, nor his non-therapeutic miracles. Nor does any parable deal with his remarkable forgiving of sins or his activity on the sabbath.

His crucifixion is not hinted at. It is said in the parable of the Wicked Husbandmen that the landowner's son is rejected and killed by the tenants—but he is not crucified.

Nor is the resurrection of Jesus taken into account.

What does have a secure place in the narrative material is the climactic future—the parousia of Jesus (the SM) and his judgment. But, again, what is elucidated is not the heavenly Lord himself, but what his return is going to mean: there will be a judgment, the judgement will reward the faithful and punish the unfaithful, and it will come as a surprise. The *that* and the *how* of the judgment are thus the subject of elucidation in some of the parables, but not the judge himself.

The motif in the parable of the Talents that the coming judge is harsh and exacting, is, in a sense, a christological trait, but little is made of it. The same is true of the sinister severity of the master in the mashal of the Servant in Authority and of the bridegroom in the parable of the Ten Virgins.

The striking result of our study is thus that neither Jesus himself, as a riddlesome prophetic-messianic figure in Israel, nor the different elements of his activity and fate on earth are the object of questions and elucidation in the narrative meshalim in Matthew. There has obviously not been interest in taking up these latter motifs and elucidating them with parables.

B. *Mark: Material*

4:1–20 The Sower. What I said above about the Matthean version applies in Mark as well. No christological interest, no interest in Jesus.

4:26–29 The Seed Growing Secretly. The sower may be Jesus, but in that case he is just a representative of all who "sow the word" and wait for the harvest God will send. No christological interest or Jesus-interest.

12:1–12 The Wicked Husbandmen. The parable is not allegorized here to the same extent as in Matthew, but it remains basically the same: the son whom the owner of the vineyard sends at the end is certainly Jesus. He is not, however, the object of the narrator's interest; he is not elucidated.

13:32–37 The Watchful Servants. The master of the house who goes on a journey and comes back is certainly Jesus (the SM). But no interest in him is noticeable; of interest is only the fact that he will return at an unknown point of time and suddenly.

Commentary

With regard to the parables in Mark, we notice the same situation as in Matthew: no parable elucidates Jesus himself or any of the characteristic elements of his earthly ministry, only his future return and the last judgment.

The parable of the Talents is not found in Mark.

C. *Luke: Material*

7:31–35   The Playing Children. The fact that Jesus (the SM) came eating and drinking, without being received, is mentioned in the interpretation (v. 34). In the same way as in Matthew, the parable elucidates Israel's disobedience towards God's messengers, the severe ones as well as the joyful ones, most recently John the Baptist and Jesus.

12:35–38   The Watchful Servants. The master returning from a wedding banquet is certainly Jesus (the SM). The parable elucidates both the duty to be ready for the parousia and the rich reward Jesus is going to give those who are.

12:39–40   The Burglar. The thief who comes at an unexpected hour represents Jesus (the SM), who is not elucidated, however, just mentioned. The focus is on the necessity of being ready.

12:41–46   The Servant in Authority. The master who returns and sees whether the servant in authority is properly at work is, of course, the judging Jesus (the SM). That which is elucidated is the master's principles of reward and punishment at his final accounting with his servants, both the conscientious ones and the negligent.

13:23–30   The Closed Door. The owner of the house who has to open the door or keep it closed is certainly the judging Jesus (the SM). Mention is made in the parable that he once ate and drank with those who are now knocking at his door and that he taught in their streets. Here the earthly activity of the earthly Jesus is hinted at. But it is just mentioned as an argument; it is not elucidated.

16:19–31   The Rich Man and Lazarus. The motif that somebody may return from the dead to warn the surviving appears at the end of the parable. The proposal is, however, rejected: if people do not listen to Moses and the prophets, neither will they be convinced if someone rises from the dead (v. 31). This may well allude to Israel's unresponsiveness toward the message of Christ's resurrection, but it does not further elucidate the content of this message.

19:11–27   The Pounds. The nobleman who goes to a distant country and then returns must be the Jesus of the parousia and judgment. When he comes back, he rewards two faithful servants for their stewardship and punishes a bad servant for his laziness; the focus is on the last one. The nobleman's demands and his judgment are presented in the narrative, and one of his characteristics is accentuated: he is called a harsh man with inexorable demands.

20:9–19 The Wicked Husbandmen. The owner of a vineyard
sends in turn three slaves to collect his share of the produce of the
vineyard, all in vain. When finally he sends his beloved son and the
tenants throw him out and kill him, the owner destroys them and
gives the vineyard to others. The son is in this case Jesus; the identification is developed in the commentary that follows (vv. 17–19) in
the words about the stone which the builders rejected. In this parable Jesus' story is treated. The part of the story primarily elucidated
is the rejection and killing of the son and the punishment that will
follow upon that crime. The son himself is only mentioned as sent
by the owner of the vineyard and killed by the tenants.

Commentary

Jesus' parousia and final judgment are dealt with in the narrative
meshalim in Luke as well: some parables elucidate the fact that these
events will come unexpectedly and inexorably and that reward and
punishment will be assigned. The severity of the judge is stressed.
The motifs are essentially the same as in Matthew.

With regard to the *earthly ministry* of Jesus, there are a couple of
formulations touching upon it in the Lukan parable material. Jesus'
outreach in Israel is characterized in the application of the mashal
of the Playing Children (he came "eating and drinking"); here Luke is
in agreement with Matthew. Moreover, in the parable of the Closed
Door, those who are knocking remind the master of the house that
he ate and drank with them and taught in their streets. This must
refer to Jesus.

But this is just incidental mention. The person of Jesus is not
directly taken up for *discussion and elucidation* in any one of the Lukan
parables either; nor is his earthly ministry, his crucifixion (apart from
the allusions to the killing of the son), or the resurrection (we only
find a possible hint of the message of the resurrection in the mashal
of the Rich Man and Lazarus).

A Fact That May Give Clues

I have here put forward an observation: there is an astonishing
difference in content between those sayings of Jesus (meshalim) which
are of an aphoristic type (logia) and those of a narrative type (parables). We find in the logia material a long series of sayings which

present in a straightforward and unreserved way Jesus' own person and earthly activity, indicated both in general and in specific terms; but we do not meet anything of that kind in a single one of the parables.

It is true that we cannot expect the secret of Jesus' person to be elucidated in detail in any parable—the question who he was and how he was to be regarded; the synoptic parables never characterize their role figures in detail.[4] Still, we could well expect that Jesus' situation and position, his powers and tasks during his earthly ministry, would be elucidated. A long series of aphoristic meshalim address these themes, without restrictions. We could reasonably have a similar expectation in the matter of Jesus' horrendous end on earth—his humiliation, suffering, and death on the cross—and the miraculous resurrection. But nothing of all this is taken up for elucidation in the synoptic narrative meshalim, in spite of the fact that so many aphoristic meshalim address these very topics.

The narrative mashal in the gospels can have a very concrete *focus*. At times the synoptic Jesus teaches about his listeners and opponents. They may be alluded to in the pictorial material and even elucidated; so, e.g., in the parables of the Two Sons, the Wicked Husbandmen, the Feast, the Lost Son. As to Jesus himself, we get a glimpse of him in the parables of the Wicked Husbandmen, the Closed Door in Luke, and perhaps the Feast in Matthew. He is, however, just hinted at; neither he nor his earthly ministry is *elucidated*.

Jesus was an enigmatic figure in Israel. His ministry included provocative traits (e.g., the exorcisms, the forgiving of sins and the healings on the sabbath), and his suffering and crucifixion were catastrophic and horrendous. These themes, so problematic and difficult to understand, must have needed explanation. The fact that we do not find any narrative meshalim treating such themes in the gospels must mean that neither Jesus himself nor early Christianity created any parables about them. Where such questions have been asked, they have obviously been answered in direct speech: in declarative aphoristic meshalim, a number of which I have quoted above.

Moreover, why has the *parousia* a secure place in the narrative meshalim, but not the mysterious resurrection (a possible allusion in

---

[4] See Gerhardsson, "Illuminating the Kingdom: Narrative Meshalim in the Synoptic Gospels", in *Jesus and the Gospel Tradition* (ed. H. Wansbrough; JSNTSup 64; Sheffield: JSOT, 1991) 266–309, esp. 275–7.

one parable is all)? Part of the explanation is certainly that Jesus himself dealt with the parousia in a number of parables; hence only new formulations were needed here, presumably together with some additional texts. The crucifixion and the resurrection, on the other hand, were not elucidated by Jesus in any parable, and the gospel material shows that they were not introduced into the parable material by the teachers in early Christianity either.

My observation harmonizes well with what I have pointed out elsewhere in an article on the way in which the parables of Jesus were handed on in early Christianity. Granted that they were preserved with a certain margin for variation in wording, yet they seem to have been transmitted in a conservative way. They have retained the framework of form and content which they had in the teaching of Jesus himself. And the new parables, which may have been formulated to supplement existing material, are obviously not essentially different from the old ones; nor do they seem to be numerous.[5] The observation I have made in this article leads to the same picture.

Enough of that. I have presented an observation which poses a problem, the solution to which may provide additional clues for our study of the gospel tradition: Why is there in this respect such a clear difference between those dominical meshalim which are aphoristic and those which are narrative? Does the difference reveal something about the way in which Jesus expressed himself and taught? Does it reveal something about the way in which early Christianity used Jesus' logia and parables respectively? Did the aphoristic and the narrative meshalim have different Sitze im Leben in Jesus' activity? Or in that of early Christianity? Were the two types of text transmitted in essentially different ways? Or does the difference to which I have drawn attention here reveal that the phases in the theological development of early Christianity are reflected differently in different types of material? I hope that the debate can give answers to this set of questions.[6]

---

[5] See "Illuminating the Kingdom", 294–304.
[6] Stephen Westerholm polished my English; I thank him.

FIRST-CENTURY HOUSES AND Q'S SETTING

Peter Richardson

Introduction

Setting in Judaism

David Catchpole argues that "in terms of the fundamental beliefs of Judaism the Q Christians were a conservative grouping", marked by a concern for "inclusion and association and inseparability" from features of Judaism such as the temple.[1] Though Pharisaism concerns them, the woes do not separate Q's community from either temple or law (p. 276). "The tradition seems throughout to be comfortable within Judaism, uneasy about Pharisaism, and, in view of the rarity of any comment on the authority of the law (Q 16:17), not at all preoccupied with the problem which threatened to tear apart other early Christian communities" (p. 277); "we have a picture of a community whose outlook was essentially Jerusalem-centred, whose theology was Torah-centred, whose worship was temple-centred, and which saw (with some justice) no incompatibility between all of that and commitment to Jesus" (p. 279).[2] This conservatism should neither be equated with nor set against Pharisaism, nor any specific group within Judaism; it may merely express a "common—and conservative—Judaism", characteristic of many Jews.[3]

The *realia* of early Christianity and second-Temple Judaism, as exposed in recent archaeological research in the Galilee and the Golan, suggest that Catchpole's views are correct.[4] This present

---

[1] David R. Catchpole, "Tradition and Temple", chapter 9 in *The Quest for Q* (Edinburgh: T. & T. Clark, 1993) 256–79, originally published in W. Horbury, ed., *Templum Amicitiae: Essays on the Second Temple presented to Ernst Bammel* (JSNTSup 48; Sheffield: JSOT, 1991) 305–29. This quotation is from pp. 256–7.

[2] See also C.M. Tuckett, "Q (Gospel Source)", in *ABD* 5.567–72, especially 570–71. "Q's polemic is directed against only a part of the Jewish community among which the Q community existed" (p. 570).

[3] E.P. Sanders, *Judaism, Practice and Belief, 63 BCE-66 CE* (London: SCM/ Philadelphia: TPI, 1992) Part II.

[4] Peter Richardson, "Enduring Concerns: Desiderata for Future Historical-Jesus Research", in William E. Arnal and Michel Desjardins, eds, *Whose Historical Jesus?* (ESCJ 7; Waterloo, ON: Wilfrid Laurier University Press, 1997) 296–307.

homage explores how my interests and his—both substantially altered
from our interests as students almost forty years ago—now intersect.
I will discuss archaeological data from towns and villages, which can
help define a realistic context within town life in the Lower Galilee
and the Golan that offers a plausible concrete setting, and will argue
that thinking coherently about some of this evidence might lead to
a more refined view of some of Q's emphases.[5]

Archaeological and Architectural Setting

Archaeological work has for a century or more deeply influenced
understandings of the setting of early Christianity, through analyz-
ing inscriptions, Christianity's urban setting,[6] architecture of early
synagogues,[7] religious and social structures, adaptations of houses for
religious activities,[8] voluntary associations[9] and specificity of settings.[10]
The gains have been substantial and continue to accumulate.

For obvious reasons, NT studies has concentrated on Paul and
focused on major cities, especially in Asia Minor and Greece: Paul's
(and also Ignatius's) letters, for example, reflected their social settings
in the household, set against the rich tapestry of Greek culture and
urbanism. The model of urban, upper-class Hellenistic and Roman
houses that followed from this analysis of setting has illuminated how
house churches developed in cities such as Ephesus, Corinth and

---

[5] See recently Jonathan L. Reed, "Galileans, 'Israelite Village Communities,' and
the Saying Gospel Q", in Eric M. Meyers, ed., *Galilee through the Centuries* (Duke
Judaic Studies Series 1; Winona Lake, IN: Eisenbrauns, 1999) 87–108. His approach
and mine cohere; I agree with his criticism of Richard Horsley, *Galilee: History,
Politics, People* (Valley Forge, PA: TPI, 1995) and *Archaeology, History, and Society in
Galilee: The Social Context of Jesus and the Rabbis* (Valley Forge, PA: TPI, 1996).
Specifically, I emphasize the similarity of Galilean traditions to *Judean* practices.

[6] See Wayne Meeks, *The First Urban Christians* (New Haven: Yale University Press,
1983).

[7] For example, Dan Urman and Paul V.M. Flesher, *Ancient Synagogues. Historical
Analysis and Archaeological Discoveries* (SPB 47.1–2; Leiden: Brill, 1994); Lee I. Levine,
The Ancient Synagogue (New Haven: Yale University Press, 1999).

[8] L. Michael White, *Social Origins of Christian Architecture*, (2 vols, HTS 42; Valley
Forge: TPI, 1997).

[9] John Kloppenborg and Stephen G. Wilson, eds, *Voluntary Associations in the
Graeco-Roman World* (London: Routledge, 1996).

[10] Helmut Koester, ed., *Ephesos. Metropolis of Asia* (HTS 41; Minneapolis: TPI,
1991); Helmut Koester, ed., *Pergamon, Citadel of the Gods* (HTS 46; Minneapolis: TPI,
1998); Karl Donfried and Peter Richardson, eds, *Judaism and Christianity in First-
Century Rome* (Grand Rapids: Eerdmans, 1998).

Rome. Sometimes, however, this urban Roman model, predicated on one set of local conditions, has been applied to other settings, without sufficient consideration of social and architectural and cultural factors in these other locations.[11] Neglecting the local particularities of each region in which Christianity became rooted and projecting a model derived from an Asian setting on all early-Christian developments will not do.

Recent attention to the rise of the Jesus movement in Galilee, Judea and South Syria has not much utilized *realia* associated with the movement, in part simply because no *realia* can certainly be associated with it in these early stages.[12] While the same is true of Paul and his communities, however, this fact has not prevented Pauline scholars from making substantial gains in understanding Paul's social location in Greece and Asia Minor. There is still a need, however, to move beyond generalities to a refined social description of the setting of both Jesus and the subsequent communities that shaped the earliest gospel materials, based on a nuanced understanding of relevant physical evidence.

The Jesus-movement in Palestine was lodged for some time within Palestinian Judaism. To what extent does first-century Palestinian Judaism reflect, and in turn shape, the movement's social setting and literary products?[13] How did the early Christian movement develop in northern Palestine—Galilee and Gaulanitis? Within what architectural setting did its development occur? How did the Q movement fit into its religious and socio-cultural setting? Here I will focus on housing, because it is antecedently likely that the movement among the first two generations of Jesus' followers was essentially a house-based movement and I will suppose that Q's setting was not identical to Paul's.

---

[11] For one important alternative, Robert Jewett, "Tenement Churches and Communal Meals in the Early Church: The Implications of a Form-Critical Analysis of 2 Thessalonians 3:10", *BR* 38 (1993) 23–43.

[12] On "housing", John J. Rousseau and Rami Arav, *Jesus and his World. An Archaeological and Cultural Dictionary* (Minneapolis: Fortress, 1995) make a beginning.

[13] Other areas and cultures influenced particular gospels: eastern Syria for Thomas, the Aegean for Luke, the Decapolis for Mark, etc.

Local Housing and Religious Life in the Galilee and Golan

Housing

Palestinian housing has begun to receive some attention in recent years. Archaeological excavations explore housing with increasing frequency, though archaeological reports do not always emphasize housing as an innately important feature of the site. Since houses were often occupied for centuries, their evidence is usually rather complex. The evidence is now being sifted in fresh ways, though data for the study of first-century houses is still somewhat sparse and not broadly available.[14] Here I will describe three sites—Yodefat, Gamla and Cana—among the several available that inform us of first-century houses in Galilee and the Golan (others are Capernaum, Gush Halav, Sepphoris, Meiron and Chorazin), followed by observations on how this material might contribute to a reading of Q.[15]

The northern parts of the land, especially Galilee and Gaulanitis (with related regions in Auranitis, Trachonitis, Batanea and Hulitis), though less than half of Herod the Great's kingdom, comprised most of the regions of Antipas and Philip, and later of Agrippa I and II, during and after the time of Jesus.[16] These northern regions—especially the towns—were likely Q's context. Yodefat in Galilee and Gamla in the Golan, both well excavated though not yet well published, are the most important sites, sharing two important features: both were destroyed by Vespasian in 67 CE and both subsequently remained deserted. Both offer pristine first-century sites where excavation of the housing has been an important goal, so they get scholars as close to the setting of Jesus as is currently possible. I add Cana, though it continued to be occupied much later, for its intrinsic interest.

---

[14] Yizhar Hirschfeld, *The Palestinian Dwelling in the Roman-Byzantine Period* (Jerusalem: Franciscan Printing Press/IES, 1995), mixes times and places in its broad chronological sweep. Santiago Guijarro, "The Family in First-Century Galilee", in Halvor Moxnes, ed., *Constructing Early Christian Families* (London and New York: Routledge, 1997) 42–65, focuses on four types of houses: simple, courtyard, big mansion (*domus*), and farmhouse; see also Santiago Guijarro Oporto, *Fidelidades en Conflicto. La Ruptura con la Familia por Causa del Discipulado y de la Mission en la Tradición Sinóptica* (Plenitudo Temporis 4; Salamanca: Pulicaciones Universidad Pontificia, 1998) chapters 11–12.

[15] Reed, "Galileans", 94, for sites and periods.

[16] Peter Richardson, *Herod, King of the Jews and Friend of the Romans* (Columbia, SC: University of South Carolina, 1996) chapter 6.

Yodefat

Yodefat lies on a steep hill half way between the Mediterranean Sea and the Sea of Galilee, concentrated on a bald hilltop, with a narrower southern extension on a plateau about 30 metres lower.[17] The small town (about 40 dunams or 4 hectares = 10 acres), built around a Hellenistic fortified farmstead,[18] had flourished since the Hasmonean resettlement of Galilee in the second century BCE. Though without a natural water supply, there were walls, cisterns and buildings that formed the basis of the later town. The earliest Jewish village was contained within the late-Hellenistic fortifications, but it grew as it attracted new settlers, so that the southern slope and the lower plateau dated mainly from late-first century BCE to first-century CE, perhaps under Herod the Great (40–4 BCE), Antipas (4 BCE–38 CE) or Agrippa I (38–44 CE).[19] Josephus strengthened the defences of Yodefat and built additional walls to resist Rome's forces during the early stages of the Revolt of 66–74 CE, taking advantage of the steep hillsides that dropped down into the surrounding wadis.[20] The town fell on 20 July 67 CE, after a 47-day siege.

Occupation was densest on the hilltop, while parts of the plateau were used for industrial purposes: pottery, oil and wool.[21] Rock-cut cisterns—some immense—were distributed around the site, with the largest concentration around the hilltop; most were domestic installations, either with rock-cut stairs or an opening for a storage jar. There were two large open rectangular pools, one on the plateau and one on the northern saddle. The cisterns and pools were crucial to the town's existence, for Yodefat survived entirely on collection and storage of the winter rains.

---

[17] Josephus claims the town's population was 40,000, though it could have held no more than 10,000 during a siege and its normal population was probably about 2000.

[18] I will ignore the important Hellenistic stage.

[19] The expansion of the town represents significant development, so formulations of Galilean social history that emphasize the accumulation of land and wealth in relatively few hands, with the squeezing of the lower middle class, may need modification.

[20] The excavations, especially in 1999, show this hurried strengthening of the defences clearly.

[21] Excavations in 1999 disclosed intensive pottery manufacturing in the southeast area; earlier excavations discovered an almost complete olive press in a cave outside the east wall, with crushing stone, weights, pressing pits, slots for beams; loom weights and fine decorated spindle whorls were found at various residential locations.

Houses—mostly first century CE—have been excavated throughout the site. The houses were relatively simple, one or two stories,
rough masonry construction, almost no hewn stones, not even around
the openings; no mortar to bond the masonry, no plaster or stucco
wall finishes. The walls would have been bonded with and finished
in mud plaster, all of which has disappeared. Second floors and roofs
would have been constructed from small locally cut wooden beams,
with sticks and branches and mud forming the finished floor and
roof surfaces. No stone beams or arches were found, and no roof
tiles.[22] Ground floors were equally simple, of beaten earth or roughly
leveled exposed bedrock, occasionally plaster or rough flagstone.

The lower plateau (roughly a third of the total area) had an orthog-
onal street pattern between two north-south wadis. On the east, a
narrow street two metres wide and surfaced with stone chips ran
immediately inside the wall; at other points (e.g., the steeply terraced
housing on the northeast, inside the wall at the Roman ramp, and
on the west side of the plateau) houses abutted the wall directly or,
in several cases, were cut through by the wall, suggesting that at
these points the town wall was hurriedly constructed under threat
of attack.

Little evidence of public facilities emerged—neither agora nor public building—except for the largest cisterns and the two large open
rectangular pools. The one inside the walls had rock-cut steps and
balustrade at one corner. These communal water storage facilities
must have been used for such purposes as watering animals, doing
laundry, or emergency water supplies (as Josephus reported). There
was a public building at some stage, either Hellenistic, perhaps destroyed during the Hasmonean period, or Jewish, or both. Several
column drums, several capitals, one piece of architrave and one mon-
umental doorpost—found in disparate locations—demand a public
building of some sort. If so, it was probably on the now-bare hilltop, where some of the Hellenistic period rock-cuttings may eventually offer a sensible reconstruction of such a building.[23]

Evidence of Jewish ritual concerns was common. Numerous stone-
cut cups, bowls and jugs, in a wide variety of shapes and sizes,

---

[22] Arches and basalt beams were common in the volcanic areas of Golan and
parts of the Negev, where different building materials and methods were used.
[23] The denuded hilltop was the reason that the site, identified since the 19th century, had been thought archaeologically unpromising.

implied a widespread concern for ritual purity and a common wish to avoid impurity in everyday utensils. [Widely-distributed evidence of stoneware has been found throughout the Holy Land and in varied social locations, so it is no longer possible to argue that only one group—Pharisees, for example—were concerned with ritual purity.] In addition, two plastered *mikvaoth* (ritual bathing pools) in adjacent houses in the southeastern area pointed to purity concerns. Both stoneware and *mikvaoth* imply strong domestic attention to purity; both underline the continuity between Galilean and Jerusalem purity concerns. Indeed, some of the stoneware may have originated in Jerusalem. Much the largest group of coins was Hasmonean, likewise suggesting close links with Jerusalem.[24]

Housing was of several types. Terrace housing was excavated on the steep east slope just inside the wall, similar in form and construction to the housing at Gamla and Cana (see below). The foundations and lower floors were rock cut; houses were generally two stories; upper-level houses were built on the walls of the houses below, so at some places the walls were three stories high. Buildings abutted the walls with no intervening street; the owners higher up used rooftops in lower houses as an additional living area, so that housetops were part of the living space.

An unexpectedly different room was discovered in 1997 among these terraced houses. A length of almost five metres of frescoed plaster wall in a simplified geometric first Pompeian style was found, alongside a painted plastered floor. This evidence of a wealthier and higher-status owner is unusual in a rural, peasant town in the Galilee; the nearest Jewish analogies are Jerusalem mansions or Herod's palaces.[25] The fresco is the most vividly painted intact first-century wall in Israel; the painted plastered floor is unique in Galilee. Was this a peristyle house? Was the rest of the house consistent stylistically? Were there other similar houses, forming a continuously differentiated social scale in town, or was this house unique?

Where the slope was less steep the houses followed the contours

---

[24] Reed, "Galileans", 97; similar numismatic evidence appears at Cana and Gamla and numerous other sites. See Reed's general observation, "Although the number of sites with abundant first-century evidence is limited, the existing finds consistently mirror the finds of Judea and are remarkably homogeneous with regard to religious indicators" (p. 100).

[25] Note especially the wealthy "priestly houses" in Jerusalem; villas at Jericho, Herodium, Masada, Machaerus, Caesarea Maritima.

closely, with floors adjusted to suit the levels. The foundations and floors were sometimes rock-cut; one floor was roughly plastered on bedrock. The rooms were a little larger than in the terrace housing, and more artefacts illustrative of daily life were found in this area. Short lanes off streets provided access. Two houses with private *mikvaoth* formed a complex that could be reconstructed in more detail.[26] Floors were rock cut or beaten earth or roughly paved; rock-cut cisterns were filled by water from the roofs; at ground level, a collecting pool and channel survived. An adjacent cave for storage or a shelter for animals was integrated into one house; there was an oven (*tabun*) in one courtyard and a small olive crushing installation in another. One *mikveh* had a room of its own, the other was in a rock-cut cavity adjacent to a cistern; both appear to have had their own sources of running ("living") water. Beside this complex was the large open pool, on which the neighbourhood focused. A narrow street separated these houses from the town wall, and a lane gave access to other houses whose plans could be read from rock-cuttings. Outside the wall was a cave with an industrial-scale double press olive-oil installation; the *mikvaoth* inside the wall might mean it operated under conditions of ritual purity.

On the lower plateau, simple first-century housing was excavated with one- or two-room houses laid out orthogonally. One larger unexcavated house was discerned from rock-cut remains half a metre to a metre high (front door and all four walls); it may have been planned around a central courtyard, though it had collapsed into the cisterns below. On the northwest near the Roman siege-ramp another housing complex showed the vigour of the Roman siege. Houses were built against the wall, which had been occupied over a long period and reconstructed from time to time (late-Hellenistic houses overlaid by first-century BCE and CE houses, with blocked-up doorways, changes in plan, and casemate rooms filled during the siege to strengthen the defences). A kitchen was the most revealing room, full of pottery broken during the siege, with a *tabun* (oven) and a piece of stone table top or kitchen "counter", all on a beaten earth floor with an adjacent bedrock floor at a higher level.

---

[26] "Echoes from the Ancients," a prize-winning video produced by WXXI in Rochester, includes a 3D visualization of these houses predicated on my sketches as site-architect for Yodefat.

Gamla

Gamla was similar. The town was built on a much earlier Bronze Age site, on a ridge between two very steep ravines with rivers. Yet there was no permanent water supply by aqueduct; cisterns supplied Gamla's water needs. Like Yodefat, the town had flourished from its Hasmonean rejudaization onwards. The earliest housing was in the northeast, but it expanded into new neighbourhoods to the south and west. Most housing was terraced, with the rear wall of a lower house acting as the front wall of a house higher up the slope. Gamla was easily defended on three sides by the ravines, but the natural approach from higher land to the east required extra efforts, so that during the Revolt the ridge was cut away. As at Yodefat, Josephus added a new casemate wall before the Roman attack, using a combination of existing and new walls. He described a round tower high on the northeast corner where the casemate wall met the ridge. These precautions worked well, for Gamla survived a seven-month siege in the spring of 67 CE before Vespasian took it in the fall of that year.

Early in the excavations a public building was uncovered, which served various religious purposes associated with a synagogue: a simple multi-purpose communal building, with columns, varied capitals, complex entrance, niche in one corner (possibly for the torah scroll), separate large *mikveh* with water channel and connecting *otzer*, and small *Beth ha-Midrash* for study and education, acting as part of the casemate wall. Recently another community building was discovered (whose presence was long anticipated from a lintel lying on the surface),[27] whose purpose is uncertain, for the structure has no obvious Jewish analogies. It seems impossible that it was a second synagogue, since it had three equal-sized rooms side by side, connected by doorways; all the inner rooms opened onto a broad space through wide openings framed by decorated pilasters. Had the building been found in a Roman context, it might have been thought dedicated to Rome's Capitoline Triad! That is obviously impossible, and all that can be said so far is that Gamla had more complex and organized social-religious facilities than are usually imagined for a rural townsite.

Gamla's neighbourhoods, like Yodefat's, were somewhat differentiated, some wealthier than others. The excavators identified a

---

[27] The lintel had a central rosette with flanking palm trees.

higher quality neighbourhood on the west, a Hasmonean neighbourhood (perhaps no longer in use at the time of the revolt) on the
upper hillside, a neighbourhood around the synagogue, and still other
neighbourhoods lower down the hill. The buildings in the wealthy
neighbourhood were larger, better constructed, better finished, had
frescoed plaster surfaces, with more artefacts, and even a paved courtyard of dressed stones. A street running up the hill (*clivus*) had wide
stairs, and adjacent houses included industrial activities such as olive
oil or flour production. A complete first-century CE olive oil installation occupied its own building, with two large industrial-scale presses,
an adjoining "office", and an attached *mikveh* to ensure ritual purity.
Perhaps olive oil was produced for use in the Jerusalem Temple.[28]
The oil factory was roofed with slabs of columnar basalt about two
metres long, supported by an intermediate longitudinal arch to create
a single large room. Most houses—and even the recently discovered
public building—were also roofed with columnar basalt supported
on consoles projecting from the walls.

The older northeast houses were smaller (time of Herod or earlier), had plastered floors within which were washing and purification
installations, including a low pool and a bathtub; one was a *mikveh*
with a floor of undressed stones in front.[29] Near the synagogue,
houses survive to about four or five metres: rooms typically had small
cupboards incorporated into one or more walls; in some cases stairs
to a second floor have survived. The simplicity of the domestic organ-
ization in such simple housing can still be appreciated; no rooms
were specifically set aside for dining or "public" entertaining.[30] More
significant was the concern for ritual purity, both publicly alongside
the synagogue, privately within the Hasmonean housing and in the
western neighbourhood.

Khirbet Cana

With Khirbet Cana the situation is different.[31] Whereas Yodefat and
Gamla were destroyed in 67 CE, most structures at Cana were occu-

---

[28] A hoard of Tyrian shekels from the time of the revolt, possibly connected with
this, was found outside the door of this factory.
[29] See S. Gutman, "Gamala," *NEAEHL* 2.459–63.
[30] Hirschfeld, *Palestinian Housing*, 24–44, seems to suggest *triclinia* and entertaining
areas were regular features, but there is little evidence of either in simple early houses.
[31] Excavations began in 1998; see the web page http://www.nexfind.com/.

pied through a number of periods. The town lies about two kilometres southeast of Yodefat, across the Beth Netofa valley from
Sepphoris and due north of Nazareth. It was identified as NT Cana
in the Byzantine period, and soon became a pilgrimage site, exploit-
ing the Fourth Gospel's description of Jesus' turning water into wine.[32]
Cana sits on a rocky hilltop visually controlling one of the most fer-
tile areas in the holy land, an area long known for wheats and grains.
The site was occupied through a very long period, with peaks of
settlement in early Roman and Byzantine periods and smaller peaks
in the Iron Age and early Arab period. The visible structures are
mainly Roman and Byzantine: a rectangular structure 45 by 80
metres covered the crown of the hill in the Byzantine period, likely
the monastery referred to in the literature. The housing on the slopes
outside the monastery walls was occupied from early Roman to
Byzantine; structures under the Byzantine structure were Roman.

Cana was undefended before the metre-wide monastery walls were
built; it occupied about 20 or 25 dunams on the upper slopes of
the hill,[33] most of which derived from the early Roman period or
earlier. Evidence of clear resonances with Yodefat and Gamla has
emerged after two years' excavation. Stoneware, in two cases turned
on a lathe rather than chiseled, was used. This concern for ritual
purity was accentuated, as at both Yodefat and Gamla, by *mikvaoth*:
one *mikveh*—in use up to the Byzantine period though its date of
origin was much earlier—has been excavated and three other possible
mikvaoth have been identified. One (potentially first-century) *mikveh*
had been abandoned because the mason carelessly broke through
into a large bell cistern, making both cistern and *mikveh* useless.

On the steeper eastern and western slopes early-Roman or late-
Hellenistic houses were reused up to the Byzantine period. They

---

[32] A Byzantine-period pilgrimage cave was excavated in 1999, with crosses and
inscriptions on a plastered ceiling, covered by a later layer of plaster. The cave had
a plastered bench through which one damaged stone-cut basin still poked, while a
second broken stone-cut basin was discovered below the plaster and a third stone-
cut basin was lying on the floor. The plastered bench had space for six stone cut
jars. It seems that a deliberate effort was made in the Byzantine period to develop
Cana as a pilgrimage site, though it was somewhat off the beaten track. Later,
Kefar Cana (which also has first-century remains) replaced Khirbet Cana, because
it was on the main road to Tiberias.

[33] There was a "suburb" (still undated), halfway up the slope, of about 12 dunams.
In total, Cana was about 35 dunams (3½ hectares or 8 to 9 acres). Gamla was
about 60 dunams (6 hectares or 15 acres); Yodefat was about 40 dunams (4 hectares
or 10 acres).

were terraced in much the same way as at Yodefat and Gamla; on
the east slope a party wall between two houses had joist supports
for the floor of the house lower down the slope. It is still too soon
to sketch in any detail the urban layout at various periods or to
describe differentiated neighbourhoods, but it is clear that the first-
century town was about the same size as the late-Roman or early-
Byzantine towns.

Eleven family tombs, all loculi type, have been examined in a very
preliminary way and appear to be early-Roman Jewish tombs. All
but one shared a slightly unusual entrance, having a vertical shaft
without steps or other obvious means of access from ground level.
None was decorated, though several were embellished architecturally
with walls and water installations and perhaps monuments on the
surface level. Forty-two loculi were identified, but the total number
was substantially greater, since several tombs or chambers could not
be entered.

Cana, like Yodefat and other first-century sites, had a public reservoir on the saddle north of the townsite, at a level where it was of
relatively little use except to water animals. A complex entrance system utilized this saddle near the public reservoir.[34] Despite the fact
that Cana was unwalled, there appears to have been a double gateway, with both an informal "gate" (between bedrock and a large
standing stone) and a formal gate (with ramped approach and two
right-angled turns). These are still unexcavated, so it is unclear from
what period this arrangement derived. From the northern saddle,
travellers descended either to the southwest or to the southeast, and
joined the main Galilean road system six kilometres to the south
across the Beth Netofa valley, where major roads connected to
Tiberias, Sepphoris and Ptolemais. Alternatively, one might take a
minor road northwest to Yodefat.

Social Setting of Q

The Origins of Q

Some opening presumptions might be stated at the outset.[35] (1) Q
is not the product of "wandering charismatics" but of a sedentary

---

[34] Two roads joined beside a large reservoir in the saddle of the hill, similar to
Yodefat.
[35] Since I do not work regularly with Q, I gratefully acknowledge assistance at

scribal setting.[36] (2) While stages in Q's composition can plausibly be posited,[37] (3) Q profits, nevertheless, from analysis as a carefully structured and complete document in its final—if not original—stage, (4) so that Q is not so much *Kleinliteratur* (*pace* Harnack, et al.) as a careful composition.[38] (5) Cynicism, which many consider relevant to Q's origins, was a near neighbour to Antipas's and Philip's territories.[39] Despite substantial recent contributions, I have not yet found a convincing analysis of the setting of Q; it is more often assumed than analyzed,[40] and one of those assumptions has tended to be the multi-ethnic but essentially Greco-Roman character of the Galilee, where Q likely was written.[41]

I have begun in the first part of this paper with the concrete and "real" evidence from first-century towns and villages in the region.[42] What follows is a modest contribution to concretizing Q's social setting.[43] It starts from Kirk's reconstruction of Q's macro composition: "Each macro composition articulates, aggressively and *protreptically*, a

---

an early stage in the development of these ideas of three recent graduates of the Centre for the Study of Religion in the University of Toronto, William E. Arnal, Willi Braun and Alan Kirk. It has also been an advantage to work adjacent to John Kloppenborg and Leif Vaage of the Toronto School of Theology, whose work on Q has stirred such interest.

[36] William E. Arnal, "The Rhetoric of Deracination in Q: A Reassessment," Ph.D. dissertation (Centre for the Study of Religion, University of Toronto, 1997), who emphasizes economic issues such as a Roman policy of urbanization, more effective collection of taxes, monetization, cash-cropping, and consolidation of holdings (chap. 6); Arnal suggests Capernaum as a place where a village scribe might have produced the earliest stratum of Q. See also John S. Kloppenborg, *The Formation of Q: Trajectories in Ancient Wisdom Collections* (Philadelphia: Fortress, 1987).

[37] Kloppenborg, *Formation*.

[38] Alan Kirk, *The Composition of the Sayings Source: Genre, Synchrony, and Wisdom Redaction in Q* (NovTSup 91; Leiden: Brill, 1998), building on Kloppenborg, *Formation*, 323–4.

[39] Leif Vaage, *Galilean Upstarts: Jesus' First Followers According to Q* (Valley Forge, PA: Trinity Press International, 1994). While I am not persuaded by the "wandering cynic" hypothesis, it can be granted that there were cynics in the Decapolis, even perhaps in Gaulanitis and Lower Galilee.

[40] John S. Kloppenborg Verbin, *Excavating Q: The History and Setting of the Sayings Gospel* (Minneapolis: Fortress, 2000), forthcoming, may deal with these questions in more detail.

[41] Burton L. Mack, *The Lost Gospel. The Book of Q and Christian Origins* (San Francisco: Harper Collins, 1993), chapters 4, 11.

[42] K.C. Hanson and Douglas E. Oakman, *Palestine in the Time of Jesus. Social Structures and Social Conflicts* (Minneapolis: Fortress, 1998), chapters 2 and 4, for other social aspects.

[43] In contrast, Reed, "Galileans," 103–8, has undertaken to refute Horsley's "Northern Israelite" traditions in Q; for a different critique, see Halvor Moxnes, "The Historical Context of Jesus Studies," in *Biblical Theology Bulletin* (1998) 1–15.

set of social interests. Q is a particularistic 'boundary' text whose paraenesis functions both to *recruit* and *resocialize*."[44] Others will evaluate his claims in detail; to my mind, Kirk makes attractive and illuminating sense of Q, so I build on his "ring composition," despite my general reservations about such approaches.

Macro composition

Kirk argues for four main compositional macro units that collectively form a single larger composition. My summary strips away a few elements irrelevant to my purpose, though his overall scheme is still represented, sometimes by summaries of compositional units; the highlighting of words and phrases is mine.

I Q 3:7–7:35

John introduces Jesus, including his baptism, John and Jesus together (3:7–9, 16–17, 21–2)
   Temptation narrative (4:1–13)
      Inaugural sermon; love enemies, judge not (6:20b–49)
Central saying   *Disciple not above teacher* (6:40)
        Trees, fruit, builders
      Healing of Centurion's child (7:1–10)
Jesus' ministry, speaks of John, John and Jesus viewed together (7:18–35)

II Q 9:57–10:22

Homelessness, give up family and patrimony (9:57–8)
   Lord of harvest sends labourers, "I send you" (10:2–3)
      Peace, houses/cities accept; houses/cities reject; towns, cities (10:4–11)
Central saying   *More tolerable for Sodom than that city* (10:12)
      Woes, cities reject (Chorazin, Bethsaida, Capernaum); cities accept (Tyre, Sidon); towns, cities (10:13–5)
   Receives you, receives me, receives him who sent me (10:16)
Exalted Son of the Father, new family (10:21–2)

III Q 10:23–13:35

Sightedness, presence, prophets and kings (10:23–4)
   Prayer: household, daily bread, debts, poverty, purity (11:2–13)
      Beelzebul controversy (11:14–23)
        Unclean spirit (11:24–6)

---

[44] Kirk, *Composition*, 399, his italics.

Central saying   *Last state worse than first* (11:26b)
     Demand for sign controversy (11:29–35)
   Official purity apparatus and cult: temple, tithes, wealth, pollution (11:39–52)
Blindness, withdrawal, Jerusalem prophets (13:34–5)

IV Q 12:2–22:30

Followers judged by hostile authorities (12:2–12); followers anxious about
food and drink (12:22–34)
   Servants, master, rewards and punishments (12:35–46)
     Judgment and families sundered (12:49–59)
       Mustard seed and leaven (13:18–21)
         The narrow door and Banquet parable (13:24–9)
Central saying   *Last first, humble exalted* (13:30; 14:11)
             Banquet parable and discipleship (14:16–24, 26–7, 34–5)
         Lost sheep, lost coin, law and divorce, mustard seed (15:4–10; 16:16–18;
         17:5–6)
     Judgment; divisions and separations (17:23–37)
   Servants, master, rewards and punishment (19:12–25)
Followers judge Israel; followers eat and drink in kingdom (22:28–30)

In Kirk's display of Q, its macro-structure flows from John's relationship with Jesus in the wilderness by the River Jordan in unit I, to
a familial setting among towns and cities, contrasting three towns
that oppose Jesus with two (actual? potential?) that approve him in
unit II. The emphasis on households continues in unit III, where
the poverty and purity concerns of households favourably disposed
to Jesus contrasts with Pharisees' purity and torah concerns and also
with Jerusalem's treatment of prophets. In unit IV, Q continues to
emphasize household activities associated with daily life in a rural
and agricultural setting: eating and drinking, masters and servants, divisions within families. Thus Q progresses in an orderly way
from a remote setting in Judea (I) to a town/city setting somewhere
in regions contiguous to the north end of the Sea of Galilee and
Phoenicia (II), through an emphasis on household concerns (III–IV),
some of which focus on purity (III), while others focus on status
relationships, rewards and punishments, within an agricultural context (IV). Curiously, none of the four central sayings in Kirk's macro-
composition is fundamental to the social description; I take the reason
to be that these sayings characterize central elements in Jesus' message as recalled by Q, and are not elaborative or adaptive features
of the Q scribe, introduced to apply Jesus' central sayings to his
community. To put it differently, the scribe of Q is freer in the surrounding materials to introduce features that directly reflect his own

setting, though it would be incorrect to suggest that the surrounding material is therefore entirely redactional or secondary.

Q's emphases as an indication of its setting

Of course, only a careful redactional and compositional analysis can
disentangle those elements in Q that most directly reflect its setting.
In place of such a fine tool, of the sort that Catchpole has wielded
with distinction, I use a blunt tool and gather a few elements together
to assess the coherence of the picture of Q. My interest is not in
the redaction but in the reflected setting and its correspondence to
archaeological, architectural and religious features found in the representative towns briefly surveyed above.

Households

Q's core imagery is house and householder as models for community behaviour. A householder returns from a wedding feast to find
lights burning and rewards his faithful servants (Q 12:35–8); a householder punishes unreliable servants (Q 12:42–6); a careless householder's house is broken into (Q 12:39–40); a householder answers
the door cautiously after dark (Q 13:25–7); a householder rewards
and punishes servants for their handling of monetary affairs on his
behalf (Q 19:12–26).[45] A [one-room] house lit by a lamp functions
as an analogy for the eye (Q 11:33–6); a house on a rock is an
analogy to doing Jesus' words (Q 6:46–9); an orderly and swept
house is an analogy for exorcism (Q 11:24–6).[46]

Poverty, debts, and supply of daily bread are endemic issues within
some households (Q 11:2–13), while other wealthier households have
servants and labourers, who are subject to domestic punishments
and rewards (12:35–6; 19:12–25). Some followers leave the domestic responsibilities of ploughs and graves (Q 9:57–62) to take up temporary accommodation in others' houses, where they are provided
for (Q 10:4–11), perhaps sundering familial relationships to acquire
new ones (Q 12:49–59; 10:21–2). The Q community throughout presupposes householders in towns and villages or as small landowners,
with servants as factors in the domestic economy of the household,

---

[45] The realism of the picture of the servant who hides his talent resonates with
archaeological evidence of buried coin hoards (Gamla, above).
[46] For a similar analogy, drawing on the roughness of rural floors, see Q 15:8–10,
Lukan *Sondergut*.

suggesting that Q's immediate context lies less among the dispossessed or itinerant than among those who have houses and, in some cases, land.

The earlier description of small northern towns corresponds to and amplifies Q's core emphasis on the household within rural town life. Towns' social organizations were tight and close, with houses packed together into a relatively dense matrix, where—if it was hilly, as many townsites were—houses shared common walls for different levels of floors and roofs, where living and working activities were in the courtyards overlooked by roofs, where the roof of one house was an important addition to the living space of another (Q 12:3; LkR in 17:31). Small Palestinian townscapes were dominated by conglomerations of housing, with some variety in building types—though not comparable to equivalent Roman towns—that might have stretched to a multi-purpose communal building and a few other public facilities.

Agricultural imagery

Q presumes plentiful harvests that require labourers (Q 10:2), oxen (Q 14:18–9), with sowing and reaping, gathering into barns and granaries (Q 12:24–8), winnowing and threshing (with burning of chaff; Q 3:17; cf. Q 17:35). These presuppose a crop-farming background in either Lower Galilee (for example, Beth Netofa or Jezreel valley) or Gaulanitis, both of which provide a rich agrarian context that responds well to Q's ethos.[47] Q's neglect of the natural imagery of lakes, fishing and boats (slightly present in Q 17:2, 6; 11:11) suggests that the Sea of Galilee is outside Q's field of vision, just as its neglect of grapes and olives (slight allusion in Q 6:44) suggests that Upper Galilee is beyond its view.

Towns and Villages

Q was interested in the city, naming polemically Chorazin, Bethsaida and Capernaum (within a few kilometres of each other), and pointing in a surprisingly positive way to Tyre and Sidon (Q 7:1–9; 10:13–15). Jerusalem also is mentioned polemically (Q 13:34–5; cf. 11:51), though probably proverbially, as Tyre and Sidon may also be. The polemic against Capernaum, Bethsaida and Chorazin is

---

[47] Were it not that more general considerations pull the setting towards either Galilee or Gaulanitis, other farming areas in Judea, Batanea, Auranitis or Peraea would be possible.

surprising, for otherwise Q's setting might naturally gravitate to that region. Because the polemic is rhetorically gratuitous, these towns cannot be the actual setting of Q.[48]

The strong man in his house (*aulê* = peristyle? Q 11:21–2) hints at a kind of house found in cities, though the new evidence that an agrarian town such as Yodefat could have a sophisticated upper class house, possibly a peristyle house, calls for careful consideration of the degree of uniformity of houses in a particular town. Further, the commonplace observation that the Synoptics never mention Tiberias or Sepphoris (Antipas's capitals)—used to claim that Jesus was not interested in the city—must be qualified with the observation that Q mentions Bethsaida, and even Tyre and Sidon.[49] Generalizing from the omission of Tiberias and Sepphoris that the tradition is hostile to all cities is unwarranted and misleading. Attention to Galilee coupled with silence on its capitals must be balanced by consideration of Gaulanitis and mention of its capitals. Galilee and the Golan are equally good candidates for Q's setting; indeed, Q's description of the kingdom divided against itself (Q 11:17–18) resonates with the division of Herod's kingdom between his two sons, specifically with the consequences of that division during their tense later years or during the middle years of Agrippa II.

The *agora* is the backdrop for children's games (Q 7:32) and for Pharisees' activities (Q 11:43).[50] Community proclamation occurs in cities (*poleis*;[51] Q 10:8–12; cf. 10:1), which either accept or reject the messenger (Q 10:13–5; cf. Matt 10:23). Followers must enter by the narrow gate, as in a walled town (Q 13:24 should perhaps be taken in its Matthean form; Matt 7:13–4)[52] or even an unwalled town, Yodefat, Gamla and Cana provide relevant examples. Towns near the capitals offer a highly suitable setting for Q.

---

[48] In his argument for Q's location at the north end of the lake, Arnal relies on these allusions too much.

[49] Mark also mentions Caesarea Philippi (Philip's other capital).

[50] None of the three towns surveyed above has evidenced an *agora*, though all must have provided for communal sale of goods.

[51] *Polis* properly alludes either to capitals of the brothers Herod, or Decapolis cities (Beth Shean, Hippos, Gadara), or coastal cities (Dor, Ptolemais), though Matthew (11:20) thinks Chorazin, Bethsaida and Capernaum are *poleis*. Only Bethsaida would qualify.

[52] Luke has it in a household setting.

Ritual Allusions

Baptism. In Q the ascetic John warns of Isaiah's vision of judgment to come and separation of the wheat from the chaff (Q 3:2b–4, 7–9, 16–17, 21–2). While his baptism now is by water, at the end it will be by fire and Spirit (Q 3:16). So Jesus comes to John for baptism (Q 3:21–2), a rite intended for the children of Abraham, and by extension for those not genetically Abraham's progeny (Q 3:7–9). John reappears in the account, thinking of Jesus in terms of Isaiah's description of the one to come (Q 7:18–28); the sociable townsperson contrasts starkly with the wilderness ascetic (Q 7:33–4). Still, the Jesus of Q, true to his Baptizer roots, threatens metaphorical fire and baptism (Q 12:49–53), the result of which is division among members of the household and fire upon the earth.

This emphasis on baptism seems not to accord well with the sociogeographic setting that I am proposing for Q, until we recall the widespread provision for ritual immersion in *mikvaoth*. Purity concerns, including rituals dealing with uncleanness, were common within the towns that I consider within the horizon of the Q-community, so one possibility is that baptism in this earliest period would be thought appropriate in a *mikveh*, or in another water source such as public reservoirs.[53] While John's baptism was in the wilderness, "this generation's" baptisms took place in towns and public places (Q 7:31–5).

Eating and drinking. Q uses differences in eating and drinking as fundamental elements in the John/Jesus contrast: John ignored the table; since Jesus did not (Q 7:33–4; cf. Q 10:7) he was thought a glutton and a drunk like tax collectors and sinners. Similar allusions appear in the Great Supper parable (Q 14:16–24), the account of Diaspora Jews ("east and west") sitting at table (Q 13:28–9), and negatively in the eschatological sayings about the Son of Man (Q 17:27). Luke emphasizes this theme redactionally in the Marriage Feast parable (Q 12:36, Lukan *Sondergut*) and the closed door (Q 13:24–7, "we ate and drank in your presence").

This emphasis on eating and drinking within Q's social situation occasionally implies substantial dining rooms (e.g., "reclining" as in *triclinia*) for communal activities. While it is not impossible that wealthy

---

[53] *Didache* 7:1 requires baptism in "living water" (cf. Lev 15:3) and contrasts this with ordinary cold water, hinting at the use by this community of *mikvaoth* for baptisms.

followers of Jesus had such rooms, and while occasionally a Palestinian town might have houses with *triclinia* or second-floor rooms for entertaining guests, this was probably uncommon.[54] If no *triclinia* were available, where did community social/religious activities occur? Though we have no direct evidence that followers of Jesus used community buildings—like Gamla's—there is no reason for this not to have happened. The issue, of course, is the point at which an early-Christian group had become sufficiently marginalized or "self-identified" that it could no longer do so. Since Q and the community that spawned it came before the "parting of the ways", there is no reason to exclude Q's community from use of such multi-purpose communal facilities.[55]

Woes and purity. The woes (Q 11:39b-52) clearly reflect Q's setting: ritual purity of utensils (cleaning the outside and/or inside, Q 11:39b–41), tithing (Q 11:42), synagogue attendance (Q 11:43; cf. 12:11–12), corpse impurity (Q 11:44; cf. also 11:47), torah interpretation (Q 11:46, 52), relationship to prophets (Q 11:47–51). The community's relaxed handling of ritual and quasi-ritual issues is striking. Q's arguments—more subdued than Matthew's polemical expansion of the woes (Matt 23)—were directed against Pharisees and *hoi nomikoi*, but the community certainly participated in tithing, interpretation of torah and recognition of prophets, and probably also in ritual purity activities, synagogue attendance, and avoidance of corpse impurity.[56] If so, it would not seem strange if the community used local synagogues for communal meals.

Prayer. Finally, the document produced for this community contains a strong injunction to regular prayer (Q 11:2–4; cf. 11:5–8, 9–13), the clauses of which emphasize purity, poverty and debts.[57]

Summary. This sketch of Q's reflections of its social and geographical setting suggests the following. Q was part of an agriculturally ori-

---

[54] In Morocco, 500–year old Berber village houses, similar to Palestinian houses, commonly include a second- or third-floor "guest room", the only decorated room in the house, which was exclusively to entertain visitors. Hirschfeld, *Palestinian Dwelling*, s.v. "Upper-level" and "Living-Rooms", observes the same pattern.

[55] Peter Richardson, "Early Synagogues as Collegia in the Diaspora and Palestine", in S.G. Wilson and John Kloppenborg, eds, *Voluntary Associations in the Ancient World* (London: Routledge, 1996) 90–109.

[56] Catchpole's more positive understanding is better than Kirk's impression of deep-seated antagonisms towards purity concerns.

[57] Catchpole holds Q 11:5–8 to be original, not Lukan redaction.

ented community involved in grain farming and related pursuits in Lower Galilee or Gaulanitis. It was set in a town, one in competition with those towns condemned by Jesus, possibly walled, and in a location where Tyre and Sidon were within the situational horizon. Houses and householders were a dominant factor in the town. There was a synagogue, which may have been used for the group's ritual activities: eating and drinking, prayer, baptism and ritual purity.

Conclusion

Some features discussed above could reflect a stage prior to Q, perhaps a stage identified with the sayings of Jesus, so that these features reflect Jesus' setting, not Q's. This is a valid reservation, but two further observations may be made: first, even if this were the case, Q's overlay was largely consistent with the earlier setting, for most of the indications cohere into a clear picture; second, and by contrast, the setting of the "historical Jesus" would weight differently factors such as the importance of fishing, the Sea of Galilee, Jesus' trips to the "other side", a more positive attitude to Capernaum, and so on. I have deliberately left uncertain whether Galilee or the Golan is the likelier geographical location, partly because I cannot decide and partly because at this juncture more studies of these questions are needed.[58] Some indications ("other side", allusions to Tyre and Sidon) pull towards Lower Galilee; other indications (especially Bethsaida) pull towards Gaulanitis.[59]

The social and geographical setting of Q can be identified more precisely than is usually thought. Q was set naturally in towns (and cities?), not within the activities of wandering charismatics. The major social referent was the householder, some of whom were masters with servants. They worked within a region where grain crops were a common source of income. The community was familiar with and tolerant of concerns for ritual purity and the cleansing of utensils; it was a group where baptism—perhaps even the use of *mikveh*—was observed, where eating and drinking were important rituals, and thus a group that had found a solution to carrying on such activities.

---

[58] Similarly, Ivan Havener, *Q. The Sayings of Jesus* (Good News Studies 19; Wilmington, DL: Michael Glazier, 1987) 42–5.

[59] Perhaps continuity with the historical Jesus makes Lower Galilee the most logical, if not the only, choice.

RESURRECTION IN Q?

N.T. Wright

Introduction: Multiple Agnosticisms

New Testament scholars working in different fields often appear to live in parallel universes with little contact between them. We need to specialise if we are to go deeper into our chosen areas; and the multiple non-academic pressures on scholars, not least those who, like David Catchpole, have given of themselves generously to the wider concerns of both academy and church, mean that most of us can scarcely keep up in a small field, let alone across the whole spectrum of early Christianity and related topics. Scholars who, like the present writer, spend much of their lives working on Paul rarely venture across the street to visit those who work on Q, and vice versa.

All this may be inevitable, but I find it regrettable; and there are times when to cross the street, if only as a gesture of interest and support, may be worth while. It is, of course, risky. The book of Proverbs (26:17) warns that to meddle in someone else's quarrel is to take a stray dog by the ears. The high degree of current specialisation means that one may expect, as the least reward for one's pains, to be told to stick to one's own last, to mind one's own business.

But of course it is our business. By comparison with other academic fields—second-Temple Judaism, for instance—the study of the early church and its writings is a small field, with few primary sources and a small geographical and chronological framework. If it is true that a document or tradition existed that corresponds to what people today call Q, and if it is claimed that this document reflects the religious and theological interests and hopes of a community in the middle of the first century, those of us who have worked on documents that we actually possess and communities for which we have first-hand evidence are bound to take notice, especially if these hypothetical documents and communities are claimed to hold significantly different views from those commonly ascribed to early Christians. The large and often high-profile growth of Q studies in recent years,

especially in America, has gained much of its energy from the underlying hypothesis that Q, or some form of Q, represents and embodies not only an *earlier* version of Christianity than that which we find
in the written gospels from which we deduce its existence, maybe
even an earlier version than that of Paul, but a significantly *different*
one. In this different version, that which is emphasized in what are
now the canonical texts of the New Testament plays little role, and
that which is downplayed in the canon plays a greater role. Thus,
as in the triple tradition, and perhaps in Q itself, so in contemporary scholarship, the privileged are to be overthrown and the humble exalted, the orthodox to be confuted and the heretics vindicated,
the first to be last and the last first.[1]

Just as many scholars (including, perhaps, David Catchpole himself) remain unaccountably agnostic about some things of which I
am quite convinced, so I find myself wanting to return the compli-
ment on this particular subject. I have never been fully convinced
that the Q hypothesis does justice to the evidence, but nor have I
been convinced that any of its rivals succeeds notably better.[2] More
particularly, in company with several who do believe in the existence of some kind of documentary Q, I find it impossible to believe
that we can now discern developmental layers within it which involve
significant theological shifts and transformations. In part, I confess,
my scepticism at this point arises from an obvious hermeneutic of
suspicion. When, a generation ago, Siegfried Schulz proposed a development from an early Q with a low Christology to a later one

---

[1] Luke 13:30; Matt 19:30; 20:16; Mark 10:31; *Barn.* 6:13. I have written briefly
about some recent work on Q in *The New Testament and the People of God* (hereafter
NTPG) (London: SPCK, 1992) 435–43; *Jesus and the Victory of God* (hereafter *JVG*)
(London: SPCK, 1996) 35–44. Among the key works, from different points of view,
are J.S. Kloppenborg, *The Formation of Q: Trajectories in Ancient Wisdom Collections*
(Philadelphia: Fortress, 1987); C.M. Tuckett, *Q and the History of Early Christianity*
(Edinburgh: T. & T. Clark, 1996); and, of course, David R. Catchpole, *The Quest
for Q* (Edinburgh: T. & T. Clark, 1993). Perhaps the most strident exponent of the
new American Q school is B.L. Mack, *The Lost Gospel: The Book of Q and Christian
Origins* (San Francisco: HarperSanFrancisco, 1993); cf. too. L. Vaage, *Galilean Upstarts:
Jesus' First Followers according to Q* (Valley Forge, PA: TPI, 1994).
[2] The work of W.R. Farmer remains seminal, though inevitably controversial:
see his *The Synoptic Problem: A Critical Analysis* (London: Macmillan, 1964). More
recently, but equally controversially, see, for instance, M.D. Goulder, *Luke—A New
Paradigm* (Sheffield: Sheffield Academic Press, 1989); A.J. McNicol et al., eds., *Beyond
the Q Impasse—Luke's Use of Matthew* (Valley Forge, PA: TPI, 1996). On recent alternatives to Q see the discussion in Tuckett, *Q*, ch. 1, and the other works referred
to there.

with a high Christology—a proposal eagerly picked up by Eduard Schillebeeckx—the coherence between the literary theory and the theologically desired result was too close for comfort.[3] When, today, we find scholars passionately advocating the wholesale revision of our picture of early Christianity, and our agendas for contemporary Christianity, so as to minimize supposedly "apocalyptic" elements in favour of "sapiential" ones, and "discovering" in the process that "early Q" just happens to fit that agenda, similar scepticism is in my view quite justified.[4]

I do not think, in fact, that within the history of first-century Judaism—and that, if anywhere, is where earliest Christianity belongs, and with it, *ex hypothesi*, Q—it is possible to separate out what we loosely call "apocalyptic" and "sapiential" streams of thought and play them off against one another. Too many counter-examples, from 1QS through the Wisdom of Solomon to the *Didache*, taking in books like Matthew and James *en route*, stand in the way of such a facile analysis, though that is a topic for another day.[5] Thus, though the subject to which I now turn may properly belong within what is sometimes labelled "apocalyptic", it should not be supposed to be the property of only one narrowly defined group within either Judaism or early Christianity. I propose to consider Q and Resurrection.

This is of course nicely ironic. Many New Testament scholars, including many for whom Q's existence and demonstrability has become an article of personal faith and academic orthodoxy, are at least as agnostic about the resurrection of Jesus as I am about Q. Indeed, one of the attractions of Q in some quarters today is that it seems to say nothing about Jesus' death or resurrection, thus apparently providing evidence of a flourishing type of early Christianity for which those (Pauline?) emphases, so strikingly reinforced in the canonical gospels, were unimportant.

There are, of course, mediating positions here as elsewhere. I think, for instance, of Marcus Borg's insistence that Jesus really was

---

[3] S. Schulz, *Q. Die Spruchquelle der Evangelisten* (Zürich: Theologischer Verlag, 1972); E. Schillebeeckx, *Jesus: An Experiment in Christology* (London: Collins, 1979).
[4] The most sophisticated attempt in this genre is that of J.D. Crossan, most recently in *The Birth of Christianity* (San Francisco: HarperSanFrancisco, 1998); see my article review, *SJT* 53 (2000) 72–91.
[5] See, briefly, N.T. Wright, "Jesus", in *Early Christian Thought in its Jewish Context* FS M.D. Hooker (ed. John Barclay & John Sweet; Cambridge: CUP, 1996) 43–58.

raised from the dead even though nothing happened to his body.[6] Perhaps this is rather like saying that though Q may have existed, it was never a document but rather a loose collection of oral traditions, or even of ideas in people's heads. Nobody, after all, has ever seen Q; we only deduce it from its apparent effects. It only appears, one might argue, to those who believe in it, and perhaps it takes a special literary-critical grace to have that sort of faith or experience. But somewhere amidst these multiple agnosticisms the question should, I think, be posed: is it really true that Q, as it stands (insofar as it does), has no interest in the resurrection?[7]

The question is seldom raised, and, when raised, normally answered quite swiftly. Two leading Q scholars dismiss the possibility;[8] one recent writer makes a brief case in favour.[9] Q, of course, notoriously lacks both a resurrection narrative as such and the specific predictions of resurrection that are prominent in the Markan tradition.[10] It seems to me that there is more to be said—even though, of course, as with the gospel tradition as a whole, so with Q material in particular, the resurrection, whether of people in general or of Jesus in particular, is not a prominent theme. If, in investigating this possibility, crossing the street as I do so to where the Q specialists live, I may seem like a neighbour giving unwanted and unnecessary advice on how to dig the garden, I trust that David Catchpole at least will take this contribution to ongoing controversy, not least in relation to Christology and community, in the spirit in which it is meant.

1. *Future Hope in Q*

As is well known, several of the sayings in which Matthew and Luke overlap warn of imminent judgment.[11] These passages fit naturally

---

[6] See N.T. Wright and Marcus Borg, *The Meaning of Jesus: Two Visions* (London: SPCK, 1999), ch. 8.

[7] In what follows, when I refer to Q, the reader may understand the proviso "if, that is, it exists".

[8] J.S. Kloppenborg, "'Easter Faith' and the Sayings Gospel Q", *Semeia* 49 (1990) 71–100, at p. 90 (the "metaphor" of resurrection is "fundamentally inappropriate to the genre and theology of Q"); B. Mack, "Q and the Gospel of Mark: Revising Christian Origins", *Semeia* 55 (1992) 15–39.

[9] E.P. Meadors, *Jesus the Messianic Herald of Salvation* (WUNT 2.72; Tübingen: Mohr, 1995) 307–8.

[10] Mark 8:31; 9:9; 9:31; 10:34, with parallels in each case.

[11] I follow the convention of referring to Q passages by their Lukan numbering,

into the world of first-century Judaism, with its prevailing sense that history, particularly Israel's history, was accelerating towards a moment when Israel's God would judge the nations, and the wicked within Israel, in order finally to right the wrongs with which the world, and Israel in particular, had been plagued.[12] The reasons why there are so many of these warnings in Q cannot be examined here; but we should note that within the worldview where they make sense, namely that of second-Temple Judaism, warnings of this sort would always at least imply, as their correlate, that God's people, the "righteous", the "poor", the "saints", or whoever, would be rescued, saved, and vindicated precisely in and through this judgment on their wicked contemporaries. And one of the main ways in which this vindication was conceived was precisely resurrection.[13]

It is not simply a risky argument from silence, therefore, but a safe conclusion to say that where we find stern warnings of judgment we should also hear promises of vindication, salvation, and perhaps even resurrection. There are sufficient passages where this implication peeps out for us to be clear on the point. Thus, for instance, the saying about people seeing Abraham, Isaac and Jacob sitting down in the kingdom of God with a great company is designed as a warning, but clearly contains the promise that there will be such an event and that some—presumably including Jesus himself, and those who have faith in him and/or follow him—will share it.[14] And any first-century Jew hearing of a coming feast in which Abraham, Isaac and Jacob would be sharing would understand this in terms of the patriarchs, and presumably a great many others besides, being raised from the dead. This is obviously the case with the references to future resurrection and judgment in Q 11:29–32, which we shall examine in the third section below.

Staying with the patriarchal theme, I think it is likely that the Q saying of John the Baptist about Abraham would also be heard within Judaism and early Christianity as a prediction of resurrection. Q 3:8, a passage whose very close wording makes it a classic

---

without thereby implying agreement with the mainstream view in which the Lukan form of the sayings is held to be closer to the original Q.

[12] On the context and content of such sayings see *NTPG* ch. 10; *JVG* ch. 8.

[13] See *NTPG*, 320–34. I review this evidence more fully in my forthcoming book *The Resurrection of the Son of God* (London: SPCK), and presuppose this review in what follows.

[14] Q 13:28–30.

example of the evidence on which the Q hypothesis is based, warns against presuming to say "we have Abraham as our father", and emphasizes the warning with the promise that "God is able to raise children for Abraham from these stones". The word for "raise" here, ἐγεῖραι, was well known in early Christianity as one of the regular words for the resurrection, and would quite likely be seen as an indication that when God raised Abraham himself from the dead a great family would be raised with him from quite unlikely sources—a very similar point, in fact, to that which is being made in Q 13:28–30.[15]

This is clearly the meaning, too, of Q 12:4–7 and, in conjunction with that passage, 12:8–9 and even perhaps 12:10. Telling people not to be afraid of those who can kill only the body is clearly telling them that there is a future life beyond the death of the present body—precisely the point to which the martyrs had clung in the Maccabaean period and afterwards.[16] Coupling with this promise the double-edged promise and threat that the Son of Man (Luke) or Jesus himself (Matthew) will acknowledge and deny those who acknowledge and deny him in the presence of the angels of God (Luke) or the heavenly Father (Matthew) likewise clearly implies a future life beyond the grave, since part of the point of the saying is that those who confess Jesus may face death for doing so.

It is possible that the challenge to trust God for clothing (Q 12:28) is also at least a veiled promise of resurrection. The grass in the field is thrown into the furnace, but God can be trusted for future clothing.[17] And the treasure in heaven which Q 12:33 encourages

---

[15] Cf. too, interestingly, Rom 4:16–17. For ἐγείρειν cf. Luke 7:14; 9:7, 22; 20:37; 24:6, 34; Paul has more than thirty uses of it. The background includes Dan 12:2 (Theodotion); LXX Sir 48:5. This point is valid even though, as Davies and Allison point out, ἐγείρειν ἐκ τινός is a Semitism meaning "to come to be born" (W.D. Davies and D.C. Allison, *A Critical and Exegetical Commentary on the Gospel According to Saint Matthew* [3 vols. Edinburgh: T. & T. Clark, 1988–97] 1.308). The question is what a first-century Jewish Christian would have heard in the phrase.

[16] See e.g. 2 Macc 7; Wis 2:1–3:9. On the Wisdom passage, which despite the popular impression teaches future resurrection for the dead as well as present immortality, see *NTPG* 329–30, and the discussion in my forthcoming *The Resurrection of the Son of God*.

[17] Compare and contrast the sayings in *Gos. Thom.* 21 and 37, where, in one interpretation at least, nakedness is a metaphor for the disembodied state (*contra* e.g. R. Valantasis, *The Gospel of Thomas* [London: Routledge, 1997], 93–4, 112–3, who suggests that the clothes represent social conditioning). The saying in Thomas (36) which precedes the second of these passages is a version of the Q saying which warns against anxiety over clothing. On clothing as a metaphor for resurrection cf.

its hearers to seek and store up, a treasure which neither theft nor corruption can spoil, goes well not so much with a notion of a disembodied immortality but with the promise of new creation, stored up at present in the heavenly places, ready to be brought to birth in a new, incorruptible life.[18]

In this context, and granted the second-Temple Jewish setting, the promise about losing one's life in order to gain it (Q 17:33) can only refer to resurrection. Coupling this saying, as Matthew does, with the challenge to take up the cross and follow Jesus (Matt 10:3–8; Luke 14:26–7) brings home the force of this: the challenge to martyrdom, to death at the hands of the pagans (which is what taking up the cross meant in the first century), would at once imply the promise of resurrection the other side of death.[19]

Finally, the last saying in Q arguably envisages the resurrection in a characteristically second-Temple Jewish fashion. In Q 22:30 Jesus promises his followers that they will sit upon thrones, judging the twelve tribes of Israel. This is one of those cases where the Matthaean parallel (19:28) appears more primitive, since it specifies twelve thrones, ignoring the embarrassment of Judas;[20] but precisely the Matthaean saying emphasizes that this will take place "in the regeneration, when the Son of Man shall sit upon the throne of his glory".[21] Even if the Lukan version is considered the more original, at the time the saying circulated it was obvious that for the prophecy to be fulfilled not only would Jesus need to be alive and present, but the twelve tribes, of whom ten were of course still geographically dispersed, would need to be miraculously gathered. A first-century Jew, faced with that proposal, would naturally, I suggest, assume that this would be accomplished through the resurrection.

---

e.g. 1 Cor 15:53–4; 2 Cor 5:3. Q 12:28 echoes the promise of new covenant life in Isa 40:7–8.

[18] Cf. again the contrast of corruption and incorruption in 1 Cor 15:42–54.

[19] The unusual word ζωογονήσει in Luke 17:33 should probably be rendered "bring to life" rather than merely "keep". *Pace* e.g. J.A. Fitzmyer *The Gospel According to Luke X–XXIV* (AB 28A; New York: Doubleday, 1985), 1172, "will give life to it" is not the same as "will preserve it alive".

[20] So e.g. Fitzmyer, *Luke*, 1419.

[21] In Josephus *Ant.* 11.66, παλιγγενεσία, "regeneration", is used in the sense of the rebirth of the Jewish nation after the exile.

2. *The Dead Raised Already*

Within this broad-based Q theme of future judgment and vindication, with overtones of future resurrection, there are also signs that
Q regarded the raising of the dead as something that was happening in the present time as well. Jesus' answer to John the Baptist
offers a list of the messianic activities Jesus has been performing, and
within the list we find the claim that "the dead are raised" (Q 7:22).[22]

Within its present gospel contexts, this presumably refers back to
previous healings which Q itself does not, of course, relate. For Luke,
this means the raising of the widow's son at Nain (7:11–17, immediately preceding this pericope); for Matthew, the obvious reference
is to Jairus's daughter (Matt 9:18–26). The raising of the dead as
one of the signs of the Messiah is attested in Qumran as well, in a
passage remarkably similar to Q 7:18–23.[23]

In Matthew's version of the Mission Charge, this messianic work
is shared with the disciples. Matt 10:8 commands Jesus' disciples to
"heal the sick, raise the dead, cleanse lepers, exorcise demons", while
Luke's parallel charge (10:2–12) merely has "heal the sick" (Q 10:9).
Although this cannot therefore be counted as a Q saying, it seems
to be part of a developing Q tradition expanded by either Matthew
or an intermediate source (Matthew's version of Q?).

Related to this, but more significant for our purpose, is the striking saying "Leave the dead to bury their dead" (Q 9:60, with identical wording in Matthew 8:22). I have explored elsewhere the way
in which this saying may represent a radical move on Jesus' part,
setting the call of the kingdom (in Luke) and following him (in
Matthew and Luke) as a higher priority than one of the most sacred
duties of family loyalty.[24] Here I want to note the way in which the
Q saying resonates with the other material studied above. If those
who are not following Jesus are "dead", it appears that those who
are already following him are in some sense "alive"; Luke at least
would presumably comment, in the light of 15:24, 32 that this life,

---

[22] The phrase echoes the LXX of Isa 26:19.
[23] 4Q521:12 (the Messiah will "heal the badly wounded and will make the dead
live, he will proclaim good news to the poor and . . . he will lead the . . . and enrich
the hungry"); also frag. 7 l. 6, where the Messiah, or perhaps God, "gives life to
the dead of his people". Text, and short bibliography, in F. García Martínez and
E.J.C. Tigchelaar, eds, *The Dead Sea Scrolls Study Edition* (Leiden: Brill, 1998), 2:1045–7.
[24] *JVG* 401, with reference to the work of Hengel and Sanders.

found by those who repent and follow Jesus, is in some sense res-urrection life, life from the dead. I think the Q saying as it stands already implies this; the Q context, warning that to follow Jesus is to have nowhere in the present world to lay one's head (Q 9:57–8), indicates that Jesus is offering a future world, to be anticipated in the present, in which a new kind of life has burst upon the scene.

A case can be made, therefore, for the following view, granted a reasonably traditional understanding of Q. Q understood the imme-diate future crisis not just as a moment of terrible judgment, but as the time of vindication and resurrection. This future resurrection, in which the righteous would be vindicated and would share the feast of Abraham, Isaac and Jacob, was already anticipated in the pre-sent in two ways: the actual raising back to life of recently dead per-sons, and the new life, a form of metaphorical life from the dead, enjoyed by Jesus' followers. And all this leads to the harder, but more important, question: does Q after all have anything to say about Jesus' own resurrection?

3. *The Sign of Jonah*

We return to the passage I postponed earlier.[25] Q 11:31–2 offers an unambiguous statement of the future resurrection. The Queen of the South, and the people of Nineveh, "will arise at the judgment with this generation and condemn it". This is a further instance of the phenomenon examined in part 1 above, where Q affirms the future resurrection—in this case, of non-Jews, which ties in nicely with Q 13:28–30. The implication is that "this generation" will also arise at the judgment; as frequently in both second-Temple Judaism and the New Testament, there is an implicit tension between the universal resurrection (some to be saved, others to be condemned) and the resurrection seen as the specific gift for those who are saved.[26]

But what about the sign of Jonah itself?[27] Matthew is in no doubt what this sign is: Jonah was three days and nights in the belly of

---

[25] I assume for the purposes of the following that Matt 16:1–2a, 4 is Matt's ver-sion of Mark 8:11–12, into which Matt has inserted in v. 4 the reference to the sign of Jonah, to correspond with his 12:39. On this point see Catchpole, *Quest*, 244, discussing various options.

[26] For the former in the NT, cf. e.g. John 5:29.

[27] In what follows I am in implicit dialogue with Catchpole, *Quest*, 241–7.

the sea monster, and in the same way the Son of Man will be three days and three nights in the heart of the earth (12:40, quoting the LXX of Jonah 2:1). Matthew does not make the point more explicit, but it is clear enough none the less: when the Son of Man emerges from his three days and three nights of burial, that will be the sign to this generation, the only sign they will be given. During Jesus' ministry, in other words, there will be nothing to compare with the great event which will immediately follow it; and that event, the resurrection of Jesus himself, will function as the sign that will be sufficient to condemn those who do not believe.

Luke's version of the saying (11:30) is briefer and more cryptic: Jonah became a sign to the people of Nineveh, and in the same way the Son of Man will be a sign to this generation. A case can be made out for seeing this as a deliberate abbreviation of the Matthaean text, in line with Luke's insistence elsewhere that Jesus was raised *on* the third day, not after it.[28] Most, however, prefer to see Matthew's version, with its characteristic theme of the fulfilment of scripture, as the more developed, and Luke's as nearer a hypothetical Q original. But does this mean that Luke's saying has a significantly different meaning from Matthew's?

I think not. The immediately following references to the resurrection both of the Queen of the South and of the people of Nineveh creates a presumption that this is the theme of the "sign" as well.[29] Jonah hardly became a "sign" simply by, or in, his preaching; nor is it likely that the "sign" refers to the fact of Jonah's being sent from afar, or even from heaven.[30] The "sign" can only be a reference to Jonah's extraordinary escape from the sea-monster.[31] The resurrection of the Son of Man, seen as future from the perspective of the saying in the mouth of the pre-Easter Jesus, will be the equivalent "sign". That Luke at least thought like this seems to be clear from the end of the parable of the rich man and Lazarus: if they do not hear Moses and the prophets, neither will they believe even if someone were to rise from the dead (Luke 16:31, coming not long

---

[28] So e.g. McNicol, *Beyond the Q Impasse*, 181, citing Luke 9:22; 18:31–33; 24:7, 21.

[29] Luke 11:31, 32, using the two regular NT resurrection verbs ἐγερθῆναι and ἀναστῆναι.

[30] *Pace* Fitzmyer, *Luke* 933–6.

[31] Catchpole's suggestion that the "sign" is actually "no sign at all" (*Quest*, 245–6) seems to me a subtlety that would have passed by a first-century reader, or indeed a hearer of Jesus.

before Luke's discourse in ch. 17 about the coming Son of Man).

This is not the place to open a new discussion of "the Son of Man" either in Q in general or in this text in particular.[32] But certain comments may be made by way (I hope) of further elucidation of the strong hint of resurrection in this passage.

(a). There is more evidence than used to be thought for a messianic understanding of "Son of Man" in the Jewish world of the first century. To look no further, the re-reading of Daniel 7 in 4 Ezra 11–12 makes it clear that this was how Daniel 7 as a whole (not just as the passage in which a particular "title" happens to be found) was being understood in at least some circles.

(b). The narrative of Daniel 7, seen through the lens of subsequent martyrology, envisages the suffering of God's people being followed by a mighty act of divine judgment on the oppressors and vindication of the righteous sufferers. We know from the Wisdom of Solomon, 2 Maccabees and elsewhere that the Daniel tradition was among the resources drawn on to spur righteous Israelites to resist compromise and to go to their deaths trusting in God's future vindication.

(c). The book of Daniel, specifically its twelfth chapter, became in subsequent Judaism the key text predicting the bodily resurrection. Since the underlying narrative of Daniel 11:33–5 and 12:1–3 has much the same underlying shape as that of Daniel 7:2–14, interpreted first in 7:17–18 and then in 7:19–27, and since we know that both passages were used in subsequent Jewish thinking about martyrdom and vindication, we have reason cautiously to link the apocalyptic vision of ch. 7, in which "one like a son of man" is exalted, with the future resurrection and exaltation of "the wise" and "those who lead many to righteousness" in 12:3.

Without texts that make such a link this would remain purely hypothetical (not that purely hypothetical entities have always been frowned on in New Testament scholarship). It is always risky, in any branch of history, to put together two and two and make five. But when such a hypothetical construct opens up new perspectives on existing texts, there is some reason to pursue it further. And I submit

---

[32] On "Son of Man" see *NTPG*, 291–7; *JVG*, 513–19, which I presuppose in what follows. These are of course themselves highly abbreviated and preliminary discussions, but indicate the way I think the topic should be tackled and the evidence that might be adduced.

that, read within this context of second-Temple Jewish understandings
of the Messiah on the one hand and Israel's vindication after suffering
on the other, Q 11:30 makes good sense. It can be seen as a reference to the resurrection of Jesus: a future event, from the fictive
perspective of Luke's narrative, that will function as a sign to Jesus'
contemporaries, and a past event, from the actual perspective of Q,
that was already functioning in that way.[33]

Here, then, is an otherwise missing link in Q between the promise
of a future general resurrection and the fact of present raisings from
the dead both literal and metaphorical. Though, like the rest of the
traditions of Jesus' ministry, both canonical and non-canonical, Q
has little to say about Jesus' own resurrection, we may claim to have
found not only a text which hints at it but also a wider context
within which such a hint may be thought to make sense. It may be,
after all, fundamentally appropriate to Q. And maybe Q is not, after
all, quite so far away in theology and context from the rest of the
New Testament as is sometimes suggested.

Reflections

Nothing that I have said significantly advances an argument for
believing today in Jesus' resurrection. If I am on the right lines,
though, an argument that is sometimes advanced against, namely
the existence of flourishing groups of Jesus' followers who either did
not believe in Jesus' resurrection or did not think it important, begins
to look thinner. Does my argument, though, encourage us to believe
in Q itself?

I do not think so. If I am right, there is no reason why those
who wrote, read, and preached from Q would have wanted to deny
or downplay Jesus' resurrection. If that is so we face once more the
old chestnut of possible overlaps between Mark and Q: why should
Q not have contained some of the predictions of the passion and
resurrection that we find in Mark, and in the traditions that (as we
have been taught) flow from him to Matthew and Luke? Of course,

---

[33] Cf. R.A. Edwards, *The Sign of Jonah in the Theology of the Evangelists and Q* (London:
SCM, 1971) 56: "The Q community ... understands the resurrection of Jesus as
the sign which is now of crucial significance in bringing people into the renewed
fellowship of the coming Son of Man" (italics original).

the notion of overlaps between Mark and Q requires a remarkable scholarly imagination: all we know really about Q is that it consists of the parts of Matthew and Luke that do *not* overlap with Mark.

Once we have got in our heads the notion of an existing document, however, it is not so difficult to think of it containing more than we realized, and even of Mark knowing it and responding to it in certain ways.[34] But once we extend our imaginations this far, it is not fanciful to suggest other solutions as well: perhaps Q knew Mark, or pre-Markan tradition? Perhaps Q contained all sorts of things which did not fit the theological or editorial purpose of Luke, or of Matthew, or of both? If so, how would we ever know? If (as I think) Luke used Mark, omitting some parts, editing others, and adding considerable material of his own, why should he not have done the same with his other sources as well? But have we not then sawn three parts of the way through the branch we were sitting on?

If, in short, the resurrection of humans in general (in the future), and of Jesus in particular (in the recent past), were known to, and referred to by, Q, what theological reason is there for Q not to have had its own resurrection narrative? There is, of course, no literary reason for supposing that it did. But if either Matthew or Luke had access to a different way of telling that particular story, how would we ever know that that one of them had preserved the Q narrative and the other had not? I am driven back to supposing that, though Q may have existed, it is beyond our power to know what it contained: in other words, to a puzzled agnosticism comparable to that which some scholars now profess about the resurrection itself (something may have happened, but we cannot now say what).[35] That is not my position, but it demonstrates the right of scholars to remain puzzled about things that some of their colleagues believe in. You cannot, I suggest, take Q seriously and remain agnostic about the place of the resurrection within the earliest forms of Christianity known to us. But you can take the resurrection seriously and still remain agnostic about Q.

---

[34] See Catchpole, *Quest*, 70–78.
[35]. E.g. A.J.M. Wedderburn, *Beyond Resurrection* (London: SCM, 1999).

Q 22:28–30

Christopher Tuckett

The saying in Q 22:28–30 has been something of exegetical step-child in recent Q-research. The saying has attracted more than its fair share of attention in studies of the historical Jesus.[1] Yet in studies of Q it has perhaps been more notable for the lack of attention it has received. The saying is regularly included in lists specifying what is taken as comprising the contents of Q; yet discussion of it is usually brief and is not often integrated into broader analyses of the ideas or distinctive features of Q.[2] In his magisterial study of Q, David Catchpole gave only three passing references to the saying,[3] and this has been typical of some of the (by now classic) full-length recent studies of Q (e.g. Lührmann, Hoffmann, Kloppenborg).[4] Some

---

[1] Cf., for example, E.P. Sanders, *Jesus and Judaism* (London, 1985) 98–104; R.A. Horsley, *Jesus and the Spiral of Violence* (Minneapolis, 1987) 199–208, to name but two. A detailed discussion of the tradition history of the saying is provided in the very full essay of J. Dupont, "Le logion des douze trônes (Mt 19,28; Lc 22,28–30)", *Biblica* 45 (1964) 355–392, repr. in Dupont, *Études sur les évangiles synoptiques* (BETL 70B; Leuven, 1983) 706–743 (refs. to the latter), though without any discussion of the place of the saying in Q: Dupont considers only the contexts of Matthew, Luke and Jesus.

[2] There have been one or two exceptions. The saying was the basis of the relatively early essay of E. Bammel, "Das Ende von Q", *Verborum Veritas: Festschrift für Gustav Stählin zum 70. Geburtstag* (ed. O. Böcher & K. Haacker; Wuppertal, 1970), pp. 39–50, which sought to use the saying as the basis for his theory that Q should be seen as a "testimony". However, in this he has found few supporters. His theory depended heavily on ascribing the "testamentary" language of Luke 22:29 to Q, even though there is no direct parallel to this in Matthew (on this, see below); also many of the characteristics of a "testament" are lacking in Q. For a critique, see J.S. Kloppenborg, *The Formation of Q* (Philadelphia, 1987) 29–30; A. Kirk, *The Composition of the Sayings Source. Genre, Synchrony and Wisdom Redaction in Q* (NovTSup 91; Leiden, 1998) 18, with further references.
In more recent times, there is a valuable essay on the saying by H. Fleddermann, "The End of Q", *1990 SBL Seminar Papers* (Atlanta, 1990) 1–10; and one important aspect of the saying is analysed in detail by P. Hoffmann, "Herrscher in oder Richter über Israel? Mt 19,28/Lk 22,28–30 in der synoptichen Überlieferung", in *Ja und Nein. Christliche Theologie im Angesicht Israels* FS W. Schrage (ed. K. Wengst & G. Saβ; Neukirchen-Vluyn, 1998) 253–264.

[3] D.R. Catchpole, *The Quest for Q* (Edinburgh, 1993) 45, 164, 290.

[4] If there is "blame" to be apportioned, then I would plead equally "guilty", having recently burdened others with a book on Q of nearly 500 pages and with

have cast doubts on whether the saying should be regarded as part of Q at all.[5] Nevertheless, a recent volume in the *Documenta Q* series has devoted 465 pages to documenting and assessing scholarly views about these verses and concluding that the saying in some form was part of Q.[6] Further, given the (probable) position of the saying as the "last word" in Q, and the general importance which any conclusion to a text has,[7] it is perhaps surprising that the saying has not generated more discussion than it has.

In one way, the relative silence about the saying may be understandable. There is considerable uncertainty about the exact Q wording of the saying, what the saying contained, and even for some (cf. above) doubt about whether the saying actually belonged to Q at all. Nevertheless, despite the inevitably hazardous nature of the attempt to reconstruct the wording of any Q tradition in a very detailed way, the problems surrounding Q 22:28–30 seem in general terms to be no more complex than those concerning many other Q sayings even if complete precision in the reconstruction of the saying may be impossible.

As far as the existence of the saying in Q is concerned, the all but verbatim agreement between Matthew and Luke in the last part of the saying (Luke 22:30b/Matt 19:28: "you will sit on [twelve?][8] thrones judging the twelve tribes of Israel") is surely enough to guar-

---

only a single passing reference to Q 22:28–30: C.M. Tuckett, *Q and the History of Early Christianity* (Edinburgh, 1996) 163.

[5] Cf. in recent times, M. Sato, *Q und Prophetie* (WUNT 2.29; Tübingen, 1988) 23; R. Uro, "Apocalyptic Symbolism and Social Identity in Q", in R. Uro, ed., *Symbols and Strata. Essays on the Sayings Source Q* (Helsinki & Göttingen, 1996) 67–118, on pp. 78–9; U. Luz, *Das Evangelium nach Matthäus* 3 (EKK 1/3; Zürich & Neukirchen-Vluyn, 1997) 121. As symptomatic of the general uncertainty about the saying within Q, one may refer to one of the more recent attempts to provide a comprehensive analysis of all the material assigned to Q, viz. A.D. Jacobson, *The First Gospel. An Introduction to Q* (Sonoma, 1992) 248, who concludes his discussion of the saying by stating that "if we could be sure that Q 22:28, 30 was in Q, and if we could know its location, it might shed much light on the theology of Q. Unfortunately, there are too many uncertainties to make any such inferences."

[6] P. Hoffmann et al., eds, *Documenta Q. Q 22:28, 30 You Will Judge the Twelve Tribes of Israel* (Leuven, 1998). For the discussion of whether the saying belonged to Q at all, see pp. 4–68 (with full documentation of competing views and also evaluations: all the evaluators agree that the saying should be seen as part of Q). For a much briefer summary of scholarly views on the issue of whether the saying was in Q, see J.S. Kloppenborg, *Q Parallels. Synopsis, Critical Notes & Concordance* (Sonoma, 1988) 202.

[7] Cf. Fleddermann, "End of Q", 1.

[8] It seems very unlikely that Q contained "twelve" here. The word at this point

antee the status of the saying as part of Q, at least in general terms.[9] The doubts of others about the presence of the saying in Q have in part focused on the allegedly anomalous nature of some other elements of the saying, e.g. the possible reference to "*my* (= Jesus') kingdom".[10] However, this (a) depends on the disputed reconstruction of other parts of the saying, and (b) in any case rather prejudges the issue of what Q "must" (or "cannot") contain before one decides about the wording of individual sayings in Q. Here, however, it is probable that Q did not contain a reference to "my (= Jesus') kingdom" (cf. below), so one of the objections to the saying's being part of Q may not be very strong. Other doubts about the presence of the saying in Q have focused on the apparent lack of any clear context for the saying.[11] However, the evidence does probably indicate a reasonably clear context for the saying as the final saying in Q, coming immediately after the parable of the talents/pounds (see below).

The wording of the rest of the saying is very uncertain, and almost certainly some redactional interference has taken place by both Matthew and Luke. Certainly Luke's version of the saying in Luke 22:28–30 has long been suspected of having been adapted secondarily, probably by Luke. In Luke's v. 30, the slight mismatch between "eating and drinking" in v. 30a and "judging" in v. 30b,[12] as well as the grammatical change from a ἵνα clause with subjunctives (ἔσθητε καὶ πίνητε) to a future indicative (καθήσεσθε), all combine to suggest that the two halves of the present Lukan verse have different origins. Given the ease with which v. 30a fits the present Lukan context of the discourse at the Last Supper, it is probably simplest to presume that v. 30a is a LkR addition to a previously existing v. 30b in Luke's source material.[13]

---

would seem to indicate an audience of precisely twelve disciples. Q elsewhere gives no indication of the existence of the Twelve as a distinct group among the disciples of Jesus. The word in Matthew is probably due to MattR. See the survey of views and the evaluations in *Documenta Q*, 380–425.

[9] Hence *pace* Uro, "Apocalyptic Symbolism", 79: "the verbal agreement is scarce"; similarly, Sato, *Q und Prophetie*, 23: "die Wortübereinstimmung ist im ganzen recht gering".

[10] Cf. e.g. Uro, ibid.

[11] So Luz and Uro, as in n. 5 above.

[12] *Pace* Kirk, *Composition*, 290–2, who seeks to show that the two are often connected in other texts; however, the examples he cites do not seem to imply any integral relation between the two sets of activity.

[13] See D.R. Catchpole, "The Poor on Earth and the Son of Man in Heaven. A

Luke's v. 29 is probably also most easily explained, at least for the most part, as due to LkR.[14] In Luke's v. 28, Luke's οἱ διαμε-μενηκότες may be LkR and Matthew's οἱ ἀκολουθήσαντες may preserve the Q wording,[15] though the issue may not be not so important here. Matthew's explicit SM reference in Matt 19:28 may also be redactional,[16] though as we shall see, the saying is integrally related to ideas associated with the use of the term SM elsewhere in Q. The only other remaining issue about the wording concerns the phrase ἐν τῇ βασιλείᾳ μου in Luke 22:30. The μου is widely regarded as a foreign element in Q and at home in LkR;[17] but it is uncertain if a phrase ἐν τῇ βασιλείᾳ (i.e. τοῦ θεοῦ) was present in Q (perhaps a vestige of which is still visible in the ἐν τῇ of Matthew's ἐν τῇ παλιγγενεσίᾳ).[18] This is possible though such a conclusion can only be tentative given the sparse nature of the evidence.

Re-appraisal of Matthew XXV.31–46", *BJRL* 61 (1979) 355–397, on p. 375; Fleddermann, "End of Q", 4; also *Documenta Q*, 216–95, with full documentation of alternative views.

[14] Catchpole, "Poor on Earth", 375–6, has argued for the presence of the verse in Q, claiming that it would provide a rough parallel, consisting of christological material, to Matthew's Son of Man (henceforth "SM") reference in Matt 19:28 (the SM sitting on his throne of glory). But the latter, which is almost certainly MattR (as Catchpole himself agrees and argues persuasively for), does not necessarily require the presence of Luke 22:29 in Q to explain its existence in Matthew. Some of Catchpole's other points are (persuasive!) arguments against the possibility that Matthew's SM version might represent Q. The covenantal language (cf. the use of διατίθημι) is perhaps more easily seen as LkR in light of e.g. Luke 1:72; 22:20; Acts 3:25; 7:8 (cf. Dupont, "Logion", 711; Fleddermann, "End of Q", 4; cf. too Hoffmann, in *Documenta Q*, 292). Catchpole seeks to distinguish between some of these other texts as referring to the Abrahamic or Mosaic covenant and the present verse as referring to a Davidic royal idea. This may be true, though the link with Luke 22:20 seems particularly telling (cf. Fleddermann); and since the placement of the saying in the context of the Last Supper may be LkR (cf. below: Q certainly had no account of the Last Supper), it may be easier to see this verbal/conceptual link here as also LkR.

[15] *Documenta Q*, 154–95, especially Hoffmann's evaluation on pp. 191–5; for the Lukan nature of διαμένω (cf. Luke's fondness for the use of μένω and for διά compounds), cf. too Dupont, "Logion", 713–4; Fleddermann, "End of Q", 2–3.

[16] Catchpole, "Poor on Earth", 375; *Documenta Q*, 336–79.

[17] Cf. Luke 23:42 and the general stress in Luke on Jesus' kingship: cf. A. George, "Le royauté de Jésus selon l'évangile de Luc", *Études sur l'oeuvre de Luc* (Paris, 1978) 257–82; M.L. Strauss, *The Davidic Messiah in Luke-Acts* (JSNTSup 110; Sheffield, 1995).

[18] See the discussion in *Documenta Q*, 296–335. One the evaluators, J.M. Robinson, tentatively suggests that Q might have contained a reference to the "kingdom" (i.e. of God) here (pp. 331–5: cf. too Fleddermann, "End of Q", 5), though the other main evaluator (P. Hoffmann) regards the question as indeterminate (pp. 324–31).

In sum, despite the uncertainty about the other details, it seems certain that the saying was part of Q and that it contained one key element in the promise to the followers of Jesus that they would "sit on thrones" and exercise a royal/judging function, "judging the twelve tribes of Israel".

The precise meaning of κρίνω here, and whether it means "judging" or "ruling over", has always been a key issue of debate in the interpretation of the saying.[19] It also seems clear that, at least in the context of Q, the use of κρίνω in the saying does refer to "judging" in a discriminatory way and not just to "governing".[20] Within Q, κρίνω/κρίσις seems to refer to judgment, often to the final judgment (cf. Q 10:12; 11:19; also 6:37), and the saying in Q 22:30 clearly coheres closely with e.g. Q 11:31–32 which refer to others from the past (the Queen of the South and the people of Nineveh) "condemning" "this generation" at the "judgment". The reference is clearly to an act of (negative) discriminatory judgment, not just ruling over or governing. Thus whilst the saying in Q 22:30 *might* have been meant more generally, or positively, in an earlier stage of the tradition, and almost certainly did at the later stage of Luke's use of the tradition, it would seem that, for Q at least, the saying does refer to an act of final judgment.[21]

As far as the context is concerned, the evidence suggests that this was the final saying in Q.[22] In Luke, the saying constitutes the last piece of Q material in the gospel, following the eschatological discourse

---

[19] See the survey of views in W.D. Davies & D.C. Allison, *The Gospel according to Saint Matthew* 3 (ICC; Edinburgh, 1997), 55–6, though without always distinguishing clearly between the possible meaning at different levels of the tradition. It is above all the merit of the articles of Dupont ("Logion") and Hoffmann ("Herrscher") to show clearly that the word may have been taken differently by different authors at the various stages in the tradition.

[20] *Pace* Jacobson, *First Gospel*, 247–8; Horsley, as in n. 1; also his "Social Conflict in the Synoptic Sayings Source Q", in J.S. Kloppenborg, ed., *Conflict and Invention. Literary, Rhetorical and Social Studies on the Sayings Gospel Q* (Valley Forge, 1995), 37–52, on p. 38; Davies & Allison, ibid.

[21] See J.S. Kloppenborg, "Conflict and Invention. Recent Studies on Q", in Kloppenborg (ed.), *Conflict* (see previous note), 1–14, on pp. 12–13, in relation to Horsley. (Horsley's original claim [as in n. 1] was about the possible meaning of the saying at the level of the historical Jesus, though he has mostly simply repeated this in his later essays on Q as applying to Q as well.) Also Fleddermann, "End of Q", 7–8; Hoffmann, "Herrscher", 263. For the meaning of "governing" as more likely in Luke, cf. Dupont, "Logion", 730–732; Hoffmann, "Herrscher", 258–262.

[22] See Catchpole, "Poor on Earth", 373–4; *Documenta Q*, 69–141 (all the evaluators agree that the saying should be regarded as coming at the end of Q).

of Q 17 and the parable of the pounds (Luke 19); and Luke is generally thought to preserve the order of Q more faithfully than Matthew. In Matthew, the eschatological material from Q 17 is interwoven (in a typically Matthean way) with Markan material in Matt 24; the parable of the talents (the Matthean equivalent of Luke's parable of the pounds) comes in Matt 25:14–29 and this is followed by Matthew's parable of the sheep and the goats, introduced by the SM saying in 25:31 which is clearly very close to Matthew's version of the Q saying of Q 22:28 in Matt 19:28 in referring to the "SM sitting on his throne", thus perhaps revealing a Matthean reminiscence of the original Q order. The likelihood is then that here, as elsewhere, Luke may preserve the Q order more faithfully. Hence the saying constitutes the final saying in Q, offering as it were a commentary on the eschatological material of Q 17 and Q 19. All this suggests that the saying occupied a key role in the literary structure of Q as a whole: it constitutes the final word, in a sense interpreting and putting in context all that has gone before.

In terms of the broader structure of Q, the saying can be viewed in a number of different ways, depending on one's view of any structuring in Q itself. If one is right to see the saying as forming the conclusion of Q after the eschatological material in Q 17 and Q 19, then it can be seen as a clarification of the reward promised to the "faithful/profitable servants" of the parable of the pounds.[23] The saying has also been seen as forming an *inclusio* with Q 12:2–12 as part of a macro-ring-composition comprising Q 12:2–22:30.[24] Thus the promise to judge others picks up the motif of being judged by others (12:11–12), the promise of 22:30 can be regarded as fulfilling the promises of 12:8–9 etc. However, the parallels in Q are not perhaps closest with this particular passage. There is for example little verbal overlap with 12:11–12; and, as we shall see, despite a close relationship between the ideas of 12:8–9 and 22:30, the latter verse goes one step significantly further than the earlier saying in Q 12. Even Kirk himself concedes that the unit he attempts to isolate here may exhibit less of a chiastic ring form with parallels between corresponding elements, and more of a *linear* progression, indicating a

---

[23] The links between these two traditions are well highlighted by Catchpole, "Poor on Earth", 373–4.

[24] Kirk, *Composition*, 294–7.

development and change in thought.[25] Perhaps more relevant might
be the similarity which the saying exhibits with the opening section
of Q in 3:7–9, highlighting the theme of judgement (which is on
any showing a very important theme in Q). Alternatively, one could
see the promise by Jesus at the end of Q in 22:30 as similar to, and
expanding, the promise made by Jesus at the start of his preaching
in Q, viz. in the beatitudes of Q 6:20–23, promising the "kingdom"
to the poor, the mourners and the hungry who, in the final beatitude, are clearly identified with the followers of Jesus.[26] In any case,
the links show that the saying probably occupies a key position within
Q's overall structure and hence failure to take full account of its
implications may lead to an incomplete picture of Q as a whole.

   In order to see what place the saying has within the broader context of Q, it will be necessary to consider that broader context in
a little more detail. Recent research on Q has reached a measure
of widespread agreement that a dominant feature of Q is the polemic
against "this generation" and the threat of judgment, all encompassed within a deuteronomistic view of history. According to this
view, God has continually sent his prophets to Israel but Israel has
regularly rejected them and inflicted violence on them, acts which
God has punished and will continue to punish if the people do not
repent. Many have suggested that the Q Christians viewed themselves as in a line of continuity with Israel's prophetic messengers of
the past, all of whom suffered rejection and violence. Q thus seems
to reflect a situation of Christians who have sought to address their
fellow Jews but have met with rebuff and rejection and who have
then interpreted that rejection as similar to the fate experienced by
the prophets of Israel in the past (cf. especially Q 6:23 where this
is quite explicit; also 11:49–51; 13:34–35). The Q Christians thus
perceive themselves to be in a rather marginalised situation, alien-
ated in part from the rest of society and suffering rejection, abuse
and possibly violence.

---

[25] Ibid., 294: ". . . the rhetoric of this section follows the course of an intelligible
linear progression, beginning with the opening maxim (12:2) and moving *incrementally*
though sequenced units to culminate in 22:30" (my stress).

[26] Cf. A. Järvinen, "The Son of Man and His Followers: A Q Portrait of Jesus",
in D. Rhoads & K. Syreeni, eds, *Characterization in the Gospels. Reconceiving Narrative
Criticism* (JSNTSup184; Sheffield, 1999), 180–222, on pp. 194–6. The connection
between the two would be even closer if Q 22:30 did indeed have a reference to
the "kingdom" (cf. above).

What the precise nature of the relationship between the Christian group and their Jewish contemporaries was remains unclear; indeed it may well be that the situation would have been perceived differently by different parties at the time. Some have argued that the breach between the Christian group and the Jewish community was so final that the Q Christians had given up all hope of dialogue, had turned their backs on the Jews in favour of a Gentile mission, and claimed that all that remained for the Jews was judgment.[27] Others have argued that the breach may not have been as severe, and that, at least for the Q Christians, the aim was to maintain the links with the Jewish community with very little idea of a Christian "church", separate from and distinct from the Jewish community, ever in mind.[28] What level of violence the Christian group was experiencing is also unclear. Some have claimed that intense physical violence, and even violent death itself, was being experienced. I myself have tried to argue that the violence itself may not have been quite so intense, amounting to a certain amount of verbal abuse and hostility, but not necessarily involving any great physical danger.[29] But whatever the ultimate aims of the Christian group, and whatever the precise nature of the present situation, it would seem that the Q Christians *thought* of themselves as "persecuted", rejected and experiencing the same kind of hostility as had been experienced by Israel's prophetic messengers in the past. The Q Christians thus perceived themselves to be in some kind of "liminal" situation.[30] Part of the rationale for

---

[27] Cf. D. Lührman, *Die Redaktion der Logienquelle* (Neukirchen-Vluyn, 1969), 30–1, 93; Kloppenborg, *Formation*, 148, 167 and others. See the discussion e.g. on the meaning of "this generation" in Q in Tuckett, *Q and the History*, 196–201, also the next note.

[28] See Catchpole, *Quest*, passim; also Tuckett, *Q and the History*, 425–50.

[29] Tuckett, *Q and the History*, 296–323.

[30] On the idea of a "liminal", or marginalized, situation, see especially the work of Victor Turner, e.g. his *The Ritual Process and Anti-Structure* (Ithaca, 1969), 94–130. The idea of "liminality" has been used by a number of NT scholars in recent years. Here the idea is used in a more metaphorical way: for a useful analysis, see S.R. Bechtler, *Following in His Steps. Suffering, Community and Christology in 1 Peter* (SBLDS 162; Atlanta, 1998), 118–26. (Bechtler applies such a model to 1 Peter, but much of his approach can be equally fruitfully applied to Q.)

I am less persuaded by the use of the category of "liminality" to throw light on Q in the recent article by A. Kirk, "Crossing the Boundary: Liminality and Transformative Wisdom in Q", *NTS* 45 (1999) 1–18. Kirk claims that an essential feature of "wisdom" instruction is to place the hearers in a "liminal" situation to make them more prepared to accept the new wisdom of the teacher. In this way

Q may then have been to provide some kind of strategy of "legitimation", providing a kind of "symbolic universe", to "explain" the
situation for the readers/hearers, to make some kind of sense of it
and perhaps to provide some hope for the future which would resolve
the perceived ills of the present and put them right.[31]

One way in which Q seems to do this is by making the case that
the Q Christians are not unique. Both Jesus and others have trodden
the same path so that any unpleasant experiences of the present are
nothing new. Indeed this is the whole basis for evoking the deuteronomic scheme of history at all. This is clear in Q 11:49–51 and Q
13:34–35: the whole history of Israel has been characterised by a
constant stream of rejected prophets. And in Q 6:22–23 the parallel with the present is quite explicit. Christian followers of Jesus will
suffer various times of persecution, abuse, rejection etc., and the final
clause (v. 23c) states that this is just what has happened to the
prophets in the past.

However, the theme of the rejected prophets is part of a broader
complex of motifs in Q. The prophets who suffer violence are the
messengers of Wisdom (cf. especially Q 11:49–51; cf. too 7:31–35).
Also several of the passages which employ this complex of motifs,
severally or singly, refer to Jesus as "SM" in this context. In many
of these texts, the experience of Jesus as SM serves as a prototype
for the suffering and hostility experienced by his later followers. This
is hinted at in the last beatitude of 6:22–23: the suffering endured
by the followers of Jesus is suffering endured "for the sake of the
SM".[32] It then comes out probably in the parable of the playing
children in Q 7:31–35, where Jesus as SM is set in parallel with the
figure of John the Baptist as one suffering hostility and rejection,
and also by implication with Jesus' followers (implied in the reference

---

Kirk seeks to resolve some of the tension felt by others between the strident judg-
mental preaching of John the Baptist in Q 3 and the calmer tones of the teaching of Jesus in Q 6, thus obviating any need to ascribe the two sets of sayings to
different strata within Q. The question of the need to posit strata within Q is perhaps another issue; but Kirk's analysis ignores the fact that the audiences of John
in Q 3 and of Jesus in Q 6 are *not* the same: John is preaching to people who are
not followers of Jesus, whereas Jesus is addressing those who are.

[31] On the idea of the "symbolic universe" as well as "legitimation", see P. Berger
& T. Luckmann, *The Social Construction of Reality: A Treatise in the Sociology of Knowledge*
(New York, 1966), 110–146. Also Bechtler, *Following*, 30–39.

[32] There is widespread agreement that Luke's reference to "SM" here is more
original than Matthew's "for the sake of me". Cf. Catchpole, *Quest*, 93.

to Wisdom's children in v. 35).[33] Similarly, the missionary discourse is preceded by the SM saying of 9:58 ("the SM has nowhere to lay his head"), which thus acts as an important interpretative key for the discourse itself: the experience of the SM will be the lot of his followers as well.[34] All this then reinforces what was said some years ago by Gerd Theissen in his study *The First Followers of Jesus*, arguing that the SM sayings in the tradition serve to create a "structural homologue" between the situation of Jesus and that of his followers.[35] Despite some of the criticisms levelled against Theissen (e.g. on using all strands of the gospels too indiscriminately and assuming too uniform a role of "wandering charismatics"), his thesis does seem to apply well to the use of "SM" in Q: the SM acts as a paradigmatic figure in Q, giving an example of what followers of Jesus may expect in their own lives. And indeed this conformity between Jesus and his followers is indicated elsewhere in Q, apart from the SM sayings. The end of the mission instructions in Q 10:16 states that there is a quasi-identity between those sent out and Jesus who sends them out ("whoever hears/receives you hears/receives me"), perhaps forming an *inclusio* with the start of the discourse and the SM saying in 9:58. The temptation story in Q 4:1–13 probably sets Jesus up as a paradigmatic figure to be imitated in his commitment and obedience to God and to God's word in scripture.[36] So too the fate which the follower of Jesus can expect is the cross, exactly mirroring the fate of Jesus (Q 14:27). The (isolated?) saying in Q 6:40 spells all this out explicitly if cryptically: the disciple should be like his teacher.[37]

However, all this on its own does only little to alleviate any suffering felt in the present. Such sayings note the existence of suffering and may seek to "legitimate" it at one level by placing it in a broader context of similar suffering experienced by others. Thus those suffering may not feel quite so isolated and alone. Nevertheless the suffering is not explained very much and not necessarily really alleviated.

[33] See Järvinen, "Son of Man", 201–2.
[34] Kloppenborg, *Formation*, 192; also my *Q and the History*, 183; Uro, "Apocalyptic Sybolism", 108f.; Järvinen, "Son of Man", 132–6.
[35] G. Theissen, *The First Followers of Jesus* (London, 1978), 24–9; also Järvinen, "Son of Man", passim.
[36] See my "The Temptation Narrative in Q". in F. Van Segbroek et al., eds, *The Four Gospels 1992* (FS F. Neirynck; BETL 100; Leuven, 1992) 479–507.
[37] Cf. also Fleddermann, "End of Q", 9–10.

However, in the case of Jesus, and especially Jesus in his role as SM, the statement that Jesus SM is one who suffers rejection and hostility is by no means the end of the story. The sayings implying such hostility and rejection are balanced by sayings which look to the future. Jesus as SM is the one who will play an active role in the final judgment (cf. especially 12:8–9)[38] when he comes suddenly and unexpectedly (12:40) on his "day" (17:23ff.). The precise role of Jesus as SM is debatable, with a possible distinction between activity as a witness (cf. 12:8) and activity as judge, though the two are probably not easy to distinguish. Further, the idea of Jesus as the coming SM in judgment is one that clearly has key significance for Q and may well be implied in several places even where the term "SM" itself is not used. Thus it is almost certainly implied in the references to "the coming one". Catchpole has shown very clearly how Q—and moreover what is almost certainly Q editorial activity— has invested a great deal of effort, especially in the material about John the Baptist, in indicating that Jesus is indeed the "coming one" of John's preaching whose coming will be at the final judgment.[39] Thus John announces the future activity of this figure (3:7–9); the questioned is explicitly raised later as to whether this figure is Jesus (7:19); by implication the question is answered positively by Q's Jesus, and indeed in a real sense Jesus (as SM!) already "*has* come" (7:34). Yet his activity as "the coming one" is also still future at a time when a positive response may be too late (13:35).

Yet what is the purpose of this material within Q? Very often it is said that the matter is one of *christological* concern, and the whole complex of ideas is tied up with Q's Christology.[40] In one sense this is of course undeniable: Q *is* concerned with *Jesus*—after all Q, like all the gospels, re-presents the teaching *of Jesus*.[41] Yet modern gospel study has taught us to be alert to the possibility that the gospel writers, and earlier Christian tradents of the Jesus tradition, were not recording the past just for the sake of it. The teaching of Jesus in

---

[38] Assuming, as with most, that a reference to "SM" is more original than Matthew's "I" version. See e.g. D.R. Catchpole, "The Angelic Son of Man in Luke 12:8", *NovT* 24 (1982) 255–265; also my "Q 12:8 Again", in *From Quest to Q* FS J.M. Robinson (ed. Jon Ma. Asgeirsson et al.; BETL 146; Leuven, 2000) 171–88.

[39] See Catchpole, *Quest*, 60–78.

[40] Cf. Catchpole, *Quest*, 69.

[41] On the importance of the fact that *Jesus* is the focus of attention in all the gospels, see R. Burridge, *What are the Gospels?* (SNTSMS 70; Cambridge, 1992).

the past was thought to be relevant for, and to relate to, the needs
of the Christians recording it. The same may then be just as true
with the SM (and related) material in Q. The concern may thus be
as much to do with the Christian community as with Christology.

The story line implicit in the SM sayings in Q is almost certainly
no bolt from the blue in terms of tradition history. I have tried to
argue elsewhere that the SM sayings in Q are part of a developing
exegetical tradition, based in part on Dan 7 but having its roots ultimately in the description of the "suffering servant" of Isa 53.[42]
Nickelsburg has shown how the Isa 53 passage generated a developing exegetical tradition, in part to meet the classic theodicy question of seeking to explain the apparently undeserved and unredeemed
suffering of the righteous.[43] In Isa 53 itself, some (unidentified) people are amazed at the new status of the servant figure (Isa 52:13).
In the tradition as developed later in texts such as *1 Enoch* 62 and
Wisd 2–5, the servant figure is "democratised" so that the figure
becomes, or is the representative of, a wider group of people who
have been persecuted. The amazement scene of Isa 52:13 is now
developed into a post mortem scene of judgment: those who are
amazed are the one-time persecutors of the righteous, and the once
despised figure now acts as judge. In Wisd 2–5 this is the (typical
or representative) suffering righteous person himself; in *1 Enoch* 62
it is the SM figure who represents the suffering righteous but who
can be recognised up as in some way identical with them. Thus built
into this developing tradition is an attempt to explain the problem
of apparently unredeemed suffering by claiming that, in a future
judgment scene, those currently being "persecuted" will turn the
tables on their persecutors and in turn become their judges. In my
earlier discussion, I noted the similarities and differences between
Wisd 2–5, *1 Enoch* 62 and Q, as well as the possible links with the
SM vision in Dan 7:

> There is no "SM" in Wisd 2–5, whilst "SM" is present in *1 Enoch*
> and Q. Moreover, the SM figure is slightly different in the two texts:
> in Q the SM is Jesus, whereas in *1 Enoch* the SM is the heavenly
> counterpart of the righteous. In this then Q is perhaps closer to the

---

[42] See my *Q and the History*, 266–76.
[43] G.W.E. Nickelsburg, *Resurrection, Immortality and Eternal Life in Intertestamental Judaism* (London, 1972) 62–78.

vision in Wisd 2–5 where there is a clear identity between the persecuted figure of Wisd 2 and the vindicated figure who becomes the
agent in judgment in Wisd 5.[44]

What however I failed to note in the earlier discussion was perhaps
the way in which the Q tradition also implies an element of "democ-
ratisation" in the development of this idea by applying it to more
than a single individual, though this happens in Q in a slightly
different way from that in *1 Enoch* or Wisdom. In Wisdom, the figure
of the suffering righteous man may well be a representative one and
he certainly has little identity of his own. In *1 Enoch* 62 the collective group of the suffering righteous are represented by the SM figure
who is their heavenly counterpart.[45]

In Q, there has been a clear separation of the SM figure and
others who are suffering "persecution". It is clear that for Q, the
SM figure is Jesus and Jesus alone. Indeed, as Catchpole has shown
and we have already noted, Q invests a lot of editorial effort in seeking to establish the equation between the SM figure (or the "coming one") and Jesus (cf. above). There is then no room within Q's
"symbolic universe" for the SM being a "corporate figure" in any
sense at all. Jesus and his followers are distinct. However much the
SM sayings provide a "structural homologue" with the experience
of his followers: "SM" itself remains a description of Jesus alone and
does not in itself refer to anyone else.[46]

Nevertheless, the way in which this whole "myth", or story line,
was developed may not be forgotten here. The myth seeks to provide an answer to the problem of the persecution of the righteous.
For Q, the "righteous" comprise a group of people as well, including both Jesus and his followers. Both Jesus and his followers, it is
claimed, have suffered or are suffering. The story line of the myth
then seeks to resolve the problem by claiming that those presently
suffering will be enabled to reverse the situation in a later judgment
scene and themselves act as judges over others who are currently
"persecuting" them. Something of this is clearly reflected in Q,

---

[44] *Q and the History*, 275
[45] The similarities between *1 Enoch* 62 and Matt 25:31–46, and the implications
for the interpretation of the Matthean parable, are brilliantly brought out by Catchpole in his article "Poor on Earth".
[46] Hence the Q use of the term SM provides no direct support for any theory
that "SM" itself is some kind of "generic" term, referring to Jesus and others.

though with its own peculiar features. Jesus and his followers are clearly distinguished at one level. Certainly in relation to descriptions, or "names", Jesus and his followers are different. Jesus and Jesus alone is called "SM". Thus in relation to Jesus himself, the tradition developing from Isaiah is applied via the use of the SM description (and probable overtones of Dan 7): Jesus is one who is to suffer (in relation to Q's story world—in relation to the Q Christians, Jesus has of course suffered already); but as SM he will play an active role in judging the "Israel" that has failed to respond to the Christian message.[47] It is then precisely this claim, or even assurance, that gives meaning and hope to the situation of apparently otherwise unrewarded suffering.

But, as we have seen, the "suffering" or "persecution" experienced by the Q Christians is placed on a par with that of Jesus in that they too share in the rejection and hostility experienced by him as SM. If then the future SM sayings provide some kind of explanation and legitimation for the status of Jesus, some equivalent legitimation might be expected in relation to Jesus' followers. In one way this is provided by the future SM sayings which promise positive recognition by Jesus as SM for those who have remained faithful (cf. 12:8: "whoever confesses me . . . the SM will confess"). But it is also striking that a "resolution" of the problem for Jesus' followers almost parallel with that for Jesus himself is provided by the saying in Q 22:30: just as the suffering righteous man in Wisd 2–5 will judge his one-time persecutors, just as the suffering righteous in *1 Enoch* 62 will confront their one-time persecutors in the form of their heavenly counterpart the SM, and just as Jesus SM in Q will judge others who have rejected him earlier, so too the Q followers of Jesus will judge the twelve tribes of Israel. There has thus in Q been a clear distinction drawn between Jesus on the one hand and his followers on the other. He and he alone is the SM. Yet the explanation and the resolution of the theodicy problem faced by the Q Christians in their present situation is the same as resolution for Jesus himself: just as he too will act as judge over others who have not responded, so too will they.

Two issues arise from this saying and will be briefly discussed

---

[47] Much of the polemic in Q is directed against those who have failed to respond positively to the Christian message.

here. These concern the implications for the relationship to Israel, and the implications for Christology.

First, does the saying imply anything about the relationship between Q Christians and Israel? According to Hoffmann, the presence of the saying in Q marks the basis of the fundamental breach between the Christian church and Israel. "Wer einem solchen Anspruch konfrontiert wird, kann nur mit 'nein' antworten oder aber sich bekehren . . . Es bedeutet den Abschied von Israel."[48] This may however go too far. In the first place, the language of the saying is futurist and eschatological. It is looking to the final judgment at the end of time. If there are any breaches, they are to come in the future; they are not in the present. Further, even if one accepts that κρίνω here means "judging" and not "ruling over" (cf. above), it does not necessarily refer to condemning as opposed to acquitting. In theory, an action of "judging" can involve a positive, as well as a negative, verdict. The language of the saying itself does not imply necessarily that the whole "twelve tribes of Israel" are rejected and condemned en bloc.

But second, the fact remains that this is a *future* eschatological event, even for those who might be condemned by the followers of Jesus sitting on their thrones and judging. As such it serves as much as a threat of what might be as a statement of what will inevitably happen. The saying in Q 22:28–30 probably follows on the parable of the pounds in Q 19 and may well pick up the promises (and threats) of that parable (cf. above). Yet while the saying may in one way state what it is claimed will be the case in the future in general terms, it does not necessarily work with any predetermined ideas about precisely which individuals will occupy each role in the future drama. The parable and the saying thus act just as much as a challenge to the present audience to review their own attitude to, and commitment to, the cause of Jesus. And for Q it seems clear that being committed to Jesus' cause and being part of Israel are by no means mutually exclusive! That some *in* Israel might act as judges over others, both in Israel as well as outside, seems to be implied in other claims similar to Q 22:30 which assign a judging role to the righteous, without necessarily implying that there is a radical breach with Israel.[49] That such a breach between Christian followers

---

[48] "Herrscher", 253, 264.
[49] Cf. Wisd 3:8; *1 Enoch* 38:5; 91:12; 95:3; 1QS 8:6, 10; 1QpHab 5:3–4. (For

of Jesus and the Jewish people did eventually take place is undeniable. That claims such as Q 22:30 may have contributed to such a breach seems intelligible. But it is still the case that such a breach may be a long way ahead in the future at the time of Q.

What though are the implications of Q 22:30 for Christology, especially the Christology of Q? It is very often said that the Christology of Q is above all a SM Christology, and that SM is "the" most important christological title in Q. In one sense of course this is undeniably true. Insofar as any one christological "title" is important in Q, it must be "SM" if only on the basis of the number of occurrences.[50] Yet while SM is clearly important in Q as a designator of Jesus, the saying in Q 22:30 may raise a small question about its significance in terms of Christology. Such a claim depends of course on what one means by "Christology". At one level, "Christology" refers to the identity of Jesus, who/what Jesus is or was. However, in another sense, "Christology" is often taken as referring also to the way in which Jesus is believed to be *distinctive* and *different from* other human beings.

In one sense Jesus' identity as SM is certainly important for Q's Christology in that the term serves to designate Jesus. Moreover, as we have already noted, it designates Jesus and Jesus alone and hence serves to distinguish Jesus from others: Jesus is the SM and others are not. What though is striking about the saying in Q 22:30 is that it shows that in one way Jesus' *role* in his capacity as SM does *not* serve to distinguish him from others. Rather Jesus' role as SM is one that he shares with that of his followers. Or perhaps better, the role of Jesus' followers is one that they can share with him. Just as Jesus in his capacity as SM is one who has been abused and rejected, but who will be vindicated by God and will come to judge others, so too his followers suffer a similar experience of hostility and rejection, but are promised future vindication and reward and are also promised a position where they will judge Israel. The emphasis in

---

references, cf. Luz, *Matthäus* 3, p. 129; Hoffmann, "Herrscher", p. 255.) However, one should be a little wary of adducing texts such as these as too close a parallel to the gospels: Dupont, "Logion", 723–8, points out that several of these passages imply that the righteous will be involved in carrying out a sentence of punishment *after* the act of judgment itself has been enacted (by God), rather than acting as judges themselves.

[50] "Son of God" and "Lord" appear hardly ever in Q; "Christ" is notorious by its complete absence from Q.

the SM and related sayings in Q is thus as much on the solidarity between Jesus and his followers, on the characteristics, the experiences and the future rewards that are shared as it is on features that distinguish Jesus from his followers. "SM" is thus important for Q's Christology in that it clearly evokes, and is associated with, important things said about Jesus. Yet Q's presentation shows that Jesus *qua* SM is not unique: the same function of judge at the final judgment is promised in the final climactic statement of Q to his followers as well.

In this, "SM" may not be much different from other christological "titles" in Q. Jesus is "Son of God", especially in the temptation narrative; but there too he is a paradigm for other followers who are called to be equally obedient to God's Word as Jesus Son of God is shown to be in this story (cf. n. 36 above), and elsewhere in Q followers are invited to be sons/children of God their Father (cf. Q 6:36; 11:2; 12:30). Similarly Jesus in Q is the "Lord" as the one who must be listened to and obeyed (cf. Q 6:46); but equally the Q Christians are those who can claim just as much for the status of their own preaching which brings near the Kingdom (10:7, cf. too 10:16) and rejection of which will have eternal consequences (12:10).

This is not to say that Jesus' distinctiveness is ignored completely in Q. It remains the case that, however much Jesus and his followers may be seen to be in parallel with each other, the status of his followers is mediated through Jesus himself and dependent on him. Those who will sit on thrones judging Israel are precisely those who in turn have been confessed before God by the SM (12:8). Those rewarded with such a position in 22:30 are the same as those rewarded by the master of the preceding parable who is probably someone other than God,[51] i.e. in context almost certainly Jesus. They are also those who have "followed" Jesus.[52] The relationship between Jesus and others is thus a non-reciprocal one and Jesus does have a unique role in Q. Nevertheless, it is a role of enabling others to *share* in his own position. If such a role does not have any clear "title" attached to it, that may simply reinforce the criticisms many have advanced against an approach to NT Christology which

---

[51] See Catchpole, "Poor on Earth", 374.
[52] Cf. n. 15 above for this as the probable Q wording in Q 22:28.

is too closely tied to christological "titles".[53] It is moreover a role remarkably similar in many ways, though expressed in very different language and using a very different set of ideas, to Paul's Christology of Jesus as the new Adam and as Son of God. That is of course another story. But if the suggestions made here serve to show that Q has deep roots linking it with other key NT writers, this may enhance the importance which Q must have in any studies of early Christianity, as indeed the work of David Catchpole has so amply shown.

---

[53] Cf. L.E. Keck, "Toward the Renewal of New Testament Christology", *NTS* 32 (1986) 321–343.

CREATIVE CONFLICT: THE TORAH AND CHRISTOLOGY

Morna D. Hooker

The great majority of the books of the New Testament reflect, to a greater or lesser extent, the controversies between Jews and Christians that marked the emergence of the Christian faith and its separation from Judaism. But to what extent was it Christian claims about Jesus which led to disputes between Christians and Jews regarding the torah or law, and to what extent was it disputes regarding the torah, and Jesus' relation to it, which led to the development and formulation of christological claims? This may well prove to be something of a chicken-and-egg question! Certainly the gospels suggest that controversy over the torah was inextricably linked with the question of Jesus' authority from the beginning. The purpose of this essay is to explore that link. Pressures of space mean that our exploration will be confined to the Synoptics. It is a pleasure to offer the essay as a modest tribute to David Catchpole, whose own work on the Synoptic Gospels has contributed so much to our understanding of them.

There are four distinct ways in which Jesus and the torah are related in the gospels. First, the torah—together with the prophets and the writings—is understood to be *fulfilled* in Jesus. Each of the evangelists emphasizes, in his own way, that the scriptures point forward to him. Secondly, Jesus is portrayed as himself *faithful* to the commands of the torah: he fulfils the torah in the sense that he keeps it. In both these approaches, the authority of the torah is assumed; their purpose, however, is not to stress the authority of the torah, but to emphasize the significance of Jesus. Thirdly, the teaching of the torah is from time to time *challenged* by Jesus, whose authority is demonstrated to be greater than that of the torah. Fourthly, the era of the torah is seen as *giving way* to the era of Christ. Although these last two approaches might suggest a break between torah and gospel we find, remarkably, that the links are firmly maintained. Seeming challenges to the torah regularly occur in contexts that affirm the validity of the torah; the belief that the old has been replaced by the new arises from the assumption that there is continuity between the two: even when the torah is superseded, it continues to have a role.

Mark

In order to trace what is taking place we turn first to Mark which, with the great majority of scholars, we believe to be the earliest gospel. Although Mark never uses the word νόμος (law), he depicts many controversies regarding its regulations and interpretation, and he shows how scripture in general is fulfilled in the gospel.

In his opening lines, Mark declares that his story is the fulfilment of prophecy which he attributes to Isaiah (Mark 1:2–3). This theme is echoed in the rest of the gospel in quotations—the majority of which are also taken from Isaiah—found in the mouth of Jesus. Mark does not always specify that these are quotations, but unless we suppose that he was using tradition without being aware of its significance, and that this therefore represents an early *pre-Markan* method of handling scripture, he must have considered it unnecessary to spell out its origin. Interestingly, these subsequent quotations are invariably negative: scripture is "fulfilled" by Israel's hard-heartedness and rejection of God's plan (4:12; 7:6; 11:17); judgement is inevitable (13:24–25). Even the disciples succumb (8:18). Israel's failure leads to Jesus' death (12:10–11; 14:27), and this is said to correspond to what is "written", even when specific quotations are not given (9:12f.; 14:21,49). The passion narrative itself contains clear allusions to scripture (15:24,34). The nature of these quotations suggests that the purpose underlying their use was to deal with the major theological problem created by Israel's rejection of "the gospel about Jesus Christ" and by what Mark believed to be Israel's own rejection by God.

The one quotation that stands apart from this pattern is Ps 110:1, interpreted in 12:35–7 as a "messianic" prophecy. Yet this is not cited as straightforward "fulfilment", but raised as a question which hints that "Davidic" messianism is an inadequate category for Jesus. The passage almost certainly reflects christological debates within the Christian community, as it endeavoured to explain Jesus' status by appealing to Old Testament texts.

Mark portrays Jesus as faithful to the torah: Jesus "keeps" the sabbath by attending synagogue (1:21; 3:1), orders the healed leper to carry out the procedure laid down by Moses (1:44); he celebrates

Passover in Jerusalem (14:12–16). In his teaching, Jesus appeals to the torah—to the commandment to honour father and mother (7:10); to the creation story (10:6–8); to the commandments (10:19); to God's self-revelation to Moses (12:26); to the Sh‘ma (12:29–30) and to the demand in Leviticus to love one's neighbour (12:31).

This picture of Jesus as faithful to the torah helps to demonstrate the falsity of the accusations constantly brought against him by his enemies. Accused by the Pharisees of allowing his disciples to break the sabbath law (2:23–28), Jesus appeals to the divine purpose behind the sabbath law—a purpose which is being realized in what he and his disciples are doing. The accusation brought by the Pharisees is false, because what is at issue is the way in which the sabbath law is interpreted. In the incident that follows this, Jesus counters the unspoken accusation that, by healing, he himself is breaking the sabbath, with the question "Is it lawful to do good on the sabbath, or to do evil? To save life or to kill?" Once again, Jesus points to the purpose underlying the torah; the story demonstrates that it is he who in fact observes the law—by giving life—while the Pharisees break it—by plotting how to destroy him.

The first of these stories, however, is less straightforward than the second. The Pharisees' objections are based on their interpretation of the disciples' actions as "reaping" and "threshing", and the obvious response would have been that such an interpretation was "human tradition" (cf. 7:1–23) not "divine law". Instead, Jesus is said to have appealed to the action of David and his companions in eating the shewbread, which only priests were allowed to eat (1 Sam 21:1–6). But what is the connection? The only link seems to be the action of eating, but while David's men are described as having been hungry (Mark 2:25), no explanation is given for the disciples' action. Is the meaning, then, that scripture itself does not apply the regulations with the rigidity exercised by the Pharisees? That they are losing sight of the purpose of the law by concentrating on its details? Yet the fact that Jesus is said to appeal to David is significant, for it suggests that Mark sees it as a statement about Jesus' own authority.[1] It was David and his companions who ate the shewbread, Jesus' companions who eat the grains of wheat. If David and his companions

---

[1] This incident occurs in a section—Mark 1:14–3:6—which underlines very clearly the authority of Jesus.

could break the command of the torah, how much more can Jesus
and his companions dispense with the regulations *surrounding* the law.
The comparison is christological—between David and Jesus (who,
we learn at 12:35–37 is greater than David)—but the question of
authority touches the torah. The Son of man is not subject to the
sabbath, but is Lord of the sabbath (2:28).

Leaving aside the question of what light this material might shed
on Jesus' own attitude, we can see that these stories reflect disputes
between early Christians and Jews. To the former, it seemed clear
that Jesus was faithful to the torah, and that what he rejected was
the particular interpretation of its commandments espoused by scribes
and Pharisees. Nevertheless, his words and actions presented a radical challenge to traditional assumptions about what the torah required,
and thus raised questions about his authority and identity. To non-
Christian Jews, his teaching and behaviour appeared to undermine
the torah, enabling his followers to sit loose to all its commandments.

This clash is demonstrated in chapter 7, where scribes and Pharisees
again attack Jesus because of the behaviour of the disciples. This
time their criticism concerns the disciples' failure to observe "the tradition of the elders" which demanded the ceremonial washing of
hands before eating, and once again Jesus turns the tables, quoting
Isa 29:13 to accuse his opponents of deserting the torah in order to
keep the tradition—an accusation that is then backed up with the
example of "Corban", which could be used to make void "the word
of God", the commandment to honour father and mother to which
Jesus has himself appealed.

So far Jesus is clearly in the right in the eyes of the torah and
his opponents at fault, because they allow concern for the tradition
to obscure the demands of the torah. At this point, however, Jesus
seems to challenge the torah itself, declaring that one cannot be
defiled by what one eats (v. 15), an apparent flat contradiction of
Leviticus 11. Since the saying is couched in the form "Not this, but
that", however, it may well be an emphatic way of affirming that
ritual cleanliness is less important than moral cleanliness (cf. Hos
6:6). Nevertheless, what is "less important" is part of the torah, and
Jesus is clearly understood to be challenging the attitude which devotes
so much attention to those aspects of the torah that can be easily
regulated that the less-easily definable commands are ignored. This
is radical teaching, but it is not unique: the saying in v. 15 stands
firmly in the prophetic tradition (cf. Hos 6:6; Jer 7:22f.). Mark, how-

ever, understands it as far more radical still. The "parable" of v. 15 is explained in subsequent teaching given to the disciples alone (7:17–23), and Mark adds the comment that Jesus thereby "declared all foods clean": in a Gentile Christian environment, Jesus' words were understood as annulling the Mosaic command. This interpretation clearly cannot be reconciled with Mark's overall presentation of Jesus as *faithful* to the torah. The fact that it is nevertheless found in the context of a passage where Jesus is presented as more faithful to Moses than the Pharisees demonstrates the way in which the argument developed. The original conviction that Jesus was loyal to the torah was breaking down, and Jesus' own teaching was being seen as more authoritative than that of Moses.

A similar shift occurs in Mark 10, where Jesus is questioned by the Pharisees as to whether or not divorce is permissible.[2] Jesus replies by asking what Moses commanded, but they respond by referring to what Moses *permitted*. Jesus then appeals to the divine intention for male and female expressed in the creation story (Mark 10:6–8; Gen 1:27; 2:24).[3] This time it is not Mosaic command and human tradition that are in conflict, but the "command" implicit in the Genesis texts and the permission implicit in Deut 24:1–4. The Mosaic regulation in Deuteronomy 24, which allows for divorce, is interpreted as a concession, of lesser significance than the divine plan in Genesis.[4] Once again, however, in the subsequent scene, what Jesus teaches his disciples in private appears to challenge the torah itself, since those who remarry after divorce are said to "commit adultery" (10:10–12). The antithesis seems to have sharpened and the rule set out in Genesis now precludes altogether the possibility of remarriage implicit in Deuteronomy 24. As with 7:17–23, the setting of this

---

[2] For a detailed discussion of the way in which this story is handled see David R. Catchpole, "The Synoptic Divorce Material As a Traditio-Historical Problem", *BJRL* 57 (1974) 92–127.

[3] There is an interesting parallel in CD 4.20–5.5, where Gen 1:27 is also quoted, together with Deut 17.17. This passage is sometimes understood to prohibit divorce as well as polygamy; so, e.g., Joseph A. Fitzmyer, "The Matthean Divorce Texts and Some New Palestinian Evidence", *TS* 37 (1976) 197–226. The issue there, however (as in 11QTemple 57.17–19), seems to be not marriage after divorce, but marriage to more than one wife, since David is exonerated from blame on the grounds that in his time the book of the law had not yet been opened.

[4] "Jesus' restrictive pronouncement, while radical, does not have the same force as would permitting what Moses prohibited", W.D. Davies and E.P. Sanders in *Cambridge History of Judaism* 3 (ed. William Horbury, W.D. Davies and John Sturdy; Cambridge: CUP, 1999) 656–7.

scene "in the house", where Jesus addresses only his disciples, suggests that we have here Christian reinterpretation of Jesus' teaching. Jesus' authority is again seen as greater than that of Moses.

These are the only two scenes in Mark in which Jesus appears to challenge the teaching of Moses, and the fact that both are presented as explanations of Jesus' teaching, given to the disciples in private, is significant. This was how, in time, the teaching of Jesus was understood by at least some first-century Christians. For the most part, Mark portrays Jesus as challenging the authority of the *teachers* of torah, the scribes and Pharisees. The comment at the beginning of the story, in 1:22, that he taught with authority, not as the scribes, is echoed at the end of the gospel, where it is presented in dramatic form when a scribe questions Jesus, endorses his teaching—and is then himself commended by Jesus (12:28–34): the scribes, who considered themselves the guardians of the torah, thought it their task to judge Jesus' faithfulness to torah, but Mark's story suggests that *he* was judging *them*, since his authority was greater. A few verses later, we find Jesus condemning the scribes in general, because they oppress widows while making a public show of piety (Mark 12:38–40; Exod 22:22; cf. Deut 24:17–22; Mal 3:5). In this chapter, too, we find Jesus berating the Sadducees for failing to understand the torah (12:18–27): they, too, have concentrated on the Mosaic regulations (Deut 25:5–10) and ignored the implications of the divine self-revelation in Exodus 3.

But there are hints in Mark's narrative that support the idea that he thought of Jesus as superior to the torah itself, and not just to its teachers. He makes a leper clean—something the law cannot do, though it can authenticate the cure (1:40–45); although Jesus himself commands that the Mosaic regulations should be obeyed, the healed leper does not bother to carry them out: in the new community, the torah's commands seem irrelevant, since Jesus' power is demonstrably greater than that of the torah. In the next scene, Jesus declares a man's sins to be forgiven—in marked contrast with the torah, where sacrifice and ritual cleansing are required. Here too, Jesus is depicted as claiming an authority greater than that of Moses.

Moses typology may well lie behind the feeding narratives (6:30–44; 8:1–10), and possibly the miracles on the sea (4:35–41; 6:45–52). If so, however, Mark leaves us to work this out for ourselves. But the story of the Transfiguration (9:2–8) reminds us forcefully of the continuity between Moses and Jesus, and the superiority of the latter.

Elijah, Moses and Jesus are not equals, as Peter supposes, for it is Jesus alone who is singled out by the divine voice as "my beloved Son": once they had listened to Moses, but now they are to listen to Jesus.[5]

The new situation is presented in dramatic form in Mark 10:17–22, where a man asks Jesus how to inherit eternal life. Jesus, faithful to the torah, reminds him of the Mosaic commandments, whereupon he declares that he has kept them all. He lacks only one thing, responds Jesus: he must sell everything he has, give the proceeds to the poor, and follow him. Jesus here plainly endorses the old, but offers something better, the way of Christian discipleship.

These passages suggest, not that Jesus is seen as challenging Moses by overturning his teaching, but rather that Moses is seen as pointing forward to Jesus:[6] the old era is being replaced by the new. The time for fasting has given way to the time for feasting because the bridegroom is here (2:18–20). The appointment of twelve disciples indicates that Israel is being re-formed (3:13–19); Jesus' death is seen as a covenant which brings this community into being (14:24). But the new must not be allowed to destroy the old: the old cloak must not be torn, nor the wineskins be destroyed, even though there is new wine to be enjoyed (2:21–22). Mark seems anxious that the old should be preserved: to change the image, he is determined, not simply to eat his cake, but to have it.[7]

Matthew

Matthew presents a similar picture to Mark, but the various elements in it are all intensified. The theme of fulfilment is clearly of prime importance to Matthew, and is seen above all in the ten quotations introduced by a formula explaining that events took place "in order that what was said through the prophet might be fulfilled".

---

[5] Cf. M.D. Hooker, "'What Doest Thou Here, Elijah?' A Look at St Mark's Account of the Transfiguration", in *The Glory of Christ in the New Testament. Studies in Christology in Memory of George Bradford Caird* (ed. L.D. Hurst and N.T. Wright; Oxford: Clarendon, 1987) 59–70.

[6] I have argued earlier (see n. 5) that Elijah and Moses are both seen as Jesus' "forerunners" in Mark.

[7] I have discussed Mark's use of the Pentateuch at greater length in "Mark", in *It is Written: Scripture Citing Scripture. Essays in Honour of Barnabas Lindars* (ed. D.A. Carson and H.G.M. Williamson; Cambridge: CUP, 1988) 220–230.

These various quotations all function as broadly "messianic" proof-texts: they explain who Jesus is (1:22–23; 2:15; 2:23; 21:4–5 (cf. 21:9)) and the effect of his coming (2:18; 4:14–16); describe the nature of his ministry (8:17; 12:17–21; 13:35) and the price of his betrayal (27:9). A slightly different formula introduces a similar "messianic" prophecy in 2:5–6, and another the quotation from Isa 40:3 which identifies John as the forerunner in 3:3 (cf. Mark 1:3). Other quotations showing how scripture is being fulfilled are found in the mouth of Jesus at 11:10 (= Mark 1:2); 13.14–15 (cf. Mark 4:12); 15:7–9; 21:13 (= Mark 11:17); 21:16; 21:42 (= Mark 12:10–11); 22:44 (= Mark 12:36); 24:29 (= Mark 13:24–25); 26:31 (= Mark 14:27). Elsewhere, there are clear allusions to scripture being fulfilled (11:2–6; 24:15; 26:54,56).

Jesus is depicted as living by the torah: tempted by the devil, he repeatedly quotes from Deuteronomy (4:4,7,10; Deut 8:3; 6:16,13); twice, in disputes with the Pharisees, he complains that they do not understand the saying "I desire mercy, not sacrifice" (9:13; 12:7; Hos 6:6). Clearest of all is 5:17–20, where he declares that he has come to fulfil the law and the prophets, not to abolish them. As with the Qumran community, it is law and prophets together that must be obeyed.[8] None of the commandments can be annulled. It is hardly surprising then, that Matthew modifies the implications of Mark 7 and 10. In the story of the dispute about handwashing, Matthew records, in different words from Mark's, the saying that "it is not what enters the mouth that defiles a person, but what comes out of the mouth", but it is quite clear from the subsequent conversation that "what enters the mouth" is understood to refer back to the original question about eating with unwashed hands, not to "clean" and "unclean" food (Matt 15:1–20). Jesus is not challenging the law but, as in 9:13 and 12:7, insisting that "mercy" is more important than "sacrifice".[9] The account of the question about divorce has also been modified, and the order in which the Old Testament passages are quoted has been reversed, so that the rule is mentioned before the concession (Matt 19:3–9). In his response Jesus appeals immediately to Gen 1:27 and 2:24, which he interprets as a prohibition of divorce.

---

[8] I QS 1.2–3: the members of the community are to "do what is good and right before [God] as He commanded by the hand of Moses and all his servants the Prophets" (Vermes' translation).
[9] Cf. also 23:23.

Asked about Moses' provision for divorce he replies, as in Mark, that this was because of their hardness of heart; nevertheless, anyone who divorced his wife *except for unchastity* and married someone else committed adultery. In first-century Judaism this position would not have been seen as challenging the law, but as supporting the interpretation of Shammai, who held that Deut 24:1–4 permitted divorce only on the grounds of unchastity.

In both these scenes, Matthew has retained Mark's picture of general teaching followed by teaching addressed specifically to the disciples, even though this special teaching is no longer given in private. This continues the pattern he has already set in the Sermon on the Mount, where Jesus teaches his disciples (5:1), although the crowds are present and listening (7:28). The implication is that all are invited to respond, though few will be able to accept this more difficult teaching. In 15:12–20, Jesus merely spells out the meaning of the saying in v. 11 which his disciples ought to have understood (v. 16), but in 19:10–12 the disciples' question leads to teaching on a somewhat different subject—those who adopt celibacy for the sake of the kingdom. This certainly goes beyond anything that the law required, but suggests that Matthew saw the kingdom as presenting demands far greater than the torah.

The teaching on divorce in Matt 19:3–9 is similar to that which forms the third of the six antitheses in Matthew 5. These antitheses present a contrast between what was said in the past (i.e. by Moses) and what Jesus now says. Is Jesus, like a Jewish rabbi, simply contrasting previous interpretation of the torah with his own?[10] The emphatic ἐγὼ δὲ λέγω ὑμῖν suggests that what Jesus is presenting is more than mere "interpretation" of the torah. Is he then challenging the teaching of Moses? Matthew cannot have believed this, since the antitheses follow immediately after 5:17–20.[11] In fact, none of the antitheses contradicts the teaching of Moses; on the contrary, they all intensify it. What is true of the teaching on divorce is true of the antitheses in general: *Jesus forbids what is permitted in torah, but he does not permit what is forbidden.* Not only are murder and adultery forbidden, but anger and lust as well; divorce—except for adultery—is

---

[10] Cf. D. Daube's discussion of the rabbinic formula in *The New Testament and Rabbinic Judaism* (London: Athlone, 1956) 55–62.

[11] For a recent discussion of these issues, see W.D. Davies and Dale C. Allison, *The Gospel According to Saint Matthew* 1 (ICC; Edinburgh: T. & T. Clark, 1988) 505–9.

ruled out; not only is false swearing prohibited but oaths of any
kind; the law that limited revenge is insufficient—there should be
no revenge at all; love for one's neighbour must be extended to
embrace one's enemy as well.

Although Matthew's Jesus does not challenge the teaching of Moses,
he does far more here than simply interpret its meaning, since his
words stand in contrast to those of Moses. What he is demanding
of his followers is a righteousness greater than that of scribes and
Pharisees (5:20), a righteousness greater than anything that Moses
demands. But on what authority? Matthew has already given us the
clues. In his opening chapters, the story of Herod's attempt on the
life of Jesus, the Massacre of the Innocents and Jesus' escape to
Egypt all echo the story of Moses. Now, however, Jesus emerges as
greater than Moses. Like Moses, he ascends a mountain,[12] but whereas
Moses stayed on the mountain for forty days and then descended
to pass on the teaching he had received to the people, Jesus sits
down *on* the mountain, and his disciples come to him there. If the
setting suggests that Jesus is for Matthew a "new Moses", it also suggests that he is *superior* to Moses, and that the teaching he gives is
closer to the source of divine revelation, being delivered from the
mountain itself. The teaching of Jesus is delivered to the disciples,
the people who have left everything to follow him (4:18–22)—much
as the Israelites abandoned everything to follow Moses—and they
form the nucleus of a new community (cf. 19:28). The Sermon begins
with the Beatitudes—the blessings God gives his people; like the story
in Exodus, grace precedes demand, for Moses also, when he came
down the mountain, began by reminding the people of what God
had done for them and told them of the blessings he was now promising them (Exod 19:3–7). Two short sayings then describe the role
of God's people: their task is to be the salt of the earth and the
light of the world. Both sayings contain a reference to possible failure to carry out the task—is this a criticism of Israel? Both sayings
indicate that the task is now seen as a universal one.

The teaching Jesus gives is new, because it is the fulfilment of
both law and prophets (v. 17), but precisely *as* their fulfilment, it
does not destroy them. What Jesus demands does not contradict
torah but surpasses it, because what he demands from his followers

---

[12] The phrase is used repeatedly of Moses in the LXX: e.g. Exod 19:3; 24:15;
34:4.

is nothing less than perfection (v. 48). The commands are *his* commands, as we are reminded by the repeated use of the phrase ". . . but *I* say to you . . .". To be sure, we are reminded at the end that allegiance to Jesus is insufficient, and that what is required from men and women is obedience to God's will (7:21–23); but it is *Jesus* who will sit in judgement, and who will vindicate or reject! This idea is spelt out at length at the end of the gospel, when Jesus describes the judgement carried out by the Son of man when he comes in glory as king (25:31–46). And the Sermon closes with the parable of the wise and foolish builders; the man who builds on rock is not the man who obeys torah, but the man who hears *these words of mine* and does them. The choice reminds us of the one placed before Israel after the giving of the law (Lev 26; Deut 30:15–20). No wonder Matthew ends with the comment that Jesus taught with authority, not like the scribes!

The Jesus who delivers the Sermon on the Mount does not challenge the Mosaic law: on the contrary, he confirms the law, for not an iota or a tittle will be abolished until heaven and earth pass away. Nevertheless, those who are Jesus' disciples and who belong to the new community obey *his* words—words which, like the word of God himself (Isa 40:8; Ps 119:89), will endure even *after* heaven and earth pass away (24:35). The era of the torah is giving way to the era of Christ, for "the prophets and the law prophesied" until the coming of John, whose arrival announced the coming of Jesus himself (11:7–15). This strange statement in 11:13, with the prophets preceding the law, and the use of the verb "prophesied", betrays Matthew's concerns.[13] Prophets and law are not abolished in the new era but fulfilled. When the era of Christ *finally* takes over, the torah given through Moses will no longer be necessary. But that time has not yet come, for the rule of heaven is at present subject to violent attack (11:12). In the meantime, the regulations of the law should be observed (e.g. 5:23; 17:27; 24:20).[14]

---

[13] See David R. Catchpole, "The Law and the Prophets in Q", in *Tradition and Interpretation in the New Testament. Essays in Honor of E. Earle Ellis* (ed. Gerald F. Hawthorne with Otto Betz; Grand Rapids MI: Eerdmans/Tübingen: Mohr Siebeck, 1987) 95–109.

[14] Each of these passages raises problems. How are we to understand the reference to sacrifice in 5:23, since Matthew was writing after 70 CE? Can 17:27 be construed as an attack on the regulation in Exod 30:13, or does it reflect the view that the tax should be given only once in a lifetime, not annually (cf. 4Q159)? Does

Confirmation of our understanding of the Sermon on the Mount is found in Matt 11:25–30. The thanksgiving in v. 25 reminds us of the Beatitudes: it is the νήπιοι, the simple, to whom "these things" have been revealed. In the LXX Psalms, the νήπιοι are God's faithful ones, who receive wisdom in the shape of the law (Ps 18(19):7; 118(119):130). Now the wisdom comes from Jesus, who is the source of revelation, for "all things have been handed over" to the Son by the Father (v. 27). The mutual knowledge of Father and Son is strongly reminiscent, it has been suggested, of the reciprocal knowledge requested by Moses in Exod 33:12–13 (cf. Deut 34:10), the promise of rest (v. 28) of the promise in Exod 33:14.[15] But now the mutual knowledge is between the Father and the Son. Does this passage, then, contrast the revelation to God's servant Moses and the revelation through the Son? If so, it points us in the direction of John 1:17 and Heb 1:1–2; 3:1–6: in Matthew's setting at least, this passage well deserves its description as a "Johannine thunderbolt"! The Son reveals the Father (cf. John 1:18) to those whom he chooses. The rest is now given *by Jesus*, and he summons men and women to take up *his* yoke. Jer 5:5 speaks of the torah as a yoke, and Sirach 51:26 of the yoke of wisdom, which is identified with the torah. Now Jesus offers his yoke, for he is himself wisdom (Matt 11:19); Jesus is authentic torah, "the full revelation of God and of his will for man".[16]

Matthew uses much of the Markan material we have looked at with very little alteration, but there are one or two significant changes. In 9:17 he underlines the meaning of the parable about the wine and wineskins with the words "and both are preserved". To the teaching on parables he adds the saying in 13:52 about the scribe who rightly treasures "what is new and what is old". In Matt 12:1–8 Matthew has retained the strange reference to David eating the shewbread, but has made the conversation more relevant to the matter under debate, first by noting that the disciples, too, were hungry, and secondly and more significantly by adding another example— that of the priests, who "break the sabbath" (12:5, presumably by offering the sabbath sacrifice, and so working on the sabbath, Num

---

24:20 assume that flight on the sabbath is impossible, or merely that it would offend Jewish neighbours? On this last point, see G.N. Stanton, *A Gospel for a New People: Studies in Matthew* (Edinburgh: T. & T. Clark, 1992) 192–206.

[15] See W.D. Davies and Dale C. Allison, *Matthew* 2 (1991), 271–97, and literature cited there.

[16] Davies and Allison, *Matthew* 2, 290.

28:9–10). The argument now runs smoothly: the Pharisees have failed to understand the principles set out in Hos 6:6: "I desire mercy, and not sacrifice". The priests "break the sabbath" in order to serve the temple, but "something greater than the temple is here", and that "something greater" appears to be Jesus himself, "for the Son of man is Lord of the sabbath" (cf. 12:38–42). Another interesting change is found in Matt 19:16–22 (//Mark 10:17–22), where a man asks Jesus how to possess eternal life. Instead of addressing Jesus as "Good Teacher" as in Mark, he asks Jesus "what good deed" is necessary. Matthew thus avoids the danger of interpreting Jesus' reply as a denial that he is good. There is one who is good, and his commandments are plain, and must be obeyed: nevertheless, if the man wishes to be perfect, he must sell everything and follow Jesus. The story neatly encapsulates the message of the Sermon on the Mount. Finally, we note that in 22:41–46 the question about the significance of Ps 110:1 is addressed to the Pharisees and given a new introduction: "What is your opinion about the Messiah? Whose son is he?" The implication, of course, is that he is not son of David, but Son of God (cf. 11:27; 28:19).

As in Mark, it is those who *teach* the law who are condemned, notably in Matthew 23, where Jesus pronounces woe on scribes and Pharisees. But this passage is introduced with the command to do whatever the scribes and Pharisees teach, since they sit on Moses' seat (23:1). One must do what they say, but not what they do, since their actions show them to be hypocrites.

There is just one passage in Matthew which could be interpreted as a challenge to the law itself. This is 8:21–2, where a disciple is forbidden permission to bury his father before following Jesus. Does this contradict the teaching in Matt 15:1–20 (cf. Mark 7:1–23), where Jesus himself condemns the Pharisees and scribes for not observing the commandment to honour one's parents? It seems unlikely that Matthew would have understood it in that way. Are we perhaps to suppose that the man's father was not yet dead, and that he is simply offering an excuse for postponing his commitment to Jesus? Or does Jesus' reply reflect rather the importance of the enterprise on which he is engaged? When God's call demands, then certain obligations under the law no longer apply (cf. Lev 21:11; Num 6:6; Jer 16:1–9; Ezek 24:15–18; Matt 10:37). If this is how we should understand the saying, then it is similar to others in which one demand in the law is weighed over against another.

Matthew has emphasized three of the four themes found in Mark: the fourth is firmly refuted. He has shown how Jesus fulfills the torah and is faithful to torah; he has shown also that Jesus' authority is greater than the authority of Moses; at the same time, he has stressed that Jesus in no way challenges Moses' teaching. Nevertheless, though the torah will last while heaven and earth endure, it will finally be subsumed in the era of Christ.

Yet for Jesus' followers, members of the new community, his teaching has already taken over, and nowhere is that clearer than in the closing verses of the gospel. Allusions to the Moses tradition have often been found in this story,[17] but there is one aspect of this that seems to have escaped attention. The scene is reminiscent not only of those in which Moses commissioned Joshua (Deut 31:14–15, 23; Josh 1:1–9) but, even more importantly, of Moses' own commissioning in Exodus 3, and his return in Exodus 19–20 to receive the law. In Exodus 3, Moses meets with God and is commanded to bring his people out of Egypt: when he protests that he is unfit for the task, God replies "I am with you" (Exod 3:12) and tells Moses to return with the people to the same mountain and worship him there. God then reveals his name as "I am who I am". If the parallel between that story and Matthew's has largely gone unnoticed, that is because in the latter Jesus is the one who commissions, not the one who is commissioned: it is *Jesus* who meets the disciples on the mountain that he has appointed (though Matthew has made no previous reference to this!) and who is worshipped by them there— even though some doubted, much as Moses and the Israelites doubted. Jesus has been given all authority, not only on earth but in heaven, and it is with that authority—the authority of God himself—that he acts here. It is *he* therefore, who sends the disciples out to make disciples of the nations, so creating a new community. Moses received the law and passed it on to the people, but the disciples have been instructed by Jesus, and now it is *they* who are commanded to pass on *his* teaching. The God who revealed himself to Moses was the God of the Jewish patriarchs, the God of Abraham, Isaac and Jacob, and his name was "I am"; now this God is revealed as "Father, Son and Holy Spirit", and it is into this name that all nations are to be baptized. But he is still "I am"! Moses was sent to Pharaoh with the

---

[17] For details, see W.D. Davies and Dale C. Allison, *Matthew* 3 (1997), 676–87.

promise "I am with you" (Exod 3:12), even before he understood the significance of the divine name (3:14), and now Jesus' promise to the disciples—"I am with you always"—echoes that promise and that name. The echo can hardly be accidental, for in Matt 1:23 we were told that Jesus' birth fulfilled the words of Isa 7:14, including the promise that "they shall call his name Emmanuel". The reference to this promise followed somewhat strangely after the angel's instruction to call the child "Jesus", but Matthew certainly intended to include the whole quotation from Isaiah, for he spells out the word's meaning—"God with us". He has, in fact, made one slight alteration to the LXX version, changing the singular καλέσεις to the plural καλέσουσιν: this part of the promise will be fulfilled, not at Jesus' birth, but when Christian believers come to acknowledge him as "God with us".[18] Now, at the close of Matthew's gospel, the words are fulfilled in Jesus' own promise "I am with you".[19]

Luke

In Luke, the emphasis is very much on the fulfilment of scripture, and though there is opposition from Jesus' fellow-Jews, there is no hint of conflict with the law itself. The emphasis on fulfilment is seen in the opening chapters—not, indeed, in "fulfilment" quotations, as in Matthew, but in the allusions that pervade the whole account, and which clearly show Jesus to be the fulfilment of God's promises. There are just three references to "the law", all in 2:22–24, and all referring, not to the way in which prophecies were fulfilled in Jesus, but to the way in which Jesus—through his parents—fulfilled the regulations of the law. Mary and Joseph did what the law required, bringing Jesus to Jerusalem to present him to the Lord, and making the appropriate sacrifice. They are shown to have been a pious, law-abiding family, observing the Passover (2:41), as indeed was Jesus himself, attending synagogue on the sabbath "as was his custom" (4:16). As in Matthew, Jesus quotes scripture in his conflict with Satan (4:4,8,12), for he lives in accordance with the law. At his death,

---

[18] See Graham Stanton, "Matthew", in *It is Written* (see n. 7), 205–19, at p. 215.
[19] I hope to explore the ideas set out in this paragraph in a forthcoming book on the theme of "endings".

the centurion declares him to be righteous (23:47), innocent of the charges brought against him.

Luke has just one "fulfilment" prophecy, but that dominates the first few chapters of Jesus' ministry. The long quotation from Isaiah 61 in 4:16–19 is placed in the mouth of Jesus himself, and forms the agenda for the material from 4:31–7:23. On hearing Jesus' words, "all in the synagogue" are enraged and attempt to kill him: their objection is not to anything that Jesus has yet done, but to the claim that he is the promised anointed prophet of Isaiah 61. The theme of fulfilment is implicit in Jesus' message to John the Baptist in 7:18–23 and in 9:31, where he discusses his coming "exodus" with Moses and Elijah.

Luke's presentation of Jesus in the role of a prophet serves to emphasize the continuity of what is taking place with God's self-revelation in the past. In 4:24, and again in 13:33, Jesus himself accepts that prophetic role: both passages refer to rejection and death. He is acknowledged by the people as a prophet (7:16; 9:8,19; 24:19; cf. 7:39). Specifically, he is linked with Elijah (and Elisha) in 4:25–27; the story in 7:11–17 echoes stories about Elijah and Elisha (1 Kings 17:17–24; 2 Kings 4:32–37) and 9:59–62 the call of Elisha by Elijah (1 Kings 19:19–21); the people think that he may be Elijah (9:8, 19). Like Elijah (2 Kings 2:1–12), Jesus will be "taken up" (9:51). There are hints, too, that he is seen as the prophet like Moses (cf. 9:35; Deut 18:15), for in the long journey to Jerusalem which begins in 9:51 there are possible echoes of the story of Moses.[20]

Towards the end of the story, Luke emphasizes that what happens to Jesus was "written by the prophets" (18:31; 22:37), and in the closing scenes the risen Christ explains the things written about himself in all the scriptures, "beginning from Moses and all the prophets" (24:27, 44–45).

In Luke, all suggestion that Jesus might be challenging Moses has vanished. The squabble about unwashed hands (Mark 7:1–23//Matt 15:1–20) is absent, and the argument about divorce is reduced to a single saying (16:18). Without the setting of controversy provided by Mark and Matthew, it would not have occurred to Luke's readers that the prohibition of divorce and remarriage might be held to con-

---

[20] Cf. C.F. Evans, "The Central Section of St. Luke's Gospel", in *Studies in the Gospels. Essays in Memory of R.H. Lightfoot* (ed. D.E. Nineham; Oxford: Blackwell, 1957) 37–53.

tradict Moses. Luke provides his own setting:[21] first, we have the saying in v. 16 that contrasts the era of the law and prophets, which lasted "until John", with the new era, in which the rule of God is proclaimed, and everyone is eager to accept it. The urgent necessity of proclaiming and entering the kingdom is demonstrated in Jesus' sayings to would-be disciples in 9:57–62. The saying in v. 17 makes clear that this does not mean that the law is therefore obsolete: on the contrary, what the law demands accords with the demands of the kingdom, and v. 18 is presumably meant to illustrate this! Luke is clearly not interested in the niceties of rabbinic debate, and sees the ethical issues as paramount. The parable that follows hints at the continuity between the demands of the torah and the demands of the kingdom. The rich man ignored the needs of the poor: he, like his brothers, has ignored "Moses and the prophets", but those who ignore Moses and the prophets will fail to listen, "even if someone rise from the dead" (16:29–31).

In Luke, the so-called "Johannine thunderbolt" is found in a passage which stresses the theme of fulfilment (10:17–24). It follows the account of the return of the Seventy and Jesus' vision of the fall of Satan from heaven, and it is followed, not by sayings about finding rest and accepting Jesus' yoke, but by Jesus' declaration that the disciples are blessed, because they see and hear what many prophets and kings longed in vain to see and hear.

Luke sees no conflict between the torah and the gospel. The teaching in the Sermon on the Plain (6:17–49), though similar to that in the Sermon on the Mount, is not contrasted with previous teaching. There are, to be sure, many incidents in which the Pharisees are depicted as rejecting Jesus' teaching, a theme which is continued in Acts, where "the Jews" continually reject the gospel. The Pharisees, in turn, come under attack from Jesus. But the problem of reconciling Jesus' teaching with that of Moses is no longer a real one.[22]

---

[21] The three sayings in 16:16–18 are all found in totally different settings in Matthew. Either Luke has brought the sayings together himself, or he has taken the combination over from "Q" (so David R. Catchpole, *The Quest for Q* [Edinburgh: T. & T. Clark, 1993] 235).

[22] There are, however, echoes of this controversy in Acts, where the charge of prophesying that Jesus will destroy the Temple and overturn the Mosaic teaching is brought against Stephen in Acts 6:14; his subsequent speech ignores the charge and demonstrates that it is his *accusers* who are guilty of rejecting the demands and promises of God.

The change is demonstrated by Luke's remarkable version of the saying about patching a garment (5:36). No one, we are told, takes a patch out of a new garment in order to mend an old one! The absurd image reveals Luke's concern lest the gospel be treated as a "repair job" on Judaism: he is worried, not about losing the old, but about destroying the new. The new must be recognized for what it is. The saying, absurd as it is, reminds us (like that in 16:16) that something essentially *new* has happened: its meaning now corresponds with that of the parable about new wine which cannot be contained in old wineskins (5:37–38). In view of this, v. 39 must be seen as an ironic comment, not a commendation of the old wine! Whatever the origin of this saying, it is an appropriate description of the reaction of Jesus' contemporaries to his message.

Synthesis

Can we draw any conclusions from this brief survey?

Underlying all the gospels we have tradition which indicates that Jesus spoke and acted with an authority that led to conflict during his lifetime. This authority and this conflict inevitably raised questions regarding his identity in the minds of his contemporaries. Whether or not these questions were formulated in christological terms, they would certainly have included the suggestion that he was a prophet.[23]

Mark suggests that the conflict continued in arguments between Christians and Jews, and that Jesus' authority was now being linked with particular christological claims. Jesus acted as the Son of man, as someone like David, as one with greater authority than Moses. The Transfiguration shows Jesus to be not only the successor of Elijah and Moses but greater than they, since he is the Son of God— for Mark the most significant of all the christological titles. Mark maintains that Jesus himself was in agreement with Moses, and that his only disagreement was with the interpreters of Moses. Nevertheless, he recognizes that, in the context of the Gentile mission, Jesus' teaching in effect overruled that of Moses (7:19).

Matthew has faced up to the problem that Mark failed to solve.

[23] For some of the evidence, see Morna D. Hooker, *The Signs of a Prophet* (London: SCM/Harrisburg PA: TPI, 1997).

Writing in a Jewish milieu, the situation of conflict is more obvious, the response more consistent. Matthew emphasizes the theme of fulfilment, but insists that the old has not been overthrown. His solution to the tension between old and new is to trace the continuity between Moses and Jesus in terms of partial and complete revelation. Moses instructed the Jews in what he was given, but he did not see the whole picture, which is now revealed to Christians by Jesus, who is not simply a teacher or a prophet but the source of the torah. As the controversy intensifies, so the christological claims are sharpened. Matthew develops Mark's link between the idea that Jesus is greater than Moses and the revelation that he is Son of God: Jesus is the Son who reveals the Father, he is "God with us". Of course Jesus is greater than Moses! Nevertheless, Moses' teaching is endorsed, even while it is superseded.

Luke presents a very different story. His emphasis is on the theme of fulfilment, on the way in which the story of Jesus continues the story of Israel, and on how the law and prophets and writings point forward to Jesus. Although he uses some of the "controversy stories" showing Jesus in conflict with scribes and Pharisees, there is little indication that he was involved in Jewish-Christian wrangling about possible conflicts between Moses and Jesus. His Christology is the Christology of fulfilment: Jesus is the expected prophet, the expected Messiah, he is Son of God, Lord and Servant. But the era of Jesus succeeds the era of the law and the prophets, and the demands of the torah are not relevant to Luke's Gentile community. Although in Acts Luke shows that Christians were still endeavouring to persuade the Jews that Jesus was the fulfilment of Israel's hope (Acts 28:20), the break between the Jewish and Christian communities is clear.

And what of the Fourth Gospel? To complete this survey, we would need to look at this also. Were we able to do so, we would find there the theme of fulfilment, not simply in the many references to scripture,[24] but in the introductory Prologue in 1:1–18, and in the very Johannine presentation of Jesus "fulfilling" the law by offering to men and women everything that was offered not only in the law (e.g. in the images of manna, water, light, and life[25]), but in the feasts (in particular the offering of Jesus as the true passover lamb[26])

---

[24] See 1:23,51; 2:17; 6:45; 7:38; 10:34; 12:13,15,38,40; 13:18; 15:25; 17:12; 19:24,28,36,37; 20:9.
[25] 6:5–59; 4:1–15; 7:38–39; 19:34; 1:1–18; 3:19–21; 11:25 etc.
[26] 1:29,36; 18:28; 19:36.

and in the worship of the temple (4:23). Jesus is clearly greater than Moses and the torah—indeed, this theme dominates the gospel (1:17–18)—but there is no contradiction between old and new, since the same divine λόγος, which spoke in creation and through Moses, was "made flesh" in Christ (1:14). Moses pointed forward to Christ (5:39–47; 7:19–24), who is far greater than himself—and than Abraham too—since he is "I am" (8:58).

Many studies have shown that John's gospel reflects conflict between Christians and Jews, and some have attempted to trace the way in which his theology evolved from that situation.[27] It is surely no accident that Matthew, also facing opposition from fellow-Jews,[28] and attempting to hold together old and new, developed a profound Christology which, though it is not spelt out in the Johannine manner, is remarkably similar.[29] Christology like this would certainly have led to further controversy, but controversy itself was undoubtedly one of the creative forces which helped to shape this Christology.

---

[27] See, in particular, John Ashton, *Understanding the Fourth Gospel* (Oxford: Clarendon, 1991).

[28] The situations are not, of course, identical. In John's time, the split between the two communities has taken place, and the opponents are "the Jews", not "the Pharisees".

[29] Similar also, it should be added, to many Pauline passages, written after similar arguments with his fellow-Jews.

GOSPEL GENRE, CHRISTOLOGICAL CONTROVERSY AND THE ABSENCE OF RABBINIC BIOGRAPHY: SOME IMPLICATIONS OF THE BIOGRAPHICAL HYPOTHESIS

Richard A. Burridge

Introduction

It is a privilege and a delight to contribute this essay in honour of David Catchpole. I first met him at the British New Testament Conference in September 1986, when I was delivering a paper which contained the first public airing of the substantive idea of my doctoral work on the genre of the gospels.[1] I little expected to find myself a year later appointed as Lazenby Chaplain to the University of Exeter, whereupon David invited me to do some New Testament teaching with him in the Department of Theology. It was through this experience of teaching together both in the university and in extra-mural activities that I came to appreciate David's passion for the traditio-historical method of studying the gospels. At the same time his support and encouragement for me to finish my doctorate and get it published was as constant as it was helpful.

Therefore I have chosen to draw on this material and develop it further in this essay to look at how my work on gospel genre might affect our chosen area of christological controversy. It will begin with a brief summary of my argument about gospel genre and biography, which leads to the concentrated christological focus on the person of Jesus. We then consider some implications of this for christological development and controversies. Finally we will discuss the question of why no biographies were written of other Jewish rabbis in the first century; this notable absence suggests that the biographical

---

[1] I have to admit it was David's Somerset County Cricket Club sweatshirt which attracted my attention as a fellow supporter! Many of our subsequent debates on the New Testament, including some of the ideas in this chapter, were conducted on days out at the cricket—and I wish him many happy days at the Taunton ground in his future retirement.

genre of the gospels itself contains a christological claim about Jesus of Nazareth.

1. *The Genre of the Gospels*

The major focus of David Catchpole's work has been to use the historical method to analyse the gospels, to understand the redactional interests of the evangelists and to get behind them to their sources, especially the "double tradition" of material shared by Matthew and Luke, known as "Q".[2] The ultimate aim, however, is to go further into the process to discover the original teachings of the historical Jesus: thus, in a typical Catchpole phrase, he says of the sermon by Jesus in Nazareth, "while the words are the words of Luke, the voice is surely the voice of Jesus."[3] Many a time I have watched David take a class through a complex section of gospel material, such as the Beatitudes, on the blackboard, analysing it and reducing it to the pure, golden nugget of authentic material from Jesus. Such an approach is often described as treating the gospels as though they are "windows" through which we look to that which lies "beyond" or "behind the text". Thus Q is to be found behind the canonical gospels—and the historical Jesus beyond that. The gospels are seen as windows onto both the early Christian communities and their debates and also to Jesus himself.

One problem with such an approach is the sheer diversity of reconstructions offered by those who look "through" the "window"—see for example the multitude of interpretations of Q itself.[4] Equally the variety of accounts of the historical Jesus are sometimes thought to "reflect" as much of the scholar's own views as those of Jesus. Thus the image moves from window to "mirror" in which what one may think is seen through or "behind" the text is actually one's own concerns "before" the text, like a mirror reflecting back what is actually "in front" of it. The traditional historical method depends upon

---

[2] David Catchpole's major articles on Q are collected together and expanded in his, *The Quest for Q* (Edinburgh: T. & T. Clark, 1993).

[3] D.R. Catchpole, "The Anointed One in Nazareth", in *From Jesus to John: Essays on Jesus and New Testament Christology, in Honour of Marinus de Jonge* (ed. M.C. de Boer; Sheffield: JSOT, 1993) 230–51; quotation from p. 251.

[4] Contrast, for example, Catchpole's work with that of J.S. Kloppenborg, *The Formation of Q: Trajectories in Ancient Wisdom Collections* (Philadelphia: Fortress, 1987).

a communication model of author–text–reader, where the reader attempts to get back through the text to the original author's intention or situation. Since we do not know who wrote the gospels, when, where or why, more recent literary approaches have stressed the impossibility of getting back behind the text to the author; instead there is just text and reader.[5] But, it may be asked, are all responses made by a reader to the text equally valid? Can we make texts mean what we want them to mean in such Humpty Dumpty fashion?

Both approaches tend to ignore the question of genre: what kind of glass is the text; window, or mirror—or something different? The issue of genre is absolutely crucial to any kind of communication theory. TV or radio broadcasts must be decoded by a receiver using the same frequency or system as that in which they were transmitted. Interpreting legends as though they were history, or soap operas as though they were real life leads to misunderstanding them. Thus genre is a key convention governing both the composition and interpretation not just of texts, but of all communication. It is an "agreement", often unspoken or even unconscious, between writer and audience, author and reader about the expectations and conventions in which the work communicated is composed and understood.

Thus before we can read the gospels, we have to discover what kind of books they might be. It is therefore rather a shock to discover scholars like Karl Ludwig Schmidt and Rudolf Bultmann affirming that the gospels are "unique" forms of literature, *sui generis*, of their own genre—and that this approach dominated gospel studies for most of the last century.[6] In contrast to this approach, I compared the gospels with ten examples of ancient biography from fourth century BCE rhetorical encomia (Isocrates and Xenophon) through the major biographical writers (like Plutarch and Suetonius) to the 3rd century CE forerunners of the novel (Lucian and Philostratus). This showed that while ancient biography was a diverse and flexible genre, it still had a recognizable "family resemblance" in both form and content.

---

[5] See, for example, S.D. Moore, *Literary Criticism and the Gospels: The Theoretical Challenge* (New Haven: Yale University Press, 1989).

[6] See K.L. Schmidt, "Die Stellung der Evangelien in der allgemeinen Literaturgeschichte", in *EUCHARISTERION: Studien zur Religion und Literatur des Alten und Neuen Testaments* (ed. H. Schmidt; Göttingen: Vandenhoeck und Ruprecht, 1923), vol. 2, 50–134; R. Bultmann, *The History of the Synoptic Tradition* (Oxford: Blackwell, 1972), see especially p. 374.

From a formal or structural perspective, they are written in continuous prose narrative, between 10,000 and 20,000 words in length,
the amount on a single scroll; unlike much modern biography, they
do not cover every part of the subject's life and times in detail, preferring a barely chronological outline starting with the birth or public debut and ending with the death, with topical material inserted
to portray a particular understanding of the subject. Given the ancient
interest in how a person's death encapsulates their life, often this
will be dealt with in great detail. The gospels' narrative structure,
length and mixture of anecdote and sayings fit quite happily in this
genre and their concentration on Jesus' last days and death is typical of ancient biographies.[7] This means that the gospels have a particular focus on the person of Jesus of Nazareth derived from their
literary genre.

2. *The Christological Subject of the Gospels*

However, the subject of the gospels has produced considerable debate
over the years which takes a different view. Various proposals for
their "real" subject include God, the Kingdom of Heaven, the early
Christian preaching, discipleship, or specific concerns of each different
community, assumed to be behind the gospel. Nonetheless, for most
of the last century, the one thing most scholars agreed was that they
were not about Jesus: "there is a lack of focus on the hero . . . It is
not a biography of Jesus but a story of God bringing salvation to
his people."[8]

In fact, detailed analysis of the verbal structure of the gospels
reveals exactly the opposite. Every sentence in English and in ancient
languages must have a subject—the person or thing doing the action
of the verb. Analysis of the subjects of the verbs can be extended
from one sentence to a paragraph and then across a whole work.
Most narratives, ancient or modern, have a wide variety of subjects,
as different people come to the fore at different times. It is particularly characteristic of biography that the attention stays focused on

---

[7] This is a very brief summary of the argument of my doctoral studies; see R.A.
Burridge, *What are the Gospels? A Comparison with Graeco-Roman Biography* (SNTSMS
70; Cambridge: CUP, 1992) for fuller detail.
[8] E.P. Sanders and M. Davies, *Studying the Synoptic Gospels* (London: SCM, 1989)
288.

one person. My analysis has demonstrated that in ancient biography around a quarter or a third of the verbs are dominated by one person, the hero; furthermore, another 15% to 30% of the verbs can occur in sayings, speeches or quotations from the person. So too in the gospels: Jesus is the subject of a quarter of the verbs in Mark's gospel, with a further fifth spoken by him in his teaching and parables. Matthew and Luke both make Jesus the subject of nearly a fifth of their verbs, while about 40% are spoken by him. About half of John's verbs either have Jesus as the subject or are on his lips.[9]

Thus we can see clearly that, as in other ancient biographies, Jesus' deeds and words are of vital importance for the four evangelists as they each paint their different portraits of Jesus of Nazareth. Since the gospels are a form of ancient biography, we must interpret them with the same biographical concentration upon their subject to see how each evangelist portrays his understanding of Jesus. For this reason, I followed up my work at Exeter on the genre of the gospels with a study of the four gospels as christological narratives, using the traditional images of the four faces or living creatures (the human, lion, ox and eagle of Ezekiel 1 and Revelation 4–5) as symbols not of the evangelists themselves, but rather of their understandings of Jesus.[10]

To return to our earlier images, the gospels are not primarily a window onto the historical Jesus or the early Christian communities, nor a mirror to reflect anything we place before them. They are more like a piece of stained glass. Of course, we can look through stained glass to that which lies the other side—but what we see is shadowy and coloured by the glass. Equally, we can sometimes catch our own reflection in the glass. But principally, stained glass is about the image in the glass—the picture or portrait, assembled by the artist within a relatively limited compass and using all the various possible colours and shapes to communicate their particular understanding of the subject or person depicted. In the case of the gospels as ancient biography, that subject is Jesus—and so the gospels are nothing less than Christology in narrative form, the story of Jesus.

---

[9] For diagrams of all this data, see *What are the Gospels?*, Appendix, 261–74.

[10] R.A. Burridge, *Four Gospels, One Jesus? A Symbolic Reading* (London: SPCK/Grand Rapids: Eerdmans, 1994).

This is true at the micro-level of every word, passage or pericope as well as the macro-level of the overall narrative flow.

3. *Christological Controversy and Genre*

Given this biographical concentration upon the person of Jesus in the gospels, one would expect the genre of the gospels to play a major part in studies of Christology—both in terms of its own development and its role in controversy among early Christians and Jews. Surprisingly, these are two notable areas where there is very little discussion of the genre of the gospels.

a) *The Development of Christology*

The development of New Testament Christology has been a very productive area with many key books published over recent decades. The emphasis has moved from the development "of" Christology, to the "Christology in the New Testament" and more recently to a stress on the "Christologies" of the New Testament. What is common to most of these studies is the use of various tools of historical analysis—using the texts as "windows" to reconstruct the understandings of Jesus which lie behind the various texts. Any literary analysis is confined mostly to things like the christological titles used in the various New Testament books to describe Jesus—but even here the emphasis is upon which titles may have been used by which groups among the early Christians, again what we are calling the "window" approach.

This began with an evolutionary approach to Christology, pioneered by the History of Religions theories of Wilhelm Bousset and, later, Rudolf Bultmann.[11] Taking the texts as windows, they looked "through" them to the origins of Christology in a Palestinian primitive Christianity believing in Jesus as a messianic figure, descended from David and being the Son of Man, as opposed to the primitive Hellenistic Christianity which saw Jesus in terms similar to pagan deities.

A typical study of the christological "titles" is seen in C.F.D.

---

[11] W. Bousset, *Kyrios Christos: A History of the Belief in Christ from the Beginnings of Christianity to Irenaeus*, German original published in 1913 and revised in 1921; ET was not until 1970 by J. Steely (Nashville: Abingdon, 1970); Bultmann, *History of the Synoptic Tradition*.

Moule's *The Origin of Christology*, looking first at four "descriptions of Jesus" as Son of Man, Son of God, Christ and Kurios; he then goes on to the "corporate Christ" looking particularly at Pauline phrases, including the body and the temple. After a survey of the rest of the New Testament, he goes on to the death of Christ and the theme of fulfilment and a discussion of Christ's "distinctiveness". He concludes by arguing against the History of Religions approach of Bultmann and others that "development is a better analogy than evolution for the genesis of New Testament Christology".[12] While Moule recognises a variety of understandings of Jesus in the New Testament, the different genres of the various books do not feature at all, nor whether any particular type of book lends itself particularly to the argument. Instead, the various books are like quarries from which to extract the titles.

James Dunn follows a similar strategy for *Christology in the Making*, looking at the titles of Son of God, Son of Man, last Adam, Spirit or Angel, the Wisdom of God and the Word of God. He also talks of "development" over the first century,[13] but once again there is no attempt to look at the different genres of literature. Raymond Brown provides an introduction for lay people into high and low, conservative and liberal Christologies and traces a development from Jesus' own Christology, or self understanding, to a variety of Christologies in the New Testament in terms of Jesus' second coming, resurrection or pre-existence.[14] Despite Brown's general concentration on the gospels, here too there is no attempt to deal with their overall form or genre as christological narrative; instead, once again they are merely a source for the various christological ideas Brown discusses.

Ben Witherington III began by looking at *The Christology of Jesus*,[15] but more recently stresses plurality in his *The Many Faces of the Christ: The Christologies of the New Testament and Beyond*.[16] This begins with some historical background on pre-Christian Jewish Messianism and moves onto Jesus' self-understanding, drawing on his previous work.

---

[12] C.F.D. Moule *The Origin of Christology* (Cambridge: CUP 1977); quotation from p. 135.

[13] J.D.G. Dunn, *Christology in the Making* (London: SCM 1980, 2nd edn 1989); quotation from p. 248.

[14] R.E. Brown, *Introduction to New Testament Christology* (London: Chapman, 1994).

[15] B. Witherington III, *The Christology of Jesus* (Minneapolis: Fortress, 1990)

[16] B. Witherington III, *The Many Faces of the Christ: The Christologies of the New Testament and Beyond* (New York: Crossroad Herder, 1998).

When he comes to the rest of the New Testament, Witherington argues against any developmental or evolutionary view, preferring to describe a variety of Christologies, or "many faces of the Christ", where early views of Jesus do not necessarily imply a "low" Christology, nor later writings a "high" one. Like the other books of this type, he also makes no use of the genre of the gospels, nor of any other New Testament literature.

Another blow to the History of Religions type of evolutionary accounts of Christology arising slowly from pagan sources was dealt by Larry Hurtado. In his *One God, One Lord*, he looks at the interest in angels and personified divine attributes in Judaism, and the shift given to Christology very early on by the first Christians' religious experience of Jesus.[17] This time the "window" is particularly directed towards early Christian worship. Unfortunately, such an account also has no room for the literary nature of the gospels.

Most recently, the development of genre and narrative approaches to the gospels have finally begun to impinge on this debate. Thus, in a new set of *Essays on Christology in Honor of Jack Dean Kingsbury*, entitled *Who do you say that I am?*, Ben Witherington recognizes that one area where "distinct progress has been made" since his previous work "is in genre studies". He notes that "the crucial work of R.A. Burridge has provided a strong case" for the biographical genre of the gospels.[18] In the same volume, Leander Keck rightly notes that there is no such thing as a "single 'Christology of the New Testament'", but many Christologies and goes on to point out that they are "expressed in quite diverse literary forms", from titles and parables right up to entire gospels. Furthermore, not only do the gospels contain christological forms, but "they also build Christology into their narrative structures, thereby creating a 'show and tell' Christology".[19] In another collection sharing the same title, David Hancock argues that not only do the gospels provide a sufficient and authoritative source for Christology, but that they also give it "narrative force",

---

[17] L. Hurtado, *One God, One Lord: Early Christian Devotion and Ancient Jewish Monotheism* (London: SCM 1988).

[18] B. Witherington III, "The Christology of Jesus", in M.A. Powell and D.R. Bauer, eds, *Who do you say that I am? Essays on Christology in Honor of Jack Dean Kingsbury* (Louisville: Westminster John Knox, 1999) 1–13; quotations from p. 2.

[19] L.E. Keck, "Christology of the New Testament: What, then, is New Testament Christology?", in Powell and Bauer, eds, *Who do you say?*, 185–200; quotation from p. 186.

stressing that story should "form the genre in which the Gospels are read and interpreted".[20]

Thus the history of the study of Christology in the New Testament over the last century has mostly concentrated on the gospels as "windows" into the historical development, although with the occasional attempt to "reflect" in them some contemporary descriptions of Jesus. Given the christological nature of the biographical genre of the gospels, it is surprising that this aspect has made so little impact on the discussion. However, the last examples might lead us to begin to expect more literary use of the gospels' biographical genre in future discussions of Christology.

b) *The Parting of the Ways*

The second area of surprising omission concerns the debate about the so-called "Parting of the Ways" as the early Christian movement and what became Rabbinic Judaism grew apart after the Jewish war of 66–70 and the Bar Kochba revolt of 132–35. Many accounts of this separation stress the importance of Christology as a dividing factor. Therefore, one might have expected the biographical nature of the gospels with their concentrated christological focus to feature in the various discussions, but actually this is not the case.

Thus Bruce Chilton and Jacob Neusner use the New Testament as a window into first century Jewish practices and beliefs, describing early Christianity as "(a) Judaism".[21] Dunn's account of *The Partings of the Ways* works its way through the four pillars of Second Temple Judaism, Jesus and the Temple, Paul and the Covenant to reach the climax of his discussion of the christological issues in the relationship of Jesus to God in chapters 9–11.[22] Throughout, the New Testament documents are treated as a source for the period, but not their literary form. This omission is all the more surprising in the light of Dunn's earlier article, from a 1982 symposium, "Let John be John: A Gospel for its Time" where he does bring together Christology

---

[20] D. Hancock, "The Christological Problem", in *Who do you say that I am? Christology and the Church* (ed. D. Armstrong; Grand Rapids: Eerdmans, 1999) 1–24; quotation from pp. 12–13.

[21] B. Chilton and J. Neusner, *Judaism in the New Testament: Practices and Beliefs* (London: Routledge, 1995), *passim*, e.g. pp. 4–9.

[22] J.D.G. Dunn, *The Partings of the Ways: Between Christianity and Judaism and their Significance for the Character of Christianity* (London: SCM 1991).

and relationships among Christians and with "the Jews" in his consideration of John as a gospel.[23]

In the same 1982 symposium, Graham Stanton argued for Matthew as a creative "interpreter" of the sayings of Jesus.[24] By the 1989 Durham-Tübingen symposium, Stanton is stressing the role "Matthew's Christology" plays in the separation between Jews and Christians, looking particularly at the charges that Jesus was a magician and a deceiver—but again with no treatment of the writing or genre of the gospel as a whole.[25]

The oddity of this omission of the role played by the christological nature of the gospels in the parting of the ways is further strengthened by the recognition that both Christians (especially Jewish Christians) and their (non-Christian) Jewish opponents shared a respect for and use of the scriptures. Judy Lieu indicates one possible answer in her account of Justin Martyr's use of the scriptures in christological debate with Trypho, where she notes that Justin knows he must debate "on the basis of the scriptures accepted by the Jews (56.16; 68.2)", unlike later writers who use the gospels.[26] Martin Hengel discusses the way Christians claimed the Septuagint for their scriptures, while Philip Alexander notes that "the books of the heretics", *sifrei minim*, alludes to Torah scrolls copied out by Christian scribes which *Tosefta Yadayim* 2.13 and *Tosefta Shabbat* 13 (14):5 did not consider to have the same sanctity as "genuine Torah scrolls".[27] Dunn sees this shared experience of interpreting scripture as a common heritage even for Jews and Christians today and a "cause for hope in Jewish/Christian relations".[28] However, such comments do run the risk of reflecting in the mirror of the text a modern concern placed in front of it, namely relationships between Jews and Christians today.

---

[23] J.D.G. Dunn, "Let John be John: A Gospel for its Time", in the 1982 Tübingen symposium, *The Gospel and the Gospels* (ed. Peter Stuhlmacher; Grand Rapids: Eerdmans 1991) 293–322.

[24] G.N. Stanton, "Matthew as a Creative Interpreter of the Sayings of Jesus", in *The Gospel and the Gospels*, ed. Stuhlmacher, 257–72.

[25] G.N. Stanton, "Matthew's Christology and the Parting of the Ways", in *Jews and Christians: The Parting of the Ways, AD 70 to 135* (ed. J.D.G. Dunn; Grand Rapids: Eerdmans 1999), 99–116.

[26] J.M. Lieu, *Image and Reality* (Edinburgh: T. & T. Clark, 1996) 125.

[27] M. Hengel "The Septuagint as a Collection of Writings Claimed by Christians: Justin and the Church Fathers before Origen", in *Jews and Christians*, ed. Dunn, 39–83; P.S. Alexander, "'The Parting of the Ways' from the Perspective of Rabbinic Judaism" also in *Jews and Christians*, ed. Dunn, 1–25, see especially pp. 11–15.

[28] Dunn, *The Partings of the Ways*, 252–3.

One person who does examine the implications of this shared use of scriptures for the literary form of the gospels is Wolfgang Roth who examines the use of what he calls "the Pharisaic canon", the "law and the prophets", in the gospels to contrast what he considers are two types of gospel—the Synoptics and John.[29] While the contrast he draws is interesting, it is not sufficient to demonstrate different genres for John and the Synoptics.

Thus despite the significance of the biographical genre for the christological focus of the gospels, this aspect hardly features in both the usual accounts of the development of New Testament Christology/ies and of the debates between early Christians and Jews over Christology which led to the parting of the ways. Instead, nearly all the scholars discussed have been using the gospels as windows to get behind the text to the first century debate and parting of the ways, although there are also hints of a "mirror approach" when modern concerns about anti-Semitism after the holocaust are reflected in the discussion. Once again, however, the "picture in the stained glass", the portrait of Jesus determined by the genre of the text, is almost totally missing. In both of these areas, the christological implications of the biographical hypothesis could make a significant contribution.

4. *Rabbinic Material and the Absence of Biography*

This almost total ignoring of any consideration of the overall form and story of the gospels in the light of their biographical genre is all the more remarkable given the frequent comparison of individual gospel stories with rabbinic material. In our work together, David Catchpole would often give students gospel pericopae in parallel with comparable rabbinic anecdotes to assist with traditio-historical analysis. Once again, both the gospel texts and the rabbinic material are being used as windows to get behind the text to the kinds of stories and events typical of teachers in the first century.

Thus, Rabbi Michael Hilton and Fr. Gordian Marshall OP worked together to produce *The Gospels and Rabbinic Judaism: A Study Guide* to demonstrate the similarities between some of Jesus' sayings and

---

[29] W. Roth, "To Invert or Not to Invert: the Pharisaic Canon in the Gospels" in *Early Christian Interpretation of the Scriptures of Israel: Investigations and Proposals* (ed. C.A. Evans and J.A. Sanders; JSNTSup 148; Sheffield: Sheffield Academic Press, 1997) 59–78.

passages from rabbinic sources. They begin with the Great Commandment, comparing Mark 12:28–34 and the parallels in Matt 22:34–40
and Luke 10:25–28 with a *Sifra* passage from Rabbi Akiba on Lev
19:18, *Gen. Rab.* 24.7 (on Gen 5:1) and the famous story from the
Babylonian Talmud, *Shabbat* 31A, of the different reactions from
Shammai and Hillel when asked to teach the whole law to a Gentile
enquirer standing on one leg: Shammai chased the questioner away,
while Hillel repeated the Golden Rule as the sum of the whole
Torah, with the rest as commentary, but still to be learned. Further
passages are noted, leading up to Hilton's conclusion that here is
"Jesus at his most 'rabbinic' engaged in lively debate and answering
some of the same questions as the rabbis".[30] Subsequent chapters
compare passages from the gospels with rabbinic material on the
synagogue, parables, halakhah in the saying about an ox in the pit
(Matt 12:11–12; Luke 14:5), the sabbath, divorce and forgiveness.

Similar comparisons emerge from the results of an international
symposium comparing Hillel and Jesus held in Jerusalem in June
1992.[31] No less than eight chapters or 170 pages of the published
papers are devoted to comparisons of just the sayings of Jesus and
Hillel! Once again the Golden Rule traditions are carefully compared,
here by Philip Alexander who concludes that "the overriding feeling is one of astonishment at the convergence of the two traditions".[32]
Similarly, B.T. Viviano compares and contrasts Hillel and Jesus'
teaching on prayer, concluding that Hillel is more creation-centred
and sapiential as against Jesus' apocalyptic urgency.[33] Other chapters examine the difficulties in reconstructing sayings of both Jesus
and Hillel, as well as some Qumran material and questions of transmission and interpretation.

Philip Alexander has devoted many studies elsewhere to such rabbinic writings, and is keen to enable New Testament scholars to han-
dle this material carefully.[34] He has collected together some rabbinic

[30] M. Hilton with G. Marshall OP, *The Gospels and Rabbinic Judaism: A Study Guide* (London: SCM, 1988) 34.
[31] J.H. Charlesworth and L.L. Johns, eds, *Hillel and Jesus: Comparative Studies of Two Major Religious Leaders* (Minneapolis: Fortress, 1997).
[32] P.S. Alexander, "Jesus and the Golden Rule" in *Hillel and Jesus*, ed. Charlesworth and Johns, 363–88; quotation from p. 388.
[33] B.T. Viviano, "Hillel and Jesus on Prayer" in *Hillel and Jesus*, ed. Charlesworth and Johns, 427–57.
[34] See for example, P.S. Alexander, "Rabbinic Judaism and the New Testament" *ZNW* 74 (1983) 237–46.

stories and anecdotes to compare "Rabbinic Biography and the Biography of Jesus". He concludes, "there are parallels to the individual pericopae, and at this level similarities are very strong. In terms of form, function, setting and motif, the Rabbinic anecdotes are very close to the Gospel pericopae, and there can be little doubt that both belong to the same broad Palestinian Jewish tradition of story-telling."[35]

Thus, at the level of Form Criticism, looking through the "window" of the text to the first century context, the parallels between the gospel pericopae and the rabbinic anecdotes are very close. Since Bultmann and other Form Critics saw the gospels as just a collection of such stories, strung together like beads on a string, we might expect the rabbinic stories to be similarly strung together to form accounts of Hillel, Shammai or others, to give us some more stained glass portraits.

Yet, this is precisely what we do *not* find, much to everybody's surprise. Thus Philip Alexander concludes his study of "Rabbinic Biography and the Biography of Jesus" thus: "there are no Rabbinic parallels to the Gospels as such. This is by far the most important single conclusion to emerge from this paper . . . There is not a trace of an ancient biography of any of the Sages . . . This is a profound enigma."[36]

Jacob Neusner has devoted much study to this question. In 1984 he began with *In Search of Talmudic Biography* in which he notes the importance of attributing a saying to a particular rabbi—notably Eliezer. Yet despite this material, he states that "there is no composition of tales and stories into a sustained biography".[37] He followed this with an analysis of *Why No Gospels in Talmudic Judaism?*, confronting the question of why the rabbinic traditions contain no biographies and nothing like the gospels about Jesus. He provides many examples of the stories about sages, but which were never compiled into biographical narratives or gospels: they are "the compositions no one made".[38] His next study on *The Incarnation of God*

---

[35] P.S. Alexander, "Rabbinic Biography and the Biography of Jesus: A Survey of the Evidence" in *Synoptic Studies: the Ampleforth Conferences of 1982 and 1983* (ed. C.M. Tuckett; JSNTSup 7; Sheffield: JSOT, 1984) 19–50; quotation from p. 42.

[36] Alexander, "Rabbinic biography and the Biography of Jesus", 40.

[37] J. Neusner, *In Search of Talmudic Biography: The Problem of the Attributed Saying* (Brown Judaic Studies 70; Chico: Scholars, 1984) 2.

[38] J. Neusner, *Why No Gospels in Talmudic Judaism?* (Atlanta: Georgia, 1988) 33–8.

was a detailed treatment of the idea of incarnation, both of the Torah and of God—but he stresses as before: "While the two Talmuds present stories about sages, neither one contains anything we might call a 'gospel' of a sage or even a chapter of a gospel. There is no sustained biography of any sage."[39] Finally, he answered the claim of some similarities between the gospels and other Jewish material with *Are There Really Tannaitic Parallels to the Gospels?*[40]

Lastly, we return again to the symposium on *Jesus and Hillel*. In chapter 2, A. Goshen Gottstein from the University of Tel Aviv deals with the question, "Jesus and Hillel: Are Comparisons Possible?" He comes to the same conclusions as Neusner: "We must be reminded of some basic differences between the nature of Talmudic literature and the nature of the Gospels. We have no Talmudic Gospel of any Rabbi." He then refers to my book, *What are the Gospels?* and accepts its conclusions: "Following Burridge's discussion, the present discussion assumes Gospel writing to be a form of biography." Thus Goshen connects the two main parts of this essay together, linking my work on the gospels' genre to that of Alexander and Neusner on rabbinic stories: "One could therefore ask why we do not have any instances of rabbinic biography".[41] To this question, therefore, we must now turn at long last. Why is that, while both rabbinic stories and gospel pericopae can be used as windows onto the first century context, biographical portraits were only painted of Jesus?

5. *Literary Reasons: The Genre of Rabbinic Material*

The first area to consider for possible reasons why there are no rabbinic biographies is literary. We argued above that genre is crucial for the composition and interpretation of texts. Therefore, as with the gospels, we need to start with the issue of the genre of the rabbinic traditions.

Most of the rabbinic material is comprised of anecdotes, which are more about a rabbi's teaching than his actions. Many of the stories are composed mostly of dialogue which leads up to actual say-

---

[39] J. Neusner, *The Incarnation of God: the Character of Divinity in Formative Judaism* (Philadelphia: Fortress 1988) 213.

[40] J. Neusner, *Are There Really Tannaitic Parallels to the Gospels? A Refutation of Morton Smith*, South Florida Studies in the history of Judaism, No. 80 (Chico: Scholars, 1993).

[41] A.G. Gottstein, "Jesus and Hillel: Are Comparisons Possible?" in *Hillel and Jesus*, ed. Charlesworth and Johns, 31–55; quotations from pp. 34–5.

ing or ruling of the rabbi, with any narrative just at the start to set
the scene. In this way, the rabbinic material is more like Q or Gospel
of Thomas, i.e. it has the genre of sayings, *logia*, more than biographical narrative. Thus Philip Alexander tries various methods to provide an analysis of rabbinic anecdotes, attempting to use form, point
and content in his classification of seven main types:

- Precedents—stories which may begin with *ma'aseh* and lead up
  to a ruling.
- Exempla—stories commending certain virtues.
- Responsa—answering a question from a disciple or enquirer.
- Scholastic debates—disputes between authorities over halakhah.
- Encomia—aiming to praise a certain master.
- Miracle-stories—stories often told of the earlier masters.
- Death stories—developing later, especially of martyrdoms.[42]

He also argues that the rabbinic stories have an "intensely oral character . . . against the more prosy 'written' style of the gospels". They
are "extremely compressed, allusive, witty, dramatic and learned";
more like bits from a play to be performed than a text to be read,
intended for oral circulation, not in written form.[43]

Neusner makes a similar point. *In Search of Talmudic Biography* is
subtitled "the problem of the attributed saying"—and it is "sayings"
which comprise this material. In *The Incarnation of God*, Neusner applies
a "taxonomy of narrative" to the material and finds "five species of
the genus narrative". He calls them parable, precedent, narrative setting for a saying, scriptural story and sage story.[44] The problem with
this is that "narrative" is neither a genus nor a genre in itself according to most literary theory of genres, and his five "species" are not
clearly identified by generic features as subgenres.

However, the basic point is clear, that the rabbinic anecdotes are
directed more towards sayings than actions. The question then needs
to be asked whether this generic character would prevent their being
complied into an ancient biography. However, ancient biography
was not all composed of narrative and actions. One possible comparison is with Lucian's *Demonax* which has a brief preface and account
of the philosopher's life, followed by a large number of anecdotes

---

[42] Alexander, "Rabbinic Biography and the Biography of Jesus", 21–4.
[43] Alexander, "Rabbinic Biography and the Biography of Jesus", 42.
[44] Neusner, *The Incarnation of God*, 214.

all strung together, each composed mainly of dialogue leading up to a pronouncement or decision by the great sage—yet it is still called a "life", *bios*. In fact, the *Demonax* is more loosely structured with less integration of teaching and activity than even Mark's gospel.[45]

However, the concern particularly for precedent does tend towards a more narrative biographical form. The Jews believed that a teacher's example could be as important as his words. Thus, in the absence of a ruling by a legal authority, it was permissible to report a rabbi's actions and to deduce from them what his legal position would be on the matter. This gives the precedent, or *ma'aseh*: "it happened that Rabbi X did such and such". From the master's action, something of the Torah could be learned. Thus stories are told of Rabbi Akiba following his master, Rabbi Joshua, into the toilet to see how he relieves himself and there he learned three things (to sit north and south, to sit not stand, and to wipe with the left hand, not the right). When Ben 'Azzai expressed some surprise that he should "take such liberties with your master", R. Akiba explained that "it was a matter of Torah, and I needed to learn". Ben 'Azzai then followed R. Akiba into the toilet and learned the same three things, which he duly passed on to R. Judah. Similarly, R. Kahana hid under his master's bed and was so impressed with what is euphemistically termed his master's "chatting with his wife, and joking and doing what he required" that he cried out "One would think that Abba's mouth had never before supped the cup!" When his master, somewhat surprised to find his pupil under the marital bed, told him to get out "because it is rude", Kahana's reply was also "Master, it is Torah, and I need to know".[46]

So the imitation of the master is a way of knowing Torah, and so it becomes an imitation of God. Thus the crucial point here, as Neusner says of the sage-story, is that it provides "a good example of how one should behave".[47] He repeats the same point elsewhere: "The sage is always represented as exemplary".[48] Similarly, Alexander notes how these stories "hold up the conduct of the rabbis for emulation".[49]

---

[45] See my discussion of the *Demonax* in *What are the Gospels?*, 166, 170–1.
[46] Babylonian Talmud, *Berakoth* 62a (London: Soncino Press, 1948) 388
[47] Neusner, *The Incarnation of God*, 216.
[48] Neusner, *Why No Gospels in Talmudic Judaism?*, 52.
[49] Alexander, "Rabbinic Biography and the Biography of Jesus", 38.

One obvious example of this sort is the story of the death of a sage. Alexander notes that rabbinic literature is not interested in "wonderful birth-stories" but "does show a steady interest in how the Sages died". Usually it is either a death-bed scene which allows for the last instructions or "ethical last will and testament" or a martyrdom, which provide another form of exempla.[50] This exemplary purpose was very common for much of ancient biography, and we noted above the tendency to describe the subject's death at some length to reveal their true character. Neusner sees the stories of the deaths of sages with a similar function: "How a sage died—the death-scene, with its quiet lessons—likewise presented a model for others."[51]

Thus although the rabbinic material is more anecdotal and based more on sayings than are the gospels and some other ancient lives, it still contains enough biographical elements (through sage stories, narratives, precedents and death scenes) which would have enabled an editor to compile a "life of Hillel" or whoever. Such an account would have been recognisably in the genre of ancient biography and have looked quite like works like the *Demonax*. Literary and generic reasons alone are therefore not sufficient to explain this curious absence of rabbinic biography.

6. *Theological Reasons: The Christological Focus of the Gospels*

In the end, biography directs the audience's attention at the life and character of the person being described. We are back to the image of stained glass, where the skill of the artist is in representing a portrait through limited means and the focus must be centred on the subject. The decision to write a biographical account of Jesus thus has important christological implications. Equally, the failure to write, or even compile from the various anecdotes available, any biographies of the rabbis also has significant implications.

Neusner argues that this is because the individual sages are not at the centre of attention:

> *Sage-stories turn out not to tell about sages at all; they are stories about the Torah personified.* Sage-stories cannot yield a gospel because they are not about sages anyway. They are about the Torah. Gospels by contrast tell the

---

[50] Alexander, "Rabbinic Biography and the Biography of Jesus", 24.
[51] Neusner, *Why No Gospels in Talmudic Judaism?*, 62.

life of a human being . . . The sage story, dealing with the individual, homogenizes sage with sage. The gospel does just the opposite, with its focus on the uniqueness of the hero.[52]

Neusner's answer thus has two key components—that the sages or rabbis are seen as a collective group, being not significant as individuals, and that centre stage belongs not to them as human beings but to the Torah.

Alexander makes the same point:

The obvious answer is that neither Eliezer nor any other Sage held in Rabbinic Judaism the central position that Jesus held in early Christianity. The centre of Rabbinic Judaism was Torah; the centre of Christianity was the person of Jesus, and the existence of the Gospels is, in itself, a testimony to this fact.[53]

Similarly Rabbi Michael Hilton says:

The Gospels can thus be regarded as a kind of commentary on Jesus' life, in much the same way as the Rabbis comment on biblical texts. What is central to the Gospel writers is the experience of resurrection . . . And what is central to the rabbinic texts is the experience of revelation, the feeling that God's will is known and available to be derived from the text of the Torah.[54]

This is not to say that sages are not important. Indeed, notes Neusner, they can be seen as "equivalent to a scroll of the Torah: He who sees the disciple of a sage who has died is as if he sees a scroll of the Torah that has been burned (y. Moed Qatan 3:7.X)." The Sage is "at the same level of authority as the Torah".[55] However, this is only true in as much as he represents and embodies the Torah and the whole community; there is no uniqueness or individuality about the rabbi to commemorate for his own sake. So he concludes his study thus: "our rapid comparison of the Gospels of Jesus Christ and the Torah of our sages of blessed memory yields a simple point of difference. Individual authors, Matthew, Mark, Luke, John, tell the story of the unique individual. A consensus of an entire community reaches its full human realization in the sage, and the writing down of that consensus will not permit individual traits of rhetoric."[56]

---

[52] Neusner, *Why No Gospels in Talmudic Judaism?*, 52–3, his italics.
[53] P.S. Alexander, "Rabbinic Biography and the Biography of Jesus", 41.
[54] Hilton and Marshall, *The Gospels and Rabbinic Judaism*, 13.
[55] Neusner, *Why No Gospels in Talmudic Judaism?*, 20 and 45.
[56] Neusner, *Why No Gospels in Talmudic Judaism?*, 72

Similarly, Goshen Gottstein in comparing Jesus and Hillel stresses that individual rabbis are not to be venerated, nor separated from other rabbis. Furthermore:

> Gospel writing would be the product of the particular religious under-standing of the messianic, and therefore salvific, activity of Jesus. The lack of Gospels in rabbinic literature would then be a less significant issue, since no salvific claim is attached to any particular Rabbi.[57]

Further on in the same symposium, David Flusser from the Hebrew University of Jerusalem compares the "self awareness" of Jesus and Hillel; while Hillel understood himself as a representative of human-ity and an exemplar, Jesus had a high self-awareness of himself as Messiah.[58]

Thus the literary shift from unconnected anecdotes about Jesus as a teacher, which resemble so much of the rabbinic material, to com-posing them together carefully in the genre of an ancient biography is making an enormous christological and theological claim. In the end, rabbinic biography is not possible, because no rabbi is that unique and is only important as he represents the Torah, which con-tinues to hold the central place. To write a biography is to replace the Torah by putting a human person in the centre of the stage. The literary genre makes a major theological shift which becomes an explicit christological claim—that Jesus of Nazareth is Torah embodied, or as Jacobus Schoneveld puts it, "Torah in the Flesh".[59]

Conclusion: Gospel Genre as Christological Claim

This paper has suggested that many traditio-historical studies treat the gospels as "windows" through which they look to what lies behind or beyond the text in the first century context of the historical Jesus or early Christian communities. More recent literary approaches see the text more like a mirror, reflecting our concerns from in front of

---

[57] Gottstein, "Jesus and Hillel", 35
[58] D. Flusser, "Hillel and Jesus: Two Ways of Self-Awareness", in *Jesus and Hillel*, ed. Charlesworth and Johns, 71–107.
[59] J. Schoneveld, "Torah in the Flesh: A New Reading of the Prologue of the Gospel of John as a Contribution to a Christology without Anti-Semitism". in *The New Testament and Christian-Jewish Dialogue: Studies in Honor of David Flusser* (ed. M. Lowe; Emmanuel 24/25; Jerusalem: Ecumenical Theological Research Fraternity in Israel, 1990) 77–93.

it. However, the study of literary genre confronts us with the question of what is the nature of the text itself. Genre analysis shows that the gospels are written in the form of an ancient biography, with a concentrated focus on the person of Jesus of Nazareth. Like a piece of stained glass, it is their portrait which is most important. Yet the christological implications of this literary genre have been ignored in most recent writing on New Testament Christology.

Furthermore, it is common to see Christology as a boundary marker, helping to develop a sense of identity and separation from Judaism in the construction of early Christian identity during the period of "the parting of the ways". However, in this debate too, the christological implications of the gospels' biographical genre have also not been realized.

The significance of these implications is increased by a comparison of the gospels with rabbinic material. Both gospel pericopae and rabbinic anecdotes can be used as windows into the first century context. However, although the rabbinic tradition contains all the biographical anecdotes and raw material, no "Lives of Hillel" or Eliezer were ever compiled. Only with respect to Jesus were the various individual pieces assembled to form a portrait in their own right—a fact of theological and christological importance. In concentrating the readers' attention upon the person of Jesus through writing a biography, the early Christian gospel writers were asserting something which was never said of a rabbi—that he was centre stage as the embodiment, or even replacement of Torah, a unique individual revealing God in his deeds and words, life, death and resurrection.

The desire to make this deliberate christological claim forces the early Christian writers to move out from the Jewish tradition of stories and anecdotes to use a Greek genre of continuous biographical narrative. The actual writing of a gospel was a christological claim in itself and also contributed towards the "parting of the ways" between the early Christians and the developing rabbinic tradition.

TOWARDS A CRITICAL APPROPRIATION OF THE SERMON ON THE MOUNT: CHRISTOLOGY AND DISCIPLESHIP

Robert Morgan

If teaching one's grandmother to suck eggs risks getting them all over one's face it will seem rash to talk about reading the Bible, i.e. to offer some suggestions about Christian theological interpretation and appropriation, to an older friend and senior colleague who shared the responsibility for teaching New Testament in Ninian Smart's Lancaster department in the 1960s and 1970s. We had earlier sat together as beginners in Ernst Bammel's seminar at Cambridge, and both continued (and continue) to benefit hugely from Charlie Moule's friendship and generous encouragement. But that stable nurtured a variety of foals, and my topic and manner of handling it touch on some of the theological, hermeneutical, and ethical differences between us.

The *Festschrift* genre allows the odd personal note. Grey hairs now nodding in harmony may recall different styles on the Lune when a Pauline-Lutheran-Käsemannian Celt saw a more sternly Matthean moralist gradually becoming more liberal as a result of meticulous engagement with the tradition of Jesus' sayings. Others have found there a queue leading to loss of Christian theological identity but David's synoptic Christology owed more to Luke's adoptionist tendency than to his hypothetical sources.

The *Festschrift* permits a personal note, but dressing it up in dubious parallels from New Testament theology looks self-indulgent. The justification is that the connection between the texts and their modern interpreters is at issue in what follows. One controversial aspect of a Christian *theological interpretation (Sachexegese)* of the New Testament is *Sachkritik*—theological criticism by the interpreter of a part of the biblical witness where it apparently expresses inadequately the gospel it means to proclaim.[1] Granted the theological diversity in the New

---

[1] This view of *Sachkritik*, accepted by Bultmann in his appeal to Luther's criticism of the Epistle of James and the Revelation of John (*Theology of the New Testament*

Testament, some writings will resonate with some interpreters better than others. Since scripture is not infallible, readers may in principle criticize it at certain points while remaining loyal to its witness as a whole. Believers do sometimes criticize their scriptures and do so in the light of their own (provisional) understandings of the gospel. This means not only in the light of their intellectual and moral experience, but in the light of their christologies: when like Luther "we urge Christ against scripture" our own provisional understandings of Christ are brought into play, open to correction but also ready to question and challenge the text. Today the practice of historical study affects most theologians' sense of who Jesus was and is. Historical criticism has thus been and is an instrument of theological criticism of the Bible and the doctrinal tradition.[2] But those who engage in *Sachkritik* of their scriptures constantly return to these definitive writings and seek to understand them afresh. Hence the choice of Davidic territory on which to illustrate some "Pelagian" suggestions about our common task. More discourse on method is a response to the limitations of an armchair discussion. If our efforts at writing theology or speaking of God are at best mere traces of events which (some say) cannot be objectified, the fall-back position is to write *about* theology instead.

1. *Interpreting Matthew Theologically*

The words *exegesis* and *interpretation* are sometimes used synonymously, but exegesis directs us to difficulties in the text, whereas the word interpretation turns the spotlight towards the interpretative process and makes the interpreters themselves more visible. Even where textual indeterminacy is repudiated the word hints at different possibilities. Within such limits as are set by the text itself interpreters are free to choose what *kind* of interpretation they will attempt. Interpretations are often not simply right or wrong, though some are more and some less appropriate. There are different *kinds* of understanding as well as different kinds of texts, and they reflect the different *aims* which interpreters may have.

---

2 [London, 1955] 238) goes beyond the immanent criticism of what is said, on appeal to what is meant—which he advocated in the 1920s against Barth.

[2] Cf. from our shared Lancaster years *The Cardinal Meaning* (ed. M. Pye and R. Morgan; Leiden, 1973) 59–101; *The Nature of New Testament Theology* (ed. R. Morgan; London, 1973) 42–52.

In the phrase "theological interpretation" the adjective signifies an interpretation which aims to speak of *God*. That is easily trivialised in a culture where God is no longer self-evident, the word much abused, and its logic ignored, but rightly understood it implies more about the interpreter than is to be expected in the writing of history or even literary criticism. Whether confessing or denying, obeying or rebelling, worshipping or rejecting, speaking appropriately of God leaves no place for neutrality, granted the meaning and reference of this word.

To speak authentically of God is not merely to describe or analyse others' talk of God (that has its place), but to respond to God. It is to acknowledge the mysterious reality, however fragmentarily understood, and so to recognize an obligation to wonder and worship—or to resist. This typically happens in religious contexts, and most theology is a function of some religious community, but not even Paul on the Areopagus restricted religious worship and talk of God to the recipients of special revelation, and the Paul who wrote Rom 1:21 could even assume a general knowledge of God.

He could scarcely be so sanguine today. The peculiarity of *theology* among intellectual disciplines today is the widespread doubt, denial, or redefinition of its subject-matter. But precisely because this is sharply contested, the new interest across the humanities in the contribution of the readers, i.e. interpreters, acquires special significance here. The biblical witness is heard in different keys, according to how the subject-matter is understood and evaluated by the reader.

A theological interpretation of the Sermon on the Mount will thus seek to communicate its religious message (i.e. from God, about God, having God and humanity *coram Deo* as its subject) in a way that is true both to the text itself and to the modern interpreter's own responsive and engaged understanding of God. This implies some identification with the intention of the text, but that need not be explicit. Theological interpreters share many assumptions with those outside their theological circle, and can use the methods of literary criticism and history, sometimes thickened with philosophical terminology[3] to articulate the subject-matter of the texts. Whether they wear their hearts on their sleeve will depend on context and audience—

---

[3] Notably F.C. Baur's adoption of Hegel's metaphysics of history to make his reconstructions of the past speak of God, and Bultmann's use of Heidegger's analysis of human existence to articulate the modern Lutheran and existentialist theology that guides his interpretation of Paul.

a lecture is not a sermon—but what makes either work properly theological, i.e. authentically speaking of *God*, is the interpreter's account
of the subject-matter of the text and consequent attitude to it.

That confessional view of Christian theology is contested. Some
distinguish between first-order religious speech and second-order
theological speech, arguing that the latter's critical and analytic
activity implies nothing about the speaker's own relation to the
subject-matter. It is true that much excellent theological scholarship
is quite far removed from theology proper and that this is different
again from the direct address of a sermon, but in a secular culture,
where only religious communities and those influenced by them talk
seriously of God, to describe the subject-matter of scripture in this
way rather than as Israelite, Jewish and early Christian religion, is
(unless the phenomenologist's *epoche* or bracketing is intended) to place
oneself within Tillich's "theological circle", however loosely. The
word "God", rightly used, implies an attitude of worship, whereas
"religion" can be described and analysed by historians and philoso-
phers of religion, without any implication concerning their own attitude to it. In practice a sympathetic historian of religion who does
not stand within the tradition might so imaginatively enter the world
of the text as to catch or purport to catch its echoes of transcend-
ence. Much scholarly writing on the Bible could be classified either
as theological interpretation or as history of religion, with only the
intentions of authors and readers telling the difference. The only
point at which some historical theologians go beyond the bounds of
historical reason in their attempts to appropriate and communicate
what the text is about is when they engage in a *Sachkritik* which is
more than immanent criticism of a text and is based on their own
current understanding of the Christian gospel.[4]

In comparison with historical descriptions and explanations, and
philosophical or sociological or literary analyses, a systematic or even
historical theology (including Old and New Testament *theologies* which
make use of these disciplines) are usually written from within the
circle of those who take the word God to refer to the transcendent
reality identified by their tradition. If religious texts are heard differently
according to how the subject-matter is understood and evaluated,

---

[4] Hence the reservations expressed by N.A. Dahl in his (1954) classic review of
Bultmann's *Theology* (n. 1), reprinted in *The Crucified Messiah* (Minneapolis, 1974)
94, 127.

interpretations which presuppose and acknowledge (however weakly or indefinitely) the reality of God are now best called "theological interpretations". The generic label "New Testament theology" has been weakened and rendered ambiguous by including histories of early Christian thought which do not presuppose the reality of God.

The theological interpreters' presuppositions are often unspoken, and their historical and literary methods are those of their colleagues in these other disciplines. There is therefore no difficulty in doing such work outside ecclesial contexts, such as in modern universities. Not even the point at which interpreters' confessional commitments become more visible, as they go beyond historical description and engage in *Sachkritik*, bars them from secular contexts. Those who silently identify with the witness of the text in agreeing with it about its subject-matter, but disagree with something it *says* or *implies* about this, produce rational arguments for their opinion, drawn from the wider tradition and from contemporary knowledge and moral insight. They acknowledge the dangers of their own preconceptions suppressing an uncomfortable witness,[5] but trust the truth of the gospel to emerge in the religious community's on-going engagement with its tradition in the light of contemporary experience. Theological decisions are ultimately the community's responsibility, but the rational arguments by which these are (usually) reached may be conducted anywhere and by anyone sufficiently informed. Theological interpretations of the New Testament are normally guided by religious commitments, but they can be rationally assessed by anyone because the interpreters use ordinary linguistic, literary, historical, and social-scientific methods. Their application, however, and the choice of interpretative concepts, and consequently the resulting interpretations, are guided by an interest in making the text's talk of God intelligible and persuasive today. That means they reflect (as will become clear in what follows) an opinion about what is authentically Christian and what is not.

The 107 verses of Jesus' teaching in Matt 5–7 are largely concerned with how to live. They show the moral aspect of Jesus' teaching and

---

[5] Hence Barth's opposition to the *Sachkritik* advocated by Bultmann. A similar theological concern underlies Krister Stendahl's attempts to hold the historical task of New Testament theology apart from the hermeneutical, and Schlatter's restriction of this discipline to the historical (in his sense) task.

they speak of God. Matthew can elsewhere seem to subordinate theology to morality, making God's judgment a sanction and motivation to good conduct, but here God is the overarching reality, and
the moral teaching of God's will an aspect of God's rule: the injunction to seek first God's rule and his righteousness (6:33) is paradigmatic. Matthew, and behind Matthew Jesus, insist on the moral
aspect of their religion, rather than religious grounds and sanctions
for morality. Their Jewish theocentricity has not always been preserved in subsequent readings of this gospel.

Our title, however, proposes not the doctrine of God but Christology
as the first term by which to open up the Sermon on the Mount,
and that is a category not suggested by these chapters. Interpreters
are free to choose their conceptual tools for understanding a text
and their choices will be guided by their own aims as well as by
the character of the text itself. They must not do violence to the
text as allegorical interpretation stands accused of doing, but like
Origen theologians seek meanings which correspond to (and sometimes correct, or may be criticized by) their own pre-understanding
of what it is about. Loyalty to both the New Testament text and to
the Christian interpreter's own sense of its subject-matter allows respect for authorial intention because unlike the Christian Old Testament these texts and their theological interpreters both bear direct
witness to a recognisably Christian faith. The historical meaning of
Matthew is therefore unlikely to undercut Christian theological interpretations, even when tensions between its first and our twenty-first
century accounts of Christianity call for *Sachkritik* or (more likely) self-
criticism.

Interpreters use concepts which fit both the text and their own
interpretative needs and aims. Morality is an obvious candidate for
the Sermon on the Mount, but the text subordinates that to its talk
of God. In preference to either, our title proposes Christology and
discipleship to help us appropriate its message. The shift is not great
since Christology is as much talk of God as of Jesus,[6] and calls for
the correlative concept discipleship, as talk of God calls for talk of
human being. Most Christian talk of God is either explicitly or im-

---

[6] Cf. J.M. Creed (quoted by D.M. MacKinnon in a foreword to the reprint of
The Divinity of Jesus Christ [London, 1964] 10–11): "To say that Jesus is Lord and
Christ is . . . an affirmation of faith about God, Man and the world, no less than
an affirmation about the historic Jesus of Nazareth himself."

plicitly christological, whether by being trinitarian or by some alternative modern route.[7] It also often speaks at the same time of the human being under faith, i.e. discipleship. There is no explicit Christology in these chapters apart from the title "Lord" at 7:21f., but the Sermon is part of a larger text whose central theme is christological: the story of Jesus, Son of David—Son of God, who will save his people from their sins (1:21). "Christology and discipleship" can be justified as identifying the Sermon in its larger literary context. However, this choice of concepts is motivated also by the present interpreter's understanding of Christianity and his wish to test this against the witness of a central portion of Christian scripture. Making Christology and discipleship a key to these chapters is intended to acknowledge their moral dimension while blocking the moralistic understandings of Christianity which Matthew might seem to encourage. If the evangelist himself misunderstands Jesus in that way then *Sachkritik* will be an unfortunate necessity.

Our title refers to "critical appropriation" and that has been explained as critical theological interpretation: *Sachexegese*, including *Sachkritik*. This theological practice relates the text's talk of God to the understanding and worship of God advocated by the interpreter or found in contemporary Christianity. It does not pretend that these are or ought to be identical, as uncritical readings do. It expects the text to challenge contemporary Christianity, but holds open the possibility that the text may be in some respects theologically defective and itself open to challenge in the light of some other understanding of the truth of the gospel. The aim of the whole operation is to enable the text to inform and strengthen the interpreter's own understanding of God and Christianity, normally by clarifying the witness of this central piece of Christian tradition, but possibly also by challenging it—since disagreement with respected traditions can also be part of a learning process. Either way this kind of New Testament study is a critical theological activity, not merely prolegomena to that.

Interpretation begins with the interpreter who brings questions and interests to the text. But any modern Christian interpretation of scripture is already partly shaped by these texts before it begins. The belief in God in Christ which guides theological interpretations of

---

[7] E.g. Schleiermacher's account of the essence of Christianity in which "everything is related to the redemption accomplished by Jesus of Nazareth" (*The Christian Faith* [1831; New York, 1963] 52).

Matthew has already been shaped in part by Matthew's presentation of that faith. Some preliminary account of Matthew is therefore the best way into this hermeneutical circle. It will confirm that
the doctrinal category "Christology", chosen as an interpretative aid,
fits the text itself. Relevant aspects of modern Christology will then
(§2) be introduced to show how this also can assist in the appropriation of these chapters' witness. The two terms in our title through
which we approach the text thus refer not only to Matthew's understanding of Christianity but more emphatically to what is being advocated here as an appropriate way to understand Christianity today.
A modern interest determines the choice of questions asked. However,
attention to the text suggests a first step: to relate the moral material of the Sermon to the larger christological context provided by
Matthew's gospel as a whole.

Matthew understands that Jesus seeks and proclaims the will of his
Father (6:20; 7:21; 12:50; 18:14; 21:31; 26:42). This moral aspect of
what some call Matthew's "Christian Judaism" is so important to
him that he gives a strong moral emphasis to Jesus' decisive (if also
most elusive) phrase "the kingdom of God/heaven". This is transmitted by Matthew who makes it into his own central theological
term, as is apparent in his alteration of Mark's Pauline God-word
"the gospel" to "(this or the) gospel *of the kingdom*" at 4:23, 9:35 and
24:14. He prefers not to follow Mark's use of the word "gospel" at
Mark 1:1, 15; 8:35; 10:29 (if he knew it), and greatly increases (to
fifty) the instances of "the kingdom of heaven/God". But a new *moral*
emphasis is evident in the way Matthew associates "righteousness"
with the phrase at 3:15; 5:3–10, 20; 6:1, 33; 21:32 (cf. 3:2), and also
in his formulaic introduction to certain parables. The eschatological
note which was probably dominant in Jesus' own use of the phrase
(however exactly this is interpreted) yields to an ethical and ecclesiological emphasis, without that eschatological dimension being lost.
Thus "the kingdom of God is like" is sometimes better paraphrased:
"this is what discipleship is like here and now", than "this is what
will happen in the future". Even where the latter meaning is prominent, as in the parables of the tares and dragnet (13:24, 47), Matthew's
concern is primarily ethical; eschatological judgment is there an ethical sanction. When his focus is eschatological Matthew usually connects
judgment to the (eschatological) Son of man rather than to "the kingdom of heaven". The sons of the kingdom are indeed judged at 8:12

(MattR), but the emphasis here is on the kingdom of heaven as the place of eschatological salvation (v. 11). It is no doubt anticipated in the eucharist (26:29). The kingdom from which evildoers will be rooted out by the angels sent by the eschatological Son of man (13:41) is not the kingdom of God, but that of Jesus, i.e. the church.

Matthew's re-interpretation of "the kingdom of heaven" is visible in the Sermon on the Mount. It can be defended as true to Jesus himself in two respects: for Jesus as for Matthew this theological and eschatological term announced salvation rather than judgment, despite Matthew's attribution of it to John at 3:2; and secondly, Jesus' teaching was strongly moral. It is hard to find authentic Jewish or Christian talk of God which is not ethical as well as eschatological, but Matthew's connecting the moral aspect of Jesus' teaching with this kingdom phrase is new. It forges a synthesis which (so far as the surviving evidence allows us to say) was not characteristic of Jesus himself. Matthew is perhaps closer to Jesus' actual usage when he associates ethics with God as Father and Creator (e.g. 5:45), rather than when he fuses his own and Jesus' moral concern with Jesus' phrase "the kingdom of heaven (God)" or when he reinforces the moral aspect of Jesus' teaching by frequent repetition of the judgment theme. Jesus no doubt shared this belief, and could utter dreadful warnings (Matt 11:20–4; 12:41–2), but most historians would agree with Luke (if he knew, and therefore was critical of Matthew)[8] that the earlier evangelist has changed the emphasis and the tone of Jesus' teaching.

Matthew emphasized the moral requirements of his own and his community's religion, and is convinced that this agrees with what the disciples had learned from Jesus. But does he base this on his Jewish trust in God who gave the law as a moral and ritual norm, or does he align it more closely with the person of Jesus himself, i.e. to his Christology? And how historically and theologically true to Jesus was he in this respect?

Studies of Matthew's understanding of Jesus' attitude to the Jewish law[9] have rightly emphasised the importance for Matthew of the law interpreted through the love-commandment, and have contrasted his views with those of Mark and Paul. He defines Christian morality by reference to Jesus' teaching (7:24–7; 28:20), but understands this

---

[8] As I think, in agreement with E. Franklin, *Luke: Interpreter of Paul, Critic of Matthew* (Sheffield, 1994).

[9] E.g. W.R.G. Loader, *Jesus' Attitude towards the Law* (Tübingen, 1997).

as fulfilling (5:17) or perfectly interpreting the law which is not merely a Mosaic (Mark 7:10), but divine command (Matt 15:4). It is clear that he distrusts those who relax the law (5:19), and he probably means by "lawlessness" (7:23; 13:41; 23:28; 24:12) moral laxity. As a God-given guide the law remains a bulwark against bad behaviour. What is said about Jesus' words at 7:26f. presumably extends to the law that he interprets. Where it is ignored disaster will follow. But that does not make the law, given to Moses and interpreted (surely not replaced) by Jesus, the basis of morality. It contains God's will but is not an adequate account of this, as Jesus' interpretations show, and does not provide the disciples' motivation for keeping it.

The main reason for Matthew's enlargement of Mark was probably to include the "all things whatsoever I commanded you" that he portrays the risen Jesus, now invested with "all authority", telling his disciples to teach all subsequent disciples to observe (28:20). That includes pre-eminently the teaching compiled in this first and largest discourse. Matthew's emphasis on the law in some of these traditions from Jesus' earthly ministry, modified and refocused after his death, can be partly explained by his opposition to (hypothetical) charismatics who were calling Jesus "Lord" but behaving badly.[10] If these "false prophets" (7:15) appeal to Jesus they should hear what he said—and do it. Jesus' words are the criterion of authentic speech and action in his name (cf. 7:22), but morality is related more closely to the person than to the law he interprets. In that respect the charismatics are right. To address Jesus as Lord is a necessary but not a sufficient condition of discipleship. It is perhaps the false prophets' behaviour which leads Matthew to insist on the Lord's true identity by recourse to what in his earthly ministry he taught.

Both the conclusion to the Sermon and the conclusion to the gospel lay great weight on doing what Jesus said, and Matthew understands this to include interpretation of Torah. But neither passage authenticates Jesus' teaching by referring to the law as the grounds of his authority. However the Antitheses of 5:21–48 are to be read, the decisive passages 7:24–7 and 28:20 point not to the law but to Christology as the ground and authority for his teaching (7:28; 28:18). Unlike Paul in Antioch (Gal 2:11–14) and Galatia, Matthew never poses the law and Christ as alternatives. The conventional term

---

[10] Cf. E. Schweizer, "Observance of the Law and Charismatic Activity in Matthew" *NTS* 16 (1970) 213–30.

Antitheses perhaps overpresses the adversatives in 5:21–48. But even if Matthew avoids Paul's antithetical formulations, taken to breaking-point by Marcion, it is clear where his ultimate loyalties lie, and that Christology (God's presence in Jesus), not the earlier gift of the law, is the key to his theology and ethics.

It is generally agreed that for Matthew the teaching of Jesus is important on account of who the teacher is. Jesus has been intro-duced in 1:1–4:6 as the Davidic Messiah Son of God, whose birth happened as a result of God's Holy Spirit. He has been identified as himself "God with us" who will save his people from their sins (1:20–3). The moral aspect of this Christology begins to unfold in the Sermon on the Mount. It is fairly prominent in the succeeding chapters, and is strongly underlined by the penultimate line of the gospel. Matthew probably sees himself as "a scribe discipled to the kingdom of heaven" (13:51) who transmits the tradition of Jesus' moral guidance which does not abolish but fulfils the law and the prophets (5:17). His account of Jesus' teaching emphasises God's moral rule and respects the law which can be summed up in the two-fold commandment to love God and neighbours (22:36–40) or even in the "golden rule" (7:12), but the focus is always on Jesus himself, who is followed (and addressed "Lord"), not on his teach-ing in isolation from the person. In Mark Joseph of Arimathea is said to have been waiting for the kingdom of God (15:42); Matthew changes this to "discipled to Jesus" (27:57). He could not imagine an orientation to God's rule that Jesus taught other than as disci-pleship to the messianic teacher himself. Some of the most powerful moral teaching he records occurs in an account of the last judgment (25:31–46) in which the eschatological stage is occupied by Jesus himself. Without Christology there is no play; without Hamlet, no *Hamlet*.

The logic of Matthew's theology compels us to base his under-standing of Christian morality primarily on his Christology rather than on the law which Jesus interprets. This requires a middle term, the interpretative category second only to Christology, and correla-tive with it: discipleship.[11] The Sermon is addressed in the first place to disciples (5:1) even if (as today) it is overheard by the crowds

---

[11] On this still the best essay is by U. Luz, "The Disciples in the Gospel accord-ing to Matthew" (1971). ET in G.N. Stanton, ed., *The Interpretation of Matthew* (Edinburgh, [2]1995).

(7:28). Both the Beatitudes and the so-called Antitheses describe discipleship in ideal terms, as do the sections 5:13–20 which intersect them. As is the case (with different nuances) in Mark, John, and especially Luke, the moral emphasis in Matthew's gospel is thus the concrete application of discipleship. Matthew's presentation of Jesus and implied account of Christianity draws on resources available in his tradition, including the God-given law. But his book is about Jesus, God's saving revelation to his people, and he redefines the people of God by reference to discipleship.

There can be no question of driving a wedge between Christology and belief in God when interpreting this gospel. For Matthew as for later orthodoxy they are inseparable. To say that Jesus is the saving revelation of God sounds more Johannine (1:18; 8:19; 12:44f.; 14:9) than Matthean, and it is true that Matthew does not weave what he wants to say about God's saving revelation into a dramatically new portrait of Jesus. John's new and fictional presentation of Jesus' teaching may even have been related to what Matthew was opposing. Nevertheless, to separate what Matthew says about Jesus from what he believes about God, or to reduce that to the messianic idea of Jesus as God's human agent, is true neither to Matthew nor to the ways he has until recently been read in the Christian church.

That separation stems from our modern common-sense instinct to understand Jesus in purely human historical terms. New Testament Christology is then seen as a selection of mythological ideas appended to this historical figure in the light of post-resurrection experience—and easily peeled off by the modern critic. Modern historians of religion proceed in this way because it leads to the kind of historical reality they seek and expect to find on analogy with their own experience. But the theological interpreter cannot dismiss Matthew's own logic so lightly. The evangelist makes no such disjunction between the Jesus of history and the Christ of faith. Jesus is understood by Matthew as not only God's human agent or Messiah, but as in some sense God's presence with the disciples. No doubt this is a post-resurrection perspective but Matthew interprets the earthly ministry of Jesus in this light. The experience of the abiding presence of the risen Jesus with his disciples (28:20) stands behind Matthew's interpretation of the earthly Jesus himself as "God with us" (1:23). A rabbinic saying attributed to R. Hanania ben Teradion about God's presence resting between two people sitting together studying the Torah is christified at 18:20, and Matthew's traces of wisdom Christology (Matt 11:19, 28f.; 23:34 cf. Luke 11:49) point in the same direction. To talk about Jesus is, for Matthew if not for some of his modern interpreters, to talk of God—a perspective only more explicit in John's gospel and subsequently expounded in patristic Christology and trinitarian theology, and preserved in all orthodox Christian talk of the divinity of Christ, and in simple belief in the Trinity and Incarnation.

Matthew's talk about Jesus is at the deepest level talk about God, not merely talk of a first-century teacher and prophet, even though much can be said about Jesus at the level of history which Matthew would not say about God. The reverse should then also be true. Even though Matthew knows who God is quite apart from the final revelation of God in Jesus, this knowledge is decisively affected by what is now known through the life, death, and resurrection of Jesus. Certainly God was already known as Creator and Judge, heavenly Father, and present with his people. But now all authority is given to the risen Jesus, probably as Son of man (if 28:18 echoes Dan 7:13, LXX);[12] and knowing God as Father is dependent on the revelation of God by the Son (11:27). The wisdom of God at work in creation is now heard speaking (11:28f.) and acting (11:19, cf. v. 2) in Jesus, and it is Jesus who is present with his disciples to the end of the age. Scripture is read in new ways in the light of its fulfilment in Jesus (5:17–48 etc.). God's rule is not only preached by and signalled (12:28) by Jesus, but somehow embodied in him. If it echoes Dan 7:13 (LXX) Matt 28:18 evokes its kingdom associations. The royal ideology evoked by the (to Matthew important) Son of David title is transformed by being associated with Jesus' healing activity (9:27, 12:23, 15:22, 20:30f., 21:15). And the poor in spirit and persecuted disciples possess the kingdom now (see the present tenses at 5:3,10) by attending to Jesus.

It remains true that there is very little explicit Christology in the Sermon on the Mount and that its moral teaching is there related more directly (as it was by Jesus himself) to trusting God and obeying God's will. But the introduction of this post-resurrection Christian doctrinal category into our interpretation is required by the gospel as a whole, of which the Sermon must be understood as a part. Even though a comparison with his main source Mark reveals a shift

---

[12] Cf. O. Michel "The Conclusion of Matthew's Gospel" (1950). ET in Stanton, ed., *Interpretation*.

to ecclesiological and ethical interests, Matthew also requires Christology as its primary interpretative category because he too speaks primarily of Jesus and relates Jesus to God and to human salvation. It is therefore appropriate to see how chapters 5–7 fit into his overall design and to make Christology our primary interpretative concept here too.

Modern New Testament scholarship has had much to say about both Matthew's Christology and his moral concern. It has often related these, rightly recognising that chapters 5–7 contribute to the gospel's rendering of Jesus' identity. It has also done something quite different: it has lifted (some of) the teachings of Jesus out of their narrative context in order to understand the historical figure of Jesus himself. That legitimate historical exploration is not relevant to descriptions of *Matthew's* Christology, but it is arguably relevant to *modern* Christology. If so that historical quest should also be relevant to modern theological interpretation of Matthew's gospel, because this is not merely historical description of Matthew but integrally related to modern Christology and preaching and to other Christian use of scripture. How is that relevance to be understood?

Interpreting the Sermon on the Mount theologically relates the witness of this text to contemporary Christian belief and practice. The first step has been to clarify Matthew's own talk of God which is rooted in his scripture and expressed in the moral accent he gave to the "gospel of the kingdom". In "Christology" we have an overarching concept which can encapsulate Matthew's talk of God and characterise the narrative (including the teaching) which unfolds the identity of Jesus. Using this interpretative concept also forges a link between the content of the text (and the intention of the evangelist) and the theology of the modern Christian interpreter.

The use of doctrinal *loci* in New Testament theology, rightly criticized by Wrede[13] from his "history of religion" standpoint, originated in and is justified by the need of New Testament *theologians*, i.e. theological interpreters, to forge such links in order to communicate what they agree with the text and author is its subject-matter. The introduction of this traditional category into our interpretation

---

[13] *Über Aufgabe und Methode der sogenannten neutestamentlichen Theologie* (Göttingen, 1897; repr. Darmstadt, 1975). ET in Morgan, ed., *Nature.*

of the Sermon is a constructive move made with a theological purpose. It helps fuse the horizons of the text and the modern interpreter who chooses it, encouraging a reading of the text in tune with traditional Christianity and it is none the worse for that—despite the discomfort of some not very cultivated despisers. It resists a modern misreading of the Sermon and the whole gospel as a more or less historical account of a merely historical figure. Matthew *can* (with a few adjustments) be read in that way, and often is. The text *is* about a historical figure and contains plenty of historical information, but to impose a humanistic Christology on Matthew is to do violence to the text. A way must be found to do justice to its elements of truth without distorting Matthew's actual witness.

This post-Enlightenment reading of the gospel as a more or less historical record has also rightly affected the way even orthodox Christians think of Jesus. But infusing the traditional Christology with some historical realism is quite different from replacing it with a merely historical portrait. That too yields a theological interpretation of Matthew's text when it is connected with a (non-trinitarian) understanding of Christianity in which Jesus teaches us about God, and inspires us, while not himself being "God with us" now, the risen Lord who is with his disciples to the end of time. But however Christian and theological, this is a misreading of Matthew, and for all its elements of truth should not satisfy anyone who wants Christian faith to be normed by scripture. To appeal to scripture alone, or to scripture and tradition, is to appeal to the *texts*. That means to the history they contain *and* to the interpretations they provide, not simply to the history behind the text. Whether the truth and credibility of Christianity do in fact depend on this significant continuity with past witness, and how much is necessary, cannot be argued here. To appeal only to the history which may lie behind the text misses out what Matthew and most Christians after him have considered most important in this story: God with us. The moral teaching of Jesus (says Matthew) informs Christian faith and practice when read within this larger christological context of which it is a necessary aspect. Without that it is merely an impossible ethic.

The dogmatic framework of subsequent Christianity has protected Matthew's christological witness by teaching Christians to read these chapters as they read the Johannine discourses, as the life-giving words of the divine Saviour, not merely as the wisdom of a Galilean rabbi. However, over the past two hundred years the traditional

expressions of that framework have lost much of their former credibility. It has become more natural to think of Jesus in historical
rather than dogmatic terms, and so to read the gospels as history
or history-like narratives. This has the merit of doing better justice
than before to one part of the old dogmatic formula (truly human)[14]
and to the historicizing intentions of Matthew (and especially Luke),
even though it does less than justice to Matthew's witness as a whole.

A case might be made for discarding Matthew's and the rest of
New Testament and patristic Christology, and revisioning Christianity
by basing it on the religion of Jesus, rather than retaining the version in which Jesus is seen as the saving revelation of God (cf. John
14:9) or "God with us" (Matt 1:23). The text of scripture is important only for what it bears witness to, in this case to the person
behind and above and beyond the text. What matters is "the real
Jesus". But the "real Jesus" is not the "historical Jesus"[15] (to borrow
a misleading because ambiguous phrase). The reality of that person
cannot be reduced to any historian's reconstruction. Many believers
claim that the Jesus identified by the gospel as the crucified and
risen Lord who is present with his disciples is more real to them
than the modern reconstructions. And yet those historical reconstructions are also relevant to the identity of Jesus, and the question
remains how to insert what is true in them into a modern Christology
and into theological interpretation of this gospel.

A theological interpretation which sets the Sermon in an Enlightenment rather than a Matthean christological context is attractive to
modern readers and has common-sense on its side. The moral teaching of Jesus has a clearer relationship to the Galilean teacher and
healer than to the christological ideas of the evangelist or the later
doctrinal tradition. But the perspective of the text has first claim on
its theological interpreters. The only justification for challenging this
would be if it seemed to fall short of its subject-matter: Jesus himself. But Jesus himself is beyond all our interpretations, theological
and historical. In making a critical judgment (*Sachkritik*) about an
aspect of Matthew's Christology modern interpreters depend on their
own, informed as this is by Matthew and by other witnesses, and
also perhaps by their historical study of Jesus. It is by this round-

---

[14] As even Martin Kähler acknowledged: see his *The So-called Historical Jesus and
the Historic Biblical Christ* (1892; ET Philadelphia, 1964) 46.
[15] Rightly J.P. Meier, *A Marginal Jew* 1 (New York, 1991) 21.

about route that modern historical Jesus research can contribute to christologically shaped theological interpretations. We must therefore turn to modern Christology and the place of historical Jesus research within it.

2. *Two Eyes and Lenses in Modern Christology*

At a local discussion group well-known for turning wine into water, a colleague who had written a commentary on Matthew gave a paper on Matthew's theology. Someone asked the speaker why he had chosen to speak about *Matthew*. It is *Jesus* people want to know about, he insisted. The speaker growled that Matthew is what we've *got*.

Presumably he meant Matthew's gospel, or its implied author, but the objector had a point. The *text*, which is the biblical scholar's primary concern, is not what interests most readers, and critics who stop at this level of the theology of the evangelist (or his social location or the text's literary character) are not satisfying their customers, and here at least the customers are right, even if ignorant. Most people will think of Jesus rather than the evangelist when we speak of the Sermon on the Mount. Even if further instruction convinces them that the route back to Jesus lies through the witness of the evangelists they will repeat that it is Jesus they want to know about.

But the objector also was imprecise. If he was calling for more historical research on Jesus that was hardly necessary in the present state of the discipline, stuffed as it is with books claiming to tell the historical truth about him. Given much bogus history careful attention to the history of the synoptic tradition is refreshing. The speaker rightly implied that historical knowledge of Jesus is to be found (if at all) at the end of a long process. But he might have turned the tables in a more time-honoured way by insisting that very little such knowledge is available, and that it remains quite uncertain, and that in any case this is *not* what most people want from New Testament scholars. The knowledge of Jesus that Christians claim and seek to deepen through study of the gospels is accessible only through an amalgam of history and theology, not by historical research alone.

The dialectical theology's objections to the older life of Jesus research finds little support today. The earlier objections of Ritschl[16]

---

[16] *Justification and Reconciliation* 3 (ET Edinburgh, 1874) 3; cf. 414.

and Kähler[17] to its hypothetical and speculative reconstructions are
still worth pondering and apply to most of the latest examples, but
they never justified Bultmann's repudiation of interest in historical
knowledge about Jesus other than the crucifixion. Many Christians
agree with some non-Christians in wanting to know what can be
known about Jesus by historical research, while denying that this will
tell the whole truth about him. This historical knowledge has influenced
but does not correspond to the texture of Christian faith. It is surely
possible to make some historical judgments which are independent
of religious evaluations, but the historian's procedures remain remote
from how most Christians read the gospels.

Neither enquiry is wrong in its own terms, and some will want
to relate their two approaches to the gospels. Since Christology offers
the larger picture and history a person identified by a few very probable facts it is more promising for theologians to fit their historical
knowledge and sensibility into their larger christological frameworks
which speak of God, the world, and salvation than to reconstruct a
highly speculative "historical Jesus" and try to relate this construction
to a "Christ of faith" that has lost or lost interest in its historical
components. Christians need a picture of the one Christ which is
true to what they can know by historical research and also expresses
their religious conviction that to have seen him is to have seen the
Father. New accounts of this *vere Deus, vere homo* are possible when
the divinity of Christ is understood formally as a claim to the decisive
saving revelation of God in Jesus, not as a description bound to
conflict materially with anything we could recognize as truly human.
The gospel evidence is sufficiently ambiguous to permit hypotheses
about Jesus and Christian origins which are both historically plausible and compatible with the traditional dogma. These can meet in
a Christology reflecting modern knowledge and sense of historical
reality. Whatever can be known about Jesus can be incorporated
within a faith-picture. But attempts to replace a Christology true to
the many dimensions of Christian faith with historical reconstructions
that are inevitably largely imaginative are either attacks on traditional Christianity or else written from a Christian apologetic perspective. Such bogus history is unlikely to persuade critical enquirers.

In making a distinction between gems of reliable historical infor-

[17] Op. cit.

mation about Jesus which can be included in larger christological constructions, and historical reconstructions which are highly speculative and provide no firm basis for faith, and then accepting the former while remaining sceptical about the latter, contemporary believers are in tune with the gospels themselves. Despite their relative proximity to the events the evangelists were less interested in the question of historical accuracy than we are, despite Luke 1:1–4 and John 19:35, 21:24, but they all include genuine historical information about Jesus within the christological frameworks which serve their religious aims, and they probably all reject or correct or supplement alternative constructions of Jesus' life and death.[18] Modern historians certainly, and modern theologians perhaps, have to distinguish between more and less reliable historical material in the gospels. Our question is what importance that critical historical work has for modern Christology and for modern theological interpretation of Matthew.

If this task were simply to communicate Matthew's message there would be no need to go behind the text and to ask about the historical reliability of the evangelist's portrait of Jesus. In many religious contexts that is still an unnecessary complication, beset with uncertainties. But theology is a critical discipline and must ask about the truth or adequacy of any portrait of Jesus in its tradition, even those on which the subsequent tradition most depends. Theological interpretation asks about the truth and adequacy of biblical statements, not only about their meaning. It is at least possible that Matthew's portrait may have to be criticized as in some respects untrue to what the interpreter perceives as the reality of Jesus. Historical conclusions can contribute to the formation of such theological judgments. The contested results of historical research are rarely strong enough on their own to bear this burden of theological criticism, but they may provide evidence in support of alternative modern Christologies whose advocates might have to criticize Matthew.

Some theologians welcome historical criticism of the gospels but repudiate theological criticism (*Sachkritik*) of documents on which all subsequent Christian theology depends. It is dangerously subjective and erodes these necessary traditions. The danger of modern prejudices overcoming the witness of scripture to the gospel is the price

---

[18] Even Mark presupposes and perhaps criticizes an earlier narrative, whether written or not.

paid for allowing historical reconstruction a role in Christology and
admitting that no human testimony is immune from criticism. If it
is *Jesus* that the gospels are interpreting, it is hard to protect them
in principle from challenges made by historians, however few of these
are in practice likely to be upheld, on account of the state of the
evidence. Borrowing these critical historical arguments to serve the
frankly theological purpose of communicating the Christian truth of
Matthew's gospel while expressing some reservations about Matthew's
theology is audacious, but has a long pedigree in nineteenth-century
theology. All theological interpretation looks for some harmony
between the witness of the text and contemporary understandings of
God and Christianity (*Sachexegese*). But it must also be free to recognize tensions and contradictions between these two poles. A biblically-
based theology must take these seriously, must allow itself to be
questioned by the awkward text, but also must finally be free to criticize any text it judges inadequate to the gospel it is seeking to express. If one thinks that Matthew misrepresents Jesus in some dangerous
detail, such as in his presentation of Jesus' attitude to his fellow-
countrymen, or the harshness of his emphasis upon God's judgment,
or the law-centred character of his moral teaching, the appropriate
vehicle of theological criticism is one's admittedly uncertain historical judgments. This uncertainty introduces a proper note of caution
and provisionality.

   Historical appeals to Jesus are only one instrument of theological
criticism, alongside moral judgment and enlarged knowledge of the
world. Critical theological judgments are usually made from further
outside the particular text under consideration. For example, Luther
owes his distinctive understanding of the gospel to his reading of
Paul, and he criticizes the Epistle of James in the light of this. That
is open to the response, "But I am of James!" and the debate may
grind to a halt. One attraction of appeals to historical conclusions
about Jesus (where available) is that both the evangelist and the modern theological interpreter claim to be speaking of the same Lord
Jesus whose earthly ministry and passion and resurrection provide
the key to his identity and so to the truth of the gospel. Here the
debate continues, because most historical judgments about Jesus are
uncertain. Theological interpretation of scripture allows this debate
to fuel the reflection of the Christian community seeking the Spirit's
guidance. It does not resolve disputes in a way that short-circuits
that process of discernment.

Our "two eyes of modern Christology" refer (1) to any past Christian witness to Jesus (such as Matthew's) and (2) to modern historical research on Jesus. On its own the latter encourages humanist Christologies which deny the divinity of Christ. Even where the trinitarian shape of Christian belief has been maintained, historical study has contributed to (and stemmed from) a new sensibility. Christians now quite naturally and rightly think of Jesus as a historical figure, not as a quasi-angelic visitor to earth, even when they confess him Lord and God, because they find in him crucified and risen the decisive revelation of God.

The main point of our analogy with two eyes wearing contact lenses or spectacles is again to emphasise the contribution of the perceiving interpreters. It does not explain *how* the two eyes perceive one Jesus, but it does suggest the extra dimension over a purely historical portrait or even a dogma-inspired ikon. Even without spectacles, two eyes yield 3-D. Bifocals would provide a better analogy for the way that close historical readings of the text contribute constructive and critical contributions to theological portraiture,[19] but that would place too much weight on the spectacles which are mere instruments to help the eyes, and would also replace the Christian's perception of one Lord Jesus with two pictures, one historical and the other Matthean or other past theological interpretation. An act of theological interpretation today is aware of both, but aims beyond both to a perception which the interpreter can believe corresponds to the reality of Jesus who can be known today. That will be an expression of the interpreter's own Christology, informed but not destroyed by critical historical research.

It is the interpreter with two eyes that matters. One lens in our analogy refers merely to the doctrinal concepts which conceptualise and help our first eye to see and describe what Matthew is saying in a way that corresponds to the insights of this ancient author *and* his modern Christian readers. The other lens represents the modern techniques by which reliable historical information is derived from the text. Neither lens is more than a means to an end and both serve ends which on their own fall short of the goal of the theologian and the Christian reader of scripture. Each of them serves a "single

---

[19] On "theological portraiture" see E. Farley, *Ecclesial Reflection* (Philadelphia, 1982) 193–216.

vision" which on its own does not yield an adequate modern Christian apprehension of Jesus.

Most descriptions of Matthew's thought by historians of early Christian religion and theology, improperly called theologians, have rightly used only the first eye to see and first lens to conceptualise what the author was saying. Historical Jesus research rightly uses the second eye and its lens to see through the tradition, and reconstructing its Jewish and early Christian contexts to risk a few inferences about the man from Nazareth. The commercial success of this second kind of writing suggests a real interest and perhaps even a spiritual need, however wretchedly this is sometimes satisfied with bad history and worse theology. What are needed instead are theological interpretations of the text which communicate its religious meaning in a way that evokes appropriate religious responses (whether positive or negative) to Jesus, i.e. God in Jesus, today. These forge a link between the modern theological interpreter's eye and the theological claims of the text by using (lens 1) concepts such as "Christology" which are appropriate both to the text and to the aims of the interpreter, and also by using (lens 2) modern historical methods. These methods help gain knowledge of the historical figure Jesus, who is now confessed in faith as risen and present with his disciples today. Neither the lens nor the pictures they project are the real Jesus whom the interpreter hopes may communicate himself to the heart and mind receptive to the revelation of God which is mediated by interpretations that facilitate such disclosures.

Even assisted with the lens of modern historical methods this second eye does not contribute much detail to a critical theological interpretation of scripture, but it reinforces the reality to what is seen by faith and described in Christology. Occasionally what the historian's squint picks up under close analysis of the tradition and its history may challenge what the other lens discloses as Matthew's message. Critical theologians' interpretative efforts may then include a few correctives. But it remains primarily Matthew's message which communicates Jesus from faith to faith, with or without correctives.

Neither Matthew's message (the text) nor the mediator of God to whom he bears witness (his subject-matter or *Sache*) should be confused with the doctrinal concepts some theological interpreters use to articulate this message in a way that fits their own doctrinal pigeon-holes. That redescription has often been found useful but can only be a hindrance to Christians who do not easily understand their own faith in such traditional terms. The reality of Jesus perceived today by faith (where and when God wills) is beyond all the faith-pictures that modern believers construct from the texts with the help of such instruments and maps or instructions as doctrinal concepts provide.

One further suggestion emerges from the theological decision to use both eyes and both lenses in the process of so redescribing the text of Matthew as to hear and understand what he is saying: where Matthew's meaning is uncertain because the text is ambiguous, theological interpreters may select the reading most in accord with their own conclusions about the historical figure that Matthew is interpreting. At times Matthew seems historically more accurate than Mark, and both evangelists stand close enough to the history that they are interpreting to be given the benefit of the doubt, other things being equal.

3. *From Precept to Practice*

The optical analogy was intended to resist the view of theological interpretation as getting doctrine out of the text. It is rather a way of reading the text which respects (and may well share) its basic assumptions about God in Jesus, and uses appropriate categories to aid understanding.

But the limits of the exercise must be recognized. If Christian theology aims to speak of God in Jesus, and that calls for the response of worship, a published interpretation of Matthew can be no more than a trace of some past act of interpreting the gospel, or information about the interpreter's own encounter with the text.[20] It is the process of engaging with relevant texts in a relevant way that may lead to disclosure; the words which reflect this engagement are no more than scripts and stage-props. We have identified two main components and the instruments appropriate to each, and have suggested one point at which the minor key or half-blind eye (historical Jesus research) might impinge upon the major component, but the aim is to nurture on-going acts of interpretation, not to achieve "results" which would make further interpretative activity superfluous.

---

[20] Cf. R. Bultmann, *Jesus and the Word* (1926; London, 1958) 13, on his encounter with history, which is surely an encounter with the texts he considers the earliest traditions.

This is because it is *in* acts of interpretation that disclosures may happen, not *through* results or other dead information, useful as this sometimes is. The aim is to keep the theological conversation going.

The doctrinal concepts often used in theological interpretation are not a cage or net in which the fishy reality (*ichthus*) is captured, but rather a lens whose symbolic patterns have helped make the subject-matter approachable in past acts of interpretation, and may be most likely to succeed in the future. To insist on Christology as the main lens for reading the Sermon on the Mount is to say that it is the living Jesus we wish to hear and understand. And that means to follow and obey, which is why discipleship is the necessary correlate to Christology. But neither these terms nor their application to Matthew is the goal of our analysis. Matthew's Christology and his understanding of discipleship offer controls against misreading the text. But they are not themselves theological interpretation, as some New Testament theology (so-called) has suggested. They might even be a distraction, deceiving us into supposing that this is where New Testament studies should lead—to the point where the exegete hands over the baton to the systematic theologian. The theologian might well protest against this conception of New Testament theology that far from completing the first lap the historians have been going off in another direction or possibly chewing the baton. Their contribution is helpful only if it accompanies the theologian's efforts, gently assisting in the understanding of the texts and sharply warning of abuse.

Theological interpretations (or their traces) vary in shape and scale from short sermons to major commentaries. Here a few observations must suffice to illustrate what has been proposed; their unsystematic character reflects the way that pre-understandings, exegetical conclusions, cross-references to other relevant traditions, and the interpreter's own life-experience, all swirl around in Christians' reflection on their scriptures. Theology can sprout from close attention to philological detail (as Hoskyns learned from Schlatter, to whom Kittel dedicated the *Wörterbuch*), but biblical theology can also work with a broader brush, content to make some essentials stand out clearly.

The fundamental question for theological interpretation today is that addressed most impressively by Bultmann: how to speak of God in a post-Christian culture. But because biblical theology normally stems from within religious communities, it finds no need to be for ever relaying foundations or engaging in apologetic strategies. It usually sees its "normal" task of communicating what each witness is wanting to say as clarifying and organizing rather than radically rethinking the biblical material. Nevertheless, for critical theologians to appropriate the witness of scripture they must reckon with the possibility of imperfection and be free to balance self-criticism with correction of a text's witness. They must also insist that some readings are more true to the underlying aim of a text than others. What will be illustrated in what follows is firstly the way the interpreters' choice of interpretative concepts (here especially Christology) helps produce readings which resonate with their own understandings of God and Christianity; and secondly how historical judgments about Jesus might affect a believer's reading of a gospel, perhaps even supporting some criticism of the evangelist's Christology.

Christology and its correlative term discipleship have been proposed as the most appropriate lens for reading the Sermon theologically because they fit both Matthew's text as a whole and the Christianity of interpreters who want their religion to be in accord with their scriptures. Other interpreters have preferred the categories of law, folk wisdom, or morality, which also fit much of Matthew's tradition and have often fitted this Jesus tradition into a modern, more humanistic version of Christianity. Both these competing versions of Christianity appeal to the text with a view to getting behind or beyond it, whether to general moral and religious truths enunciated by a much admired teacher, or to a claim that in this crucified and risen Lord (inclusive of the teaching ascribed to him) the reader might be confronted with God who is to be worshipped. Both versions respect the moral seriousness of Jesus and advocate discipleship. But the pattern of discipleship differs in each case, and the question of which is more true to Jesus must surely be answered by reference to his dedication to God. This is scarcely compatible with a merely human wisdom ethic, though Kant's categorical imperative might conceivably (as the stern daughter of the voice of God) be seen as an appropriate expression of Jesus' God-consciousness. Bultmann's Jesus is not far from this, but even Matthew's is more joyful, as was Schlatter's.

Matthew continued Jesus' worship of the one God and insisted that discipleship has moral implications. This is a large part of the message of the Sermon, but that message is not presented as a moral code. The citations of the Mosaic law in the Antitheses are springboards into a different kind of moral discourse. They are better understood, like the Beatitudes, as in effect a description of discipleship.

This is confirmed by Matthew's τέλειοι at 5:48; the redactional insertion of this word at 19:20 refers explicitly to discipleship. Only the antitheses on divorce and oaths *can* be read as laws (which must define transgression clearly, and set minimum standards) and even these point rather to dispositions (honesty, fidelity) and standards of behaviour which transcend the specified minimums. Dispositions are not subject to legislation and Matthew's summary of the law in the love commandment shows that for him even Torah is primarily a description of a relationship, the people's relationship with God and so with each other. Its prescriptions belong within that description.

Matthew expresses the two sides of this relationship primarily through his Christology and his understanding of discipleship. Jesus is the presence of God with his people and he elicits a response of attachment which Matthew does not say, but surely thought fulfilled the command of Deut 6:5. The latter like the fruit of the spirit at Gal 5:22f. is not appropriately spelled out in terms of obedience to any law, no matter how new or perfect or Jesuanic, but as following Jesus. That phrase itself calls for elaboration (and *imitatio* is an inadequate paraphrase) but it insists on the personal character of discipleship. It is only vv. 17–19 which precede the antitheses that suggest that Matthew may have seen the higher righteousness of discipleship as a "sharpening of the law". That is less wrong than claims that Jesus, according to Matthew, abrogates the law, but it is not the impression given by his gospel as a whole. Discipleship is attachment to Jesus, which has moral implications and consequences. It is not obedience to a moral code, however tempting it is to teach and communicate it in those terms.

Matthew does not formulate an ethic which stands independent of his religious beliefs and commitments. His moral teaching can be understood correctly only by being closely tied to the teacher himself who is addressed as Lord. Lifting the teaching of Matthew's Jesus out of its Matthean context and placing it in some hypothetically reconstructed context of Jesus' earthly ministry is not interpretation of Matthew's gospel. It is nevertheless a legitimate historical task, and has an important function in the critical appropriation of Matthew's gospel. Any secure results achieved in this modern quest may even correct Matthew's picture. Since Matthew's account of God with us in Jesus describes and interprets a piece of history, further historical information obtained by a critical comparison of all the sources and tentative reconstructions of the traditions behind them may at least affect our understanding and evaluation of Matthew's perspective.

For example, one might well consider the references to divine judgment in the Sermon more true to Jesus' historical teaching than the harsh emphasis on eschatological sanctions in chapters 13 and 25 (and 22:11–14). Evidently Jesus shared the general Jewish belief in God's eschatological judgment (11:22, 24, cf. 5:22), whether or not he believed this to be imminent, and could refer to it in woes on communities that failed to respond to what was now happening in and through his healings (11:20–4). The figurative reference to judgment at 7:27, predicting personal disaster for failure to attend to his teaching coheres with this and is probably authentic, but it is hard to doubt that he emphasized the good news of God, not, like John the Baptist, the threat of judgment. The later word "gospel", only rarely applied to his teaching (Mark 1:14) and de-emphasized by Matt 4:23, 9:35 (and perhaps 24:14), is an appropriate interpretative summary term. One may suspect the negativities of 7:21–3 to be secondary, and feel some sympathy for Matthew's charismatic opponents. This will lead an interpreter to place less emphasis on these verses than Matthew himself does, accepting the importance of doing God's will, but hesitating to condemn those who are less inclined to make of Jesus' teaching a new law. Matthew can be given credit for associating the similitude of judgment (7:24–7) with the person of Jesus by placing it after 7:21–3 (cf. 10:33). He does not separate his moral code from Christology and discipleship, as some of his successors do. But there are tendencies to moralism in his presentation which can be criticized by reference to the probably quite unmoralistic person he is interpreting.

Matthew's positive association of the teaching of Jesus with the person may also be seen in the Beatitudes. These are addressed to disciples and describe their discipleship, but are perhaps intended to reflect the character of the teacher too. At 11:29 Jesus also is described as πραΰς (cf. 21:5), and tells his disciples to learn from him. It goes without saying that he too belongs to the righteous poor, can lament, hungers to fulfil all righteousness, is merciful, pure in heart, a peacemaker—and finally is persecuted for righteousness' sake. There is implicit in the Sermon a picture of the teacher, and the teaching is not rightly understood if it is separated from the person of the teacher and preacher and healer who is identified in the summaries which form an *inclusio* around this and the collection of miracle-stories which follows it (4:23; 9:35). This connexion is not strong enough to justify interpreting discipleship in terms of imitation but it requires our understanding of Jesus' teaching to be emphatically oriented to the person of the master.

If in this indirect way the moral teaching of the Sermon can be seen as contributing to Matthew's portrait of Jesus, and by its critical appropriation to the Christologies of his readers, the question for theological interpreters is how to conceptualise that appropriately.

The moral emphasis of the Sermon raises the question of moralism, just as the emphasis on the law in 5:18f. invites the charge of "legalism". Both can be answered by reference to the more appropriate categories of Christology and discipleship. Comparison with Luke 6:21f. does indeed suggest that Matthew (or his predecessor) has moralized the Beatitudes, as he has moralized their key phrase "the kingdom of heaven". But he preserves their note of joy and celebration, which most historians think characteristic of Jesus (cf. 11:18f.), and by placing them at the beginning of the Sermon he too gives priority and precedence to God's saving grace within the Sermon, as in the gospel as a whole. Obedience to God's will is emphasised, but set in a context which gives priority to God's gift and call. This is analogous to Jewish "covenantal nomism", but Matthew does not (apparently) see the Mosaic covenant as foundational for his community's relation to God. It is therefore initially surprising that he emphasises the abiding significance of the law so strongly, and it is tempting to interpret the second "until" clause in 5:18 as setting a time-limit to that.[21] But Matthew's understanding of this verse must cohere with v. 17, and with the "Antitheses". Both of these are ambiguous, but they seem to imply (as v. 19 does more clearly) that the law of Moses was still valid for Matthew. On the other hand both v. 17 and the Antitheses do in a sense subordinate the law to Jesus himself. As its true and authoritative interpreter Jesus is not merely a scribe but in some sense sovereign with respect to it. That does not mean that he abolishes it or even (in Matthew's view) that he breaks it, but Jesus and his words are what define God's will (7:21–6).

What Matthew has Jesus say about the law follows and is subordinate to Jesus' proclamation of the kingdom which at 4:17 has not lost its eschatological urgency. Matthew's subsequent emphasis on

---

[21] So J.P. Meier, *The Vision of Matthew* (New York, 1979).

the moral aspect of this God language has been justified above as true to Jesus' teaching as a whole. However free of moralising Jesus may have been he was clear that God's rule and claim had a strong moral dimension. He probably expected its public manifestation in the future, without specifying when,[22] but surely thought it a present hidden reality, available for those who trusted in God and lived under God's rule, doing his will. There is no reason to doubt Matthew's historical credibility about that. But this does not explain the prominence given to the law in this chapter, a prominence which leads some to suppose that he understood God's will primarily in these terms.

It is perhaps because there was some dispute in the early churches about the content of God's will in the light of the Messiah's coming, and his behaviour and teaching, that Matthew insists, against some appeals to the Spirit or risen Lord (7:21f.), on the importance of the tradition—both scripture and what was remembered of Jesus' sayings. But his text has, rightly or wrongly, fuelled Christian moralism, and that poses both the historical question of his understanding of the relation of Jesus to the law of Moses, and the theological question of the place of this law in Christian ethics. Does Matthew see Jesus as "sharpening the Torah" and if so is this a misunderstanding of Jesus requiring theological criticism?

By "Christian moralism" is meant the tendency to define Christianity in moral terms, or at least to give undue emphasis to this aspect and so distort the gospel of grace. It is part of Paul's legacy that any emphasis upon the place of law in Christian faith and life is open to the suspicion of moralism. The charge against Matthew maybe opened with his alleged "moralising" of the Beatitudes.

In their probably more original form preserved by Luke the emphasis falls on their second halves—the promises made to people who find themselves (not by choice) in difficult situations: poor, hungry, bereaved, persecuted. In Matthew the element of finding oneself in unchosen situations remains (bereaved, persecuted), but the emphasis has in general shifted to the first half and there is almost a sense here of virtues to be cultivated, or a depiction of Christian character. That is how the passage has been read, and has become a

---

[22] As I have argued in *The Biblical World* (ed. J. Barton; London, 2001) forthcoming.

centrepiece of Christian scripture. In Matthew, however, it is not implied that we have to work at becoming merciful, pure in heart, peacemakers etc. Rather it is as though these characteristics emerge from the fact of following Jesus as disciples, and this corresponds to the unselfconsciousness that is described later in the Sermon. Here discipleship is the theme, more than eschatological reversal, and that explains the present tense of the kingdom of heaven in vv. 3 and 10. Its christological orientation (explicit in v. 11) is not a matter of deliberate and self-conscious imitation of Christ. Christian character is the consequence of following him, which for Matthew includes observing his commands (28:20) and learning from him (11:29).

Discipleship is more explicitly thematised in 5:13–16. The second person address here follows vv. 11f. and the sequence supports the view that discipleship (living under God's rule as a follower of Jesus) is central to the Beatitudes and to the Antitheses. It involves "good works" (v. 16) and it would be absurd and unmatthean to contrast following Jesus with its moral content and implications. "Good works" are sufficiently general not to require explication in terms of fulfilling the law's demands, or even the teaching of Jesus himself, but the references to the law (vv. 17f.) and commandments (v. 19) which follow do suggest an orientation to this which stands in some tension with some of his teaching about discipleship and its moral demands (e.g. 8:22; 11:29) and criticism of the scribes and Pharisees (23:4). The care Matthew takes to avoid any suggestion that Jesus breaks or disregards the written law[23] is explicable as cautious conservatism, but confirms the impression that this was more important to him than to most New Testament writers, including Luke and James.

Matthew's view, however, is hardly to be called nomist. The highly Matthean v. 17 subordinates the law and prophets to Jesus himself, and the introduction to the Antitheses (v. 20) speaks of "righteousness" rather than the law, allowing the elaborations which follow to clarify the position of the law in Christian discipleship. they must be understood in a way that does not abolish the law (v. 17) and their interpretation depends in part on whether Matthew's ἐγὼ δὲ λέγω ὑμῖν is taken (as it usually is) as a strong adversative. The modern, rather Marcionite title "antitheses" has already been questioned. The contrasts may be less strong than usually thought, and these

---

[23] E.g. G. Barth (1955) in G. Bornkamm, G. Barth and H.J. Held, *Tradition and Interpretation in Matthew* (1960; ET London, 1963).

phrases perhaps better taken as introducing a gloss and translated "And what's more I tell you . . .".

It is widely agreed that Jesus' comments here, preserved in the tradition and only given their shape by Matthew, go to the root of the law's intentions and confront the heart with God's will rather than measure the act by it. Laws generally define minimums, and that remains true even for the law which regulates the covenant people's relationship to God. Jesus' comments cannot be understood through the category of law, even if it is hard to doubt that Jesus, like Paul, understood the law to contain an authoritative statement of God's holy will and moral requirement. To call this transcending the category of law (cf. Gal 5:23b) an ethic of intention (*Gesinnungsethik*) would undermine both the act and the goal which are certainly important for Matthew and probably for Jesus, but this section of the Sermon, like the Beatitudes, does reveal a disposition rather than impose a set of moral rules.

There is no reason to criticise Matthew's understanding of Jesus here, as would be necessary if "sharpening of the Torah" were the most adequate description of this higher righteousness. The addition of the clause "except for πορνεία" to the prohibition of divorce may well reflect the practicalities of a church seeking to be guided by Jesus' teaching, and perhaps a wish to avoid apparent conflict with Deut 24, but one can scarcely say that Matthew makes Jesus into a moral legislator. The law, especially the Decalogue, provides a springboard for teaching which shows the meaning of discipleship. Certain provisions in the law (oaths) and certain interpretations of it (divorce on debatable grounds; the restriction of the neighbour to fellow-Jews) are left behind in lives of discipleship which are truthful and loving, and which Matthew sums up (v. 48) as seeking to attain their goal.

Any impression of legalism or moralism in this chapter derives from vv. 18 and 19, but in v. 18c Matthew as editor probably sets a limit to the abiding validity of the law, while declining to define this, and v.19 looks like a piece of earlier Jewish-Christian tradition (polemic against Paul's gentile mission?) which he could not omit. His own position is defined by framing these sayings with vv. 17 and 20ff., where the still valid law is relativised. Theological criticisms of Matthew's moral stance in this chapter have perhaps been unduly influenced by a particular reading of Paul. But it is not obvious that Matthew understood "the mind of Christ" less well than Paul. Both of them give priority to the love commandment, Matthew in its twofold form (22:37–40). It is hard to find anything in the Sermon on the Mount which could not count as loving either God or neighbour. The "righteousness" required by God in Matthew differs from Paul's soteriological usage and usually refers to life under God's rule. At 6:1 it is applied to religious practices. To be a disciple is to be religious—and in quite conventional ways (6:1–18). This love of God expressed partly in love for the neighbour (6:2) is taken for granted and only mentioned in the context of some always necessary instruction about misuse of religion (cf. 23:5).

The section on not caring (6:25–34) is also a specification of the individual's relation of loving trust towards God. The chapter lacks any explicit Christology but this passage gains much of its Matthean force from the impression given by the whole gospel that it corresponds to the character of the Son of man himself, who has nowhere to lay his head and seems unworried by this. The picture of Jesus as the truly free man and the corresponding freedom of the disciple, unstressed by Matthew for reasons already noted, has points of contact with Stoicism, but the stance of both Matthew and Jesus is rooted in a relationship with the heavenly Father and in the service of God which loving God entails. The "therefore" of v. 25 links this section on freedom from cares to (v. 24) serving God, and all that is said about prayer and forgiveness in chapters 6 and 7 reinforces this relationship to God. What is said about the heart (6:21) and the sound eye (6:22) is also based on this.

One verse that cannot be subsumed under love of God and neighbour, or under the freedom of disciples to serve God joyfully, is the defensive-sounding 7:6. But this piece of common-sense or popular wisdom hardly needs criticizing, however uncharacteristic of Jesus it sounds. Missionary effort can be misdirected. What matters is knowing when to be guided by this maxim and when (more usually) not—and that is to say that it cannot be treated as a general rule. If Matthew understood it as such he could be criticized, but the little dogs of 15:21–8 allow us to think that he did not. Like the probably inauthentic criticism of "false prophets" which follows (7:15), the healthy warning in 7:6 confirms that disciples need to be as wise as serpents as well as innocent as doves (10:16) in a world of ravenous wolves, dogs, and pigs. The proverbial language of Jesus evidences a sturdy realism and can be transferred without cultural adjustment to a very different world. This partly accounts for the continuing impact of the Sermon.

Making discipleship rather than law the key to all these injunctions leaves more room for the moral discernment which is needed in receiving and acting on them. This is particularly evident in the history of the interpretation of one of the most discussed verses of the whole Sermon: resist not evil (5:39)—the basis of Christian pacifism. Even if this were a universally applicable law there would be a question of its interpretation. Matthew was clearly referring to personal morality, not to social or political action. One might argue that Jesus himself was advocating non-resistance to Rome, which was a social and political act—and might criticize Matthew on that basis. The real basis for this criticism would be a particular understanding of the Christian gospel, but a historical argument (about Jesus) would provide the instrument of theological criticism. That does not make it a general law applicable to nation states, and it is doubtful whether it should be treated as a *law*, even for individuals. We are often (perhaps usually) right to resist evil, and turning the other cheek might be a form of passive resistance. And yet the blunt imperative challenges the hearer, and the general point about not insisting on one's rights is obviously Christian and often an appropriate expression of discipleship. A theological interpretation should leave room for the challenge of the maxim to be heard and thought about, as a clear and unambiguous law need not be, and also leave room for those whose response to the Word of God heard in this verse leads them into the powerful Christian witness of pacifism. The danger of too much history and authorial intention is that these may go beyond their legitimate role in testing the spirits and instead may quench or extinguish them. The text must be allowed its freedom to generate interpretations which go beyond anything its author intended or previous interpreters "recepted" ("received" will hardly do justice to *Rezeptionsgeschichte*).[24] We should also consider how hugely the impact of this v. 39 is magnified by its proximity to v. 44: love your enemies, and perhaps by an incorrect "perfectionist" understanding of v. 48. At this point too the guidance on discipleship curls back towards the example of Jesus, who resisted not evil, turned his cheek to the smiters, and hardly opened his mouth, except (adds Luke) to pray for those who persecuted him.

---

[24] On this cf. M. Bakhtin, *Speech Genres and Other Essays* (Texas, 1986) 4.

Caution in treating the injunctions of the Sermon as general rules or laws which always apply confirms the choice of Christology and discipleship rather than law or even morality as overarching interpretative concepts. It also raises a question about the terms obedience and command. Unlike Paul, Matthew does not describe faith or discipleship as obedience to Christ, though one might argue that this is implied in the disciples' addressing him as Lord and seeing him as king, and that as it goes without saying that God is to be obeyed, so this must extend to Jesus as God with us. Obedience to (hearing and doing) Jesus' words is required at the end of the Sermon and at the end of the gospel the verb "command" occurs (cf. 17:9). But since Matthew sees himself free to interpret and even alter the Jesus tradition that he has received, this obedience to these commands is not quite like obedience to a law. Room is left for the discernment of God's will, and that is part of discipleship; and the Christ known from the gospel and in his little ones and present with his disciples until the close of the age remains the criterion.

Even more discussed in Christian history than 5:39 is 5:8. The vision of God which lies in the future, beyond Christology and discipleship, can serve to remind us of the relativity of our conceptual instruments. The ultimate goal of theological interpretation lies beyond even the most engaged and responsive talk of God. The purity in heart that characterizes discipleship is but the prerequisite of this promise. A contemporary of Matthew wrote (in a passage which became normative for subsequent Christology) of believers having beheld the glory of the only-begotten Son, full of grace and truth. Adding that no one has ever seen God he insisted that the only-begotten Son (or: God) who is in the bosom of the Father made him known or revealed him. Matthew's present-day faith in God in Jesus is much closer to John's than their different symbols and strategies might suggest. John's believing in Jesus and experience of the Paraclete corresponds to Matthew's account of the disciples illuminating the present-day followers' life in the company of Jesus. This reality of discipleship is not soured by Matthew's colourful expectation of judgment in the future. That "high" Christology of the apocalyptic Son of man is probably at the root of both the Johannine and the Matthean theology of the present Christ, and Matthew's account of God with us in Jesus gains reality and credibility from being drawn from the historical memory of what he said and did and suffered. The Sermon on the Mount clarifies the demands of discipleship by placing them in the context of a Christology which articulates the gift and demands of God's rule. To reduce this to a moral code, even a Christian moral code, would change its context and so its texture.

It is perhaps ironic that a protest against New Testament theology being reduced to history has spoken mainly about history and the history of the tradition. History can become a vehicle for speaking of God only when the interpreter identifies with the witness of the text, as happens in much Christian reading of scripture. What theology learns from the past, both positively and negatively, constructively and critically, is indispensable, but the imagination and the will which are engaged when speaking of God take believers beyond the limits of historical reason and into the realms of art and literature. To speak of God is to speak of beauty, as well as of goodness and truth, however controverted all three are in an age that is rightly suspicious of extravagant claims. Renewed attention to the rhetoric of the New Testament has therefore become important for New Testament theology. Experience confirms that it is the persuasive power of the language which makes the Sermon on the Mount and the epistles of Paul such potent vehicles of God's word, more than their theological or moral argumentation, and much more than dead historical information. The exhortation to let the dead bury their own dead scarcely applies to New Testament theologians as they rightly insist on the necessity of historical criticism. But it may contain a warning to any of us tempted to go no further than criticism—unlike our honorand who has recently written a book about the resurrection people that he himself exemplifies, earning the admiration, affection and gratitude of his students, friends and colleagues.

ELIJAH WITH MOSES, OR, A RIFT IN THE PRE-MARKAN LUTE[1]

Michael Goulder

For about a decade I have been pressing the case that his early followers saw Jesus as a prophet. In "The Pre-Markan Gospel"[2] I noted
that, while Mark himself saw Jesus as the Son of God, his Gospel
contained a wealth of incidents in which Jesus behaved like Elijah
or Elisha. Later, in *A Tale of Two Missions*[3] and "A Poor Man's
Christology",[4] I drew attention to the number of passages where he
acts like Moses, fulfilling the prophecy of the "prophet like Moses"
of Deut 18:15, 18, cited at Acts 3:22f.; 7:37. In this essay I point
to a fact which has been staring me in the face, but which I con-
trived to ignore: all the Elijah-Elisha incidents are in Mark 1–8, and
all the Moses incidents are in Mark 9–13. This neat division is significant, and susceptible of an interesting explanation.

The tracing of allusions, whether to Elijah and his successor or
to Moses, is a delicate business; for our concern is not just with
Mark but with the tradition which he received. Our primary evidence must be similarities with the Markan narrative: but it seems
proper to include two further elements in our assessment, each with
due circumspection. First, there are three other evangelists who are
more remote heirs of the same tradition and whose wording may
sometimes give us a pointer to thinking in the Church of Mark's
generation. Second, all arguments of this kind are cumulative: the
more we find with confidence, the more confident we become of
less clear instances. But cumulative structures may easily be houses
of cards; and by importing non-Markan evidence we risk reading in
Matthean or Lukan perspectives.

---

[1] It is an honour to be asked to contribute to the present volume. David Catchpole
has been a friend for more than twenty years, the kindest and most courteous of
colleagues. All too often we have been sparring partners over Q, but I could not
have wished for a fairer or more straightforward opponent.
[2] *SJT* 47 (1994) 453–472. The article was a revised version of a paper given to
the Pre-Synoptic Seminar of SNTS at Bethel in July 1991.
[3] *A Tale of Two Missions* (SCM: London, 1994) 132.
[4] *NTS* 45 (1999) 348.

Elijah – Elisha

Mark saw John the Baptist as Elijah, the ninth century prophet who had been taken alive to heaven (4 Kgms 2:11), and whose return was prophesied in Mal 3:22. He says, "As it is written in Isaiah the prophet, ἰδοὺ ἀποστέλλω τὸν ἄγγελόν μου πρὸ προσώπου σου, ὃς κατασκευάσει τὴν ὁδόν σου· . . . John came baptizing" (1:2, 4). It is Mark 1:3 which actually cites Isaiah, and the reference in 1:2 is primarily to Malachi: ἰδοὺ ἐγὼ ἐξαποστέλλω τὸν ἄγγελόν μου καὶ ἐπιβλέψεται ὁδὸν πρὸ προσώπου μου (3:1). John is found wearing the same clothes as Elijah had in his last days, like a prisoner coming out of gaol: ζώνην δερματίνην περιεζωσμένος τὴν ὀσφὺν αὐτοῦ (4 Kgms 1:8), cf. Mark 1:6, ζώνην δερματίνην περὶ τὴν ὀσφὺν αὐτοῦ. In Mark 9:11–13 Jesus virtually seals the identification. The disciples ask why the scribes say that Elijah must come first, before Jesus' resurrection. He replies, "Elijah indeed comes first and restores everything (ἀποκαθιστάνει πάντα) . . . But 1 say to you that Elijah has come indeed, and they did to him what they would, as it is written of him." Mal 3:22–3 said, "ἰδοὺ ἐγὼ ἀποστέλλω ὑμῖν Ηλιαν . . . ὃς ἀποκαταστήσει the heart of the father to the son . . ."

The identification seems clear: John was the Elijah of Malachi's prophecy. But what passage of scripture is in Mark's mind when he says, "as it is written of him"? "They" did to John what they would by murdering him, as Mark tells in 6:14–29; and the tale of his death there bears a family likeness to Elijah's fate in 3 Kgms 19. Then there was a weak king Ahab hen-pecked by a vengeful wife Jezebel, just as now the weak king Herod is manipulated by his vindictive wife Herodias. Both women have their knife into the man of God, and Elijah says, "I, even I, only am left; and they seek my life to take it away". Jezebel and her spouse "would" (ἤθελον) kill Elijah; it was not until his second life-chapter that their successors carried wish into action.[5]

The link is instructive, for it shows us both Mark's familiarity with the Elijah stories and also his expectation that his audience will pick up unstressed references. There is only one element in the Jesus nar-

---

[5] So J. Gnilka, *Das Evangelium nach Markus* I (1989), 249. Markus Öhler, *Elia im Neuen Testament* (1997), 45–6, prefers a general reference to the tradition of prophetic suffering; but the wording, "they did to him whatever they wished", seems rather specific.

rative which can be shown on verbal evidence to be a "fulfilment" of 3–4 Kgms, but there are a number of family likenesses, like the Jezebel-Ahab/Herodias-Herod likeness.

In 4 Kgms 4:42–4 "a man passed through from Baithsarisa and brought the man of God twenty barley loaves of the firstfruits and cakes; and [Elisaie] said, δότε τῷ λαῷ καὶ ἐσθιέτωσαν. And his servant said, Why should I give this before a hundred men? And he said, δὸς τῷ λαῷ καὶ ἐσθιέτωσαν, for the Lord says this, They shall eat and shall leave surplus (καταλείψουσιν). And they ate and left according to the word of the Lord."

There are two familiar parallel stories in Mark. In 6:30–44 there are large hungry crowds, five thousands, and the disciples urge Jesus to dismiss them. He says, Δότε αὐτοῖς ὑμεῖς φαγεῖν. They ask, Are we to go and buy 200 dinars of bread? But Jesus takes the five loaves they have, and the crowd ate (ἔφαγον), with twelve basketfuls of surplus. In 8:1–10 we have the similar feeding of the four thousand. The wording is less close to 4 Kgms, but the story runs in the same way: the disciples' scepticism, Jesus' confidence, the feeding of many with seven loaves, the surplus at the end.

The stories treat Jesus as a kind of Elisha *redivivus*: we may leave aside the riddle of there being two of them, and the differences of the numbers. It is true that Elijah also performs a feeding miracle with the widow of Zarephath (3 Kgms 17:13–17), but the two Gospel stories are much closer to making Jesus a new Elisha. Mark is aware of such a view, and is resistant to it. At 6:15 he records that "Others were saying that [Jesus] was Elijah; and others that he was a prophet like one of the prophets"; and at 8:28 he has the disciples report exactly the same two speculations. Stories like the two feedings carry with them suggestions of just such a prophetic Christology.[6]

In the same chapter, in 4 Kgms 4:8–37, Elisha performs a signal miracle by raising a dead boy to life; and again there is a parallel in Elijah's raising of the widow's son in 3 Kgms 17. Mark tells a

---

[6] Morna Hooker, *The Gospel according to St Mark* (1991), 164, notes the 2 Kings 4 parallel but says: "the most important background . . . is the story of God's provision of manna for Israel in the wilderness". She justifies this comment by reference to rabbinic expositions of Exod 16; but Mark's story raises hardly any echo with the manna narratives (they also took place in the desert). Her reference to John 6 is ironic in that John inserts the detail that the five loaves were of barley bread. Gnilka I, 262f., goes with the grain of the story: "Die Mose- bzw. Manna-typologie konnten wir nicht ermitteln, dafür aber die Vorgabe der Geschenkwunder der Elija-Elischa-Tradition, insbesondere 2Kön 4,42–44"—cf. also p. 257.

similar story in the raising of Jairus' daughter (5:21–43), but the detail is closer to the Elisha narrative. There the mother comes to request the prophet's help, as the father does with Jesus. Gehazi is sent ahead, but reports that the child has not awakened, just as Jesus says, "The girl is not dead but asleep". Elisha puts the family away and goes in to treat the child alone, as Jesus excludes the mourners. None of these features applies in the Elijah story: Jesus is behaving like a new Elisha.[7]

The parallel is sufficiently striking (for these are the only two raisings of dead children in the OT), but there are also traces of 4 Kgms 4 elsewhere in the Gospel tradition. Matt 10:8 says, "Raise the dead", and Luke has an echo of it at Luke 10:4. Elisha told Gehazi to go direct to the house and to exchange no blessings with passers-by (4:29); and so Jesus says, "Greet no one on the way". The raising of the woman of Shunem's son is a familiar text to third generation Christians.

Another element in the same story which recurs in the Gospels is the expectation of hospitality for a man of God. The Shunamite woman furnishes a prophet's chamber where he may stay regularly, and she provides for him. Perhaps this has also been influential: the disciples are told to take no provisions with them on mission, and whatever house receives them, there they are to stay, and not move from house to house (Mark 6:8–11).

Although Mark 5 is closer to the Elisha raising story, there are reminiscences of the Elijah parallel in Mark 7. Elijah went from the land of Israel to "Sarepta in Sidon" (3 Kgms 17:9), where the widow feeds him: her son falls ill with "an exceedingly great illness" (17:17), and she requests the prophet to save the child, which he does. In Mark 7:24 Jesus leaves Palestine for the borders of Tyre, and at 7:31 passes through Sidon. In the meantime he is approached by a Syro-Phoenician woman requesting him to expel a demon from her daughter, which he does. The reminiscence is striking, being the only occasions in the Gospels and in the OT where a healing is reported of a Gentile outside the land of Israel.[8] Luke comments, "there were

---

[7] Robert A. Guelich, *Mark 1–8:20* (1989) 344, makes so bold as to suggest that "Mark most likely found this story as a sequel to the raising of Jairus' daughter in a miracle collection . . . the two stories draw special parallels between Jesus' ministry and that of Elijah/Elisha". The feeding follows the raising directly in 4 Kgms 4: the order is reversed in 3 Kgms 17. But so slight a sequence is probably coincidental.

[8] Gnilka I, 291f.; K. Kertelge, *Die Wunder im Markusevamgelium* (1970) 152.

many widows in Israel in the time of Elijah . . . yet Elijah was sent to none of them, but to a widow at Sarepta in Sidon" (Luke 4:25–6).

Elijah's powers are also testified in 4 Kgms 1. King Ahaziah has fallen from an upper-story window, and sends to enquire of Baal-zebub the god of Ekron whether he will recover. Elijah intercepts three successive delegations, and pronounces a sentence of death on the king because he has not relied on the God of Israel but on this Lord-of-the-flies/dung. In Mark 3:22 scribes from Jerusalem say that Jesus "has Beelzebul/Beelzebub, and is expelling demons through the prince of demons". There is no known Jewish text in which Beelzebul/Beelzebub is the name of a demonic spirit. It is difficult therefore not to see some link with the Elijah story. The old Syriac and Vulgate MSS of Mark read Beelzebub: the LXX reads Βααλ μυιῶν in 4 Kgms 1. We may think that in a pre-Markan phase Jesus had been accused of exorcism by demonic power, and this had then been aligned with the Elianic alternative, the God of Israel or Baal-zebub. The further comments on the divided house (Heb זבל) could then have suggested a change to Beelzebul.[9]

With such a concentration of echoes, it is difficult to know where to draw the line. In Mark 1:12–13 Jesus goes into "the desert for forty days, being tempted by Satan; and he was with the wild beasts, and the angels ministered to him". It is often thought that Mark has Adam in mind: he was tempted by the serpent, later called Satan, and the animals were with him and subject to him. On the other hand there does not seem to be much other Adam symbolism in Mark; Genesis does not use the word "tempted" (nor the name Satan); and the desert, and the forty days, and the ministering angels are not in Gen 2–3.[10] But in 3 Kgms 19:4–8 Elijah is forced to flee from Jezebel: he goes in the desert (ἐν τῇ ἐρήμῳ) a day's journey, and the angel of the Lord tells him to get up and eat, and he goes in the strength of that food forty days. A little earlier he was fed by the ravens, which suggests good relations with the wild creatures.

---

[9] Dieter Lührmann, *Das Markusevangelium* (1987), 75 says: "Der Name Beelzebul kann also dem Leser schon den Hinweis auf 2Kön 1,1–17 assoziieren: Wogegen Elia eingeschritten war, das geschehe—so der Vorwurf der Schriftgelehrten—auch bei Jesus, ein wahrhaft 'schriftgelehrter' Einwand!"

[10] Later traditions can help the Adam image. The serpent is identified with Satan from Wisd 2:24; the animals are on speaking terms with Eve in *Vita Ad* 37–39 (though one of them bites Seth); angels feed Adam and Eve in *b. Sanh* 59b. For a critique see Robert H. Gundry, *Mark* (1993) 58f.

Elijah was not tempted; but then Mark does not seem to regard Jesus' temptation as important—it is not specified, nor is he said to have overcome it.

In Mark 1:16–20 Jesus calls his first disciples, four fishermen from their boats and nets. Elijah also called his first disciple, Elisha, from his work as he was ploughing (3 Kgms 19:19–21). The link in Mark is too frail to carry the weight of an argument. But it is not many years before it is clear that the Church read 3 Kgms 19 as the paradigm of Jesus' call to discipleship. Elisha asked first to kiss his father farewell, and received a dusty answer: in Matt 8:21 (cf. Luke 9:59–60) a disciple asks first to go and bury his father, and is told, "Leave the dead to bury their dead".[11] At Luke 9:62 a similar hesitant aspirer is told, "No one putting his hand to the plough and turning back is fit for the kingdom of God". So it is quite likely that Mark's tradition too saw the call of Elisha as the model for the call of Jesus' four first followers.

I may mention finally Jesus' cleansing of a leper (Mark 1:40–45). There are two such cleansings in the OT: of Miriam in Num 12, and of Naaman in 4 Kgms 5. But the resemblance to Num 12 ends there: Miriam is a woman, and God is punishing her, first with the leprosy and then with seven days exclusion from the camp. Naaman on the other hand is a man, and he comes to Elisha with a confident petition for cleansing, like Jesus' leper with his "Lord, if thou wilt . . ." Again the text is not close enough to give a clear judgement; but Matthew suggests that the association was familiar in the 70s. He has Jesus bid the Twelve, "raise the dead, cleanse the lepers . . ." (10:8). The anticlimactic sequence follows the order of 4 Kgms: 4 Kgms 4 the raising of the dead child; 4 Kgms 5 the cleansing of Naaman. At Matt 9:36, just before, Jesus has pity on the crowds, scattered as sheep not having a shepherd, like the Israelites in 3 Kgms 22:17; and in Matt 10:11–17 follow instructions reminiscent of Elisha's arrangements at Shunem. The Church saw Naaman's cleansing as a foreshadowing of Jesus' leper.

So much evidence must incline us to think that behind Mark 1–8 stands a Christology quite different from the one which Mark held himself. To him Jesus was the Son of God (1:1,11; 3:11; 5:7; 14:62;

---

[11] If David had been right about Q, here would have been evidence of a pre-Markan use of the Elijah typology!

15:39): but to Jewish Christians, both those of the Pseudo-Clementine tradition and those later condemned as Ebionites,[12] Jesus was a prophet, possessed by the Spirit from his baptism till his passion. The picture underlying Mark 1–8 is that of "Elijah, or one of the prophets" which Mark himself rejects. Perhaps it was even noticed that in 4 Kgms 2:9 Elisha asked Elijah at the Jordan for a double portion of his spirit, and this was granted as he saw heaven opened and the divine chariot and horses. Jesus' career then develops as an apparent fulfilment of the two great wonder-working prophets: forty days with the angels and animals in the desert, calling his first disciple from his work, healing a leper, exorcising in the power of God and not Beelzebub, raising a dead child to life, expecting bed and board for a man of God, feeding thousands with a few loaves, responding to a parent's request for a sick child in the Gentile Sidon area. Even if all these parallels are not in the mind of early Christians, surely enough are to make the picture plausible.

What then may we think was the development of ideas? It is likely that John the Baptist saw himself as the prophesied Elijah: he was baptizing, and those accepting his baptism were thereby to escape the great and terrible day of the Lord. But with his execution there came no Day of Judgement, and his mission was taken over by Jesus, his most charismatic follower. At first perhaps the movement asked, If John was Elijah, who is Jesus?; and so tales were told of him assimilated to the Elisha stories. But with time John became a memory, and Jesus took on the colours of both figures. Mark does not like this: to him John was Elijah all right, but Jesus is the Son of God. Only the stories he tells give the background Christology away.

The Elijah/Elisha-type stories finish at Mark 8: the Transfiguration story in Mark 9 may recall distantly the mountain visions of 4 Kgms 2 and 6, but the verbal echoes are with Moses. Elijah is mentioned twice again in Mark: once in Mark 9:11–13, the passage on John as Elijah discussed above; and the other the mysterious comment at the crucifixion, "See, he is calling Elijah!" (15:35). But of stories recalling the exploits of Elijah and Elisha there is an end.

---

[12] Irenaeus, *A.H.* 1.26.1–2; expounded in my "A Poor Man's Christology".

Moses

Jewish expectations were focused not so much on "one of the prophets", or Elijah, as on "the prophet" (John 1:21).[13] These hopes were based on Deut 18:15, "A prophet from among your brethren like me shall the Lord your God raise up for you: to him you shall hearken (αὐτοῦ ἀκούσεσθε)". This text (and the similar 18:18) were familiar to early Christian preachers; Luke sets them in the mouths of both Peter (Acts 3:22–3) and Stephen (7:37).

Mark 9:2–8 describes the Transfiguration. Peter, James and John see Jesus transformed in glory, and "Elijah with Moses" talking with him. The divine voice says to them, "This is my beloved Son: hearken to him (ἀκούετε αὐτοῦ)". This happens "after six days", when Jesus took his three named disciples into a high mountain apart; rather as Moses took Aaron, Nadab and Abihu with him, along with other unnamed elders, apart up Mount Sinai, and the glory of the Lord settled as a cloud on the mountain for six days (Exod 24:1,15–16). In Mark Peter proposes to make three tabernacles, as the cloud appears overshadowing (ἐπισκιάζουσα) the scene; in Exod 40 Moses completes the Tabernacle, and the divine glory-cloud overshadows it (ἐπεσκίασεν, 40:35).

So many Mosaic details—the six days, the mountain, the three named disciples, the tabernacles, the glory-cloud, the overshadowing, the command to hearken—make clear that behind Mark stands a tradition maintaining that Jesus was the promised prophet like Moses. Mark has touched it up, intruding "my beloved Son", as at 1:11, in place of "This is the prophet [like Moses]". Elijah does not belong in the picture. He is inserted clumsily, Ἡλίας σὺν Μωϋσεῖ, which soon reverts to the normal sequence, "one for Moses and one for Elijah". With so much Elijah-type material behind him, Mark is linking it on to his Moses-type material.

In Mark 9:14–29 Jesus and his three followers go down the mountain to a sad spectacle: a crowd mills about a boy stricken with a dumb spirit, which the other disciples have been unable to expel. There is a reminiscence of the scene in Exod 32 when Moses and Joshua come down from the glory-cloud on Sinai to a similar scene of faithlessness with the people carried away. This is one of many

---

[13] Oscar Cullmann, *The Christology of the New Testament* (1959) 13–50.

occasions when Moses was driven to despair. On his deathbed he would say, "It is a perverse generation (γενεὰ ἐξεστραμμένη), sons in whom there is no faithfulness (πίστις) (Deut 32:20 LXX); and on another occasion, "How long (ἕως τίνος) shall I suffer this wicked assembly?" (Num 14:27). Jesus comments, Ὦ γενεὰ ἄπιστος, ἕως πότε πρὸς ὑμᾶς ἔσομαι;[14] Both Matthew and Luke adapt this to Ὦ γενεὰ ἄπιστος καὶ διεστραμμένη (Matt 17:17; Luke 9:41) to bring Jesus into line with Moses at Deut 32:5, γενεὰ σκολιὰ καὶ διεστραμμένη.

In Mark 9:38–41 John tells Jesus of an exorcist using his name, and that the disciples had stopped him (ἐκωλύομεν) as an interloper: Jesus countermands this (μὴ κωλύετε αὐτόν), for he who is not against him is for him. The story recalls the scene in Num 11:24–30.[15] The spirit of the Lord has fallen not only on the seventy elders round the tent but also on Eldad and Medad, who were elsewhere. Joshua says, "My lord Moses, stop them (κώλυσον αὐτούς)", but Moses declines, wishing that the same gift of prophecy might befall all the Lord's people.

In Mark 10:1–12 Pharisees ask Jesus if divorce is permissible. Jesus first appeals to Moses, and they reply that Moses sanctioned divorce, citing Deut 24:1, 3. But Jesus uses Moses to transcend Moses. To him marriage is a yoking together by God, and remarriage is legalised adultery. Moses did indeed permit divorce, but only for the hardness of Israel's heart: in Gen 1:27; 2:24 he laid down the fundamental principle whereby in marriage man and woman become one flesh, and it is this which settles the matter. So here for the first time Jesus appears as the prophet like Moses, not overriding but transcending his predecessor, legislating for the people of God with divine authority.

A second instance of this follows in Mark 10:17–31. A rich man asks Jesus what he should do to inherit eternal life. As over divorce, Jesus asks in return what commandments had been given in the Torah; and the reply lists a part of the Decalogue (Deut 5:16–20). All this the man had done from his youth. "You are missing one thing", says Jesus, "Go, sell all you have, and give to the poor". So Jesus is again the prophet like Moses, not destroying but fulfilling the [spirit of] the Law. When Matthew has set out the "fulfilment"

---

[14] Gnilka II, 47.
[15] Gnilka II, 61.

of the second table of the Decalogue in Matt 5, he has Jesus in Matt 6 bid all his followers similarly to lay up treasures in heaven.

Mark returns to Mosaic paradigms in Mark 12, where there is a series of controversies. Sadducees come to question Jesus' belief in the resurrection (12:18–27). They cite Moses' law on levirate marriage (Deut 25:5), and tell a story intended to show an implied contradiction. Jesus silences their mockery by denying any marriage relations hereafter; and once more quotes a further word of Moses, "I am the God of Abraham . . ." (Exod 3:6), to justify his doctrine. The prophet like Moses knows his master's teaching in depth, and can always produce the telling counter which puts the enemy to flight.

In the following pericope (12:28–34), a friendly scribe asks which is the first commandment in the Torah. Jesus replies citing a combination of Deut 6:4–5 and Lev 19:18; as the man is not trying to trap him, he feels free to give the answer direct. The profundity of Jesus' response draws the man's admiration—this is surely right. After that there were no more questions. Jesus has shown himself to be the prophet like Moses, able time after time to see resolutions to any difficulties, and to draw the heart of his predecessor's teaching into new and clear rulings for the Church.

Perhaps we should add a final example from Mark 13. When the initial birthpangs are done, and the abomination has taken its stand, and the Great Tribulation is over, and the signs in heaven are past, the Son of Man will come and gather (ἐπισυνάξει) his elect from the end of the earth to the end of heaven (ἀπ᾽ ἄκρου γῆς ἕως ἄκρου οὐρανοῦ, 13:27). In similar vein Moses promised, "If your diaspora should be from the end of heaven to the end of heaven (ἀπ᾽ ἄκρου τοῦ οὐρανοῦ ἕως ἄκρου τοῦ οὐρανοῦ), the Lord your God will gather you" (συνάξει, Deut 30:4). We may think that here also the prophet like Moses is at work. Moses foresaw the gathering of Israel from the four quarters of the world in the long hoped-for return: his successor foresees the ultimate gathering of the elect at the παρουσία.

Thus from Mark 9 to Mark 13 we seem to have a sequence of incidents recalling the Moses tradition: like the Tannaitic midrashim, they run from Sinai to the end of Deuteronomy. We may wonder whether there are any such stories in Mark 2–8. Perhaps we should think of two: the sabbath stories in 2:23–3:6 and the traditions of the elders in 7:1–23. But the feel of these stories is different: they are there to justify the Pauline churches' laxity over sabbath and their rejection of the oral Torah—Jesus is not so much a prophet like Moses as an objector to legalistic bondage. He does not use Moses to transcend Moses, and there is no incident where he behaves like Moses, as in the three stories in Mark 9.

A Rift in the Pre-Markan Lute?

So sharp a division challenges us for an explanation. Our first instinct should be to look to Mark himself: can we think of any reason why he might have decided to corral all the Elijah/Elisha type stories into his first eight chapters, and all (or almost all) his Moses type incidents in chapters 9–13? We might think that this arrangement gave a happy climax, but that can hardly be an adequate answer. Mark himself rejected any prophet-like-Moses Christology: to him Jesus was the Son of God who "came"—he is a Pauline incarnationalist. Furthermore he did not think that Jesus was Elijah: that was John the Baptist. So we are forced to push the question back to the pre-Markan period: can we think of any explanation for the growth of two independent complexes, each with a prophetic Christology, one like Elijah/Elisha and the other like Moses?

There is a second feature of the Markan Gospel's division at 9:1 which may be relevant. In Mark 1–8 *in general* the disciples are heroes. Peter, James and John leave their nets and their families, and follow Jesus at his word. Jesus goes to Simon's house and heals his mother-in-law. Simon and his friends find Jesus alone and accompany him on a preaching tour. He supports their behaviour in not fasting, and in plucking the corn. He chooses the Twelve and gives surnames to Peter and the Zebedaids. It is to those about him with the Twelve that Jesus entrusts the mystery of the kingdom. He takes Peter, James and John into Jairus's house to witness the raising of his daughter. He sends the Twelve out on mission, and they cast out demons and heal many sick people. The disciples go with him to Caesarea Philippi, and Peter makes the great confession, "You are the Christ".

It is true that there is a down side to this general picture. The disciples are sometimes a foil to their master: without faith in the storm, not expecting any miraculous feeding, distressed and astonished at the walking on the water, not understanding about the loaves. Nor is Peter without fault in 8:31–3: he dares to rebuke Jesus, and is called Satan for his pains. Nevertheless the overall impression left by Mark 1–8 is that the disciples, and in particular Peter, James and John, are not unworthy to be the Lord's followers, and in due course the leaders of his Church.[16] Their faults are venial faults, and may be read largely as throwing Jesus' faith and power into higher relief.

There is no such sympathy in these chapters for Jesus' family. They (οἱ παρ' αὐτοῦ) hear of his success and go out to lay hands on him, for they said, "He is out of his mind" (3:21). They stand outside when he is preaching, calling him away from his vocation; and he says that those sitting round him, those who do God's will, are his true brother and sister and mother (3:31–5). It is they who are spoken of in 4:11–12 as those who are outside, and whose fate is to look and not see, to hear and not understand.[17] Jesus' message is not heard at Nazareth, and he says, "A prophet is not without honour except in his home country and among his relatives and in his house" (6:4). Jesus' relatives, and those in his house, are his family.

There are no more anti-family incidents in 9–13, but on the other hand the image of the disciples is markedly worse. They are terrified at the transfiguration, and Peter makes a silly remark. They discuss among themselves what the resurrection from the dead is. They are unable to cast out the dumb spirit through not having prayed. They discuss which of them is the greatest. John tries to stop a man exorcising in Jesus' name. They try to turn away children from being blessed by him. Peter wants his reward for having followed Jesus, and James and John want the seats next to him in heaven. They are amazed and frightened as they near Jerusalem. Mark 9–10 give a sustained picture of the disciples, and especially of Peter, James and John, as bone-headed, self-interested and unspiritual. If we include Mark 14, they are overconfident, uncommitted and cowardly as well. We did not get this impression in Mark 1–8, even if their faith occasionally trembled, especially in boats.[18]

---

[16] The much more hostile attitude to the Twelve in later chapters must imply that Mark himself was critical of them; and this may account in part for the negative elements in Mark 1–8. Mark was a Pauline, and followers of the Twelve pulled rank too often (1 Cor 1:12; 4:1–8; 2 Cor 11:22).

[17] M.D. Goulder, "Those Outside (Mark 4:10–12)", *NovT* 33 (1991) 289–302.

[18] The image of the Twelve, and especially Peter, James and John, as the heroes of Mark's story, was normal until the 60s. It was breached by J.B. Tyson, "The Blindness of the Disciples in Mark" (1961), and other works such as T.J. Weeden,

These contrasts lie across the same faultline at Mark 9:1 as the Elijah/Elisha and Moses contrast, and they suggest a possible explanation for the latter. There were two groups of Jesus' followers in the very early Church, and back even into his lifetime: the Twelve led one group, and Jesus' family led the other. John 2:12 says that his brothers went down to Capernaum with him, and John 7:1–9 imply that his brothers were in contact with him during his ministry. John is strongly hostile to the brothers (they did not believe in him, and are aligned with "the world", 7:5–6); but despite his antipathy, the contact is clear. The tradition of resurrection appearances in 1 Cor 15:5–7 includes an appearance to James, Jesus' brother, apparently in the first weeks, perhaps days, after Easter. Luke paints a scene of devotion after the Ascension, at which the brothers are present (Acts 1:14).

When Paul goes up to Jerusalem in the middle 30s he meets only two "apostles", Cephas and James (Gal 1:18–19). Fourteen years later James is mentioned first at the "Council" meeting, although the mission to the circumcision is said to have been entrusted to Peter (Gal 2:8–9). Acts 1–12 represents Peter as the leader of the early mission, but according to 12:17 he left James in charge of the Jerusalem church in Herod's time; James seems to take the chair at the Council in Acts 15, and to be in sole authority thereafter (21:17–26). Gal 2:12 suggests that he and Peter were colleagues, but that he had the stronger principles and character.

All this seems to point to a consistent picture. Jesus joined the Baptist's movement, and after his execution became its leader, moving to Capernaum, where Peter and others lived. At first his family were lukewarm, and the Twelve were his community; but with time James and the other brothers were impressed by his success, and joined the movement, at least in its last weeks.[19] We may think therefore that there was a gradual change in the leadership of the metropolitan church: from Peter and the Zebedaids to Jesus' brother James with Peter and John, and finally to Jesus' family only. To the Paulines Peter was a weak, rather friendly character, and Mark and

---

Mark—Traditions in Conflict (1971). But Tyson and Weeden did not note the intensification of the anti-Twelve tendency from Mark 9.

[19] John Painter, *Just James* (1999), has recently argued for a view of James more positive than has been usual. Although he sometimes presses the evidence, he is right in saying that we have too easily swallowed the anti-James propaganda in Mark and John (11–34).

John feel ambivalent about him and the Twelve; but James was a stickler for the Law, and they both have their knife into him and his brothers. Matthew and Luke do their best, in rather different ways, to heal the wound.

It is not unknown for such changes to be resented and resisted, and it is easily believable that two complexes of tradition developed among followers of the two leaderships. Partisans of the Twelve told stories of the Galilean ministry, colouring their accounts of Jesus' wonders with tints from the Elijah/Elisha legends; they represented the Twelve, and in particular the three Pillars, as heroes of the faith, and they did not mind including a few hints that Jesus had had no help from his family. James and Jude had not been around during the Galilee period, though they had joined the movement in its last months, going up to the capital. In any case their interest was in their brother as the prophet like Moses, and they assembled stories which depicted him as such. If the Twelve emerged as less than ideal, well, it was a tradent's duty to present the truth, warts and all; in fact especially the warts, if the Twelve were reluctant to cede the hegemony into the abler hands of the family, Jesus' proper successors.

Such a proposal would account for the structure of Mark's Gospel in several ways. First it would explain the "doublet" relation of the baptism and transfiguration narratives. Both these stories describe a voice from heaven saying, "You are/This is my beloved Son", a parallel noted in every commentary. No doubt Mark has substituted his own Christology, Jesus as Son of God, for what lay in the tradition: but why the duplication? For the Twelve, this was the trigger for Jesus' ministry: it happened at his baptism by John, and the voice is likely to have said, "You are my servant whom I have chosen, in whom I am well pleased" (Isa 42:1; Matt 12:18). For the family it happened later. Jesus had gathered a few companions, and took them, as Moses had, up a mountain: there, with full Mosaic colours, the revelation was made, probably in the form, "This is the prophet [like Moses]: hearken to him". Thus both complexes were able to open with a divine revelation, and Mark has two revelations, one half way through his story.

It is a platitude that Mark consists of three elements: a Galilean ministry leading up to the scene at Caesarea Philippi in 8:27–9:1, and then the Passion, 14–16, preceded by a long introduction, 8:27–13.35. No doubt Mark has made this his own, but we are hardly to think that it is all his own construction. No: it was given him. The Passion story was the oldest element, its incidents being remembered, and later recited, each year at Christian Passover/Easter. But the Passion was but the climax of a longer story. The followers of the Twelve knew the tales of the Galilean ministry, and would tell these with a 1–2 Kings gloss on them; the story ended with Peter's confession, and the party's move to Jerusalem (8:31). The family knew of incidents en route to the capital, and relayed these as proclaiming the Deuteronomic prophet. Maybe individual pericopae, as in chapter 11, were common to both traditions; but in general Mark took the easy option, following first the Galilee-Twelve story and then the Jerusalem road-family story. He took them in blocks, just as Luke took Mark and Matthew in blocks.

A third point is significant. Gal 2:11–14 suggests that it was James who insisted on the Law being observed at Antioch. Both Josephus and Hegesippus speak of James as a pious Jew respected by pious Jews. Josephus says that those most devoted to the Law—i.e. the Pharisees—protested at his execution in 62;[20] and Hegesippus presents him as a pattern of Jewish ascesis.[21] How natural then that the family traditions in Mark 9–13 should picture Jesus as a new Moses! He is not one to revoke the sabbath (Mark 2:23–3:6), or to impugn the tradition of the elders (7:1–23). He always honours the Mosaic legislation, but "fulfils" it, bringing out the profound elements which resolve superficial problems and confound logic choppers. The Jesus of Mark 9–13 would be the natural hero of the Law-observant James.

This is not the first time that a tension has been suspected between Jesus' family and the three leaders of the Twelve. Suspicious minds have been over 1 Cor 15:5–8 with a fine-tooth comb, and have speculated on a double tradition of appearances:

ὤφθη Κηφᾷ	ἔπειτα ὤφθη Ἰακώβῳ
εἶτα τοῖς δώδεκα·,	εἶτα τοῖς ἀποστόλοις πᾶσιν
[ἔπειτα ὤφθη ἐπάνω . . .]	[ἔσχατον δὲ πάντων . . .]

Perhaps there were two appearance traditions, one to Peter and then the Twelve, with a competing one to James and "all the apostles"— that is a rather larger group including Jesus' family. But in time the

---

[20] *Ant.* 20.9.1.
[21] At Eus. *E.H.* 2.23.4–7. According to 23.10–16 leading Jews asked James not to preach Jesus' Messiahship.

two leaderships came to terms, and their lists were combined. Paul's addition of a third element to each list enables him to take his rightful place. Such a suggestion has its plausibility, and may serve to buttress the more impressive case set out above.[22]

When I was invited to take part in this volume to honour David, I was working on a thesis on Rom 1:3–4, and suggested submitting this. The editors pointed out courteously that David and I had shared in work on the synoptic gospels over many years, and that a gospel study would be more suitable. I am fortunate that a new gospel hypothesis occurred to me, if rather at the last minute; and that it fits the volume's title so neatly. For it is about Christology, two forms of the Church's first, prophetic Christology. It is about controversy, for it seems to uncover a controversy between the partisans of the Twelve and those of the family. And it is about community, the Markan community which combined the two and adapted them.

BIBLIOGRAPHY

Cullmann, O., *The Christology of the New Testament* (London: SCM, 1959; German 1957)

Gnilka, J., *Das Evangelium nach Markus* I–II (EKK II/1–2: Zürich, Braunschweig/Neukirchen-Vluyn, Benziger/Neukirchener, ³1989)

Goulder, M.D., "Those Outside (Mark 4:10–12)", *NovT* 33 (1991) 289–302

———, *A Tale of Two Missions* (London: SCM, 1994)

———, "The Pre-Markan Gospel", *SJT* 47 (1994) 453–472

———, "A Poor Man's Christology", *NTS* 45 (1999) 332–348

Guelich, R.A., *Mark 1–8.26* (WBC 34A; Dallas: Word Books, 1989)

Gundry, R.H., *Mark: A Commentary on his Apology for the Cross* (Grand Rapids: Eerdmans, 1993)

Hooker, M.D., *The Gospel according to St Mark* (BNTC; London: Black, 1991)

Kertelge, K., *Die Wunder Jesu im Markusevangelium* (SANT 23; München: Kösel, 1970)

Lührmann, D., *Das Markusevangelium* (HNT 3; Tübingen: Mohr, 1987)

Öhler, M., *Elia im Neuen Testament: Untersuchungen zur Bedeutung des alttestamentlichen Propheten im Neuen Testament* (BZNW 88; Berlin/New York: de Gruyter, 1997)

Painter, J. *Just James: The Brother of Jesus in History and Tradition* (Edinburgh: T. & T. Clark, 1999)

Pratscher, W., *Der Herrenbruder Jakobus und die Jakobustradition* (FRLANT 139; Göttingen: Vandenhoeck & Ruprecht, 1987)

Tyson, J.B., "The Blindness of the Disciples in Mark", *JBL* 80 (1961) 261–8

Weeden, T.J., Mark—Traditions in Conflict (Philadelphia: Fortress, 1971)

---

[22] There is a full discussion in Wilhelm Pratscher, *Der Herrenbruder Jakobus und die Jakobustradition* (1987) 29–46; Pratscher cites a formidable list of scholars who have supported the rivalry hypothesis from von Harnack to Lüdemann, and he accepts it himself.

CHRISTOLOGY, CONTROVERSY AND COMMUNITY IN THE GOSPEL OF JOHN

Marinus de Jonge

The Centrality of Christology in the Fourth Gospel

Christology is without any doubt the main theme of the Fourth Gospel (20:30–31); it is developed in many debates of Jesus with his opponents and in discussions with his disciples. It stresses, repeatedly and in a variety of ways, the uniqueness of the relationship between Jesus as the Son and God as the Father—a theme also highlighted in the Prologue in 1:1–18. There is a particular "Johannine" Christology, characteristic of a specific community (or group of communities) which, to a considerable extent, derives its identity from that Christology. The Johannine Epistles show how this Christology remained the central issue in the life of the community(-ies) and how it became necessary to rethink and redefine it in order to safeguard it against misinterpretation.[1]

In the story told by the Gospel of John "the Jews" play an important part as opponents of Jesus. There are also Jews who sympathize with Jesus (so, for instance, Nicodemus in chapter 3) but who somehow miss the mark. Some Jewish followers of Jesus have an inadequate faith (as in 8:30). A select group of disciples, however, are repeatedly and intensively instructed by him (especially in chapters 13–18). They receive the promise that, after Jesus' return to the Father, they will be guided by the Spirit of Truth. This will remind them of all Jesus has said and lead them to a full understanding of who Jesus is (so, for instance, 14:26; 16:12–15). The Johannine community sees itself in continuity with this group of intimate friends of Jesus, insiders instructed in the true understanding of Jesus' identity,

---

[1] I cannot deal in detail with the problem of the relationship between the Epistles and the Gospel. There certainly is a difference in emphasis, also in Christology. Nevertheless the conflict reflected in 1 and 2 John has left traces in the Gospel in its present form (see n. 17). See my "Variety and Development in Johannine Christology", *Jesus: Stranger from Heaven and Son of God* (SBLSBS 11: Missoula MT: Scholars, 1977).

led by the Spirit, and sent out into a hostile world (15:18–16:4; 20:21–22).

Historical Explanations of the Unity and Variety in Johannine Christology

In recent scholarship different answers have been given to the question whether, and to what extent, the controversies and debates in which Jesus plays a central part reflect controversies and debates taking place between the Johannine community and others in and (particularly) outside the larger group of followers of Jesus. The answers are often related to the problem of the origin of the Fourth Gospel: can we detect various stages in its composition and do these stages in turn reflect decisive events in the history of the community for which it was written? Is it, then, possible to trace different stages in the development of Johannine Christology and to show how the Johannine Christians responded to questions asked and objections raised by in- and outsiders in various circumstances? By way of introduction it may be helpful to mention a number of different approaches to these questions.

M.C. de Boer

A survey of different views on the relation between communal history, composition history and the variety in Johannine Christology is found in Martinus C. de Boer, *Johannine Perspectives on the Death of Jesus*.[2] His own reconstruction of Johannine communal history in his second chapter (pp. 43–82) is most indebted to those of J.L. Martyn[3] and R.E. Brown,[4] two scholars whose views have been very influential in recent scholarship on the Fourth Gospel.

De Boer distinguishes four phases in Johannine history: (1) mission to the Jews ("low" Christology); (2) expulsion from the synagogue (after which a "high" Christology developed); (3) martyrdom for "high" Christology; Gentile converts; contact with other groups; (4) schism (Johannine Epistles) followed by the dissolution of Johannine Christianity. In accordance with this, he distinguishes four perspec-

---

[2] CBET 17; Kampen: Kok-Pharos, 1996.
[3] In *History and Theology in the Fourth Gospel* (Nashville: Abingdon, 1968; 2nd ed. 1979) and *The Gospel of John in Christian History* (New York: Paulist, 1979).
[4] Especially in his *The Community of the Beloved Disciple* (New York: Paulist, 1979).

tives on Jesus' death, connected with at least four distinct editions of the Gospel, each one composed in the Johannine School. He stresses that this seemingly complex but actually simple theory is the result of efforts to account for the evident literary and theological tensions and inconsistencies in this Gospel.

In his "Conclusions" De Boer makes an important additional observation: "It is important to note that the later phases of Johannine history retained the perspectives of earlier ones. . . . Earlier perspectives were not rejected but "recontextualized" by new perspectives. The earlier ones thereby took on new and richer meanings, even if they could not entirely shed the old meanings. Furthermore, "new" perspectives were also presented as "old" truths, as the development of ideas latent in the inherited tradition itself but not previously seen or exploited (for which reason they could be incorporated into the new edition of the Gospel tradition)." On the other hand, De Boer also says that "while Johannine writers 'recontextualized' previous perspectives in rewriting the Gospel under the pressure of changing communal situations, they did not themselves attempt, or at least did not themselves achieve, a synthesis".[5]

Thus, according to De Boer, the Johannine community was able to combine various christological approaches and to incorporate the elements they contributed in a comprehensive, yet not fully integrated perception—and that at the level of the assumed redactions as well as at the level of the Gospel in its present form. His additional observation, however, raises the question whether a presentation of the reconstructed development of Johannine Christology that begins with a supposed stage 1 and works its way down to the Gospel in its present form, will ever give an adequate description of the variegated Christology at the final stage of the Fourth Gospel. Should we not rather work our way backward, starting with the Gospel as it lies before us—as well as looking at the information given by the Johannine letters? Theories of literary development reflecting stages in the history of the community go some way in explaining the tensions in and between the Christological statements in the Gospel. But much remains, of necessity, hypothetical and we may ask whether

---

[5] See pp. 314–15. On "recontextualization" see also the stimulating article by J. Zumstein, "Der Prozess der Relecture in der johanneischen Literatur," *NTS* 42 (1996) 394–411.

there are other ways to explain the genesis of the particular Johannine view on Jesus.

P.N. Anderson

A new attempt has been made recently by P.N. Anderson in his *The Christology of the Fourth Gospel. Its Unity and Disunity in the Light of John 6.*[6] Like everyone he wants to understand the tensions and meanings associated with the unitive and disunitive aspects of Johannine Christology. He is not satisfied with theories of literary development (whether in terms of sources-composition-ecclesiastical redaction [Bultmann] or by assuming different stages of redaction). In the end, however, he assumes two editions of the Gospel by the same author. He also regards reconstructions of the history of the Johannine community as too speculative. He rather makes use of what he terms "cognitive and other related studies pertaining to the origin and character of dialectical thinking."[7]

Of course, Anderson cannot dispense with hypotheses either. He speaks of an "evangelist" rather than a group or a "school"; this person had access to Jesus-tradition that was at least partly different from that preserved in Mark and the other Gospels; he may even have been an eye-witness himself. His Christology should be called conjunctive and dialectical. This person is in constant dialogue with the tradition (Anderson speaks of "a cognitive dialogue" between earlier perceptions and later experiences). He also tries to evoke a believing response from his audience by his linear-progressive and circular-repetitive style, constantly adding correctives responding to developments in the community. He also tells his story in such a way that groups and individuals outside the community may feel addressed. And, finally, he is aware of the dialectical nature of any Christology, and the tensions inherent in any view of Jesus.

I do not think that one can really speak of an individual person responsible for the Gospel or that it is possible to delineate an independent "Johannine way back to Jesus"—let alone that we may assume that the evangelist was an eye-witness. Also Anderson's picture of the process that finally resulted in John 6 in its present form, is at least as complicated and, therefore disputable, as those of his

---

[6] Tübingen: Mohr, 1996/Valley Forge PA: Trinity Press International, 1997.
[7] See p. 253, and, in general, his "Conclusions" on pp. 252–265.

predecessors. His concentration on the final text has, however, to be welcomed, and also his awareness of multiple factors playing a role in the genesis of the Fourth Gospel as we know it.

If we think in terms of a group rather than an individual (as I think we should), that group is bound to have had a complicated and at times stormy history which left its stamp on that community and on the Gospel. It is reasonable to assume that it tried, time and again, to define its views on Jesus by telling and retelling the story of his life on earth. What we have before us in the present Gospel is still concerned with the questions that had to be answered along the way, in debates with several sets of opponents and discussions within the community. It is the product of a community looking back but also looking round, wanting to face the challenges of the day and to come up with formulations relevant for the present situation. What may, indeed, have been discovered and formulated at various stages of the community's search for the truth concerning Jesus' relation to God, continues to play a role, but now as part of the present testimony.

B.W.J. de Ruyter

A third recent approach to the problem under discussion is that by B.W.J. de Ruyter in his doctoral dissertation *De gemeente van de evangelist Johannes: haar polemiek en haar geschiedenis.*[8] After a discussion of some twelve reconstructions of the history of the Johannine community he concludes that the only way to determine the historical situation in which the Fourth Gospel originated is to analyze its Christology. John's emphasis on the unity of the Son and the Father is the corollary of the belief that the Son of man, as eschatological judge and descendant of God, had already come in the earthly Jesus. The implications of this belief are spelled out in numerous discussions with all sorts of opponents. In all forms and at all levels this points to a fierce polemic between the Johannine community and other Christian circles from which it has become separated. De Ruyter is very radical in his conclusions: "The only polemic in which the writer of the Gospel is engaged is that against the Christians of inadequate faith." And: "From John's perspective the rejection of

---

[8] *The Community of John the Evangelist: Its Polemic and Its History* (Delft: Eburon, 1998)—defended in the University of Leiden on 9.9.1998. Supervisor: Professor Henk Jan de Jonge. For a summary in English, see pp. 198–203.

the unity of Jesus and God places his Christian opponents on equal
footing with the adversaries of Jesus who rejected Jesus during his
public ministry."[9] For that reason, and for no other one, those in
opposition to Jesus in the Gospel are portrayed as "the Jews", "the
Pharisees" etc. Of course, the situation for which the Fourth Gospel
was written presupposes earlier stages: separation from the synagogue, the formation of Christian communities with Jewish and
Gentile members and the coming into being of a radical group experiencing a realized eschatology, but none of these stages is of real
importance for the central argument of the Gospel. The only situation that can still be traced with certainty is that of a radical defensive polemic after the separation of the Johannine communities from
mainstream Christianity (alluded to as excommunication in John 9).

De Ruyter analyses the present form of the Gospel, and concentrates on an explanation of its Christology. He does not discuss the
Johannine Epistles, because he is of the opinion (wrongly, I think)
that the disputes described there belong to a later stage in the history of Johannine Christianity. Neither the earlier history nor later
developments really matter. De Ruyter's concentration (and his caution) are to be commended, but the result is a two-dimensional rather
than a three-dimensional picture of Johannine Christology. It is quite
possible that elements used earlier in debates with Jewish opponents
were taken up in later inner-Christian polemic, but we can no longer
trace the connection. He does not explain why John's picture of
Jesus' debates and discussions is so complex, and why so many different figures appear on the scene—not only Jewish followers of Jesus
who fail to meet Johannine standards, but also various sympathizing Jews and, most often, Jewish leaders and Pharisees. Also, the
Jewish leaders present Jewish objections to Jesus, not Christian ones.
Are all these different persons puppets in the hands of the evangelist just to bring home one thing, the inadequacy of the faith of
Christians not belonging to the Johannine group? The position
defended in this dissertation seems to be too extreme.

The Basic Question

The present study takes its starting point in the Gospel as it lies
before us. It uses Jewish terms commonly employed in early Christian

---

[9] See p. 201.

statements about Jesus (as Christ, Son of God and Son of man), but explains and develops them in a process of elaboration and radicalisation. In this process an important role is assigned to controversies with Jewish opponents, discussions with sympathizers who, in the end, prove to be outsiders, and to "Lehrgespräche" between the Johannine Jesus and his disciples (the insiders). The result is a specific, very characteristic Johannine Christology of a community that sees itself as standing in the tradition of the disciples in the Gospel.

The question is why the author(s) of the Gospel chose to develop his (their) particular, radical Christology by means of a number of different stories of interchanges of Jesus with all these people. In that connection one will ask whether these stories reflect in any way the situation(s) in which the Johannine community found itself at the end of the first century CE.

Given the scope of the present essay, I shall concentrate on a number of central issues, illustrating them with some examples.[10]

The Central Christological Issue: Jesus, the Son sent by the Father as his Final Envoy

What does the Fourth Gospel say about Jesus as the Christ, the Son of God, the Son of man—three very important designations in the first three Gospels and (with the exception of Son of man) also in early Christianity in general? In passing we shall also have to look at the terms "king" and "prophet". We shall discover that for "John" (if we may use this designation for the sake of convenience) the right interpretation of all these designations hinges upon a proper assessment of Jesus' words and actions. Jesus reveals his true identity in

---

[10] All along I have used considerations put forward in the essays collected in my *Jesus: Stranger from Heaven and Son of God*, and in some later studies; they are listed in the bibliography at the end of this essay. (See also the more detailed exegesis in my recent commentary [in Dutch] *Johannes. Een praktische bijbelverklaring* (Kampen: Kok, 1996.)

As will become evident, the present essay takes one step further on the way chosen in my "Jewish Expectations about the 'Messiah' according to the Fourth Gospel," *Jesus: Stranger from Heaven*, 77–116. There I emphasized that Johannine Christology is developed not only in contrast with Jewish thinking but also with other Christological views. I also stated there that the Fourth Gospel gives theological reflection on the real issues in the debate between Christians and Jews than provide arguments in an acute struggle (pp. 99–100).

I thank M.C. de Boer, H.J. de Jonge and B.W.J. de Ruyter for criticizing an earlier version of this paper and helping me to express myself more adequately.

these words and actions, but only those to whom it is given are able
to know who he is; they are the true children of God (1:10–13;
3:3–4). In the Gospel they are represented by an inner circle of disciples (6:67–71); these often do not fully understand what they hear
and see (2:22; 12:16, cf. 20:9) but, after Jesus' departure, they are
allowed to regard his words and his works in the proper perspective—thanks to the guidance of the Spirit of Truth. Jesus' discussions with his disciples before his death in chapters 13–17 occupy a
pivotal place in the Gospel. The Spirit "will teach you everything,
and remind you of all that I said to you" (14:26). He will even dis-
close the many things Jesus could not say to them during his life,
because they could not bear them (16:12–15).

   John takes his readers on a voyage of discovery during which they
meet many people reacting to Jesus, as well as Jesus himself reacting to them. The readers will do well to note who says what, and
in what sense particular terms are used. They will also have to bear
in mind that not everything can be made clear in one story, and
that only gradually Jesus' true identity is disclosed. And, just as the
disciples in the Gospel, the readers can only grasp who Jesus is in
the light of the completion of his mission on earth. Finally: at the
end of their journey they will do well to retrace their steps. The
Fourth Gospel has to be read time and again, in a continuous process
of discovery.

Jesus as the Christ

For John Jesus is the Christ. The common expression "Jesus Christ"
is found in 1:17; 17:3 (there with the addition "whom you have
sent"). The "first ending" of the book (20:30–31) stipulates explicitly that it was written "so that you may believe that Jesus is the
Christ, the Son of God." The signs that Jesus performed in the presence of his disciples, and to which they testified, have been recorded
to warrant this. One should note the combination ὁ χριστός—ὁ υἱὸς
τοῦ θεοῦ, also found in Martha's exemplary confession "I believe
that you are the Christ, the Son of God, the one coming into the
world" (11:27). These two designations belong together, and the second helps to determine the meaning of the first (cf. also Mark
14:61–62).

   For John ὁ χριστός is a term that plays a significant role in Jewish
(and Samaritan) expectation. It is one of the terms used by Jewish

emissaries when they ask John the Baptist who he is.[11] He denies being the Christ (1:19–28 and, particularly, 3:28). In Johannine perspective he himself "was not the light, but he came to testify to the light" (1:8). He declares: "I myself have seen and have testified that this is the Son of God" (1:34).

Andrew, one of Jesus' first two disciples, tells his brother Simon: "We have found τὸν Μεσσίαν (1:41); the author adds "which is translated Anointed (χριστόν)." Only here, and in 4:25 in the context of Samaritan expectations fulfilled by Jesus (see also 4:19, 29, 42), is the transliterated Aramaic term used. The statement in 1:41 is followed by "We have found him about whom Moses and the prophets wrote" in 1:45 and "You are the Son of God! You are the king of Israel" in 1:49. These disciples are right, but they have only just begun their journey of discovery. The section ends with words of Jesus about "greater things than these" yet to be seen (v. 50), and about an open heaven and "angels of God ascending and descending upon the Son of man" (v. 51).

In the Fourth Gospel ὁ χριστός is an important term in Jewish expectation, which has been taken over and applied to Jesus by Jesus' followers right from the beginning. The use of this term for Jesus marks the dividing line with "the Jews" (see the comment "for the Jews had already agreed that anyone who confessed Jesus as the Christ would be put out of the synagogue" in 9:22). For this reason it is very important that Christians realize what they mean when they maintain that Jesus is the Christ.

To this purpose chapter 7 portrays Jesus as reacting to a number of statements by Jews about the coming of the Christ (7:27, 31, 41–42, cf. 12:34). These statements are clearly considered representative, but they are formulated in such a way that Jesus is able to indicate what is specific for Christian belief. I cannot go into detail here, but central is the notion that Jesus does not speak and act on his own. His teaching is that of the One who sent him. The One who sent him is absolutely reliable; Jesus is God's final envoy to the world (7:16–18, 27–29).

---

[11] It is used parallel to "the prophet" and "Elijah".

Jesus as Prophet and King

At this stage a few remarks on John's use of "the prophet" and "the king (of Israel, of the Jews)" are in order. In 1:21 we find "the prophet" as alternative of ὁ χριστός. The same juxtaposition occurs in 7:40–43 where some people in the Jerusalem crowd hail Jesus as "the prophet" and others declare that he is "the Christ". The latter contention is disputed on the grounds that the Christ, as descendant of David, should come from Bethlehem; since Jesus comes from Galilee he does not qualify. For John this whole discussion is off the mark. Jesus' earthly descent is of secondary importance if not irrelevant, once it is established that he has come from God, and speaks and acts in the name of God (7:16–18, 27–29 mentioned above—implicitly describing him as more than a prophet).

In 6:14–15 the people present at the multiplication of the loaves regard this as a "sign" and conclude from that: "This is indeed the prophet who is to come into the world." Because they want to make Jesus king by force he withdraws, seeking the solitude of the mountain. This is not the way he wants to be king, and the many discussions of Jesus with the crowd in the rest of chapter 6 make clear that the designation "the prophet" may lead to fundamental misunderstanding. "The prophet" is the prophet like Moses announced in Deut 18:15–22 and expected to come in the last days. Anyone who interprets Jesus' words and actions along the lines of Moses' "signs", particularly his giving of manna, "the bread from heaven" (6:31), does not really understand who Jesus is. He himself is the Bread from Heaven, given by his Father. "This is indeed the will of my Father, that all who see the Son and believe in him may have eternal life; and I will raise them up on the last day" (v. 40). "The prophet" (or "a prophet"—see 9:17, also 4:19) is not an adequate term to characterize Jesus; one should see him as the Son of the Father, completely dedicated to the Father's cause.

Anyone thinking in terms of Jesus as a prophet, runs into difficulties, as the discussions among the Jews/the Pharisees (and between them and the man whose eyes were opened by Jesus) in 9:13–34 show. One has to distinguish between good and false prophets, using the criteria laid down in Deut 18:15–22 and 13:1–5. Essential for a good prophet is that he serves God and obeys his commandments. The decisive point in the rejection of Jesus by the majority of "the Jews" is here that Jesus has broken the Law in healing this man on a sabbath. The man born blind persists: "If this man were not from God, he could do nothing" (v. 33). He is expelled (v. 34), and in that situation Jesus meets him again. He confesses Jesus as the Son of man, after Jesus has revealed to him that he is the Son of man (vv. 35–38), explaining that he "came into the world for judgment, so that those who do not see may see, and those who do see may become blind" (v. 39).

Here we may briefly compare the discussion between Jesus and Nicodemus in chapter 3. Nicodemus is one of the many who came to believe in Jesus because of the signs he was doing (2:23). He addresses him as "a teacher who has come from God" on the grounds that "no one can do these signs that you do if God is not with him" (3:2). We may compare here Exod 3:12 (Moses) and Jer 1:19 (Jeremiah). What Nicodemus says is not wrong: Jesus is a teacher sent by God (7:16–18, 27–29) and his signs should be accepted as works performed on God's authority and with God's help (chapter 9). One should say more, however, as becomes clear in vv. 11–13, 14–21, and also vv. 31–36. Jesus is the Son of man, descended from Heaven; he is the Son sent by the Father into the world. About him can be said: "The one who is from above is above all. He testifies to what he has seen and heard" (vv. 31–32). The Gospel adds: "Yet no one accepts his testimony." This not only applies to Jesus' opponents, but also to sympathizers like Nicodemus (v. 11, cf. 2:24–25).

Jesus' kingship comes to the fore in his confrontation with Pilate in 18:33–38 (cf. 19:8–11) and in the story of his condemnation and crucifixion as "the king of the Jews"—a term used by non-Jews (18:18–19:30). Here the Fourth Gospel takes up a theme found earlier in the Synoptics. In the beginning of the Gospel we hear the confession of Nathanael, "truly an Israelite in which is no deceit", but still a beginning disciple: "You are the Son of God! You are the king of Israel" (1:48–49). In 12:12–16 the crowd in Jerusalem greets Jesus as "the one who comes in the name of the Lord, the king of Israel." We are told that only later, after Jesus' glorification, the disciples understood the true meaning of this event.

In chapters 18 and 19 one is allowed to see Jesus' kingship in the proper perspective. It is not an earthly kingship; Jesus says: "My kingdom is not of this world" (v. 36, cf. 6:15). Its essence is "to testify to the truth"; this is the sole purpose of Jesus' coming into the world (v. 37). Jesus the king is a witness to the truth, God's supreme and final envoy (the term "prophet" is avoided).

Pilate remains an unbeliever. He yields to the pressure of "the Jews", but does not give in in the matter of the inscription on the cross. Written in no less than three languages, it proclaims to the world that Jesus of Nazareth is "the king of the Jews" (19:19–22).

Jesus as Son of God and Son of man

The Christian designation Son of God for Jesus, going back (among other things) to terminology connected with anointed kings from the family of David (cf. 1:49), is further defined in the Fourth Gospel. The starting point is the expression "God sent his Son in order that . . ." (which is not specifically Johannine, see Gal 4:4–7; Rom 8:3–4; Mark 12:1–9). It stresses God's initiative as well as the close relationship between him and the Son whom he commissions to carry out a mission at the turn of the ages. Again the Gospel is at great pains to bring out the true meaning, thus radicalising (we may also say: intensifying) this "Christology of mission".

Central is the emphasis on the Son's unity, in dependence, with the Father. We find this time and again, in the discussion with the sympathizing Jew Nicodemus (3:14–21, cf. 31–36) as well as in fundamental debates with the Jewish authorities who oppose Jesus (chapters 5, 8 and 10, and also in different settings in chapters 6 and 7). To mention a few aspects: God as sender of the Son is repeatedly called "the Father" (5:23, 37); the Son does nothing "on his own" (5:19, 30); he does God's will (4:34; 5:30) and performs God's work (4:34; 5:36). His words are the words of the Father; the Father works through him, so Jesus tells his disciples (14:10). Father and Son are united in love (5:20)—the Son sent out by the Father remains continually in contact with his Sender (5:19–20, 30). "The Father and I are one," says Jesus in 10:30, and he adds: "Believe the works, so that you may surely know that the Father is in me and I am in the Father" (10:38).

The divine origin and the unique authority of Jesus' words and actions are underlined by means of the repeated use of "from above" and "from heaven" (3:13, 31; 6:31–58), that is "from God" (6:46). Particularly in Jesus' discussions with his disciples in chapters 13–17 we hear that Jesus came from God in order to return to him again at the completion of his mission (13:3; 14:2–4, 28; 16:28). This unity of Sender and Envoy, Father and Son presupposes God's initiative and Jesus' complete identification with his Father. For the Fourth

Gospel it is self-evident that the Father is greater than the Son (14:28).[12]

Yet, Jesus' Jewish opponents accuse him in debates of blasphemy. They tell him that he has to be stoned "for blasphemy, because you, though only a human being, are making yourself God" (10:33, cf. v. 36; 5:18). The final accusation of the Jews before Pilate is: "We have a law, and according to that law he ought to die, because he has claimed to be the Son of God" (19:7). Jesus' reply to this charge, in 5:19–30, 31–47 as well as in 10:34–38 (referring back to earlier statements in this chapter), underscores that it was the Father himself who took the initiative in making the Son his plenipotentiary on earth. He has given all judgment to the Son (5:22), and therefore Jesus declares: "I can do nothing on my own. I judge and my judgment is just, because I seek to do not my own will but the will of him who sent me" (5:30). It is clear that the Johannine community took this criticism, voiced here by Jesus' Jewish opponents, very seriously. Also that, in clarifying the issues involved, it tries to avoid aberrations and to keep the radical Christology it advocates on the right track.

In referring to Jesus as "Son of man" the Fourth Gospel takes up another common Christian designation also found in Jewish sources. The fact that John maintains this unusual Greek expression, found only as a self-designation in Jesus' own mouth (in 12:34 taken up by his interlocutors), shows that he follows early Christian usage and relies on tradition. A number of times "Son of man" is found where Jesus is also identified as Son of God (1:50–51; 3:13–21; 5:19–29; 6:27, 53, 63 and 6:40; cf. 12:34 where the crowd connects "Son of man" with "the Christ"). What does "Son of man" bring out that is not expressed by "Son of God"?

We may point to 5:27 where the Son exercises judgment as "Son of man"; all emphasis is on the fact that the judgment, traditionally expected in the future, takes place now.[13] One should compare 9:35–38 where, as we have seen, "Son of man" is presented as a more adequate interpretation of "being from God" (v. 33) than

---

[12] For a full discussion of all aspects of the relationship between God and Jesus we would have to look more closely into the Logos-Christology of the Prologue and the "I am"-texts. In the present context this would carry us too far.

[13] See further "Christology and Theology," esp. 1850–1851.

"(the) prophet". In vv. 39–41 Jesus adds: "I came into the world for judgment."

Next, as has often been noted, "Son of man" is used in contexts speaking of Jesus' exaltation. The Son of man will ascend to heaven (3:13; 6:62, [1:51], cf. 20:17); he will be glorified (12:23; 13:31, cf. 7:39, and 17:1 "Glorify your Son"); he will be "lifted up"—an expression that denotes both Jesus' elevation onto the cross and his return to God in heaven (3:14–15; 8:28; 12:31–34). The Johannine community must have regarded the traditional designation "Son of man" as specifically appropriate where Jesus' return to God at the completion of his mission had to be expressed. This would be a return in glory, but of one who had died on the cross. The remarkable double meaning of ὑψωθῆναι is typically Johannine.[14]

Characteristic Features of Johannine Christianity according to the Fourth Gospel

The Christology developed in the Fourth Gospel is meant for and functions within a particular "Johannine" community. The readers of the Gospel, whether belonging to that community or interested in it, are urged to realize that any other view on Jesus' mission and his relationship to God, is inadequate or even wrong. This is a Christology of a particular community; orienting itself towards the testimony of the disciples and guided by the Spirit of Truth which plays a prominent role in chapters 14–16. At the same time the Fourth Gospel sketches the development of this specific Christology as the result of (sometimes heated) controversies between Jesus and *various* opponents and sympathizers among his Jewish contemporaries. The overall picture presented by the Gospel is very complex; it may help to look once more at some main features of that picture.

Christology and Community

Jesus' disciples occupy a key position in the Gospel, as 20:31 shows.[15] At the end of the Gospel we are referred back to the programmatic

---

[14] Compare 6:51b–58 where "the food that endures for eternal life, which the Son of man will give you" of v. 27, is further defined as the flesh of the Son of man that he will give for the life of the world.

[15] There is no space to discuss the special position of the "Beloved Disciple" in chapters 13–20, and chapter 21 in particular.

statement in 2:11 "Jesus did this, the first of his signs, in Cana of Galilee, and revealed his glory; and his disciples believed in him." However much they still have to learn, during their wanderings with Jesus in Galilee and Judea, through Jesus' teaching during his last meal with them, and in the school of the Spirit after his departure, later he sends them out into the world, as the Father has sent him, and gives them the Holy Spirit, with the authority to forgive and to retain sins (20:19–23).

There is a sharp contrast between the disciples and those who remain outsiders. Of them it is said: ". . . after Jesus had said this, he departed from them and hid from them. Although he had performed so many signs in their presence, they did not believe him" (12:36b–37). Among those who failed to see and to understand what these signs were meant to reveal were not only his opponents, but also people who believed in him, even among the authorities, but who did not confess him because of the Pharisees for fear that they would be put out of the synagogue (vv. 42–43). The sympathizers among the Jews may be said "to believe in him" (see also 2:23; 7:31; 8:30; 10:42; 11:45; 12:11, cf. Samaritans in 4:39), yet true faith is only found among the disciples.

They are the ones who receive further instruction in chapters 13–17. With regard to Christology we have already noted how much attention is paid to the completion of Jesus' mission. So, for instance, right at the beginning in 13:3, "Jesus, knowing that the Father had given all things into his hands, and that he had come from God and was going to God . . ." We may also recall the discussion between Jesus and his disciples in 14:5–11 that centres around the unity between Son and Father, using the terminology of "mutual indwelling". "Believe me that I am in the Father and the Father in me", we read in 14:11 (cf. 10:38).

A little later this unity is extended to the unity between Father and Son and the disciples (14:18–24; 15:1–11; 17:20–26). This will enable the believers to live in perfect love and to do the works Jesus did, and even greater works than these (14:12). The Son, returned to the Father, continues his work through those whom he commissioned to be his envoys. He, together with the Father, will be present in them, while the Spirit, sent by Father and Son, guides the believers and renders assistance (14:15–17, 25–26; 15:26–27; 16:4b–11, 12–15). We cannot go into details here; the important thing is to see how the (admittedly unique) bond between Father and Son

is, in a subtle way, extended to include the disciples, as representatives of the (insider) group of true believers.

The corollary of this is a strong sense of distance and even of
alienation from those outside, designated as "the world" (see 15:18–
16:4 and 17:14–16). "The world" will hate the disciples, just as it
hates Jesus. "I have given them your word, and the world has hated
them because they do not belong to the world, just as I do not
belong to the world," says Jesus to the Father in 17:14. Jesus was
sent into the world (3:17) as "Saviour of the world" (4:42), but only
a minority consisting of believers responded positively; "the world"
gave a hostile reaction.

Christology and Controversy

The other side of the picture is that the Fourth Gospel's radical
Christology takes shape in the controversies with people who oppose
Jesus and with sympathizers who, in the end, do not belong to the
true believers. Again we shall do well to look more closely at the
ways the debates are portrayed, and at the different people involved.

We may rightly ask whether we are allowed to speak of discussions or debates, if these terms presuppose at least some common
ground. All along dialogues end as a monologue, and always Jesus'
statements are the ones that really matter. If we look at chapter 7
in particular, we note that various opinions about Jesus are expressed
by groups of people that are not clearly defined. Repeatedly we hear
about "the crowd(s)" who wonder(s) who Jesus is, and how his words
and actions should be judged (vv. 10–13, 20, 31, 40–44). In vv.
25–30 we find "some of the people of Jerusalem." Both groups are
distinguished from "the Jews", here and elsewhere clearly people in
authority who are opposed to Jesus (vv. 13, 15–24; in vv. 11 and
35 their position is not quite clear). They seem to be the same as
"the Pharisees," or "the chief priests and the Pharisees" of v. 32,
who recur in vv. 45–52; also the term "authorities" is used (vv. 26,
48). All these people express opinions about Jesus considered to be
representative for his Jewish contemporaries. Jesus' own statements
are found, first, in a "dialogue" with his Jewish opponents in vv.
15–24 (where he refutes their objections with a particular interpretation of the Law). Next, in vv. 25–30 Jesus is portrayed as "crying
out" while teaching in the temple (v. 26, cf. v. 14), and the same
expression is used to introduce his statement in vv. 37–38. This is

Jesus' last pronouncement; he does not react to the discussion in the crowd in vv. 41–43 nor to that in the council chamber in vv. 44–52.

It is remarkable that the people who are sympathetic towards Jesus are described in a variety of ways. Sometimes they are common people (2:23–25; 6:2; 7:40–41; 8:31; 10:42; 11:45, 47–48; 12:11). Sometimes they belong to the leaders—so Nicodemus (3:1–2; 7:50–52; 19:38–42), Joseph of Arimathea (19:38–42), some of the Pharisees (9:35), many of the authorities (12:42–43). As we have seen, often this sympathy is called faith (2:23–25; 7:31; 8:31; 10:42; 11:45; 12:11, 42) and Joseph of Arimathea is called a "secret disciple" (19:38). Yet all of them eventually fall under a negative verdict (2:23–25 and 12:42–43). And as far as the great divide between "the Jews" and Jesus with his true disciples is concerned, they are clearly situated in the Jewish camp.

Some additional comments are needed on 8:30–47 and 6:60–71. In 8:30–31 we meet again Jews who believe in Jesus. Jesus tells them: "If you abide in my word, you are truly my disciples" (cf. 15:7). The following exchange of words, however, differs in no way from that in vv. 12–30 or that in vv. 48–59 where Jesus' interlocutors are called "the Jews". The people introduced in vv. 30–31 clearly are not really "disciples". They are said to look for an opportunity to kill Jesus (vv. 37, 40); even in this respect they do not differ from "the Jews" (cf. 5:18; 7:1; 8:59; 10:39 and other instances).[16] The tone in 8:30–47 is significantly sharper than that in 2:23–3:13, or also in 12:42–43 followed by 19:38–42 where Joseph of Arimathea and Nicodemus, unable to prevent Jesus' execution, at least give him a decent Jewish burial.

In 6:60–71 we hear of many of Jesus' disciples who turn back and do not follow Jesus any longer. They are contrasted with the Twelve who remain faithful, with the exception of Judas. Jesus knew beforehand that Judas was going to betray him (vv. 64; 70–71), just as he knew "from the first who were the ones that did not believe" (vv. 63–64). The backsliding disciples are, and always have been, unbelievers. No one can come to Jesus unless it is granted him by the Father (v. 65, cf. similar words spoken to the Jews in vv. 37, 44).

Those who no longer follow Jesus have earlier reacted to Jesus'

---

[16] See also 8:44 "you are from your father the devil." With 8:42–47 compare 1 John 3:14–17.

discourse on the Bread of Life, delivered before "the Jews" in the synagogue of Capernaum (v. 59), with the words: "This teaching is difficult; who can accept it?" (v. 60). Their difficulties may have been the same as those of "the Jews" in vv. 40–41, where they cannot understand that Jesus, the son of Joseph, came down from heaven, or in v. 52, where they ask how Jesus can say that he will give his flesh to eat. Yet Jesus' followers in vv. 60–66 are clearly distinguished from "the Jews" in the preceding part of the chapter, and they are said to have belonged to Jesus' "disciples" until they turned away. Twice they are said to be numerous (vv. 60, 66). Thus in many respects the picture in 6:60–71 differs from that in the other instances.

The Fourth Gospel: a book for Johannine Christians

From narrative to history

To make the step from John's "narrative world" to the situation in and for which the Fourth Gospel was written is far from easy. It is not surprising that so many different theories have been put forward about successive stages in the composition of the Gospel and/or in the history of the Johannine community. Yet Christologies do not originate in a vacuum, they address specific historical contexts. What can we say about the context of the Fourth Gospel? In the present article there is only room for a discussion of some central aspects.

On the basis of what was said earlier about "Christology and Community", we may conclude that the Fourth Gospel was primarily written for the instruction and inner strengthening of the Johannine community. It is plausible that the particular Johannine view on Jesus, and on the union between the believers and the Son of God, came into being in a long process of internal discussion and collective meditation. In chapters 13–17, reflecting the situation of the Johannine community after Jesus' departure, we read: "The Holy Spirit . . . will teach you everything, and remind you of all I have said to you" (14:26; cf. 16:12–15).

Internal discussions had, no doubt, been spurred by debates with groups outside the community. Hence the many instances of controversy in chapters 2–12. Yet the variety of ways in which the Gospel describes the reactions of all sorts of Jesus' contemporaries to him, negative or sympathetic, as well as Jesus' sovereign utterances concerning his unique mission, suggest a certain distance. This makes it unlikely that they reflect an *ongoing* debate with specific groups. The Gospel, in its final form at least, is not missionary, polemical or apologetical; it wants to reformulate essential viewpoints, and to show that some answers to the question who Jesus is, are insufficient and misleading. It concentrates on the central issues here and now.

Nevertheless, these central issues are brought up within the basic framework of controversies between "the Jews" and Jesus with his disciples. In these controversies passages from Scripture play an important role, just as typical Jewish notions are brought forward and reinterpreted. Other, earlier Christian conceptions about Jesus and his mission are found in the mouth of people who react favourably to Jesus, but are nevertheless ranged on the side of the Jews rather than among the disciples of Jesus.[17] The portrayal of the various altercations may be schematic and artificial, the arguments used are clearly still highly relevant. We have noted, for instance, that the accusations of blasphemy on the part of "the Jews" (see chapters 5, 10 and 19) remind Johannine Christians that they should be very careful in their thinking about the unique unity between the Son of God and his heavenly Father.

In short: Johannine Christology is defined and refined in a continuous reformulation of Jewish notions. It remains "Jewish" precisely where it rejects Jewish objections against Jesus and his followers. At the same time it corrects and supplements other, earlier or contemporary, attempts to show why and how Jesus may be regarded as the Messiah expected by Israel.

The Johannine community views itself as standing alone in true allegiance to God and to Jesus Christ, his Son, and it experiences the hostility of the world, which is said to hate Jesus' disciples just as they hated him. It is precisely in chapters 13–17, where the specific conflicts of Jesus with the Jews seem to recede to the background, that the hatred of the world is said to express itself as hostility on the part of the Jews, leading to expulsion from the synagogue and worse than that. "An hour is coming when those who kill you will think that by doing so they are offering worship to God" (16:2–3).

At the least this indicates that the rift between the synagogue ("the

---

[17] The unfaithful disciples of 6:60–66 form an exception. That is why I think their apostasy reflects the situation described in 1 (and 2) John, that has also left other traces in the Gospel.

Jews") and Jesus with his disciples, is still perceived by Johannine
Christians as a crucial moment in the history of their community.
Why? We may think of traumatic experiences in the past, although
I think we can reconstruct neither those nor subsequent events—
however fascinating the literary analyses and historical theories of
M.C. de Boer and his predecessors may be. It may be that contemporary Jewry, at least in the region where the Johannine Christians
lived, still constituted a challenge, but we cannot be certain. Although
certainly no longer "on speaking terms", the Johannine community
may have felt it necessary to refine its own views on Jesus in order
to avoid misinterpretations, first and foremost by insiders, though we
may not exclude that some of them were influenced by people outside the community.

At the same time, the community regarded as inadequate many
other views on Jesus making use of Jewish categories. Traditional
Christological notions were no longer considered useful or relevant,
unless radicalised in Johannine fashion. To what extent this reflects
conflicts with Jewish sympathizers or other Christian groups, in the
past or in the present, we cannot know. For sure, 8:30–47 remains
a difficult passage, but maintaining, like B.W.J. de Ruyter, that the
equation between "believing Jews" and "the Jews" in chapter 8 provides a decisive argument for the theory that the Gospel is only
engaged in a polemic against Jewish Christians of inadequate faith,
certainly goes beyond the evidence. The Fourth Gospel portrays certain Jewish Christians who do not espouse Johannine Christology (in
the past and in the present) as Jews, but this does not necessarily
reflect an *acute* conflict with them. There is no reason to assume that
whenever Jews are mentioned, either as sympathizers or as opponents, Christians of inadequate faith are envisaged.

Conclusion

It makes good sense to describe the specific Christology of the Fourth
Gospel as that of a particular community, shaped during a long
period of refining certain issues, among other things in debates with
others. It is fascinating to analyse the different stories in the Fourth
Gospel about altercations between Jesus and various Jewish contemporaries, as well as his instructions of his disciples. Misunderstanding and lack of complete insight prevail in all situations; the Johannine

community realizes that its Christology is the outcome of a long process of learning and unlearning in the school of the Spirit.

I have argued that it remains difficult to determine the situation directly envisaged in the Gospel or the earlier history of the community. After repeated consideration of the difficulties involved, I have (reluctantly) come to the conclusion that we have to be content with the general observation that it is highly likely that controversies with others, Jews and Christians, played an important role. The Gospel concentrates on the clarification of relevant Christological issues for the Johannine community itself.

BIBLIOGRAPHY

P.N. Anderson, *The Christology of the Fourth Gospel. Its Unity and Disunity in the Light of John 6.* (Tübingen: Mohr, 1996/Valley Forge PA: Trinity Press International, 1997)

R.E. Brown, *The Community of the Beloved Disciple* (New York: Paulist, 1979)

Martinus C. de Boer, *Johannine Perspectives on the Death of Jesus* (CBET 17; Kampen: Kok-Pharos, 1996)

B.W.J. de Ruyter, *De gemeente van de evangelist Johannes: haar polemiek en haar geschiedenis* ["The community of John the Evangelist: its polemic and its history"; with summary in English] (Delft: Eburon, 1998)

J.L. Martyn, *History and Theology in the Fourth Gospel* (Nashville: Abingdon, 1968; 2nd ed. 1979)

———, *The Gospel of John in Christian History* (New York: Paulist, 1979)

J. Zumstein, "Der Prozess der Relecture in der johanneischen Literatur," *NTS* 42 (1996) 394–411

Earlier studies on the Fourth Gospel by M. de Jonge:
"Christology and Theology particularly in the Fourth Gospel," *The Four Gospels 1992* FS F. Neirynck (ed. F. Van Segbroeck et al.; BETL 100; Leuven: University Press and Peeters, 1992) 1835–1853

Jesus: Stranger from Heaven and Son of God. Jesus Christ and the Christians in Johannine Perspective (SBLSBS 11; Missoula MT: Scholars, 1977), see here:

"Jesus as Prophet and King in the Fourth Gospel", 49–76
"Jewish Expectations about the 'Messiah' according to the Fourth Gospel", 77–116
"Nicodemus and Jesus. Some Observations on Misunderstanding and Understanding in the Fourth Gospel", 29–47
"Signs and Works in the Fourth Gospel", 117–140
"The Son of God and the Children of God", 141–168
"Variety and Development in Johannine Christology", 193–222

"John the Baptist and Elijah in the Fourth Gospel," *The Conversation Continues. Studies in Paul and John* FS J. Louis Martyn (ed. R.T. Fortna and B.R. Gaventa; Nashville: Abingdon, 1990) 299–308

Johannes. Een praktische bijbelverklaring (Kampen: Kok, 1996)

THE POINT OF JOHN'S CHRISTOLOGY
CHRISTOLOGY, CONFLICT AND COMMUNITY IN JOHN

John Painter

A late invitation to participate in this Festschrift has left little time to write a worthy contribution in honour of my friend and colleague David Catchpole. Because of a friendship consolidated by a time together in Cape Town in 1976 and an Australian connection, I would not willingly miss this opportunity. I have been helped by the chosen focus of the volume. It suggests a connection with my approach to John which recognises that Christology leads to conflict and the consequences of conflict contribute to the shaping of the distinctive Johannine community.

The argument of this essay is simple. It is that the development of Christology led to a conflict out of which the Johannine community was born. In the Jewish context of the first century the development of *Christology* inevitably became a source of conflict. Care is required if we are to avoid confusion because we need to distinguish three broad periods during which Christology means rather different things. As applied to the period of Jesus' ministry, if the term Christology is used it is to be understood in terms of Jewish expectations of the Messiah. To be sure, we now recognise a diversity of expectations, and John shows an awareness of a number of these, all of which remain recognisably Jewish. The evidence makes clear that Jesus faced conflict with the Jewish authorities of his day. Roman execution was facilitated by the cooperation and complicity of the Jerusalem leadership. But this may not have been because of Jesus' explicit Christology. It is unlikely that he was opposed simply because he was perceived to be the Messiah. Opposition is more likely to have been because Jesus was the leader of a popular movement that was seriously critical of the Jewish establishment, including the temple regime.[1] John (11:46–53) also suggests that the Jerusalem authorities

---

[1] The tradition of the "cleansing" of the temple in the gospel tradition sets Jesus in opposition to the Jerusalem leadership represented by the High Priest.

perceived Jesus to be a threat to the stability of the status quo because
his movement provoked Roman intervention.

That there was conflict between Jesus and the Jewish authorities
of his day is the ground out of which the developing conflict between
the followers of Jesus and Judaism is to be understood. At this point
it is necessary to notice that in the developing tradition of the followers of Jesus there is something of a transformation in the perception of Jesus as Messiah.

From Messiahship to Christology

The period following the crucifixion of Jesus is crucial for recognising the transformation of messianic expectations into Christology.
But if the Johannine Christology led to conflict, why did this Christology
develop in the first place? First, Jesus encountered conflict with the
Jerusalem authorities. The explicit development of Christology is a
crystallisation of the recognition of the superior authority of Jesus in
relation to the Jerusalem authorities. That crystallisation exacerbated
the conflict by sharpening the points of opposition. In as much as
they appealed to the law as the source of their authority, Jesus is
set in opposition to the law.

In Johannine terms it is ironical that Christology should be the
source of conflict because Christology is also the ground of unity.
Important to the Johannine Christology is the recognition of the
unity of the Father and the Son (5:17; 10:30–33) and the unity of
the believer with the Father through the Son is grounded in this
(17:20–23). But the unity of believers is dependent on a certain separation from the world (17:16). Only in this way can they fulfil the
mission of the Father through the Son for the sake of the world.
Unity is an expression of the mission of the sent one on behalf of
the sender (17:3–4, 6–8, 18, 21–23, 25).

Coming to terms with the crucifixion of Jesus involved proclaiming a crucified Messiah. Here Paul shows awareness of the scandal
of preaching a crucified Messiah (1 Cor 1:23). To do so involved a
reinterpretation of messiahship so that, from the beginning of this
period, we have a transition from the diversity of Jewish messianic
expectations into something which already gives expression to what
would become distinctively Christian belief.[2] Obviously this transi-

---

[2] Although *Christ* is the Greek translation of *Messiah*, in this essay Christology is

tion produced tensions with other forms of Judaism, even where there was no Gentile mission, as there was in the case of Paul.

After the destruction of Jerusalem in 70 CE, what had been tensions relating to messianic beliefs, developed into serious conflicts. The Gospel of John embodies traditions belonging to all three stages. Thus the Gospel alone of New Testament documents notes that *Messias* is translated *Christos* in Greek (1:41) and reflects a diversity of messianic expectations. There is also evidence of a growing rift between messianic expectations and the Christology of John.

In John 9 we meet the extraordinary situation where the narrator explains "for the Jews had already decided that if any one confesses *Christ* they would be cast out of the synagogue (ἵνα ἐάν τις ὁμολογήσῃ Χριστόν, ἀποσυνάγωγος γένηται)" (9:22) A messianic confession is hardly grounds for exclusion from the synagogue. Minimally this formulation has to mean, "if any one confesses Jesus is the Messiah". But even this does not seem to justify the penalty. In the period between the crucifixion of Jesus and the destruction of Jerusalem Jewish believers in Jesus maintained their Jewish identity in Jerusalem. Either John reflects a Jewish situation where messianic confession was rejected at an earlier stage, or John 9 reflects a later situation. The latter seems more likely for a variety of reasons. Before 70 CE we know of no situation where a confession that Jesus is the Messiah was grounds for exclusion from the synagogue.

Thus both the conflict and the birth of the Johannine community can be seen as processes rather than as simple quick events. Nevertheless, the birth of the community also provided resources for the further development of the Johannine Christology. In that development Christology again became a point of contention dividing the community (1 John 2:18–19; 4:1–6). In the early centuries Christology continued to be contentious so that the first five centuries in particular provide a history of a struggle for christological clarity in the face of what, in retrospect, can be seen as christological heresies. In this process the Gospel of John played a substantial role and was appealed to by people on all sides.[3] Thus we need to ask how far

---

used of the distinctively Christian development which takes as its foundation the affirmation that the crucified Jesus is the Messiah and that God raised him from the dead, vindicating him and revealing salvation through him. For a discussion of the complexity of the situation see my *The Quest for the Messiah* (Edinburgh: T. & T. Clark, 1991, 1993 and Nashville: Abingdon, 1993) 9–24.

[3] See T.E. Pollard, *Johannine Christology and the Early Church* (Cambridge: CUP, 1970).

those developments were inherent in the Gospel and if this might not throw light on the conflicts that the Gospel provoked.

Theology and Christology

It is sometimes noted that the New Testament as a whole has little teaching about God.[4] Some books have more to say *directly* about God than others do. In this category Revelation is comparatively rich. Comparatively, Paul also has a good deal to say directly about God. But the Gospel of John, as the story of Jesus, is limited in what it says about God. The New Testament writers generally presuppose the understanding of God found in the Jewish scriptures. By the first century this was understood to enshrine a monotheistic confession of faith in the creator of all things whose sovereign purpose in history was to be worked out in the destiny of God's chosen people, Israel. God's purpose for Israel and Israel's role in that purpose were set out in the scriptures. In the New Testament appeal is made to aspects of this confession from time to time.

But the New Testament marks new directions in understanding the purpose of God which are rooted in a transformation of the understanding of God. That transformation is expressed in the Johannine Christology. Almost everything John says about God is in relation to Jesus, especially focused on the Father-Son relationship. Christology is John's way of speaking of God at those points where the understanding of God is being transformed. The transformation introduces nothing absolutely new so that all the parts of the view can be found already in the Jewish scriptures. What changes is the balance amongst all the details that make up the understanding of God and the purpose of God. There is a new hermeneutic which

---

[4] See Nils Dahl, "The Neglected Factor in New Testament Theology", *Reflections* 73 (1975) 5–8. A number of studies have now appeared, for example, C.K. Barrett, "Christocentric or Theocentric? Observations on the Theological Method of the Fourth Gospel", in *Essays on John* (London: SPCK, 1982); M.M. Thompson, "'God's Voice You Have Never Heard, God's Form You Have Never Seen': The Characterization Of God In The Gospel Of John", *Semeia* 63 (1993) 177–205; "Reflections On Worship In The Gospel Of John", *The Princeton Seminary Bulletin* 19 (1998) 259–278; P.W. Meyer, "'The Father': The Presentation of God in the Fourth Gospel", in R.A. Culpepper & C.C. Black, eds, *Exploring the Gospel of John: In honour of D. Moody Smith*, (Louisville, KY: Westminster/John Knox, 1996) 255–73; D. Francois Tolmie, "The Characterization of God in the Fourth Gospel", *JSNT* 69 (1998) 57–75.

recognises a new centre from which all is viewed. The old centre becomes marginal and what was not central before now determines the meaning of the whole. John's Christology constitutes the new centre for understanding God, the purpose of God, the destiny of the creation and the meaning of faith.

The opening words of the Prologue of the Gospel resonate with the opening words of Genesis. That the words "In the beginning . . ." are a conscious appeal to the opening of Genesis is generally recognised and is confirmed as both works go on to deal with the creation of all things by God.[5] John rewrites the creation story, developing further the interpretation of Genesis already found in Israel's wisdom literature. The result is a transformed understanding of God, the will and purpose of God and of creation. In Genesis a process of creation leads to a completed creation celebrated by the institution of the Sabbath. In John, creation by the *Logos* appears to be instantaneous (1:3) though a continuing struggle between the light of the *Logos* and the darkness is apparent from the beginning (1:4–5). The creation of all things by the *Logos* implies that all things have the potential to become bearers of the *Logos* and this is the foundation of the possibility of the incarnation of the *Logos* (1:14). But, because of the darkness, the light of the *Logos* does not shine unambiguously everywhere. The signs in John are the moments in which the light of the *Logos* shines forth (see 2:11). But even here it not possible to say that the light shines unambiguously for all. The presence of the darkness from the beginning of the creation implies that creation is incomplete. Thus there are those who have been blind from birth (9:1). The sign narrated in chapter 9 is important, not only because the light of the *Logos* shines forth in it, but also because it is the story of the opening of blind eyes. Only those whose eyes have been opened perceive the glory in the signs (9:39–41).

From this perspective, John 5 also provides important clues. It is in this chapter that the Sabbath first emerges as an issue (5:9). Only when the healing has been completed does the narrator inform the reader "It was the Sabbath on that day". The story of the healing of the blind man follows the same pattern.[6] Only when his sight has been restored and a preliminary interrogation has been carried out

---

[5] For an earlier treatment of some aspects of this theme see my "Theology and Eschatology in the Prologue of John", *SJT* 46 (1993) 27–42.
[6] See my *Quest for the Messiah*, 213–35, 305–18.

by his neighbours, to ascertain whether or not he is "the blind man", do they take him to the Pharisees. Only then does the narrator inform the reader, "It was the Sabbath on the day" Jesus made the clay and restored the man's sight (9:14). In both stories it is the Sabbath issue that finds focus in the dialogues that follow. In John 9 the man who was blind is interrogated and thrown out of the synagogue (9:22, 34). John 9 is his story and he is the central character until 9:38.

The story of John 5 is quite different. The man healed by Jesus soon disappears from the scene. Before doing so he becomes an informer, making a point of going to the Jews to reveal Jesus' identity to them (5:15). Although Jesus had healed him, he shows no positive response. Initially, when questioned, he indicates that he does not know the identity of the person who healed him and is not slow to blame Jesus for any part he might have in breaking the Sabbath (5:11–13). Yet the offence was committed by the man. It was he who was carrying a burden (his bed) on the Sabbath. His response, asserting that the person who had healed him had told him to "take up your bed and walk" is a rather "lame" excuse. While he was unable to identify Jesus at the time, the moment he could do so, he became an informer.

Jesus is then charged with a failure to observe the Sabbath (5:16), a charge which he does not deny. Rather Jesus asserts, "my Father is working and I am working" (5:17). *Work* is precisely what is forbidden on the Sabbath as a mark of the completion of creation when God ceased from work. That God works on the Sabbath could be admitted if that work were thought to be to sustain the creation. That is, although creation is complete (Gen 2:1–3), God always works to maintain the state of no change. But John 5:17 has a different message. First, the claim "My Father is working and I am working" is clearly meant and understood to be a reference to God. Second, only one work is in view, not two. Jesus' work is the work of God and it is done on the Sabbath. Then, the work that Jesus performs on the Sabbath is to make a man whole (ὑγιής), see 5:6, 9, 11,[7] 14, 15; 7:23. It is not a matter of sustaining the status quo. Given this continuing work on the Sabbath, John suggests that the creation is

---

[7] The man who became an informer, not knowing Jesus' name, refers to him as "the one who made me whole (ὑγιής)".

not yet complete. There is no cessation of work by Jesus or the Father. The continuation towards completion is confirmed by the multiple stress on making the man whole, as he should be, thus completing the creation.

In both Genesis and John the themes of God, creation and the Sabbath/law occur together. In Genesis the completion of the creation is marked by the Sabbath. In John, at the end of the Prologue, John notes that "the law was given by Moses, grace and truth came by Jesus Christ" (1:17). Of course John knew that, according to Exod 33:17–23, the giving of the law was accompanied by the proclamation of the name of the Lord and the affirmation "I will be gracious to whom I will be gracious and show mercy upon whom I will show mercy" (33:19). In the LXX this language is related to the Hebrew *hesed w'emeth.*[8] There is a clear dependence on this language in John 1:17. Here John has separated the law from grace and truth so that the law is associated with Moses while grace and truth are identified with Jesus Christ. This distinction signals a hermeneutical controversy between John and other forms of Judaism where the law provides the key to an understanding of God and his *hesed w'emeth.* John's dependence on this Hebraic phrase is signalled by the combination of "grace and truth" which occurs only in John in 1:14 and 17.

In the place of the language of grace John characteristically speaks of the love of God. Because it is crucial for John to work out the reciprocal relationship between the Father and the Son, love, rather than grace is the appropriate term. Even more important is the way in John the relationship between the Father and the Son becomes the model for the relationship between Jesus and believers. There are also clues suggesting that ἀλήθεια should not always be translated as "truth" in John. In addition to the combination of "grace and truth" here, there is the expression "those who do the truth". This signals a more practical and less intellectual understanding of ἀλήθεια than is normal in Greek literature. It has more the sense of "acting faithfully" or, as we would say, with integrity. Here the linguistic linkage is via the Hebrew *emunah.* There is also the overlapping usage in John who speaks both of righteous judgment (ἡ κρίσις ἡ ἐμὴ

---

[8] See C.H. Dodd, *The Interpretation of the Fourth Gospel* (Cambridge: CUP, 1953) 82–3, 175–6.

δικαία ἐστιν) and true judgement (ἡ κρίσις ἡ ἐμὴ ἀληθινὴ ἐστιν), John 5:30; 8:16 and cf. 7:24. This judgement is the judgement of the light entering the world to save the world. The cross as the symbol for the grace and faithfulness of God is the key to the way God is understood with consequences for the life of faith in the world.

Simplistically we may say that, in any monotheistic faith, there is a balance between three attributes, power, justice and love. For Islam the centre of focus is on the power and will of God. Justice and love are both redefined in terms of the power and the will of God. Islam is submission to the will of God so that it is difficult to envisage debating with God concerning the justice of his ways. It is also difficult to envisage the possibility of the ignominious crucifixion of "the Prophet". The notion that God was in Christ and crucified is unthinkable where God is identified with power. The notion of power in weakness does not emerge here.

For Judaism God is known in and through the law and his defining characteristic is justice. "Shall not the judge of all the earth do right?" (Gen 18:25). The appeal is not to mercy but to justice and the more the law becomes the focus the greater the coherence of this perspective. But in early Christianity, of which we may take the Johannine form as representative, the incarnate *Logos* is the symbol for God in relation to the world and the symbol of the incarnate *Logos* is the cross which reveals the character of God in terms of grace and truth (John 1:17–18; 3:16; 17:21–26).

Although the three great historical monotheistic faiths (Judaism, Christianity and Islam) grow out of a common root, that of the Abrahamic tradition, and both Christianity and Islam are influenced by Judaism, it can be argued that something like a normative expression of each produces a different balance of the three attributes. While the three faiths are far from uniform in expression, this brief analysis may be understood as a typology that accentuates what is distinctive about the three faiths. In the actual world we find some Christians who conform more closely to either the Islamic or Judaic type but in doing so they fail to give priority to the distinctively Christian perspective and certainly miss the Johannine emphasis.

For John the *Logos* is the symbol of God in relation to the world and is known in the figure of Jesus of Nazareth for whom the central symbol is a cross. The passion story is central to the story of Jesus[9]

---

[9] Paul even characterises the gospel as the preaching of the cross (1 Cor 1:17–18, 23).

and overtly redefines John's theology. This position is justified by what the Gospel says about the relationship of the Jesus to God, of the Father-Son relationship and the role of the *Logos* in revealing God. It is especially important to recognise that the teaching of the Jesus of John is not concerned with a mass of theological and ethical detail. Like the central Christology of the Gospel, the teaching of Jesus proclaims that he is the revealer of God.[10] What he reveals *about* God is however to be seen in his own life and death. In particular, the giving of the Son reveals God's love for the world (3:16). In the words of 1 John, "In this the love of God is revealed among us, God sent his only begotten Son into the world that we should live through him." (1 John 4:9) While 1 John is not the Gospel, on this point it confirms the understanding of the Gospel. The suspicion that this is to allow John 3:16 to determine the meaning of the Gospel as a whole now needs to be addressed.

The dualistic character of John has led to the association of the Gospel with the Qumran texts where the *Community Rule* exhorts sectarians to love all the children of light and to hate the children of darkness.[11] Because the Jesus of John does not exhort the love of enemy or the neighbour, but only of "one another", it can be argued that John reflects a similar sectarian attitude to the world as we find at Qumran. But this is unjustified. There is no exhortation to hate those outside. And if John 3:16 is only one text expressing God's love for the world, it harmonises with the orientation to the world that we find in John 17:21, 23. Thus the love of the Father for the Son, which reaches out to believers, has the world as its ultimate objective.

The Centrality of Christology in John

It is generally recognised that Christology is central to the Johannine Gospel and Epistles (1 John at least). Why is Christology explicitly central in John (see 20:31) and what factors have shaped its distinctive Christology? An important part of the evidence needed to deal with this question is the Johannine language in which Christology

---

[10] On this central point Rudolf Bultmann is fundamentally correct, see his *Theology of the New Testament* 2 (London: SCM, 1955) 66.

[11] 1 QS 1:9–10.

is expressed. The distinctive nature of the language casts doubt on the suggestion that John's Christology can be traced *directly* and *explicitly* back to Jesus. In the Synoptics Jesus is reluctant to speak of himself in christological terms.[12] At best we have an implied Christology, arising from the relationship of Jesus to the coming kingdom of God.[13] Even here we need to distinguish between the Christology of Jesus himself and the Christology of each of the Synoptics and the unanimity of their corporate Christology.

The Christology the Synoptics is not particularly early . Thus we should not suggest that the less explicit and "lower" Christology is necessarily earlier and the more explicit and "higher" Christology is later.[14] Indeed, closer parallels to the Johannine Christology occur in the letters of Paul, the earliest New Testament documents, than in the Synoptics which, in the case of Matthew at least, is probably more or less contemporary with the Fourth Gospel. Nevertheless, it is likely that the Synoptic use of tradition is closer to the language of Jesus than John so that the form of John's explicit Christology represents a reflective development of that tradition and this is true also of Paul at his earlier stage in the history of the tradition.

The Distinctive Form of John's Christology

The distinctive form of the Johannine Christology can be identified in a summary fashion.[15] It is made up of a number of disparate elements. On the one hand there is the signs tradition in which Jesus is depicted in terms often related to the figure of a *theios aner* which is reconstructed from Hellenistic texts.[16] These motifs are used to

---

[12] This phenomenon led William Wrede to speak of the "messianic secret", especially in Mark (*The Messianic Secret* [trans. J.C.G. Grieg; Cambridge & London: James Clarke & Co., 1971]).

[13] See Rudolf Bultmann, *Theology of the New Testament* 1 (London, 1951) 37, and my *Theology as Hermeneutics*, (Sheffield, 1987) 104–5.

[14] Here, as commonly, where the terminology of "higher" and "lower" Christology is used, "higher" indicates the more explicit and closer identification of Jesus with God. See Paul Anderson, *The Christology of the Fourth Gospel* (WUNT 2/78; Tübingen: J.C.B. Mohr [Paul Siebeck], 1996) Appendices I & II. Anderson refers to the "high" and "low" Christologies of John. What he fails to note is that, in John, the low Christology serves the high Christology and is not independent of it. Thus, in John, those elements labelled "low" are dialectically part of the high Christology.

[15] See Anderson, *Christology*, 19–23.

[16] On the place of a *theios aner* Christology in John see *The Quest for the Messiah*,

demonstrate Jesus' divine power and supernatural knowledge. Then there are motifs associated with specific titles.

Associated with the λόγος are the motifs of relationship with God; of pre-existing creation; of identification with God (is God); as the agent of creation; as the source of life and light. The description of Jesus as μονογενής is closely related to other motifs dealing with Jesus as the revealer. This is certainly true of the Father/Son imagery, which is related to mutual knowledge; mutual love and subordination of the Son to the Father in a way that claims the revelation of the Father in the Son. The Son is spoken of using passive motifs: he is the sent one while the Father is the sender; he is the given while the Father is the giver. From the first reference to the Son of Man in John this figure is associated with the future and is identified as a heavenly figure (1:51). From the perspective of Jesus' ministry, Son of Man sayings have a reference to future and greater events. However, even though the focus may be on the ascent (lifting up) of the Son of Man, his prior descent is at least an important pre-supposition (3:13–14; 6:27, 33, 62). The ascent of the Son of Man is also depicted in passive terms, he must be lifted up (or glorified).

In John this event is inseparable from the crucifixion of Jesus though it is something more.[17] The crucifixion is the means by which the ascent and glorification takes place. It is also the event in which the Son of Man gives (will give, future from the perspective of 6:27) the food which brings eternal life. Interestingly, in a first person saying, not a Son of Man saying, Jesus says, "and the bread I will give is my flesh for the life of the world" (6:51).[18] Because the crucifixion of Jesus is understood as an essential aspect of the giving of God (3:16), as the glorification of the Son of Man (Jesus) it reveals the character of his glory. This is consistent with the exposition of the revelation of the glory of the incarnate *Logos* set out in 1:14. There it is said:

10–16. A significant criticism of this position is that such a figure is found in no text prior to John and when it is found it is a construct from a variety of texts. See Carl Holladay, *Theios Aner in Hellenistic Judaism: A Critique of the Use of This Category in New Testament Christology* (Missoula: Scholars, 1977).

[17] See "Exaltation and Glorification as Crucifixion Plus" in my *Quest for the Messiah*, 337–8.

[18] Here also we notice John's concern for the life of the world, a perspective not restricted to 3:16 or 17:21–23.

1. The glory was seen, "We saw (aorist tense) his glory". That is, it was seen in the life and actions of Jesus.[19]

2. The glory was revealed in Jesus, recognised as the unique Son from the Father. Thus the Father/Son relationship is made evident in the revelation of the glory. In that the Son is *from* the Father, the revelation of the glory of the Son is the glory of the Father (17:22), who is the origin and source of the glory (see 1:18; 14:9).

3. The character of the glory is described as "full of grace and truth". The revelation in Jesus has as its purpose to transform the believer's understanding of the character of God. The prologue sets out this objective from the beginning at the Gospel. The self-giving of Jesus, who gave himself for the life of the world, is understood as the self-giving of God (3:16; cf. 1 John 4:7–12).

Nevertheless, the activity of the Son of Man finds focus in two central aspects of the work of God, giving life (6:27) and judgement. In John 5 the future judgement is expressed in a Son of Man saying (5:27) while the giving of life is associated with the Son of God, the Son (5:25–26). Here we find an amalgam of Son (Son of God), Son of Man and I sayings.[20] What are we to make of this?

The Central Structure of John's Christology

W.R.G. Loader refers to aspects of the Christology of the Gospel as "the central structure". His identification is based on a study of a variety of passages which reveal the recurrence of various motifs. The central structure is first identified in a study of John 3:31–36.[21] From this passage five motifs are isolated which occur frequently. They are the focus of special discourses and feature in summaries in the Gospel.

---

[19] From the perspective of the Gospel it is likely that this is understood in the light of the resurrection/glorification of Jesus (2:22; 12:16) although 2:11 suggests a recognition of the glory during Jesus' ministry.

[20] See my *Quest for the Messiah*, 221–35 on John 5:17–30. In 6:27 it is the Son of Man who will give the food which give eternal life. See the development of this in "I" sayings in 6:33, 48–51.

[21] W.R.G. Loader, "The Central Structure of Johannine Christology". *NTS* 30 (1984) 188–216. See also his *The Christology of the Fourth Gospel* (Frankfurt am Main: Peter Lang, 1989), especially pp. 20–92 where the discussion is expanded as is the detail of the central structure.

(i) The reference to Jesus and God as Son and Father.
(ii) That the Son comes from and returns to the Father.
(iii) That the Father has sent the Son.
(iv) That the Father has given all things into the Son's hands.
(v) That the Son says and does what the Father has told him.
He makes the Father known. (pp. 191–2)

The centrality of this structure is demonstrated by its ability to integrate all other christological motifs in the Gospel (pp. 188, 192)

Supporting the central structure is the Son of Man cluster which legitimises the portrayal of Jesus in the Gospel (p. 209). Both the central structure and the Son of Man cluster are rooted in parts of the Son of Man tradition (p. 207). Nevertheless, only the Son of Man cluster makes use of Son of Man and where it overlaps the themes of the central structure it does so using its own distinctive language.[22] This language is clearest in 12:23, 31–34 where "the hour" (see also 2:4; 7:6, 30; 8:20) of the glorification of the Son of Man is identified with his death by which he glorifies God (12:28; 13:31–32). This is the basis of the success for his mission when the uplifted Son of Man will draw all people to himself (12:32; cf. 12:24). That gathering is foreshadowed by the coming of the Greeks (12.20–22, 24). The symbolism of glorification and lifting up (exaltation) associated with Jesus' death implies levels beyond the sheer physical event of the crucifixion.

At this point Loader elaborates the Son of Man cluster in texts that do not mention the Son of Man. He says that the glorification of the Son of Man is the prerequisite for the sending of the Spirit (7:39) and the true understanding of scripture (12:16; cf. 2:22). Thus he assumes that because the Gospel says that the Son of Man will be glorified/lifted up, reference to future glorification/lifting up can be taken as part of the Son of Man cluster even though the Son of Man is not mentioned and themes not in explicit Son of Man texts are introduced. It is also noted that in the Farewell discourses the themes of the Son of Man cluster are expressed in terms of the Son rather than the Son of Man. Nevertheless the conclusion is drawn that "the focus of the cluster remains intact" and "the cluster expresses a clear soteriology" which "is used to interpret the climax of Jesus'

---

[22] For example, the "cluster" uses the language of descent and ascent while the central structure refers to coming and going.

ministry" where "passion, resurrection, exaltation, ascension, and glorification are all seen together as one event" (p. 198).

Loader notes that "the messianic tradition is integrated within the central christological structure" but Johannine Christology involves more than messiahship (p. 193).[23] The Son of Man cluster is used to highlight the something greater yet to come from the perspective of Jesus' ministry (pp. 197–8). Thus Nathaniel's messianic confession is modified by a saying with future reference concerning seeing the exalted Son of Man. We might say that John uses the Son of Man motif to develop, perhaps even correct, the messianic confession.

Yet Loader sees the central structure, with its focus on Son and Son of God, as distinct from the Son of Man cluster, which finds its focus on the Son of Man.

Son of God and Son of Man

Loader thinks that the central structure and the Son of Man cluster are independently developed from different parts of the Son of Man tradition. Nevertheless, the Son of Man cluster is independent of and yet essential to the intelligibility of the central structure. This surely means that, in a sense, the Son of Man cluster is integrated into the central structure of John's Christology.[24] Indeed, Loader recognises considerable synthesis in the last discourses with a less developed stage of synthesis in chapters 1–13. His view of the distinctness of the two in John is based on the judgement that changes in terminology indicate a lack of synthesis (from descent and ascent to coming and going). Is it really the case that "in the cluster the descent has no more significance than to be the presupposition of all significant ascent" while "in the central structure . . . the coming is the essential presupposition of the earthly work of revelation, whereas the going is but a return to the Father"? (p. 200)

According to John 6:27 it is the Son of Man who gives the true bread from heaven. John 6:33 builds on 6:27 asserting that "For the bread of God is the one descending (ὁ καταβαίνων) from heaven to

---

[23] Loader says "there is more to know than Jesus' messiahship, and also more to know than what is expressed in the central structure." That something more is found in the Son of Man cluster. I suggest that we may also describe this in terms of the transformation from messiahship into Christology.

[24] Contrary to Loader (p. 199).

give life to the world". It builds on the Son of Man saying in 6:27 which uses the language of descent in the cluster. This is hardly a descent simply to make an ascent possible. It is the means by which he gives his flesh (his mortal life) for the life of the world. In 6:48–51 Jesus, in an "I" saying, identifies himself with the bread which came down (καταβαίνων or καταβάς) from heaven. He says, "I am the bread of life" and "the bread which I will give is my flesh for the life of the world". In the discourse the "I" sayings of Jesus take up the motifs from the Son of Man sayings. The same is true of the way "I" sayings are taken up and develop Father-Son sayings.[25] Rather than seeing tensions between different traditions in this we may recognise the evangelist's use of a variety of motifs in the development of the Christology of the Gospel. Thus the departure of Jesus is not simply his return to the Father. It is the necessary means by which the Spirit Paraclete comes to believers (16:7). Neither this verse nor 7:39 should be attributed to the Son of Man cluster.

Loader's analysis which distinguishes the central structure, with "Son" and "Son of God" sayings, from the Son of Man cluster, in which Son of Man sayings are to be found, suggests important different understandings of the two titles. While there are those who think that all the titles mean much the same thing,[26] there has been a resurgence of those who see Son of God referring to the divine while Son of Man is a reference to the incarnate Son.[27] Apart from other problems, such interpretations have trouble dealing with John 3:13 and 6:62.[28] The meaning here is clear. Only the Son of Man, who first descended to earth has, subsequently ascended into heaven. Thus the Son of Man in John is the heavenly figure of Dan 7:13–14.

---

[25] See my *Quest for the Messiah*, 221–35.

[26] See E.D. Freed, "The Son of Man in the Fourth Gospel", *JBL* 86 (1967) 402–9.

[27] This is the position of F.J. Moloney, *The Johannine Son of Man* (Rome, 1976) who accepts the titular use with reference to the incarnate Son. See also William O. Walker, Jr, "John 1:43–51 and 'The Son of Man' in the Fourth Gospel", *JSNT* 56 (1994) 31–42.

[28] Those who see a reference to a heavenly enthronement scene are not persuasive. Thus Peder Borgen, "Some Jewish Exegetical Traditions as Background for Son of Man Sayings (Jn 3,13–14 and context)" in *L'Evangile de* Jean (ed. M. de Jonge; Leuven, 1977) 243–58.

Evaluation

While Loader's study accentuates important characteristics of the
Johannine Christology it does not do justice to the integrated development of the discourses in John and of Johannine thought in the
Gospel as a whole. The composition of the Johannine Christology
is more complex and nuanced than this analysis of the central structure and independent Son of Man complex suggests. Certainly John
has used a variety of important images in the Gospel. But this is
more complex because the evangelist has worked creatively and with
some freedom to present a distinctive Christology. A good example
of the complexity can be found in John 5. Here we need to distinguish between the third person discourse where Jesus speaks of the
Father-Son relationship and of the Son of Man; and the first person language where Jesus speaks of his relationship to God in intimate terms.[29] We might well ask, what is the point of this christological
development?

The Function of John's Christology or the Point of John's Christology

Motifs used in the scriptures to portray the Law are used by John
to develop his Christology. This is already apparent in the Prologue
where the Wisdom/Law tradition is used to affirm Jesus' unity with
the Father (God). But what is the point of the affirmation of unity
and why is the Wisdom/Law tradition used? The answer proposed
here is that two dominant rival sets of symbols are set against each
other. This accentuates the conflict which emerges because, where
one asserts the reality of the symbols in terms of the Law, the other
asserts the reality in terms of Jesus. What results from this (in John)
is a radical transformation of the understanding of the revelation of
the will and purpose of God, indeed, there is a radical transformation of theology in the light of John's Christology.

Loader is of the view that John's "high" Christology should be
understood functionally (p. 202). Thus we may ask what is the meaning of "preexistence", and language about relationship to God, the
Father-Son relationship, the sender and the sent one, the meaning
of Wisdom motifs applied to Jesus (cf. Paul in 1 Cor 1:24), the

---

[29] See my *Quest*, pp. 213–52, especially pp. 226–35.

description of his role in creation and revelation, incarnation (cf. Paul in Gal 4:4), the language of "coming and going", "descent and ascent", and mission. Many of these motifs are also found in the Synoptics, though less prominently and less systematically.[30] How does John understand this language?

While Loader does not address this question directly, he has the following to say. "Oneness with the Father, whether expressed in terms of logos, mutual indwelling, or divine sonship, is interpreted in accordance with the central structure. The oneness lies in the fact that the Son does as the Father does, speaks what he has heard, tells what he has seen, and so on. In other words the divinity of Jesus is primarily functionally perceived, and implicit in it is the assumption that Jesus and God are two distinct beings, with the Son subordinate, but a heavenly being who in his pre-existence shared a unique relationship with God. . . . The model appears to be that of the wisdom-logos hypostasis, but the relationship is primarily functional." (p. 202).

Precisely what Loader means by functional in this context is unclear, first because it is qualified by "primarily". Thus he says that "the divinity of Jesus is primarily functionally perceived". Yet he refers to Jesus and God as "two distinct beings" and the Son is a subordinate "heavenly being who in his pre-existence shared a unique relationship with God . . ., but the relationship is primarily functional." Then Loader says, "Thus the fourth gospel exhibits the twofold phenomenon of having a 'high' Christology in the sense that Jesus is no mere man but a heavenly being, Son of God, and on the other hand defining the relationship with God not in substantial but in highly functional terms. Jesus is qualified as the revealer not on grounds of his being, but on grounds of what he has been and the relationship which he has." (p. 202 and see note 53 also).

---

[30] The Synoptics use both πέμπω and ἀποστέλλω to speak of Jesus' mission which is also expressed by Jesus saying, "I came . . . (ἦλθον). See Mark 9:37; 12:6; 2:17 and the parallels in Matthew and Luke. But the Synoptics do not develop a systematic understanding of Jesus based on the use of this language the way John does. In John Jesus characterises himself as the one sent and the Father as "the Father who sent me" (ὁ πέμψας με πατήρ), see John 4:34; 5:23, 24, 30, 37; 6:38, 39, 44; 7:16, 28, 33; 8:16, 18, 26, 29; 9:4; 12:44, 45, 49; 13:20; 14:24; 15:21; 16:5. The verb πέμπω is not used of Jesus apart from this formula though ἀποστέλλω is. Indeed, seventeen of the twenty eight uses of ἀποστέλλω are used of the sending of Jesus. Not one of these occurs in the formula common to the use of πέμπω. The frequent use of the formula is significant. What is its function?

This "both and" position should not be described as functional, not even primarily functional. If the revealer's function is under-girded by his heavenly being we do not have a functional Christology. That being has a function is obvious but a functional reading takes ontological statements to have only a functional meaning.[31] This does not seem to be Loader's point. Nevertheless his approach is on the right track. Much of John's christological language functions to affirm that God is revealed in Jesus' life and work. The question is whether such a reading leaves a residue of Johannine meaning untapped. If we can discover why the language was used, we may be in a better position to answer this question.

Conflict

John has drawn on diverse traditions, using them as appropriate in the development of Christology. The different titles each implies a range of motifs which John uses, weaving them together to express the overall view attained in the Gospel. Choice of titles and motifs is guided by a number of factors. First, John draws on what he finds in the tradition. Then the treatment intersects with positions that are fundamentally opposed, drawing on the central imagery of those positions but construing a different meaning. John opposes alternative views of God, God's purpose and alternative views of the nature of human life in the world. The Gospel develops its views using traditional christological resources, some of which are drawn from the messianic tradition of Judaism, and using also the central symbols of the traditions opposed. Thus Christology confronts the traditions opposed at their very heart. It is not a superficial confrontation but one in which the heart of the Johannine tradition intersects in confrontation with an alternative tradition at its very heart.

Why does Christology lead to conflict and with whom does the Johannine Christology provoke conflict? Given that the Johannine Christology is not just a repetition of what Jesus taught about himself, and that the teaching of the Gospel is not a straightforward

---

[31] See for example Rudolf Bultmann's demythologising programme set out in "New Testament and Mythology" (1941) now in *New Testament and Mythology and Other Basic Writings* (selected, edited and translated by Schubert Ogden; Philadelphia: Fortress, 1984); and *Jesus Christ and Mythology* (London: SCM, 1960 [US edition 1958]).

account of what Jesus taught, how did the teaching of the Johannine Jesus come to be expressed in Johannine terms? One likely suggestion is that, in the conflict Jesus encountered with the Jewish leaders, he pitted his authority against theirs. If their authority was seen to be the law, then Jesus can be seen in conflict with the law, at least as it was understood by the Jewish leaders. It may have been in this way that Jesus came to be set over against the role of the law. Long ago W.D. Davies argued that, for Paul, Jesus had taken the place of the law.[32] Just as the law was understood to have a cosmic role, as God's agent in creation, so now Jesus is so understood.

This suggestion also seems to be relevant to an understanding of the development of Johannine Christology. If this is somewhere near the mark, it is not surprising that the Johannine Christology leads to conflict in a Jewish context. The conflict finds expression in the Prologue (1:5, 11, 17). If the Prologue is an introduction prepared for the finished work, this is not surprising. But in the body of the Gospel the conflict does not emerge clearly until John 5. This chapter develops out of a Sabbath incident where Jesus, charged with breaking the Sabbath, makes claims that lead to a christological controversy with the Jews (5:16–18). This controversy ends with the first recorded attempt to kill Jesus.

The Shape of Johannine Christology

In the Prologue the first explicit reference to Jesus addresses him as "Jesus Christ" (1:17), a form of reference found elsewhere in John only at 17:3. This form of address may be understood in two ways. It may be taken as shorthand for "Jesus is the Christ" or, more likely, on the assumption that Christ is a personal name, distinguishing this Jesus from many others bearing the same name. Even the latter, which presupposes a non-Jewish context, ultimately presupposes the identification of Jesus with the Christ. But this was often obscured in non-Jewish contexts.

What is surprising is that there are two further uses of Christ before the evangelist explains the meaning of the term. In the intervening two uses John (the Baptist) explains, "I am not the Christ"

---

[32] See his *Paul and Rabbinic Judaism* (London: SPCK, 1965) 147–76 and especially 177.

(1:20) and those who were questioning him ask him, "Why do you baptise if you are not the Christ . . .?" (1:25 cf. 3:28). In these two references it is clear that "the Christ" is not a personal name but a title of some sort, though no attempt is made to explain its meaning. This is surprising because, when John bears witness to Jesus he does so in terms of "the lamb of God who bears away the sin of the world" (1:29, 36) and "the son of God" (1:34).[33] Nevertheless, one of the two of his disciples whom he introduces to Jesus, Andrew, reports to Simon (Peter), "We have found the Messiah" and the narrator explains "which is translated Christ" (1:41 cf. 1:42; 4:25).[34]

John piles up a number of designations to illuminate his understanding of "the Christ". But what is surprising is that the clarification of "the Christ" is held back until 1:41 and is repeated again at 4:25. Although the discussion between John and his questioners is an intra-Jewish discussion (1:19–28), the term Christ is used without reference to "the Messiah". Perhaps this explanation is held back until it is given in witness to Jesus in 1:41. Certainly the reader is left with the impression that the identification of the meaning of Messiah as Christ is important for the Gospel, especially as it is repeated in 4:25. But how does John understand the Messiahship of Jesus?

Even when we make allowance for the diversity of messianic expectations in second temple Judaism, the identification of Christ as the Messiah is the *starting point* of John's Christology. Thus, although Christ is the Greek translation of the Semitic Messiah, in John Christology is the Christian transformation of Jewish expectations. In the case of John, the christological development was instrumental in the emergence of the conflict.

---

[33] Textual variants here range from "the Son of God", "the chosen one", "the chosen Son", "the only begotten Son". While "the Son of God" has strongest textual support, "the chosen one" is the reading of greatest difficulty and has some claim to originality.

[34] In 1:41 the explanation (ὁ ἐστιν μεθερμηνευόμενον Χριστός) is commonly taken to be a comment by the narrator. See 1:42 where a different expression is used (ὃ ἑρμηνεύεται Πέτρος). Another idiom is used in 4:25 (ὁ λεγόμενος Χριστός). These should also be understood as explanations to the reader by the narrator. There is no good reason to attribute one idiom to the source and another to the evangelist. The idioms are an example of the evangelist's liking of variation of vocabulary without change of meaning. See the use of ἀγαπᾶν and φιλεῖν, ἀποστέλλειν and πέμπειν in the Gospel.

The Causes of Conflict

Lacking from John is the criticism of Jesus mixing with tax collectors and sinners characteristic of the Synoptics. Also missing is any dispute over food and purity issues and the exorcisms so common to Mark. Certainly John shares with the Synoptics disputes over Sabbath observance (Mark 2:23–28; John 5:1–18; 9:1–41). Indeed, this is the specific issue over which conflict first emerges in John (5:16), reminding us of the specifically Jewish character of the conflict. Nevertheless, the issue soon moves from Sabbath controversy to Christology (5:17–18).

In Mark Christology does not become an issue until the trial of Jesus (14:61–64), and then in traditional terms, "the Christ, the Son of the Blessed". Here "Christ" must be understood in terms of Messiah even if Jesus responds by referring to seeing "the Son of Man sitting at the right hand of power and coming with the clouds of heaven". The response of the high priest, rending his garments and pronouncing Jesus guilty of blasphemy is puzzling. The high priest himself identified the Christ with the Son of the Blessed so that Jesus' admission, "I am", means only that he admits to being the Christ. But the High Priest himself described the Christ as "the Son of the Blessed", which is a circumlocution for God. Even if we allow that the Sadduccean High Priest presumed a broad definition of blasphemy it is not easy to see how this might apply. His language must be understood in Jewish, messianic terms rather than in Christian christological terms affirming divinity.[35] But how can it be blasphemy to admit to being the Christ? Or is it Jesus' identification of the Christ with the heavenly Son of Man that constitutes the basis of the charge of blasphemy?[36]

The identification of the Christ with the heavenly Son of Man might allow for some understanding that would provide a basis for the charge. But this is neither clear nor is it developed by Mark. In clear distinction from this, the first instance of conflict in John is based on a Sabbath healing and the narrator informs us, "because

---

[35] The reference has to be understood at two levels. In the narrative the use of the language by the High Priest takes "Son of the Blessed" to be a designation of the Messiah. For Mark it has a more profound sense.

[36] Jesus' use of Son of Man could be understood as a claim to heavenly, if not divine, status.

of this the Jews were persecuting Jesus, because he was doing these
things on the Sabbath". To this Jesus responds, "My Father is working until now and I am working" (5:17). The narrator then informs
us that the Jews sought *all the more* to kill Jesus because he not only
broke the Sabbath [commandment], he also called God his own
father, making himself equal with God (5:18). This controversy
reemerges in 10:31–39 where the Jews seek to stone Jesus for blasphemy "because you being a man make yourself God" (10:33).
Conflict is concentrated in John 5–10. It continues in John 11 but
the seriousness of the charge is reduced and Lazarus, who has been
raised from the dead by Jesus, is as much the target of violence as
Jesus because the problem now in view is the following produced
through the sign of the raising of Lazarus (11:45–53; 12:9–11). This
moves back from the seriousness of the charge brought against Jesus
in John 5 and 10. It is now an expediency in response to the threat
posed by Roman intervention to a popular messianic movement.

In John, Christology confronts the Law because it is the primary
Jewish symbol for understanding God. The choice of Wisdom/
Torah motifs for the portrayal of Jesus focuses attention on the way
Christology encounters the primary Jewish symbol to modify the
meaning it conveys. In particular the Jesus of John confronts the law
on the matter of Sabbath observance. Two of the great conflict chapters deal with Sabbath controversies (John 5 and 9). In Genesis, the
institution of the Sabbath symbolises the completion of the creation.
God rested from his works. John 5 not only asserts God's continuing work but the work of Jesus also continues on the Sabbath in
order to make the man whole. Thus the first conflict concerns the
world which John asserts is in the process of being created and it
is not yet whole. Then there is a different view of God. From the
perspective of the Law, the dominant characteristic of God is justice but in the light of the Johannine Jesus the dominant characteristic of the Father is love. As a consequence, the appropriate
response to God is also transformed. Keeping the law is not enough
unless the law is seen to be encompassed in the love command.

SATAN, DEMONS AND THE ABSENCE OF EXORCISMS IN THE FOURTH GOSPEL

Ronald A. Piper

There are few places in New Testament scholarship where the inter-action of Christology, controversy and community is more apparent than in the fourth gospel.[1] It is hardly an exaggeration to claim that everything in the fourth gospel revolves around Christology. The nature of "the Johannine community" and its controversy with the synagogue have also become (despite some recent doubts)[2] regular features of Johannine study. But there are still some very puzzling aspects of the world depicted by the fourth evangelist and the conflicts he depicts. One of these is Jesus' conflict with Satan. Why, in par-ticular, are there no exorcisms in John's gospel? This essay will try to provide an answer; it will then attempt to follow up some of the implications of that answer.

The Absence of Exorcisms

It is well-known that there are many differences between John and the synoptic gospels, but often the lack of exorcisms in the fourth gospel has been considered a peculiarity which has drawn only cur-sory comment. Recently, however, discussion of this topic has begun to increase, not least through the studies of G.H. Twelftree[3] and E. Plumer.[4]

---

[1] A version of this paper was presented to the British New Testament Society in Aberdeen, September 1996.

[2] R.J. Bauckham, ed., *The Gospels for All Christians: Rethinking the Gospel Audiences* (Edinburgh: T. & T. Clark, 1998), esp. 9–48, 147–71; M. Hengel, *The Johannine Question* (London: SCM/Philadelphia: TPI, 1989) 114–24.

[3] *Jesus the Exorcist. A Contribution to the Study of the Historical Jesus* (WUNT 2.54; Tübingen: J.C.B. Mohr/Paul Siebeck, 1993); idem, *Jesus the Miracle Worker* (Downers Grove IL: InterVarsity, 1999); idem, "Demon, Devil, Satan" in *Dictionary of Jesus and the Gospels* (ed. J.B. Green, S. McKnight; Downers Grove IL: InterVarsity, 1992) 163–72.

[4] "The Absence of Exorcisms in the Fourth Gospel", *Bib* 78 (1997) 350–68.

Mark's gospel of course shows Jesus performing exorcisms from the very start of his ministry, and in this Mark is followed by the other synoptic writers. Even Q—which has hardly any thaumaturgical narrative—contains an exorcism (Q 11:14). J.P. Meier's study of the historical Jesus devotes over 500 pages to the miracles of Jesus and divides them into four categories: exorcisms, healings, raisings from the dead, and the so-called nature miracles.[5] The exorcisms and the healings are the two categories where he seems most confident of genuine activity by the historical Jesus.[6] While these are modern and perhaps artificial classifications,[7] it is nonetheless intriguing that John's gospel has examples of all the categories *except* the exorcisms. Why?

It is not initially clear whether this question can lead to anything beyond speculation. So at the start we should probably ask: how likely is it that John's silence about exorcisms is significant in terms of his purposes, situation or world view? To answer this, perhaps we need to consider the alternative. How might it *not* be significant in these terms?

One possibility is that it is simply an "accident" that John lacks an exorcism, not due to any theological motive or source deficiency. The fourth gospel cannot include everything. Nothing further of significance can be said.[8] This becomes less probable, however, if interest in the actions of Satan and the vocabulary of the demonic are not entirely absent in John and if the fame of Jesus as an exorcist was quite widespread in early Christian tradition.

Moreover, while many scholars continue to support the independence of the fourth gospel from the synoptic gospels, it is often accepted that John's gospel (at some stage) shows knowledge of synoptic traditions. Indeed, the pendulum now seems to be swinging increasingly in favour of Johannine knowledge of at least some of the other gospels.[9] It is difficult to believe that the evangelist would

---

[5] J.P. Meier, *A Marginal Jew. Rethinking the Historical Jesus*, Vol. 2: *Mentor, Message, and Miracles* (Anchor Bible Reference Library; New York, etc.: Doubleday, 1994) 509–1038.

[6] Meier, *Marginal Jew* 2.61, 727, 969–70.

[7] See, for example, D.E. Aune, "Magic in Early Christianity", in *ANRW* II.23.2 (ed. W. Haase; Berlin/New York: W. de Gruyter, 1980) 1529: "A closer analysis of the healing narratives, however, reveals that they stand in a more fluid relationship to exorcism stories than first appears."

[8] See the discussion and rejection of this view by M. Labahn, *Jesus als Lebensspender. Untersuchungen zu einer Geschichte der johanneischen Tradition anhand ihrer Wundergeschichten* (BZNW 98; Berlin/New York: W. de Gruyter, 1999) 483.

[9] See discussion in D.M. Smith, *John Among the Gospels. The Relationship in Twentieth-*

have been totally unaware of traditions of Jesus' exorcisms while at the same time being familiar with all the other aspects of Jesus' wonderworking.[10] If he relied exclusively upon a Signs Source,[11] then the question might effectively be pushed back a stage—why did the *semeia* source omit this category of wonders? There is no reason, however, to think that the author's knowledge of the tradition of Jesus' wonderworking was so restricted.[12]

Doubts about an absence of knowledge of exorcisms in the Johannine tradition are increased by other factors:

1. John certainly knew and used the vocabulary pertaining to demons and possession (John 7:20, 8:48, 52; 10:20). Judas is labelled as a διάβολος in 6:70. There are also references to Satan (John 13:27), the Devil (John 8:44; 13:2; cf. 1 John 3:8–10), the Evil One (John 17:15; cf. 1 John 2:13–14; 3:12; 5:18–19) and the Ruler of this World (cf. John 12:31; 14:30; 16:11, cf. 16:33).[13] Therefore even though John's accounts of signs are restricted in number, it is unlikely that one can claim that he recorded no exorcism simply because he

---

Century Research (Minneapolis: Fortress, 1992); and F. Neirynck, "John and the Synoptics: 1975–1990", in *John and the Synoptics* (ed. A. Denaux; BETL 101; Leuven: Leuven University, 1992) 3–62.

[10] See Plumer, "Absence", 350–4. Plumer concludes: "the possibility that St. John knew nothing of Jesus' exorcisms (or that he knew them but regarded them as unimportant) seems so remote as to be negligible" (p. 354). So also E.P. Sanders, *The Historical Figure of Jesus* (London: Allen Lane Penguin, 1993) 154: "I think that we may be fairly certain that initially Jesus' *fame* came as a result of healing, especially exorcism."

[11] See G. van Belle, *The Signs Source in the Fourth Gospel: Historical Survey and Critical Evaluation of the Semeia Hypothesis* (BETL 116; Leuven: Leuven University, 1994). R.T. Fortna (*The Gospel of Signs: A Reconstruction of the Narrative Source Underlying the Fourth Gospel* [SNTSMS 11; Cambridge: CUP, 1970] 100) considers the lack of an exorcism to be hardly accidental, "but whether it is due to conscious intent on the part of John cannot be known; it may be merely that the author of the source, or the tradition he relied on, took no interest in demons or their overthrow." Later Fortna (pp. 228–31) relates the absence of exorcism in the signs source to the absence of interest in eschatology and thus of "the victory over demons represented by Jesus' exorcism" (p. 229). See similarly J. Becker, "Wunder und Christologie. Zum literarkritischen und christologischen Problem der Wunder im Johannesevangelium", *NTS* 16 (1969–70) 443. Nevertheless, the evangelist is credited by Becker with polemicising against the Christology of the Signs Source (p. 459), so that one still is left asking why—even in summary statements—the *evangelist* maintains a silence about exorcisms.

[12] In addition to John 20:30, Plumer ("Absence", 352) rightly notes John 7:31; 10:32; 11:47; 12:37. In these cases the evangelist stresses the abundance of Jesus' miracles.

[13] Cf. also the interest of 1 John in antichrists (2:18), false prophets (4:1), and deceiving spirits (4:6).

gives a low priority to the sphere of Satan and the demonic. The fourth gospel on the contrary shows some significant interest in this area. This makes the omission of the exorcisms all the more striking.

2. Some scholars (such as E.K. Broadhead)[14] also find vestiges of exorcistic traditions in other parts of the fourth gospel.[15] It is not possible to consider these in detail here, but they do suggest that the evidence cited above might be extended. Most interesting is a possible reminiscence of the synoptic Beelzebul controversy in the accusations of John 7:20, 8:48, 52 and 10:20.[16]

3. More speculatively perhaps, one of Barnabas Lindars' last published works on John[17] argued that John actually knew an exorcism story quite similar to the cure of a demon-possessed boy in Mark 9:14–29. Lindars argued that the Mark 9 account had already been partially adapted to illustrate Christian teaching on death and resurrection and that the fourth evangelist took this further, changing it from the cure of a demon-possessed boy to the raising of a dead man, Lazarus (John 11:38–44). Moreover, Lindars declares: "It is not necessary to assume that he disapproved of attributing exorcism to Jesus, for he uses the language of demon possession without difficulty in 8.48, and Jesus' own death and resurrection win the victory over Satan (12.31)."[18]

4. G. Twelftree[19] builds upon the argument of R. Bauckham that John was written for Christian readers at large and not solely for a single community or particular audience. If this is so, he argues, then in view of the wide popular knowledge of Jesus as an exorcist, it is unlikely that the evangelist omitted exorcisms simply because of

---

[14] E.K. Broadhead ("Echoes of an Exorcism in the Fourth Gospel?", *ZNW* 86 [1995] 111–19) with regard to John 6:66–71.

[15] Note, however, that some terms associated with exorcism are absent in the fourth gospel, such as ἐπιτιμᾶν, φιμοῦν, (ἐξ)ορκίζω (see Aune, "Magic", 1530–2). For the use of ἐκβάλλω, see below.

[16] Cf. Plumer, "Absence", 353, 359–61. Although he shows reserve about some of the evidence often cited to demonstrate John's knowledge of the synoptic controversy story, he thinks that the "underlying tradition" leads ultimately to the conclusion that "this parallelism is not fortuitous but betrays St. John's knowledge of the Beelzebul controversy", albeit "seen through a glass, darkly" (p. 360).

[17] B. Lindars, "Rebuking the Spirit: A New Analysis of the Lazarus Story of John 11", *NTS* 38 (1992) 89–104.

[18] Lindars, "Rebuking", 101.

[19] *Miracle Worker*, 222. Twelftree (pp. 282–3) also cites evidence outside the New Testament that "Jesus was remembered as a powerful exorcist" (p. 282). See below nn. 58 and 61.

an alleged disinterest within a *particular* community. Similarly, it would be unlikely that a localised lack of knowledge of Jesus' exorcisms can be reasonably argued.

If therefore one is prepared to grant for at least *one* of the reasons given above that it is highly improbable that the Johannine evangelist simply did not know that Jesus performed exorcisms,[20] then how else might one explain their absence—and not only the absence of an exorcism narrative but even of *a passing reference* to Jesus performing exorcisms?[21]

Many suggestions can be offered, and a very diverse set of answers has recently begun to emerge. One possibility is to suggest that the evangelist knew the synoptic traditions but was seeking to supplement rather than reproduce those traditions.[22] Yet with regard to the issue of the absence of exorcisms, such an explanation would hardly be more satisfactory than claiming that he did not know the traditions at all. Not only does the fourth gospel record healings, a raising from the dead and nature miracles, but it also records some incidents which are strikingly similar to those in the synoptic tradition—such as the feeding miracle (John 6:1–15; cf. Mark 6:32–44), the walking on the sea (John 6:16–21, cf. Mark 6:45–52; 4:35–41), the healing of the official's son (John 4:46–53; cf. Matt 8:5–13 par. Luke 7:1–10), and possibly the cure of the sick man at the pool of Bethesda (John 5:1–9; cf. Mark 2:1–12) and the large catch of fish (John 21:4–14; cf. Luke 5:1–11). If the fourth gospel provides versions of these stories, it is difficult to believe that the *main* reason for not including exorcisms is that they were already known from the synoptic tradition.

Is it a matter of the fourth gospel having a world view which has effectively "demythologised" such concepts as "exorcism" or "demons" of "Satan"?[23] Certainly the evangelist can re-work motifs found in

---

[20] Plumer ("Absence", 353–4) also notes the attention given in the fourth gospel to Mary Magdalene, who elsewhere in Christian tradition is known as one from whom seven demons were cast out (Luke 8:2).

[21] The significance of the absence of reference from the signs summaries should not be underestimated. See also Labahn, *Lebensspender*, 482–3, on John 20:30 as a rhetorical convention.

[22] Bauckham (*Gospels*, esp. 170) rejects this formulation of the view in favour of arguing that the fourth gospel has a narrative integrity of its own. More precisely, it can be read by those who knew Mark's gospel as "complementing" Mark.

[23] See further below, esp. n. 81.

the synoptics. Some themes he can reinterpret without omission, such as Son of man. Others he omits, either entirely or almost entirely, such as the phrase "the kingdom of God".[24] Parables, narrative metaphors (often related to the challenge of the kingdom proclamation in the synoptic gospels), are effectively replaced in the fourth gospel by non-narrative metaphors which are mainly christological (Light, Way, Truth, Good Shepherd, Vine, Bread of Life). Has then the fourth gospel reinterpreted or even de-mythologised exorcisms?[25]

E. Plumer offers one such explanation (amongst many other suggestions he makes for the absence of exorcisms) which borders upon these ideas. Probably rightly, Plumer rejects as speculative the hypotheses of R.H. Strachan, D.E.H. Whiteley and others that the evangelist was a former Sadducee who thus came to Christianity not believing in angels or spirits. He also resists the idea attributed to G.H.C. MacGregor and others that the evangelist avoids exorcism accounts in order to distance himself from gnostic speculation about spiritual intermediaries. It is difficult to reconcile a theory of an anti-intermediary bias with texts like John 1:51 and 20:12. Yet these very texts seem to pose difficulties for Plumer's own explanation. Whilst most of his article is based on the premise that the evangelist was "decisively shaped by hostilities existing between the Johannine community and the Jewish synagogue",[26] he nevertheless wishes to argue that the evangelist "sought to give his Gospel a timeless and universal appeal".[27] The evangelist was colliding with many different forms of "religious and philosophical thought" which "called for the presentation of Christianity as the fulfilment not merely of Judaism but of the whole spiritual quest of mankind".[28] Demonology is considered distracting, which is why the evangelist concentrates on Satan as the main representative of evil in the world.[29] But if angelic intermediaries still have a place in the cosmology of the fourth evangelist, why not demonic ones? Does this really detract from the dualism of the fourth gospel? And the question is all the more relevant since

---

[24] Of course the idea is also re-worked into the more christologically-focused kingship of Jesus: John 1:49; 6:15; 12:13, 15; 18:33, 36–7, 39: 19:3, 12, 14–15, 19, 21.
[25] Becker ("Wunder", 436) notes how Bultmann saw *all* wonders in the fourth gospel not as events but only as revelatory images or symbols (thus "signs").
[26] "Absence", 367.
[27] "Absence", 367.
[28] "Absence", 367.
[29] "Absence", 368.

the evangelist can refer to Judas as a διάβολος and to charges of Jesus having a "demon", as noted above. Why does such language persist if it is counter to the world view of the evangelist? These questions press for answers, not to mention more fundamental observations about the pervasiveness of such beliefs in ancient Mediterranean culture. John may well have a distinctive emphasis with respect both to "signs" and to demon possession, but it is not at all obvious that it takes the form of a de-mythologising of or even reduction of interest in intermediary spirits.[30]

So let us probe a little further. In the synoptic exorcism stories, a victim is typically presented whose misfortune is explained as possession by malevolent spirits outside himself. Jesus is then presented as one who can control these spirits. Such control over spirits, though, leaves Jesus himself sometimes open to suspicion and accusations, as we see in Mark 3 or Q 11:15–23. In these controversies Jesus' opponents accuse him of being in the power of Beelzebul. Indeed persons who had the capacity to perform exorcisms or control spirits in other ways were quite liable to be suspected of sorcery and were feared as having the capacity to harm others by their magical techniques. One then has the paradox of "a possessed exorcist". This is known not just from the synoptic accounts cited above, but also from anthropological studies such as that of I.M. Lewis[31] on shamanism and spirit possession and from studies of magic in early Christianity and the Graeco-Roman world such as that by D.E. Aune.[32] This has now been taken up by many other scholars. Regarding the prevalence of "magic" in the gospel tradition, J.D. Crossan suggests that Jesus' work as a magician or wonderworker was a controversial phenomenon *for his friends* as well as for his enemies and thus was a cause of embarrassment. Following the work of John Hull, Crossan suggests that miracles "were, at a very early stage, being washed out of the tradition and, when retained, were being very carefully interpreted".[33] Thus, he writes, one should not be surprised that fewer

---

[30] Note, however, that the term "unclean spirit" is never used in John.

[31] *Ecstatic Religion. A Study of Shamanism and Spirit Possession* (2nd ed.; London/New York: Routledge, 1989).

[32] "Magic", 1522–3, 1533, where Aune relates this to Jesus working within the framework of a socially deviant millennial movement.

[33] J.D. Crossan, The *Historical Jesus. The Life of a Mediterranean Jewish Peasant* (San Francisco: Harper San Francisco, 1991) 310. He does note however that "one might almost conclude that miracles come into the tradition later rather than earlier"

miracles appear in the latest gospel, John's gospel, than appear in
the earliest, Mark. Presumably even more embarrassing than healings or nature miracles would be exorcisms.[34]

Another approach to Johannine embarrassment with exorcisms can
be found in the work of Dale Martin. Building on Lock and Dubos,[35]
Martin looks at illness in the ancient Mediterranean world and argues
that there were two main explanations of the mechanism by which
illness or disease[36] occurred: invasion (or pollution) from the outside,
and imbalance within. In invasion, illness is caused by alien forces
(such as demons) which attack the body from outside and against
which one needs protection. Healing requires expulsion of the harmful agent or pollutant from the body or the binding its influence.[37]
In imbalance, illness results when the ecosystem of the body is out
of equilibrium by some of its *natural* elements becoming too dominant
or too passive. Healing comes through moderation and re-balancing;
pollution from outside was not a paramount fear. Martin suggests
the educated classes in the early Roman period tended to conceptualise illness along the lines of imbalance; the more *popular* understanding was of invasion. Thus when he turns to the New Testament,
Martin suggests that the synoptic gospels and *most early Christians*
viewed illness as the invasion of hostile, cosmic, personal agents—
corresponding to the popular view in society at large. And indeed
a pervasive anxiety about demons was prevalent during the early
Christian era and Second Temple Period, as has been carefully docu-
mented by Todd Klutz. Klutz affirms that we should not underes-
timate the extent to which demons were believed to

(p. 310), because there is a relative paucity of multiple independent attestation in
the primary stratum. But he considers the opposite tendency more likely.

[34] As will be noted below, however, status enhancement may also accompany
magic and sorcery.

[35] D.B. Martin, *The Corinthian Body* (New Haven/London: Yale University Press,
1995) 143.

[36] "Illness" may be distinguished from "disease"; see J. Pilch, "Sickness and
Healing in Luke-Acts", in *The Social World of Luke-Acts. Models for Interpretation* (ed.
J.H. Neyrey; Peabody MA: Hendrickson, 1991) 191–2.

[37] G. Theissen (*The Miracle Stories of the Early Christian Tradition* [Edinburgh: T. &
T. Clark, 1983] 85–7) notes a distinction in the ways that demons are related to
illness. *Demonological aetiologies* of illness explain how a demon may have caused a
illness without necessarily implying "possession". Healing takes the form of binding
or fettering Satan or the harmful demon, but not the form of exorcism. *Possession*
involves the loss of a victim's autonomy to a demon and thus requires exorcism.

cause a wide assortment of evils, ranging from moral, physiological, and social disorders to meteorological disasters. To share a universe with beings such as these, moreover, is to live, if not in perpetual fear, then at least with the dreadful realisation that the dark forces that control human life might at any moment unfurl their arbitrary hatred.[38]

Exorcisms had a part in that understanding, expressing a belief that some individuals possessed both the power and willingness to protect others from the influence of these spirits. But in contrast, the fourth gospel never attributes illness to a demon or spirit.[39] Martin does not explicitly say so, but is this due to a more educated, philosophical approach in the fourth gospel? This is not far removed from the argument of H. von Lips that in the fourth gospel humankind is not defined by outside powers. John did not share, it is argued, the popular anthropology found in the synoptic gospels.[40]

Does embarrassment—of one kind or the other—then explain why the fourth gospel avoids stories of exorcism? As noted earlier, E. Plumer has recently reiterated the view that embarrassment is the *primary* (even if not exclusive) cause of the evangelist's decision to avoid stories about exorcisms. He reinforces his view by suggesting that it forms part of the fourth gospel's controversy with "official Judaism". Not only do exorcisms fail to show the uniqueness of Jesus (in view of the evidence of Josephus to Jewish expertise in exorcisms),[41] but also the evangelist wanted "to obviate any possible misinterpretation of Jesus as a magician or wonderworker".[42] In so far as Ephesus was a centre of magic in the Hellenistic world, and magic was regarded with suspicion, it was clear that the Jewish opponents might try to implicate Jesus in evil. Thus exorcism stories would have had

---

[38] T.E. Klutz, "With Authority and Power: A Sociostylistic Investigation of Exorcism in Luke-Acts" (PhD diss.; Univ. of Sheffield, 1995) 337. See also B.J. Malina & R.L. Rohrbaugh, *Social-Science Commentary on the Synoptic Gospels* (Minneapolis: Fortress, 1992) 79–80, who note that because causality was seen primarily as personal, things beyond human control were believed to be controlled by "non-human persons who operated in a cosmic social hierarchy".

[39] See, however, John 5:14 and 9:2–3 with regard to sin and illness.

[40] H. von Lips, "Anthropologie und Wunder im Johannesevangelium. Die Wunder Jesu im Johannesevangelium im Unterschied zu den synoptischen Evangelien auf dem Hintergrund johanneischen Menschenverständnisses", *EvT* 50 (1990) 300–1. Von Lips does, however, allow that Jesus is in conflict with Satan, even if not with demons. This purported "monism" with regard to the presentation of evil is not, however, actually maintained in John, as has been noted above.

[41] "Absence", 356, citing Josephus, *Ant.* 8.2.5 §46.

[42] "Absence", 358.

the potential of embroiling Christians in an acutely embarrassing debate. The evangelist skilfully side-steps this.[43]

Even though Plumer correctly identifies many of the ancient anxieties about magic, a number of questions must be put to the thesis that the very possibility of the charge of Jesus as a magician accounts for the evangelist's avoidance of exorcisms. Why then does John record explicit accusations of sorcery against Jesus (John 7:20; 8:48–52; 10:20)?[44] If the evangelist really was too skilled to become entangled in such a damaging debate, then why do these appear at all? There are no exorcisms to give rise to them, as in the Beelzebul controversy. Moreover, Plumer suggests that not only exorcisms but even "a misinterpretation of Jesus as a magician or wonderworker" is what the evangelist seeks to avoid.[45] Is this really consistent with the attention given to Jesus' signs, including healings, found in the fourth gospel?

On the contrary, the evangelist seems to go out of way on *three* occasions to show that Jesus is accused of "having a demon". Jesus comes near to accusing "the Jews" of the same (8:44). And when, at the last supper, Judas is at the point of departing to betray Jesus, John specifically relates "Satan entered into him" (13:27). The fourth gospel may not refer explicitly to *illness* in invasionist terms, but it clearly has not abandoned an invasionist approach to evil forces. There is no intellectual isolation from the popular fears of the day! Far from attempting to *avoid* any embarrassing accusations of sorcery, John effectively *highlights* these more than in the synoptics, because it puts *all* the stress on these![46] While the synoptics refer both to victims of demon possession and to a sorcery accusation against Jesus, John puts all the emphasis on the embarrassing accusations,[47] setting these forth more boldly and frequently than the

---

[43] "Absence", 358–61.

[44] J.H. Elliott ("Sorcery and Magic in the Revelation of John", *Listening* 28 [1993] 264) and P.F. Esler (*The First Christians in Their Social Worlds* [London/New York: Routledge, 1994] 138) note the distinction made between sorcery and witchcraft, following Evans-Pritchard.

[45] "Absence", 358.

[46] Rightly noted by Twelftree, *Exorcist*, 199–200.

[47] Jesus is also called a "sinner" by the Jews/Pharisees in John 9:24, and he is accused of deceiving the crowds (John 7:12, 47). Such labelling is consistent with witchcraft and sorcery accusations noted by B.J. Malina and J.H. Neyrey, *Calling Jesus Names. The Social Value of Labels in Matthew* (Sonoma CA: Polebridge, 1988) 26–7.

other gospels. If the evangelist were specifically embarrassed about the charge of sorcery, he would surely have chosen other means of highlighting the Jewish misunderstanding of Jesus. Moreover, John does not play down the magical elements in Jesus' healings, with healings at a distance (4:46–54) and the use of spittle (9:1–7). There is no sign of embarrassment here either.

This does, however, take one a step forward. It suggests that for the fourth gospel one needs to look at the theme of demons more with respect to the accusations. It is not just what is *not* present in the fourth gospel (exorcisms); it is what *is* present (demonising accusations).

The Presence of Demonising Charges

Recent study of gospel exorcisms by G.H. Twelftree has tried to take seriously the absence of exorcisms in John while also giving some attention to the charges, especially in John 7:20 and 8:48–52, where Jesus is accused by "the people" (7:20) or "the Jews"[48] (8:48, 52) of having a demon, or of being a Samaritan and having a demon (8:48).[49] Twelftree considers the charge that Jesus was a Samaritan most likely to be a way of referring to Jesus having outrageous views or teaching.[50] This may also underlie in part the charge of having

---

[48] Are these Jewish *Christians* (cf. 8:31)? See M.W.G. Stibbe, *John's Gospel* (New Testament Readings; London/New York: Routledge, 1994) 123–8; M.D. Goulder, *A Tale of Two Missions* (London: SCM, 1994) 124–5. Against this view, the following points can be made: (i) Elsewhere in the context, the opponents are simply called "the Jews" (8:48, 52), and this is also consistent with the other accusations levelled in John 7:20 ("the people") and in John 10. In John 10:19–20, John refers to a division among the Jews. "Many of them" accuse him of having a demon, while the "others" doubt it. Clearly the "believing" Jews in this case are those who *doubt that he has a demon*. (ii) The accusation that the Jews in John 8:34–59 are seeking to kill Jesus seems an extreme charge (even in satirical speech) to level against Jewish Christians. (iii) The evidence for an attack on "Jewish Christians" elsewhere in the fourth gospel is far from clear. There is no *specific* mention of James. For his part, Peter comes out no worse in the fourth gospel than in other gospels. All the closest disciples (apart from Judas) are kept safe by Jesus (17:12) and receive the Spirit (John 20:22)/Paraclete without differentiation. (iv) The fourth gospel shows a considerable awareness of the changing lines of division which Jesus was causing among "Jews" (7:12–13, 7:40–4, and even 7:50–2 after 7:48; also 11:45–6). Many of these divisions simply appear to be in flux throughout his ministry.

[49] In the following verses in John 8:49–52, focus is only on the charge of having a demon.

[50] K. Haacker ("Samaritan, Samaria: Σαμαρίτης", *NIDNTT* 3 [1978] 463) notes two main interpretations of the combined charges in John 8:48. (1) The view of most exegetes that the two halves of the accusation are related or mean the same

a demon.[51] It is a means of highlighting the deviance of Jesus (cf. Q 7:33 with respect to John the Baptist's deviant and perhaps aggressive behaviour: "he has a demon").[52]

Thus contrary to Morton Smith, Twelftree argues that the accusation of having a demon is in the fourth gospel not levelled against Jesus primarily by virtue of his magic, but by virtue of his teaching. It is questionable whether one can go as far as to eliminate *all* reference to Jesus' signs in these contexts,[53] but Twelftree is surely right that the accusation is not presented as solely related to his deeds of wonder-working. The outrage seems strongly directed against Jesus' message.[54]

This provides an important clue to why there are no exorcisms in the fourth gospel. *The language of demon possession is not in the fourth*

---

thing, drawing upon Jewish views that Samaria was a demon-possessed land. (2) The view of some who interpret Jesus' silence regarding the charge of being a Samaritan as an implicit acceptance of the closeness of Jesus to the Samaritans (Lagrange, Odebery, J. Bowman, O. Cullmann, E.D. Freed). Haacker rejects this latter hypothesis in view of the clear rejection of Samaritan views in John 4:22.

[51] Just before the first demonising accusation, the people are concerned that Jesus is "leading the people astray" (John 7:12; cf. also 7:1). Such language is also particularly prevalent in apocalyptic writings with regard to the activity of Belial/Beliar and his host of evil spirits: see L.J. Lietaert Peerbolte, *The Antecedents of Antichrist. A Traditio-Historical Study of the Earliest Christian Views on Eschatological Opponents* (Suppl. JSJ 49; Leiden/New York/Köln: Brill, 1996), esp. 194–205, 344–5.

[52] The charge δαιμόνιον ἔχειν was a means of attacking an opponent or deviant (see also Mark 3:22 Βεελζεβοὺλ ἔχει). It can depict either someone who is deviant, but marginalised and not harmful, or someone who poses a danger to others, such as sorcerers. Sorcerers, however, also had enhanced status by virtue of their power over others. The vocabulary of the fourth gospel never uses φαρμακεία, but the phrase "he has a demon" may reflect some of the confusion about Jesus' power and a hesitancy by Jesus' opponents to enhance Jesus' status any further than necessary. Perhaps this is why it is not phrased as "he is a sorcerer", but rather as "he has a demon". Yet his ability to lead others astray is clearly a threat.

[53] In both John 7:20 and 10:21 reference is made obliquely to the wonder-working of Jesus in close conjunction with the accusation.

[54] It is difficult entirely to agree with C.K. Barrett (*The Gospel According to St John: An Introduction with Commentary and Notes on the Greek Text* [2nd ed.; London: SPCK, 1978] 319) that the accusation means no more than "You are mad". An analysis of the language for deceit in John shows a striking conjunction with the accusations of "having a demon". Taking the vocabulary of lying and deceit isolated by J. Pilch ("Lying and Deceit in the Letters to the Seven Churches: Perspectives from Cultural Anthropology", *BTB* 22 [1992] 126–7), almost all of that which appears in the fourth gospel is clustered around the three demonising accusations. The main exception is δόλος in John 1:47. The other references include the uses of (1) πλανάω in John 7:12, 47; (2) ψεῦδος and ψευστής in John 8:44, 55; (3) βλασφημία, βλασφημέω in John 10:33, 36. Pilch does not include in his list σκάνδαλον, σκανδαλίζω, which is referred specifically to Jesus' *disciples* being offended or falling away (apostasy?) in John 6:61 and 16:1.

gospel related to matters of magical healing; but to rivalry. It is reserved for demonising one's opponents.[55] Similar labelling is used by Jesus against his opponents (John 8:44).[56]

But, interestingly, Twelftree himself does not seem fully to recognise the significance of this feature. He therefore feels constrained to find other (more theological, rather than boundary-related) reasons for explaining this feature of the fourth gospel, and he focuses on the *absence* of exorcisms rather than the *presence* of the accusations. He suggests three reasons for the former, which must be briefly considered if only to be rejected. Some of these may be consistent with a decreased emphasis on exorcisms, but none is really sufficient as a complete explanation for what is found in the fourth gospel.

1. Twelftree argues that John has a tendency in his gospel to opt for spectacular miracles. Exorcism stories, Twelftree suggests, are simply not spectacular enough to show Jesus as the Christ.[57]

This is an intriguing argument, not least because of the way it seems to be the direct antithesis of the argument of Crossan that magic of any sort was increasingly an embarrassment in later Christian tradition. Nevertheless, Twelftree himself should be aware that exorcisms *can* be spectacular, as Mark 5:1–20 shows when the legion of demons is exorcised.[58] Surely the evangelist could have come up with an exorcistic extravaganza without much effort!

---

[55] For labelling and deviance theory, see Malina and Neyrey, *Calling*, and "Conflict in Luke-Acts: Labelling and Deviance Theory", in *The Social World of Luke-Acts. Models for Interpretation* (ed. J.H. Neyrey; Peabody MA: Hendrickson, 1991) esp. 99–110.

[56] Cf. E. Pagels, "The Social History of Satan, Part II: Satan in the New Testament Gospels", *JAAR* 62 (1994) 26, 47.

[57] Twelftree, *Exorcist*, 141–2, 170, 189; *Miracle Worker*, 223; "Demon", 171. A variation of this occurs in Meier, *Marginal Jew* 2.637 n.18, who considers demons to be minor adversaries. Plumer ("Absence", 355–6) also suggests that exorcisms are not sufficiently unique, since there was also evidence of Jewish exorcists. Yet Plumer's view that the Evangelist was deliberately attempting to play down Jesus as a magician or wonderworker (p. 358) seemingly conflicts with Twelftree's observations about spectacular miracles being emphasised in this gospel. See also M. Labahn ("Between Tradition and Literary Art: The Miracle Tradition in the Fourth Gospel", *Bib* 80 [1999] 182–7), who ultimately rejects J. Becker's thesis that the evangelist meant to belittle the importance of the miracle stories included in his gospel.

[58] Rightly noted by Plumer ("Absence", 356). In contrast see also J.D.G. Dunn & G.H. Twelftree, "La Possession Demoniaque et l'Exorcisme dans le Nouveau Testament", *Hokhma* 5 (1992) 48–9. This article suggests a relative "silence" in the post-Easter church on the subject of exorcisms. Yet the exorcisms in Acts 8:7 and 16:16–18 (cf. 19:11–20) are noted, as well as possible allusions in Rom 15:19;

2. Secondly, Twelftree rightly notes that the fourth gospel plays down the theme of the kingdom of God. In the synoptic gospels, exorcisms are on occasions closely linked to the coming of the kingdom (cf. Luke/Q 11:20; Mark 1:39). Therefore, the argument goes, if John plays down the kingdom announcement, then one should not be surprised that it does not make much use of exorcisms.[59]

This is a rather one-dimensional approach to exorcisms, however. Why should John have *only* seen exorcisms as related to the kingdom? The link between exorcisms and the expectations of the kingdom outside the synoptics is far from secure.[60] Klutz's work confirms also that despite the prevalence of interest in demons and exorcisms no early Christian *extra*canonical writing treats exorcism as an event with eschatological connotations.[61] Surely John could have used them (as almost everything else) christologically, as part of the dualistic opposition between light and darkness, good and evil which pervades the gospel. But this leads to Twelftree's final point.

3. Thirdly, Twelftree draws attention to another contrast with the synoptic gospels. In the synoptics, he notes, the defeat of Satan is linked with exorcisms;[62] in John's gospel Satan's defeat is linked to

---

1 Cor 12:9–10; and Heb 2:4 (and outside the canonical New Testament). The longer ending of Mark (16:17) is attributed to the 2nd century. One should also note that any such alleged tendency did not prevent a wealth of exorcism narratives in the synoptic gospels or the extracanonical evidence cited by Klutz below (n. 61).

[59] Also Dunn & Twelftree, "La Possession", 49.

[60] E.P. Sanders, *Jesus and Judaism* (Philadelphia: Fortress, 1985) 134–5. Interestingly, Twelftree (*Exorcist*, 189) seems to accept Sanders' argument that there is no self-evident link between exorcisms and Messiahship: "Indeed, if Jesus was, in his exorcisms, self-evidently the Messiah then it is difficult to explain why the Fourth Evangelist does not make use of what would potentially be a useful component in his Gospel."

[61] Klutz ("With Authority", 381ff.) traces the continuation of interest in exorcism in the early church. He notes that Barnabas even sees conversion as having an exorcistic effect. Ignatius talks about Christian meetings keeping Satan at bay. Justin refers to prayer as a prophylactic against demons. Justin and Origin refer to the exorcistic efficacy of uttering certain powerful names, such as Jesus, etc. This suggests Christian and pagan exorcisms continued to occur. Celsus does not scoff at such views but actually issues countercharges of sorcery.

[62] This observation is itself not incontestable: see Aune, "Magic", 1531 n. 106, against H.C. Kee. With regard to Q 11:20, see also H. Räisänen, "Exorcisms and the Kingdom: Is Q 11:20 a Saying of the Historical Jesus?", in *Symbols and Strata: Essays on the Sayings Gospel Q* (ed. R. Uro; Helsinki/Göttingen: Finnish Exegetical Society/Vandenhoeck & Ruprecht, 1996) 119–42, who attributes the association of exorcisms with the coming kingdom to be a speciality of Q but not of Mark or necessarily of the historical Jesus.

the cross (12:31; 14:30; 16:11).[63] This is a point which shall be explored more later, but it is sufficient to observe here that however true the statement may be in itself, it is not adequate to explain why John would not include stories of or references to exorcisms. After all, John prefigures Jesus' death and resurrection through incidents reported earlier in his gospel, such as the raising of Lazarus, as noted by Twelftree.[64] Why could not exorcism stories similarly prefigure Satan's defeat at the cross in the Johannine scheme?[65]

So, where does it leave us? It is not sufficient simply to try to account for the *absence* of exorcisms in John. Any such account must also explain the clear *presence* of interest in spirits and the language of spirit possession. Therefore what needs explanation is the shift from viewing demon possession primarily as something to be healed to viewing it mainly in terms of accusations of sorcery and demonising one's opponents. It becomes an instrument of rivalry.

Accusations and counter-accusations about *who* has a demon may express a theme which more indirectly emerges elsewhere in John. That an invasionist view of evil was widespread in the ancient world has been previously noted. Connected with this is the concept of pollution and its opposite, the concept of purity. One of the relatively neglected features of John's gospel is the extent to which the issue of purity has been considered a major theme.[66] The early location of the Temple incident is not insignificant in this respect.

---

[63] Twelftree, *Exorcist*, 142, 223–4; *Miracle Worker*, 223. G.C. Nicholson, in his *Death as Departure. The Johannine Descent-Ascent Schema* (SBLDS 63; Chico CA: Scholars, 1983) 132, more specifically sees the ruler of this world judged as a direct result of the "exaltation of the Son of Man".

[64] *Miracle Worker*, 223.

[65] Labahn ("Between Tradition", 179–81) argues that miracles in the fourth gospel are generally linked to the overarching theme of conflict. In his larger work, Labahn (*Lebensspender*, 484) suggests that in John's gospel the miracles are also formulated to demonstrate a christological fulfilment of the Old Testament promises of a judge (cf. Isa 26:19). This coming judge is no longer portrayed as a warrior against demonic powers, but rather against the ruler of the cosmos directly, who in fact is already conquered. This does not explain the continuing concern John expresses for disciples for the period after his departure (17:15). Nor does it explain occasional interest in angelic intermediaries or the continuing engagement with the claims to "have a demon".

[66] From the start Jesus is declared to take away the sin of the world; he will baptise with the Spirit (but is not baptised by John); he has angels descend and ascend upon him; he replaces Jewish rites of purification with something better; he replaces the Holy Place; he refers to living water; he heals at the pool in ch 5; he is called Holy One in 6:69; he washes feet in ch. 13; he is the unblemished lamb, etc. The concern for ritual purity also emerges ironically at the trial in 18:28; see

Accusations of having a demon can be one important part of a wider
Johannine agenda of rivalry about the locus of holiness. Like these
demonising accusations, issues of purity and pollution have at their
core the question of identity and boundary—*who* is polluted and *who*
is pure.

Implications of the Accusations

It is now possible to follow up some of the implications of this analysis, and this will be done under three headings.

1. *Group Identity and Conflict*

It is striking how frank the fourth gospel is when presenting accusations of Jesus "having a demon". The Jewish opposition to Jesus
is of course a well-known feature of this gospel. The demonising of
Jesus can clearly be portrayed as an attempt by the accusing group
to affirm its own values and to assert Jesus' deviant and threatening stance. But a *Christian evangelist* is after all writing this story, so
why does he allow such a potentially embarrassing charge to remain
in such stark form, and why does he reiterate it? It certainly confirms
for his readers the extent of Jewish misunderstanding, but it also
opens up a measure of vulnerability by suggesting that some people
in his day did consider Jesus to be demonic.

Yet the accusation against Jesus does perhaps serve the author's
purposes in other respects. Stevan Davies' work on *Jesus the Healer*[67]
cites anthropological studies (by Erika Bourguignon) on experiences
of possession, arguing that possession occurs in at least two contrasting forms: ranging from demon possession to "spirit" possession,
the one malevolent and the other benevolent. Davies argues that
Jesus and his followers believed that Jesus *was* possessed—that is,
spirit-possessed.[68] In John, representatives of the established order

---

M.W.G. Stibbe, *John* (Sheffield: JSOT, 1993) 189. It also seems to mark a "boundary" when the term ἁγιάζω is applied not only to Jesus but also to disciples (John
10:36: 17:19). See J.T. Williams, "Cultic Elements in the Fourth Gospel", in *Studia
Biblica 1978*, Vol. 2: *Papers on the Gospels* (ed. E.A. Livingstone; JSNTSup 2; Sheffield:
JSOT Press, 1978) 339–50.

[67] S.L. Davies, *Jesus the Healer. Possession, Trance and the Origins of Christianity* (New
York: Continuum, 1995).

[68] Cf. Theissen, *Miracle Stories*, 88, with regard to Mark: "He is God's holy one
(Mk 1.24) and is regarded as possessed (3.20ff.)."

oppose him, yet even in these cases the power of Jesus seems to be recognised, while its source is debated. Moreover, anthropological studies suggest that possession plays a significant part in status enhancement in societies where social mobility was very limited.[69] Although Davies' study mostly focuses on Mark's gospel, he does note that in John 1:32–4 it is clear that the Johannine tradition knew of an association with the descent of the spirit on Jesus and the immediate witness that he was Son of God.[70] Even the words Jesus speaks are not his own (John 14:24). When the disciples receive the Spirit, the language of Jesus breathing upon them resonates with ideas of possession (John 20:22).[71] Thus a *positive* possession of the spirit seems to be associated not only with Jesus but also eventually with his Paraclete-led followers.[72] The issue then is not whether Jesus can be considered in some sense to possess the spirit, but rather the correct evaluation of the nature of this spirit—the *source* of Jesus' authority being a major recurring theme in John.[73]

Indeed the accusations and counter-accusations in John over the source of the spirit he possesses may be essential to the group competition depicted in the gospel. On the one hand, Jesus is accused by the "established group" of being possessed—by a demon. They ironically recognise a form of power, but seek to label it as deviant.[74] On the other hand, when Jesus attacks his opponents, he accuses them of "belonging to your father, the devil" (John 8:44).[75] In this

---

[69] Cf. I.M. Lewis, *Ecstatic Religion*, and Aune, "Magic", 1520–3, 1528–9.

[70] Davies, *Healer*, 61.

[71] Goulder (*Tale*, 123) wishes to show that John opposes a "possessionist" (Jewish Christian) understanding of a man Jesus being taken over by the Spirit. But John 1:32 and 20:22 at the very least seem to suggest that *in some sense* Jesus "possesses the Spirit". "Possessing" may be subtly distinguishable from "being possessed by".

[72] John 20:23 also recalls the Matthean references to "binding" and "loosing" (cf. Matt 16:19; 18:18). Note binding spells discussed by C.A. Faraone, "The Agonistic Context of Early Greek Binding Spells", in *Magika Hiera. Ancient Greek Magic and Religion* (ed. C.A. Faraone & D. Obbink; Oxford/New York: OUP, 1991) 3–32. Retaining the "sins" of someone "could fit easily into a larger pattern of political or social competition" (p. 17).

[73] The question of "possession/inspiration" can also be related to views of Jesus as "a prophet" (John 4:19, 44; 6:14; 7:40, 52; 9:17). The fourth gospel does not seem completely to repudiate the understanding of Jesus as a prophet, at least as a step towards the realisation of Jesus' identity. Even in John 8:40, John has Jesus describe himself as "a man who has told you the truth which I heard from God". *Contra* Goulder, *Tale*, 121–7.

[74] Aune, "Magic", 1523. Aune also notes the view of P. Samain that the charges in John 7:12 and 47 are equivalent to the more direct charge of practising magic (p. 1540).

[75] This of course follows John 8:41, in which Jesus' opponents state not only that

case a group is clearly being vilified rather than an individual: they collectively *belong to* the devil.[76]

But is there any evidence that such accusations and counter-accusations were indeed relevant or applied to Jesus' followers? One never directly sees a charge from opponents that Jesus' followers were also thought to be demon-inspired, but one does find the intriguing warning in 16:2: "They will put you out of the synagogues. Indeed, an hour is coming when those who kill you will think that by doing so they are *offering service to God.*" Does this contain a hint that believers might indeed have faced the kind of accusations that Jesus is depicted in the gospel as having faced? The Farewell Discourses make clear that believers would share with Jesus the world's hate and persecution (15:18–20; 17:14). Jesus prays for their protection in 17:15. The affirmation that they have the Spirit *of truth*, which the world cannot receive, is another possible pointer to a situation in which they needed to legitimate themselves. Such Christians must have been considered deviants and dangerous, if they were eventually expelled from synagogues. In a religious context such deviants were not infrequently described as Satanic or demonic. In an entirely different context, one finds this levelled against the Jews themselves when in Rev 2:9 and 3:9 they are labelled "the synagogue of Satan".[77] These observations are highly suggestive. Those in the synagogue must have thought that they were serving God by expelling the deviant Christians and by continuing to promote threatening behaviour towards them in view of the evil which they associated with these people. Is it not likely that this was expressed by demonisation? Is it not also possible that such Christians retaliated with counter-accusations, not dissimilar to those found in Rev 2 and 3? These must remain questions, but further evidence for the use and experience of demonisation by Johannine Christians will be considered in the final section.

---

they "have one Father, even God" (extending the previous discussion about their descent from Abraham).

[76] R.A. Whitacre (*Johannine Polemic. The Role of Tradition and Theology* [SBLDS 67; Chico: Scholars, 1982] 72–6) draws upon de la Potterie's analysis of the chiastic structure of John 8:42–47 to show that this charge lies at the centre of the group of sayings concerning the relationship of the Jews to God and to Jesus. See also Stibbe, *John's Gospel*, 47–9.

[77] A.Y. Collins ("Vilification and Self-Definition in the Book of Revelation", *HTR* 79 [1986] 310–14) persuasively rejects views that "those who call themselves Jews and are not, but rather are the synagogue of Satan" refers to Judaising Christians rather than genuine Jews.

2. World View

John's interest is not limited to demonising one's human opponents. One must also reckon with the place of the Devil/Satan/the Evil One in the Johannine world view. In John Jesus may not oppose Satan by means of exorcisms or in a temptation narrative,[78] but there is a conflict nonetheless and it is one which appears to be invested with genuinely cosmic dimensions as well as social implications.

That John frequently (even if not wholly consistently) represents *the world/kosmos* as part of the opposition to Jesus is well-known.[79] It is perhaps therefore not surprising that a reasonably distinctive way in which John's gospel represents "the devil" (which seems closely linked also to John's use of the terms Satan and the Evil One) is as "the ruler of this world".[80] Jesus' victory over the ruler of this world is announced in John 12:31, seemingly proleptically, just as it is announced in 12:23 that Jesus' hour has now come, even though the crucifixion-resurrection-ascension still lie ahead in the narrative sequence. The victory is declared again in John 14:30 and 16:11 (cf. 16:33).

This opens up important issues in Johannine eschatology. If Jesus is viewed as having conquered the ruler of this world, what exactly happens to Satan[81] and what exactly happens to "the world" in the thought of the fourth evangelist?

---

[78] Some have found the three temptations expressed in other parts of the fourth gospel, but through more human mediation (cf. John 6:15; 6:30–31; 7:1–9): see Pagels (following R.E. Brown), "Social History", 42.

[79] As J. Ashton (*Understanding the Fourth Gospel* [Oxford: Clarendon, 1991] 206–8) notes, there are two distinct oppositions implied by *kosmos* in the fourth gospel: vertical and horizontal.

[80] As J. Painter ("Theology, Eschatology and the Prologue of John", *SJT* 46 [1993] 32) notes, however, there is "no attempt to explain how it came to be that the world created by the λόγος now finds itself to be dominated by darkness".

[81] Pagels ("Social History", 52) concludes that "John . . . dismisses the device of the devil as an independent supernatural character (if, indeed, he knew of it, as I suspect he did). Instead, as John tells the story, Satan, like God himself, here appears in the form of *incarnation*. First he becomes incarnate in Judas Iscariot, then in the Jewish authorities . . . and finally in those John calls 'the Jews'." Certainly the fourth gospel and 1 John freely link human opposition with the devil/Satan/antichrists. But the claim (p. 40) that Satan never appears in the fourth gospel independently of human beings depends upon how one interprets "the ruler of this world" in 12:31; 16:11; 14:30. J.H. Charlesworth ("A Critical Comparison of the Dualism in 1QS 3:13–4:26 and the 'Dualism' Contained in the Gospel of John", in *John and Qumran* [ed. J.H. Charlesworth; London: Geoffrey Chapman, 1972] 92–3) admits that some vestiges of an older world view remain, but "the main thrust of this Gospel is that the devil has been demythologized. The reason for this Johannine characteristic is, of course, the belief that through his crucifixion Christ overcame

It is certainly not true that the eschatology presented in the fourth gospel is either entirely realised or entirely individualistic (see John 5:27 "the time is coming when all who are in the tombs will hear his voice and will come out"). C.F.D. Moule's[82] attempt to explain the tensions in the fourth gospel not primarily in redactional terms but as shifts between individual and corporate perspectives does not fully explain the Johannine claims that the ruler of this world has been conquered. This victory is not just concerned with individuals, and yet it seems to be more realised than future. David Rensberger has argued with some force that often in John's gospel the writer has a wider perspective than simply an individual's fate. A political perspective often emerges and an interest in the world at large.[83] If one extends this "cosmic" perspective further, then one again returns to the question: what exactly happens to Satan in the world view of the fourth gospel?

More particularly, in what sense has Satan been already defeated by the death and exaltation of Jesus—if the followers of Jesus are still facing opposition, as the farewell discourses make clear? Some have argued that John is simply affirming that Satan is defeated *in principle*. Satan has really lost, even though admittedly he is still active, even after Jesus' death. The reader knows Satan is still active because John 17:15–16 records: "I do not pray that you should take them out of the world, but that you should keep them from the Evil One.[84] They are not of the world, even as I am not of the world." In the world there is still tribulation, trouble and, significantly, the influence of the Evil One. Such an attitude is clearly reflected too in 1 John and 2 John. But how can Satan remain active if he has been defeated? Perhaps this is simply an unresolved tension which the fourth evangelist/final redactor, not unlike many others, simply had not worked out. His high Christology demanded that all was now complete, in the revealing activity and decisive "lifting up" of Jesus Son of God,

---

the world (16:33) so that the devil is now *defeated* and destroyed" (p. 93). It is unclear why the defeat of the devil requires demythologising him, however.

[82] C.F.D. Moule, "A Neglected Feature in the Interpretation of Johannine Eschatology", in *Studies in John: Presented to Professor Dr J.N. Sevenster on the occasion of his seventieth birthday* (NovTSup 24; Leiden: Brill, 1970) 155–60; Ashton, *Understanding*, 220–6.

[83] D.K. Rensberger, *Overcoming the World. Politics and Community in the Gospel of John* (London: SPCK, 1988).

[84] Taking τοῦ πονηροῦ as masculine, not neuter, and thus as equivalent to Satan or "the devil".

but he knew that believers still faced tribulations, deceivers and evil influences. Why the "victory" is not yet fully *effective* is simply considered unclear.

It is possible, however, to suggest that the author's world view was more coherent. In John's dualism of the heavenly and the earthly, the presence of evil is clearly more associated with "this world" (the earthly, below) than with the higher heavenly sphere. Hence the striking title: "the ruler of *this world*", in contrast to rabbinic writings where the prince of this world more commonly referred to God.[85] In the fourth gospel Satan and God (or his envoys) are not depicted as locked in battle in heaven. The battle appears to have been conducted more by God's broker entering this world.

Why should this be so? Lietaert Peerbolte notes that characteristic of some Christian eschatology was a two-stage victory of God over Satan. First, Satan falls from heaven (cf. the vision in Luke 10:18 and the dragon's fall in Rev 12:7–12 where he is "cast to the earth" with "his angels"). Later, Satan is confined to the abyss, a place of punishment (Rev 20:10; cf. also Luke 8:30–1). In the fourth gospel, Jesus' death and exaltation seem to have accomplished the initial victory. But after the death of Jesus, believers then appear to find themselves between two such events of Satan's downfall. In Lietaert Peerbolte's words: "The Dragon has been cast out of heaven but still rages on earth".[86] Thus for them part of the question of what happens now to the ruler of this world is the question of what happens now to this world.

The fate of believers is simply that they leave the world. In one sense, they leave it *in the present*, in that they *define their present identity*

---

[85] So, among others, B. Lindars, *The Gospel of John* (NCB; London: Oliphants, 1972) 433. J.E. Bruns ("A Note on John 16:33 and 1 John 2:13–14", *JBL* 86 [1967] 451–3) notes that the prince of this world is scarcely distinguishable from "the world" in Johannine writings, or from other designations such as Evil One, Devil and Satan. He notes that each of these figures is essentially a murderer and suggests that this can be compared to the Angel of Death (but not Satan) in some rabbinic writings and 2 Bar 21:23. See also A. Segal, "Ruler of This World: Attitudes about Mediator Figures and the Importance of Sociology for Self-Definition", in *Jewish and Christian Self-Definition*, Vol. 2: *Aspects of Judaism in the Graeco-Roman World* (ed. E.P. Sanders et al.; Philadelphia: Fortress, 1981) 245–68.

[86] *Antecedents*, 136. The fall to this world may be to the sphere below the seventh heaven (rather like the earthly stratosphere)—part of this world but still more mobile than simply earthly. This sublunar arena may be compared to the "air" referred to in Eph 2:2. Cf. also Philo, *On the Giants* 6–8, who locates between heaven and earth "the other element, the air" which is also filled with living beings and spirits.

as those who "are not of the world" (John 17:14, 16), who immediately participate in a unity of the Father and the Son and in the
protective pocket of fellowship characterising the believing community. The new bond of Father, Son and believer strengthens the
boundaries against the hostile world. The new commandment to love
one another further fosters close interaction within the group. The
Paraclete is given to them and opposes the world. This all provides
powerful reassurance to insiders, especially if they viewed their outside opposition as not only human but also inspired by evil forces.[87]

Followers leave the world *eventually* when they too join Jesus in
the place he has prepared for them with the Father (John 14:2, cf.
also 12:32).[88] So what care do believers have about what happens
to the world? In effect, it is simply isolated from where believers are.
It is quite possible therefore to see the victory over Satan simply as
the isolation of Satan *to* this world, not his expulsion *from* it. In this
case, there is no second stage to Satan's downfall necessarily envisaged. Satan is now defeated because he has no influence in the heavenly sphere, and in the earthly sphere he represents that over against
which they define their group, in which they have the prophylactic
protection of their community and the Paraclete, and from which
they will escape. Thus the victory over Satan is not just a "moral
victory"[89] or victory "in principle".[90] It is related to believers' understanding of their present identity as well as their destiny. But one
should not be surprised that John has no clear plan for a new world
as such. It becomes the tragic desert to which Satan is confined.
There is no expulsion of evil from it.[91] Just as evil is not banished
from individuals by exorcisms in the gospel, so also with respect to
Satan and the world. The physical body is a microcosm of the social
body, the world. What is offered is a more radical alternative: an

---

[87] *Contra* Theissen, *Miracle Stories*, 226. Plumer ("Absence", 363) cites Theissen,
but rightly notes that Satan is nonetheless perceived to be a real foe.

[88] Worship will be associated neither with the Jerusalem temple (John 2) nor
with Mt Gerizim (John 4:20–21), and even the Logos effectively finds no place in
his world (John 1:11). The world offers little for believers.

[89] Lindars, *John*, 433.

[90] R.E Brown, *The Gospel according to John*, Vol. 1: *i–xii. Introduction, Translation and
Notes* (AB 29a; New York: Doubleday, 1966) I.477).

[91] Thus the world is not inherently corrupt, unlike the Evil One. It is just controlled by bad things; it is the domain of Satan. The world can be loved in the
sense that humanity can be loved, but not in sense of that which controls it and
from which it will never be free. Rather believers become free from the world.

alternative "birth", a new life with God and fellowship with believers.

It might be objected, however, that the reference in John 12:31 to the ruler of this world being "cast out" might naturally suggest "out of this world" and therefore be more consistent with a view of the purification of this world than with the isolation of Satan to this world. It is possible to respond in at least two ways. On the one hand, it is not absolutely clear that the text here should read "cast out". Some manuscripts read "cast down", which in fact sets up a contrast (perhaps too well?) to John 12:32 about Jesus being lifted up. This would nicely fit the idea of Satan confined to the lower sphere, while Jesus is lifted up and draws others to him. On the other hand, if one accepts the stronger manuscript support (including P[66]) for "casting out", then it is necessary to ask what this means. Cast out from where?[92] R.E. Brown[93] considered this a reference not to Satan's expulsion from heaven, but to his loss of authority over this world. Brown realised, however, that this poses a problem in terms of the current influence of the Evil One over the world (cf. also 1 John 5:19).[94] He then resorted to referring to a victory *in principle* and to tensions in Johannine thought. The matter may well be simpler than this. Surely, a natural reading would be to suggest that the Evil One has lost authority over those who can now be described as no longer of the world, the children of God (John 1:13).[95] He is "cast out" in that believers define themselves over against him and his sphere of influence. It is a matter of identity.[96] John 12:32 graphically depicts the lifting up of Jesus from the earth and the drawing of his followers to himself. Satan's loss of direct authority over Jesus' followers is manifested above all in the death-resurrection-ascension of the Son of God. Yet Satan's authority has been fettered and limited, rather

---

[92] There are six uses of ἐκβάλλω in the fourth gospel (cf. also 3 John 10 with regard to Diotrephes expelling some members from the church), four of which use ἔξω rather than specifying more precisely the place from which expulsion occurs (John 6:37; 9:34, 35; 12:31). In John 9:34–35, and perhaps 6:37, *one's place in the community of faith* seems to be at issue.

[93] *John*, I.477.

[94] Brown (*John*, I.477) rightly sees that the writer is not "a hopeless romantic" who cannot recognise existing evil in the world.

[95] Cf. John 6:37: "he who comes to me I shall in no way cast out"!

[96] Note that "all" in 12:32 is modified to "sons of light" by 12:36. If Satan is eternally linked to this world, note that Jesus' kingship is not of this world (John 18:36).

than destroyed. The evangelist is still sufficiently in touch with the realities of Christian existence in the world to realise that the world (that which is "outside") is still threatening for believers.[97] It is not surprising therefore that those in the world, even if not of it, will still need reassurance and some explanation. The explanation is that the world and the "ruler of this world" are still united. The difference lies in how Christians define themselves with respect to both.

Neither evil opposition nor spiritual support has been completely de-mythologised. Supporting believers is the Paraclete, an almost angelic prosecutor of the world as well as guide;[98] and on the other side is the ruler of this world or the Evil One. Rather than de-mythologising, this is not far removed from what A. Segal suggests is a kind of polemical mythologising.[99]

Such an explanation integrates the various strands of our previous discussion about exorcisms and accusations of demon possession with John's eschatology and world view. It has not been necessary to relate this discussion to a redactional theory of stages. The fourth gospel may well have had an extended period of composition, but the redaction which is possessed today does not necessarily lack unity in its perspective on these matters. The evangelist defines and legitimates believers by demonising their opponents. Because the opponents are in large part their parent group, these opponents figure large in their world view and self-understanding, to the extent of a near (but not total) convergence of "Jews" and "the world". The break in relations has been sufficiently strong for these believers to anticipate persecution, but nonetheless they have prepared a strategy in terms of world view and community to help to cope with such fears.

They remain of course vulnerable, perhaps particularly to their parent group. In such a situation one might also expect a concern about waverers and apostates within the community of believers. Such a consequence may in fact be explicit in John 16:1 where Jesus issues warnings to keep his followers from "falling away" (σκανδαλ-ισθῆτε).[100] This takes us to the final section.

---

[97] Contrast J.L. Kovacs, "'Now shall the ruler of this world be driven out': Jesus' death as Cosmic Battle in John 12:20–36", *JBL* 114 (1995) 227–47.

[98] See J.A. Draper, "The Sociological Function of the Spirit/Paraclete in the Farewell Discourses in the Fourth Gospel", *Neot* 26 (1992) 24–7 (following Sekki's 1989 work on *ruah* in the Dead Sea Scrolls).

[99] Segal, "Ruler", esp. 266.

[100] So also with the emphasis on "abiding" in the farewell discourses.

3. *Opposition Within*

Until now, our concern has been mainly with *external* opposition to believers. There is, however, another sphere of interest: opposition and betrayal *within*. In the gospel, this is depicted most clearly in the case of Judas.[101] In the Johannine epistles, one finds the secessionists—those former Johannine Christians who went out from the parent *Johannine* group. In both cases these former insiders receive a quasi-Satanic eschatological label. Judas is called the "son of perdition" (ὁ υἱὸς τῆς ἀπωλείας) in John 17:12; the secessionists were called, amongst other things, "antichrists" (1 John 2:18, 22; 4:3; cf. 2 John 7).

Wendy Sproston[102] compared the "son of perdition" label given to Judas with similar phrases at Qumran (in the *Manual of Discipline* and *Damascus Rule*) and in 2 Thess 2. In the latter it appears equivalent to the "man of lawlessness", describing the final enemy just prior to the ultimate attack of evil before the parousia. This does not appear to be Satan himself but rather Satan's representative, whose downfall signifies the final collapse of Satan's schemes.[103]

This leads to an interesting comparison with the "antichrist" terminology in 1 John. The term, apparently distinctive to the Johannine epistles at the time, is probably used to indicate an *opponent* of Christ rather than a false messiah or prophet, although it seems to have been associated mainly with false teaching. As R. Schnackenburg argues, at this stage the idea of the antichrist is again not Satan himself. That identification belongs to a later period.[104]

Thus closely associated with the work of the Evil One in the world is the activity of these figures who are under the *particular* sway of

---

[101] But note also John 6:60–66; 15:2. With regard to Judas, I refer to my paper "Judas in the Fourth Gospel" presented to the SNTS Johannine Seminar in Copenhagen, August 1998.

[102] W. Sproston, "Satan in the Fourth Gospel", in *Studia Biblica 1978*, Vol. 2: *Papers on the Gospels* (ed. E.A. Livingstone; JSNTSup 2; Sheffield: JSOT, 1980) 307–11; also idem, "'The Scripture' in John 17:12", in *Scripture: Meaning and Method. Essays Presented to Anthony Tyrrell Hanson for his seventieth birthday* (ed. B.P. Thompson; Hull: Hull University, 1987) 24–36.

[103] Sproston, "Satan", 310; see also Lietaert Peerbolte, *Antecedents*, 75–89. In Sproston's more recent article ("Scripture", 26–30), she links Judas as "son of destruction" to the "thief" who "steals, scatters and destroys" in John 10:10. Cf. A. Reinhartz (*The Word in the World. The Cosmological Tale in the Fourth Gospel* [SBLMS 45; Atlanta: Scholars Press, 1992] 91–2), who primarily sees the thief as Satan, who has snatched Judas.

[104] *The Johannine Epistles. An Introduction and Commentary* (New York: Crossroad, 1992) 135. Cf. *Asc. Isa.* 4:1ff.

Satan—Judas in the fourth gospel and the antichrists of the epistles. In each case these seem to be former *insiders*, who are now outsiders and are treated with particular hostility and suspicion. Their titles acknowledge that they are under the direct control of Satan. There is again no question of these individuals being exorcised or cleansed.[105] The Johannine world view remains consistent here. They represent the crossing of a boundary; they are a significant part of the continuing influence of Satan in the world as it affects true believers, an influence which has not been eradicated. Those who have "overcome" the Evil One are those who remain loyal to the community (1 John 2:13–14) and who have not gone out into the world.

Therefore, just as the believers who are addressed in the fourth gospel were once considered deviants and were expelled by their parent group (the synagogue), so also in the Johannine epistles (and perhaps even hinted at with regard to Judas in the gospel) they viewed their own deviants in a similar way. In 1 John the *secessionists* are now the children of the devil (1 John 3:10), bearing the spirit of the antichrist (1 John 4:3), being antichrists (1 John 2:18, 22).[106] Once the break has taken place, the author associates murderous intent with the secessionists (cf. 1 John 3:11–15) in ways reminiscent of the description of opponents in the gospel. This must have been important for the self-legitimation of the parent Johannine community, a further declaration of the evil intent of their opponents. Through such accusations, the boundaries of the new parent group are tightened and affirmed, and the deviants are controlled, once again "in the name of community values".[107] In the accusations of being under the control of the devil, the Johannine Christians in 1 John used against their opponents the kind of language they knew—the kind of accusations they too had probably experienced.

---

[105] See also J.S. Wright, "Satan, Beelzebul, Devil, Exorcism: ἐξορκιστής", in *NIDNTT* 3 (1978) 475: "Deceiving spirits inspired false prophets (1 John. 4:1, 2), were to be tested and exposed by what they said of Jesus Christ, but apparently were not exorcized (cf. 1 Cor. 12:3)."

[106] For a further example of the use of vilification of Christian rivals by accusations of being associated with "the ruler of this world", see Ignatius' letters (*Eph.* 17:1), discussed by Collins, "Vilification", 311.

[107] See Esler, *First Christians*, 141.

CHRISTIAN COMMUNITY IN THE LIGHT OF THE GOSPEL OF JOHN

Stephen C. Barton

1. *Introduction: The Contemporary Situation and the Nature of the Church*

The history of the twentieth century is a history of calamitous failures in human neighbourliness. In consequence, there is widespread recognition today of the need to find ways of building and maintaining patterns of sociality which are life-giving. So strong are the perceived threats to human sociality that many political, social and religious leaders are turning their attention to ways of resisting the threats and making space for the renewal of society. In his Reith Lectures for 1990, for example, the Chief Rabbi, Jonathan Sacks, highlighted a number of threats to our social fabric: economic individualism, moral pluralism and the privatisation of values, the loss of institutions that sustain communities of memory and character, the shift from a traditional duty-based ethic to a secular rights-based ethic, the tendency of the religions to polarise into extremes of liberalism or conservatism, and so on. In the light of such threats, Sacks calls for the renewal of community, both at the local level of families, churches and voluntary associations, and at the national level of society now reconceived as a "community of communities".[1]

Building communities which allow all people to attain their full humanity as children of God are central *Christian* concerns also. Indeed, the vocation of Israel according to the Old Testament and of the Church according to the New is so to share in the life and love of God that it becomes the people and the place where the virtues and skills for life together among the nations are known and practised. The truthful, just and life-giving encounter between human beings in all their diversity which constitutes community is dependent upon true worship of the truthful, justifying, life-giving God. This means that true community is *a gift of divine grace*; and its quality as

---

[1] J. Sacks, *The Persistence of Faith. Religion, Morality and Society in a Secular Age* (London: Weidenfeld and Nicolson, 1991).

gift means that it is not something which we can presume upon or determine in advance. In the end, it requires more than rational planning, however important that may be. Like happiness, it often occurs in its most profound forms when and where we least expect it. It occurs when heaven and earth touch.

Because God is one and Lord of all the earth, the gifts and skills which make life together possible are available to all through God's life-giving Spirit in creation. But it is also the case that the Church is called and gifted to witness in a special way to the life together of people of every kind and condition which is the will of God. It does so *by being itself*: one, holy, catholic and apostolic. By its *unity*, the Church witnesses to the oneness of God and to the possibility of humankind in all its diversity becoming one in praise of God. By its *holiness*, it witnesses to the disciplines and virtues which make community possible, ordering its life according to the character of the transcendent God. By its *catholicity*, it witnesses to its loyalty to the whole human race past, present and future, a loyalty vital for the preservation of humanity and reflecting God's covenant loyalty to the whole of creation. By its *apostolicity*, the Church witnesses in word and sacrament to the source of both its own life and the life of the world. That source is the forgiveness of God through the death and resurrection of the divine Son—which reminds us that there can be no true community without atonement, and there can be no atonement without sacrifice.

That is to put the matter in credal and doctrinal terms.[2] But it is possible to put it in scriptural terms as well. Which observation brings us to the Fourth Gospel: and here I happily acknowledge my debt, both personal and professional, to David Catchpole for his inspirational teaching on the Theologies of the Evangelists when I was a postgraduate student in the Department of Religious Studies at the University of Lancaster in the late 'Seventies.

---

[2] See further D.W. Hardy, "God and the Form of Society", in idem and P.H. Sedgwick, eds, *The Weight of Glory* (Edinburgh: T. & T. Clark, 1991) 131–44; also, D.F. Ford and D.L. Stamps, eds, *Essentials of Christian Community* (Edinburgh: T. & T. Clark, 1996).

2. *Theological Interpretation: Not "The Johannine Community" but "Christian Community in the Light of the Fourth Gospel"*

I begin with a word about method. As with any biblical text, we can read the Gospel of John in various ways depending on our identities and interests as readers.[3] In broad terms, if our interest lies in the world behind the text, we can read the Gospel with a view to reconstructing the intention of the historical author and testing the reliability of his account of the life of Jesus. This might include asking whether or not the author of the Gospel had an interest in "community" and whether or not he wrote the Gospel for a community, the so-called "Johannine community". In fact, in Johannine interpretation over the past thirty years, significant scholarly work has been done in precisely this area, building upon the development of both form and redaction criticism in the immediately preceding generations. Now it is accepted as a commonplace that one of the reasons for the distinctiveness of John is that it mirrors the experiences of a predominantly Jewish Christian community radically estranged, not only from the wider society, but also from the society of the synagogue, even perhaps from the society of other Christian groups.[4] Hence, commentators point to the moral and ontological dualism of the Gospel, the "us versus them" mentality, the hostility towards "the Jews" and "the Pharisees", the prominence given to the theme of trial and judgment, the christological exclusivism, and so on. So, it is said, the Johannine community had the ethos of an "introversionist (or, according to some, conversionist) sect", a "beleaguered community" turned in on itself and isolated from the world.[5] It is argued, furthermore, that the history of the community can be traced from one part of the Johannine corpus (i.e. the Fourth Gospel, the Johannine Epistles, and the Apocalypse) to another, thus giving us an insight into one significant "trajectory" in the history of earliest Christianity.[6]

---

[3] Cf. R. Morgan and J. Barton, *Biblical Interpretation* (Oxford: OUP, 1988); and on John in particular, F.F. Segovia, "The Significance of Social Location in Reading John's Gospel", *Int* 49 (1995) 370–8.

[4] Representative of a substantial literature are J.L. Martyn, *History and Theology in the Fourth Gospel* (Nashville: Abingdon Press, ²1979); and R.E. Brown, *The Community of the Beloved Disciple* (London: Geoffrey Chapman, 1979).

[5] See, for example, W.A. Meeks, "The Son of Man in Johannine Sectarianism", *JBL* 91 (1972) 44–72.

[6] As well as Martyn, *History and Theology* and Brown, *Community*, see more recently, U.C. von Wahlde, "Community in Conflict", *Int* 49 (1995) 379–89.

Such an approach has undoubted value. It brings to the surface
possible hidden or overlooked social and communal factors which
may have affected the writing of the Gospel, while not necessarily
denying the powerful and creative influence of the "towering theologian"[7] whose reflection upon Jesus past and whose experience of
Jesus present shaped the tradition. It offers a window onto the emergence of a distinctive strand in earliest Christianity and gives 'evidence of the fraught "parting of the ways" between Judaism and
Christianity. More generally, it contributes to reading the Gospel
with historical imagination and with the critical distance which historical method makes possible. It is worth noting, however, that the
effect of this has been to turn traditional Christianity's high regard
for John's Gospel on its head. The Gospel which proclaims God's
universal love is presented now as barely Christian, or at least as
having a powerful "dark side".[8] As a product of the narrow, extreme
world of intra-Jewish polemic, a world opened up for us by the comparative testimony of the documents from the Qumran community,
the Gospel's value for Christian faith is salvaged only by the shift
in interpretation made possible by John's inclusion in the Christian
canon. According to Wayne Meeks, for example:

> The kind of ethos that the narrative of the Fourth Gospel seems de-
> signed to reinforce, when taken at face value in its historical rather
> than its canonical context, is not one that many of us would happily
> call "Christian" in a normative sense. One could argue that this Gospel
> has won its secure place in the affections of generations of readers and
> its profound influence on theological, literary, and moral sensibilities
> of Western culture only through an endless series of more or less strong
> misreadings.[9]

Now, Meeks may be right. He certainly represents a strong consensus
of experts in the field. But there are grounds for caution, both on
the level of historical method and on the level of critical evaluation.[10]

---

[7] The term is that of M. Hengel in *The Johannine Question* (London: SCM, 1989).
[8] See, for example, C.C. Black, "Christian Ministry in Johannine Perspective",
Int 44 (1990) 36–40; also, D.M. Smith, "Theology and Ministry in John", in E.E.
Shelp and R. Sunderland, eds, *A Biblical Basis for Ministry* (Philadelphia: Westminster
Press, 1981) 213–4.
[9] W.A. Meeks, "The Ethics of the Fourth Evangelist", in R.A. Culpepper and
C.C. Black, eds, *Exploring the Gospel of John* (Louisville: Westminster/John Knox Press,
1996) 317.
[10] See further, S.C. Barton, "Can We Identify the Gospel Audiences?", in
R. Bauckham, ed., *The Gospels for All Christians* (Grand Rapids: Eerdmans, 1998) 173–94.

First, it is notoriously difficult to correlate a text like a gospel and the putative community from or for which it was written. The problem of circularity—of constructing the Matthean, Marcan, Lucan and Johannine "communities" from a reading of the respective gospels and then of using those reconstructions to interpret the gospels—is inescapable. It is also complicated by the likelihood that any one community may have known and been influenced by more than one gospel.[11] Even if we are helped in the Johannine case by the evidence of the Epistles and the Apocalypse, the reconstruction depends still on a prior decision about the chronological sequence of the texts: whether (as with Smalley) Apocalypse-Gospel-Epistles,[12] or (as with Segovia) Epistles-Gospel-Apocalypse,[13] or (as traditionally) Gospel-Epistles-Apocalypse.[14] Second, the category "sect", drawn as it is from studies (using a Troeltschian church-sect typology) of religious groups primarily in the modern period, is prone to applications which are anachronistic.[15] It is also a category which tends to be "loaded" ideologically—for example, in its use as a term of approbation among anti-establishment interpreters who want to play up the subversive, "protest" character of John's vision over against more conservative, "early Catholic" alternatives.[16] Third, it does not do justice to the gospel genre. That is to say, whereas an epistolary text like 1 Corinthians is patently oriented towards the life, loves and hates of a particular community in a particular city, the gospels, as distinctive (because kerygmatic) "lives of Jesus", may have been intended for transmission to and between audiences of a much more mixed and plural kind, having as a primary goal, not community self-definition, so much as conversion to faith in Jesus as the Son of God.[17] In which case, the search for the putative "Johannine community" may be misplaced, and the gospels may need to be read much more lit-

---

[11] See on this, R. Bauckham, "John for Readers of Mark", in *idem*, ed., *Gospels*, 147–71.

[12] Cf. S.S. Smalley, *Thunder and Love: John's Revelation and John's Community* (Waco: Word, 1994) 57–69.

[13] Cf. F.F. Segovia, *Love Relationships in the Johannine Tradition* (Chico, CA: Scholars Press, 1982).

[14] Cf. Brown, *Community; idem, The Churches the Apostles Left Behind* (New York: Paulist Press, 1984) 84–123.

[15] See on this, S.C. Barton, "Early Christianity and the Sociology of the Sect", in F. Watson, ed., *The Open Text* (London: SCM, 1993) 140–62.

[16] Cf. D. Rensberger, *Johannine Faith and Liberating Community* (Philadelphia: Westminster, 1988).

[17] Relevant here are the recent essays in Bauckham, ed., *Gospels*.

erally (as testimonies to the life of Jesus), rather than as subtle "allegories" of early church life.

These problems of historical method are compounded by problems of critical evaluation. In particular, there is the question of whether Meeks *et al.* are being as "historical" as they claim when they drive a wedge between the text in its original historical context on the one hand and the *reception* of the text in early Christianity and subsequently in the life of the Church.[18] The placing of the wedge is evident in the apparently harmless decision to take the Fourth Gospel "at face value in its historical rather than its canonical context", a strategy bolstered by the suggestion that the history of Johannine interpretation in the Church is a history of "an endless series of more or less strong misreadings".[19] There are a number of problems here. First, Meeks conceals the fact that reading John in its "historical context" is more than a matter of taking the text "at face value", and is instead a matter of scholarly *reconstruction* often reflecting as much the "face" of the scholar as the "face value" of the text. Second, there is a privileging of the original text in its (reconstructed) historical context over readings of the text in its canonical context and in the light of its history of reception in the Church. This represents a curious "fundamentalism of the originating moment"—a kind of scholarly counterpoint to popular fundamentalisms which also like to "get back" to the original. Whereas in the popular case, getting back to the original is for the purpose of showing how bad things have got since then and how important it is to return to how things were at the start, in the scholarly case, it is for the purpose of showing how "strange" or "dangerous" is the original and how "difficult" it is to use for the theological and moral formation of all "right-thinking" people!

But perhaps there is an approach which avoids these mirror-image fundamentalisms and the crippling positivism from which they suffer. Such an approach is what I propose to offer here.[20] In general terms, I would characterise it as *a "readerly" approach* rather than an "historical critical" approach narrowly conceived. Whereas the interest

---

[18] See further, the discussion of "history and tradition" in F. Watson, *Text and Truth. Redefining Biblical Theology* (Edinburgh: T. & T. Clark, 1997) 45–54.

[19] Meeks, "Ethics", 317.

[20] See also my recent essay, "Living as Families in the Light of the New Testament", *Int* 52 (1998) 130–44.

of historical criticism is restricted to reconstructing the world behind
or the world within the text, the interest of the readerly approach
is more on engagement with the historical text *as Spirit-inspired* with
a view to individual and communal discernment, judgment and transformation. The advantages of this approach are several. First, it goes
with the grain of the text itself which comes to us, not as a bare
"historical document", but as part of the canon of Christian scripture, the regular reading of which in the context of prayer and worship constitutes the Church as a community of faith. Second, it is
more historical than "historical criticism", since, while engaging with
the text in ways that are philologically and historically informed, it
does not seek to play off the (original) historical context of the text
against its canonical context and the history of its reception. This
allows both for the possibility that the text bears unique and indispensable witness to the truth about God's ways with the world, *and*
for the possibility that the witness of the text to the truth is partial
and fragmented, and therefore that its location in the canon—with
the other three gospels, the Johannine Epistles, and so on—is an aid
to the disclosure of the truth rather than an obstacle. Third, it is
an approach which takes seriously the critical relation between canonical text *and community*: that reading John for its witness to the truth
is something we do as readers whose skills in discerning the truth
have been learnt in Christian sacramental communities which are
themselves scripture-shaped.[21]

In talking here about the witness of the text (John's Gospel) to
the truth, I am advocating, therefore, the practice of a form of critical reason which is *theological and ecclesial*. On this view, the text is
more than an historical source. It is unique (but also partial and
fragmentary) testimony to the life of the triune God. This means
that what we say about Christian community in the light of John
has to be measured against the *greater reality* of the life of the Trinity.[22]
It is not a matter of reproducing, in some flat, wooden way, "what
John says about community". For a start, John doesn't say anything

---

[21] See on this, S.E. Fowl and L.G. Jones, *Reading in Communion. Scripture and Ethics
in Christian Life* (London: SPCK, 1991). Relevant also is my essay, "New Testament
Interpretation as Performance", *SJT* 52 (1999) 179–208.

[22] See further, F. Watson, "Trinity and Community: A Reading of John 17",
International Journal of Systematic Theology, 1/2 (1999) 168–84. I am grateful to Professor
Watson for sending me his essay and for his comments on the present piece.

about "community" *per se.* Not, "In the beginning was community",
but, "In the beginning was the Word"! So what we are after is *Spirit-
inspired, creative fidelity* to the witness of John to the Word-made-flesh
in the ways we order our common life. To put it another way,
Christianity is not a personal or social *morality*,[23] but a *participation* in
the love-life of God the Holy Trinity, at the heart of which is gift,
sacrifice and doxology.

Such an approach has a number of corollaries. It means, for example, that, not only do we need to hear the Gospel of John in relation to the rest of the New Testament, but also that we have to
hear it *in relation to the Old Testament.* Both testaments together tell
the story of God (who comes subsequently to be known as triune),
and both testaments together tell the story of the people of God (as
Israel and the Church). Another corollary is that we cannot talk
about "community" without first talking about *what it means to be the
Church.* This is so, not only because the Church mediates scripture
to us by means of authoritative "performance" past and present, but
also because the Church is itself the sacramental community which
brings us into contact with God's triune life—and therefore (so long
as it is faithful to its calling) shows us what true community is about.
A final corollary is that our reflection on community in the light of
John will have *a strong eschatological dimension.* It will be oriented, like
the Gospel itself, on what God's Spirit calls us to be and to do in
the present as an anticipation of a new, heavenly reality yet to be
revealed; and, as a reading oriented on hope in a future that is in
God's hand, it will demand of us as readers and hearers an openness to ongoing judgment and transformation, both individually and
in our life together.

3. *Community as Communication: The Salvation and Judgment of the World by the Word*

Having cleared the way for a reading of John which is historically
sensitive and at the same time theologically open, I want to draw
attention to an aspect of the Gospel whose relevance to reflection
on Christian community is in my opinion quite profound but which

---

[23] Cf. J. Milbank, "Can Morality be Christian?", in idem, *The Word Made Strange*
(Oxford: Blackwell, 1998) 219–32.

remains to be fully explored. In broad terms, my suggestion is that John's Gospel provides seminal ground for considering ways in which Christian existence, both individual and communal, is *constituted (and threatened) by communicative activity* of one kind or another.[24] To put it another way, whereas Rudolf Bultmann placed *revelation* at the centre of Johannine concerns,[25] I want to say that revelation is itself part of a wider concern related, not just to the enlightenment of the individual—note how Bultmann's existentialism surfaces here—but also to the constitution and reconstitution of the people of God. That wider concern is *the salvation of Israel and the nations made possible by God's self-communication to the world through the Word-made-flesh* bringing into being a people called to live in the truth and witness to the truth.

I begin by listing ten items of data relevant to my claim about the significant communicative dimension of John's Gospel.

(a) The God of the Fourth Gospel is one who communicates with the world in love by the "sending" or "giving" of his Son (3:16) and, through the Son, seeking true worshippers to worship him in spirit and truth (4:23). Critically, for the narrative as a whole, this divine self-communication through the Son bypasses in certain ways previously taken-for-granted instruments of divine communication such as Torah (1:17–18; 5:9b–18, 39–47) and Temple (2:13–22; 4:21–24; 7:28).

(b) Jesus is identified as the divine *Logos* who, as God's Son, reveals or "makes known" (ἐξηγέομαι) the Father (1:14–18). The symbols used in John to display Jesus' identity and role are weighted heavily towards his communicative activity in mediating "life". He is the Word, the Light, the Way, the Truth, the Life, the Good Shepherd, the True Vine, the one who gives "living water", and so on. Important here also is the universal scope of the divine communication in Jesus. This culminates, at the end of Jesus public ministry, in the coming of "certain Greeks" to "see" Jesus (12:20–22), and, on the cross, the *titulus* written in Hebrew, Latin and Greek (19:19–22).

---

[24] After I came to this conclusion, I discovered that David Ford had made a very similar observation in relation to the Epistle to the Ephesians, in his recent *Self and Salvation. Being Transformed* (Cambridge: CUP, 1999) 107–36.

[25] See, for example, R. Bultmann, *Theology of the New Testament. Volume Two* (London: SCM, 1955) 49–69.

(c) The role of the Spirit-Paraclete is communicative also. He is the one who teaches the disciples "all things" by bringing to their remembrance all that Jesus has said to them (14:26). He also is the one who guides believers into "all the truth" by speaking to them "whatever he hears" (from the Risen Christ) (16:13–15). So the communicative activity of the Son is preserved and sustained by the Spirit.

(d) Just as the Son has been "sent" by the Father in the power of the Spirit at the Gospel's beginning, so the disciples are "sent" by the Son in the power of the Spirit at the Gospel's post-resurrection climax (20:21–22; cf. 17:18). In other words, the important theme of mission, of sending and being sent—a theme which embraces the Father, the Son, the Spirit-Paraclete and the disciples—has communication for the sake of the salvation of "the world" at its heart.

(e) The theme of "the truth" (ἡ ἀλήθεια)—of direct relevance to questions about the source, authority and reliability of God's self-communication—is all-pervasive: God the Father seeks those who will worship him "in truth" (4:23); Jesus is the way to the truth (14:6); the Spirit is the "Spirit of truth" (16:13); and the disciple is one whom the Spirit guides into "all the truth" (16:13). Conversely, the Pharisees are blinded by sin to the truth about Jesus (9:40–41); Pilate is blind to the truth embodied in "the man" before him (18:38); and the devil is characterised as "a liar and the father of lies" (8:44).

(f) The associated theme of communication as "witness" (μαρτυρία) is all-pervasive also: the Father witnesses to the Son, the Son to the Father, and the Spirit to the Son; John (the Baptist) witnesses to Jesus and against himself (1:19–23, 29–34; 3:26–30); the disciples—Philip and Nathanael, for example (1:43–51)—are witnesses; indeed, all the characters witness to Jesus, even those who either misunderstand him, like Nicodemus, or oppose him, like the High Priest (11:49–52) or Pilate (19:5, 14, 19–22); and of course, the evangelist himself is a witness through the testimony of the Gospel (19:35; 21:24–25).

(g) The language and speech patterns of the Gospel as a whole betray a strong communicative interest. Jesus' "riddling" speech (in παροιμίαι) the misunderstanding which meets it, and the irony which characterises so much of the narrative, are parts of a strategy of communication appropriate to the essential *mystery of the hidden-and-revealed God* at the Gospel's heart. The same may be said of the great miracles identified by the evangelist as "signs" for the way they display the divine "glory" present in Jesus (2:11). It is true also of the parabolic actions like the temple "cleansing" (2:13–22) and the foot-washing (13:1–20).

(h) The Gospel reflects a strong interest, not only in communication from heaven to earth, but also communication from earth to heaven. I have in mind here, not only the divine "descent-ascent" motif so strong in the Farewell Discourse (13:1; 17:11a; cf. 3:13–14), but also the motif of prayer: both Jesus' prayers to the Father (11:41–42; 12:27–28; 17:1–26) and also his instructions to the disciples about prayer (14:13–14; 16:23–24, 26–27).

(i) On the "horizontal" plain, there is an interest in impoverished or broken communication. One aspect of this is the contrast drawn between violent and peaceful communicative action: the peace-offering of the One who gives the sop and the intended violence of Judas his betrayer (13:18–30), the violence of Peter to Malchus in the garden and Jesus' renunciation of violence (18:10–11; cf. v. 36), and the offering of the blessing of peace at the end by the One who had been the object of violence himself (20:19, 21, 26; cf. 14:27; 16:33).

(j) Finally, there is the attention given to what makes true communication possible. This is a matter of what we may call Johannine ethos and ethics. Important here are specific qualities and practices like "oneness" (or unity), worship "in spirit and truth", "believing" in Jesus, obedience to the commandments of Jesus, love and being loved (epitomised by "the disciple *whom Jesus loved*"), following Jesus' example of humble service, "abiding" in the Son as the Son "abides" in the Father, the practice of forgiveness, and so on.

The evidence presented here is not exhaustive, but gives more than sufficient warrant for my claim that *communicative concerns lie at the heart of John's Gospel*. This is more than a claim that the Gospel itself has a communicative goal: for that is self-evident from the statement of purpose in 20:30–31 ("But these [signs] are written that you may believe . . ."). It is the stronger claim that divine and human existence and inter-relationship are represented in what may legitimately be called communicative terms. The profound implications of this for human sociality in general and Christian community in particular

290 STEPHEN C. BARTON

are what we turn to next,[26] developing in greater detail one or two of the points made above.

4. *The Oneness of God as the Communicative Ground of Community*

Much more than the other gospels, the Fourth Gospel places heavy emphasis on the *oneness* of the Father and the Son and the oneness of believers.[27] It does so because oneness is important in itself and because there are forces of division which threaten to undermine it. Oneness is important in itself because, in the faith of Israel reflected in the *Shema* (Deut 6:4–5) and celebrated daily in the temple cult, *God is one*: "Hear, O Israel: The Lord our God is one Lord; and you shall love the Lord your God with all your heart, and with all your soul, and with all your might".[28] As this confession suggests, the unity of the people is bound up integrally with the oneness of God. Anything which threatens the oneness of God—paradigmatically, the worship of idols—threatens the unity of the people. Conversely, anything which divides the people—the activity of false teachers, prophets or messiahs, for example—undermines the common witness of the people to the oneness of God. In sum, the existence of Israel was characterised by a series of mutually reinforcing unities: one true God, manifesting his presence (or "name") in one tabernacle or temple, where He is worshipped according to one calendar by one holy people who purify themselves by the observance of one torah.[29]

Against this background—which Hayward develops in relation to the concern with oneness and purity in the Qumran community—

---

[26] For an anthropological account of what constitutes human sociality, see M. Carrithers, *Why Humans Have Cultures* (Oxford: OUP, 1992), esp. ch. 4; also his essay, "Hedgehogs, Foxes, and Persons: Resistance and Moral Creativity in East Germany and South India", forthcoming in N. Roughley, ed., *Being Human: Questions of Anthropological Universality and Particularity from Transdisciplinary Perspectives* (Cambridge: CUP, in press). I am grateful to Professor Carrithers for sharing his work with me.

[27] For what follows, I am indebted to C.T.R. Hayward, "The Lord is One: Some Reflections on Unity in Saint John's Gospel", an unpublished paper presented at the New Testament Postgraduate Seminar of the Department of Theology, University of Durham, on 3 March 1997.

[28] See further, R.W.L. Moberly, "'Yahweh is One': The Translation of the Shema", in J.A. Emerton, ed., *Studies in the Pentateuch* (Leiden: Brill, 1990), 209–15.

[29] For more on this theme, see B. Janowski, "Der eine Gott der beiden Testamente", *ZTK* 95 (1998) 1–36.

the Johannine emphasis on oneness is highly significant. Taken as a whole, the Gospel represents a claim that the one true God has made his presence uniquely known in the person of a Son with whom he is one, belief in whom brings a new oneness into being, an eschatological unity of people drawn from every nation. This explains the extraordinarily christocentric theology of the Gospel. It is John's way of setting out the radical idea that Jesus is the Son of God, the Word made flesh, the one who, by virtue of his oneness with the Father, manifests God's glorious presence. The affirmation of the divine presence uniquely in Jesus is displayed in many ways. For example, Jesus is the one upon whom the Spirit "descends *and remains*" (1:32–33 *bis*; cf. 3:34–35). He unites earth and heaven as the heavenly Son of Man upon whom the angels ascend and descend (1:51). He is the temple (2:21) where true worshippers will worship the Father (4:23–24). And he is the one who manifests "the name" (i.e. presence) of God to believers and keeps them united in that name (17:6–26). Paradoxically, however, this radical claim about God's unique self-disclosure in his Son not only provides the communicative ground for the unity of a new people of God: it also provokes controversy, division and "judgment" (κρίσις). *Unity creates separation!* This helps to explain the pain of parting that John's narrative betrays. In no other gospel is the charge against Jesus of blasphemy so prominent (cf. 5:18; 10:32–39; 19:7).[30] In no other gospel is the shape of the narrative as a whole so dominated by juridical overtones, as characters in the narrative become in effect witnesses for and against Jesus' claim to oneness with God as his Son.[31]

We may explore all this further by way of a case study. In the discourse in John 10, Jesus for the first time makes the categorical statement: "I and the Father are one" (ἐγὼ καὶ ὁ πατὴρ ἕν ἐσμεν) (10:30; cf. 17:11b, 22). To understand the significance of this testimony of oneness, we need to go back to the beginning of the discourse. In the preceding episode, Jesus and the man born blind have been in sharp conflict with "the Jews" and the Pharisees (9:13–41).

---

[30] "Jesus as New Temple: Johannine Blasphemy?" is the subject of a doctoral thesis by Jerry Truex, currently in preparation in the Department of Theology, University of Durham.

[31] See on this A.E. Harvey, *Jesus on Trial* (London: SPCK, 1976); also, A.T. Lincoln, "Trials, Plots and the Narrative of the Fourth Gospel", *JSNT* 56 (1994) 3–30.

On account of the man's new communicative insight and ability imparted by his transforming encounter with Jesus—note that the man becomes a witness and teacher (9:17, 25–34)—the man is *ex*communicated (9:34; cf. v. 22; 12:42; 16:2). On hearing about this, Jesus (like a shepherd seeking out the lost) "finds" the man, catechises him, and leads him to true worship (9:35–38). Symbolically and socially, he passes from one sphere of communicative activity to another— if you will, from one "community of discourse" to another.

This transition is explored and dramatised in the polemical teaching which follows in which the Pharisees are shown (by implication) to be false shepherds in Israel (like the leaders of the nation pilloried in Ezek 34), and Jesus testifies to himself as the "good shepherd". In the first part (10:1–10), two metaphors are (rather confusingly) intertwined: Jesus is the one true door or gate (θύρα) to the sheepfold, *and* he is the shepherd of the sheep who enters by the gate! In other words, Jesus is both the way (cf. 14:6) and the one who leads the way. Those who attempt to get into the fold by other ways are imposters, and those apart from Jesus who try to lead the sheep are strangers and thieves whom the sheep will not follow. Whereas Jesus "calls his own sheep by name and leads them out", the voice of other shepherds are not heeded because they are not recognised. Jesus is on intimate communicative terms with God's people; the Pharisees have lost contact.

In the next part of the discourse (10:11–21), the single metaphor of Jesus as shepherd of the sheep comes to the fore and is developed: "I am the *good* shepherd. The *good* shepherd lays down his life for the sheep" (10:11). Three times in this section, Jesus affirms that he is the "good shepherd" (10:11 *bis*, 14a); three times also he affirms that he "lays down his life for the sheep" (10:11, 15b, 17b). The first time, a contrast is drawn with the hired hand who does not care for the sheep and runs away when danger threatens. The second time, the death of the good shepherd is presented as having a surprising consequence: the bringing in of "other sheep not of this fold" (10:16). The third time, the death of Jesus as the good shepherd is given as the reason why he is loved by the Father (10:17–18). For our purposes, it is important to point out that *the good shepherd's willing self-sacrifice in death is a communicative act*. It communicates his relationship of care for the sheep which itself springs out of his relationship of loving obedience to the Father (10:14–15, 17–18). Furthermore, it is a communicative act which has enormous *creative power*, for it brings into being a new solidarity. The oneness of the Son with the Father in laying down his life for the sheep creates a new, single flock: "I have other sheep that do not belong to this flock. I must bring them also, and they will listen to my voice. *So there will be one flock, one shepherd* [μία ποίμνη, εἷς ποιμήν]" (10:16).

But now the paradox of oneness and separation reappears. Jesus' proclamation of a new solidarity arising out of his own solidarity with the Father creates division among the Jews (10:19–21). The division is over the *identity* of Jesus, an issue which has been a point of controversy right through this central section of the Gospel (i.e. John 7–10). Some think he is demon-possessed and therefore not to be listened to (10:20–21). Others question him, wanting to know if he is the messiah. They do so, significantly, in the temple, the place of the divine presence (10:22–23; cf. 18:20). They want him not to keep them waiting in suspense any longer, and to communicate "plainly" (παρρησίᾳ) (10:24b). But the Jesus of John knows that barriers to communication exist which take time to overcome—perhaps will never be overcome. So he replies in words of judgment designed, perhaps, to dislocate taken-for-granted communicative and symbolic norms:

> I have told you, and you do not believe. The works that I do in my Father's name testify to me; but you do not believe, because you do not belong to my sheep. My sheep hear my voice. I know them, and they follow me. I give them eternal life, and they will never perish. No one will snatch them out of my hand. What my Father has given me is greater than all else, and no one can snatch it out of the Father's hand. The Father and I are one (10:25–30).

Here is the oneness of sheep and shepherd and of Father and Son. The two are integrally related, and cause offence: "The Jews took up stones again to stone him . . . 'It is not for a good work that we are going to stone you, but for blasphemy, because you, though only a human being, are making yourself God'" (10:31, 33). And, of course, they are right: Jesus is making himself God (cf. 10:34–38; also 1:1; 5:18; 20:28), but in a way they do not comprehend, for they are not of Jesus' sheep.

The point, I hope, is clear. In Johannine perspective, as in the faith of Israel, there is a profound connection between *who God is and what it means to be a member of the people of God*. In particular, the oneness of God is the communicative ground of the oneness of his people. But for John, the oneness of God has been revealed as *a more complex unity*, a unity between the Father and the Son made known by the Spirit. This unity has a communicative dimension. It is a unity of presence, of love, of will, of work, of gift, of Spirit. Furthermore, it provides the grounds for the *transformation of the people of God into a new unity*. By laying down his life in death, in obedience to the Father, the Son (as the Good Shepherd) opens up the way for an eschatological people made up of Gentiles as well as Jews: the "one flock" led by the "one shepherd" (cf. 10:16b). But tragically, this new, eschatological unity is itself a cause of offence and separation. The oneness of God communicated as gift and sacrifice is *not coercive*. As in the *Shema*, it is a summons to respond freely in wholehearted love (cf. 13:1, 34–35; 14:21, 23, 24; 15:9, 10, 12, 13, 17; 17:23–24, 26).

5. *Worship "In Spirit and Truth": The Doxological Community*

If there is a profound connection in John between the oneness of God and what it means to be the people of God, that connection is made not just a matter of belief, even if right belief (itself the expression of a concomitant interpersonal trust) is central. It is made also a matter of practice: in particular, *the practice of worship*.[32] Perhaps one of the reasons for the common tendency to play up the so-called "individualism" of the Fourth Gospel is that salvation has been seen as a matter primarily of private decision and personal illumination. Certainly, the evangelist's own statement of purpose in writing is "that you [plural!] may *believe* [ἵνα πιστεύ(σ)ητε] that Jesus is the Christ, the Son of God" (20:31). Certainly also, John's narrative is punctuated by extraordinarily dramatic one-to-one encounters with Jesus. Nevertheless, there is reason to see John differently. For example, the one-to-one encounters are encounters between Jesus and individual figures who have a very significant *representative* status: Nicodemus is a Pharisee and "a leader of the Jews" (3:1), the woman at the well is a representative Samaritan (cf. 4:9), Pilate represents Roman authority, and so on. So these individuals are not to be taken individualistically! Even the statement of purpose in 20:30–31

---

[32] For what follows, I am indebted to M.M. Thompson, "Reflections on Worship in the Gospel of John", *The Princeton Seminary Bulletin* 19 (1998) 259–78. On the "doxological" dimension of Christian faith in general, see D.W. Hardy and D.F. Ford, *Jubilate. Theology in Praise* (London: Darton Longman and Todd, 1984).

does not just focus on the importance of "believing". It goes further: believing makes possible "*life* in his name". This "life" (ζωή), or "eternal life", is more than a matter of right belief. It is the gift of God made possible through the death of his Son and imparted by the Spirit (cf. 4:14; 5:26; 6:27, 35, 53–58, 63; 7:38–39; etc.). What I want to show now is that, in Johannine perspective, this "eternal life" which comes from God as gift finds expression in true worship, and that true worship, as a fundamental communicative act whereby heaven and earth touch, lies at the heart of true community.

The obvious texts which display John's concern with true worship are those to do with the temple: in particular, the Cleansing of the Temple (2:13–22) and the encounter between Jesus and the Woman of Samaria (4:1–26). Texts relating to the temple are important because the temple is where God's presence or "name" or "glory" dwells, and therefore it is the focal point of the life of Israel.[33] True communication between God and the people of God in worship constitutes the very essence of the people's common life: its priestly polity, its economy of tithes and sacrifices, its calendar of festivals and pilgrimages, its ritual practices, and its holiness worked out in rules of purity. Because John's Gospel proclaims *God's presence in Jesus* and, after his ascension, in the Spirit-Paraclete, it is not surprising that the question of true worship becomes a prime concern, and that the temple, the festivals, the purity rules, the high priesthood, and other aspects of the cult, are a focus of attention.

Apart from the two crucial episodes mentioned, the following data reflect this attention also:

(a) The Prologue proclaims that "the Word became flesh and tabernacled [ἐσκήνωσεν] among us, full of grace and truth; we have beheld his glory [δόξαν] glory as of the only Son from the Father" (1:14). The allusions here to the presence of the *shekina* in the tabernacle of the people of Israel are unmistakable. But now, of course, God manifests his presence in Jesus (1:17b).

(b) When the blind man comes to understand that Jesus is none other than the Son of Man (from heaven), he confesses his belief by word ("Lord, I believe") and by worship ("and he worshipped

---

[33] See now C.T.R. Hayward, *The Jewish Temple. A Non-Biblical Sourcebook* (London: Routledge, 1996); also, Bernd Janowski's discussion of Israel's exilic "*Shekina*-Theology" in his *Gottes Gegenwart in Israel* (Neukirchen-Vluyn, 1993) 19–147.

[προσεκύνησεν] him") (9:38). The word of confession and the practice of worship are presented here, cameo-style, as inextricably linked. Earlier in the same episode, the blind man turns teacher and, with true insight, speaks of the importance of God-fearing piety for being in good communication with God: "[I]f anyone is a worshipper of God [θεοσεβής] and does his will, God listens to him" (9:31). The interest in worship comes through again.

(c) The Greeks who come to Philip with a request to "see Jesus" (itself an expression of openness to revelation), are described as being among those "who went up [to the temple mount] to worship [προσκυνήσωσιν] at the feast" (12:20). Again, faith and worship are made inseparable.

(d) Jesus' teaching in the Farewell Discourse about the hostility and persecution which the disciples are to expect from "the world" (15:18–16:4) reaches a powerful climax with the warning that "the hour is coming when whoever kills you will think he is offering service to God" (16:2). The word for "service" here is λατρεία, and its connotation is cultic. So the NRSV rightly translates it as "worship". We may infer from this warning that opposition to the proclamation of Christ (as one with the Father) is seen as a threat to true worship. Not just belief, but matters of liturgy and life are central concerns *on both sides*.

(e) To a degree unparalleled in the Synoptic Gospels, the Jesus of John times his ministry by the calendar and the festivals—Passover (2:13, 23; 6:4; 11:55; 12:1; 13:1; 18:28, 39; 19:14), Tabernacles (7:2), Dedication (10:22)—and locates his ministry in or in relation to the temple. Typical of the latter is Jesus' reply to the high priest in the high priest's courtyard: "I have spoken openly to the world; I have always taught in synagogues *and in the temple* [καὶ ἐν τῷ ἱερῷ], where all Jews come together" (18:20; cf. 7:14, 28; 8:20; 11:56). This testimony towards the Gospel's climax, corresponds with the testimony from scripture cited at the outset of Jesus' ministry: "Zeal *for thy house* will consume me" (2:17; cf. Ps 69:10).

The two questions this data raises are: Why does the Fourth Evangelist display this significant interest in worship? And, does he focus attention on the cult only to show that it has been rendered otiose because the presence of God has now been manifested eschatologically in the Son? On the first, we may affirm simply that John's interest in true worship is almost certainly a corollary of his summons to right (christological) belief. If that is so, then from a Johannine perspective, *the communicative acts which constitute community would have to have worship at their heart.* On the second, it may plausibly be argued that, in the light of the revelation of the Father in the Son, the role of the cult as the place of encounter with God has given way to a role of lesser (but still real) importance. Like the scriptures, Moses and John the Baptist, it bears witness to the coming of someone greater: the divine Son.

Two texts bear this out. The episode of the Cleansing of the Temple in 2:13–22 is particularly prominent in John. As is commonly pointed out, unlike the Synoptics, the Fourth Evangelist places this episode at the beginning of Jesus' public ministry, rather than after the Entry into Jerusalem. It is Jesus' first act on the occasion of his first (of three) visits to Jerusalem. Having revealed himself at the Cana wedding as the embodiment of God's presence or "glory" (2:11), he now goes to the temple in Jerusalem, the place where God's glory was presumed to dwell. There, in a communicative action of prophetic symbolism whose violence is unparalleled elsewhere in the Gospel, Jesus drives out the traders and the sacrificial livestock from the temple with a whip: "Take these things out of here; you shall not make my Father's house a house of trade" (2:16). As elsewhere in John, the action of Jesus is then explored for its significance. The tell-tale sign in the text is the repeated reference to what the disciples of Jesus "remembered" (ἐμνήσθησαν)—presumably under the inspiration of the Holy Spirit (cf. 14:26)—after the event: specifically, after Jesus' resurrection (2:17a, 22a). This interpretative "remembering" takes two forms (cf. 2:22b). The first is scriptural. In the light of Ps 69:10, and taking καταφάγεται as a double-entendre meaning both "consume" and "destroy", Jesus' action in the temple is seen as a fulfilment of the (enscripted) will of God for the preservation of the honour of God's house, and as a contributory factor in Jesus' death. The second "remembering" is dialogical. The Jews ask for a "sign" legitimising Jesus' action in the temple (ἱερόν) and in a typically riddling response which takes the communication to a different level, Jesus answers with reference to a *different* shrine, the temple (ναός) of his own body: "Destroy this temple [ναόν] and in three days I will raise it up" (2:19). Typically, again, the Jews misunderstand: so the narrator provides the interpretation: "But he spoke of the temple of his body [περὶ τοῦ ναοῦ τοῦ σώματος αὐτοῦ] (2:21).

What is the Evangelist seeking to communicate through the communicative acts and words of Jesus in this episode? Surely, that *Jesus' body—specifically, his crucified and risen body—is the eschatological temple of God*, the place where the glory of God dwells and where true worship takes place. Some see this as the *replacement* of the Jerusalem temple and therefore of cultic worship.[34] But that is by no means explicit in the text. Arguably, Jesus' action has as its goal, not the end of the temple, but its reformation and purification. An alternative reading, therefore would be to interpret the Evangelist as talking of *another, far superior* temple which, by analogy with the eschatological abundance of the water-turned-to-wine in the previous episode (2:1–11), signifies the time and place of eschatological "fullness" (cf. 1:16) present in the person of Jesus the Messiah.[35] In which case, the temple and cult in Jerusalem, once purified, serve as "signs" which, *while they last*, point beyond themselves to God's presence (for the salvation of Israel and the nations) in his Son. Be that as it may, the more fundamental point remains: the Fourth Evangelist cannot conceive of the life of the people of God apart from the reciprocal communicative acts between God and his people which we call worship; and that reciprocal communicative action is bound up now with the incarnate Logos crucified and risen.

The story of Jesus and the Samaritan Woman in John 4 develops this theme further. Taking the form, well known from the patriarchal narratives, of a wooing at a well (cf. Gen 24:10–61; 29:1–20; Exod 2:16–22), Jesus the eschatological bridegroom (cf. 3:29) encounters a Samaritan woman at the well of the patriarch Jacob. Extraordinarily, the one who can turn water into gallons of wine, is tired and thirsty: so he asks the woman for a drink. But soon the conversation gets into very deep water indeed (!), for, of course, Jesus is talking at a different level. By yet more riddling speech, he is wooing the woman to accept from him "*living* water" (ὕδωρ ζῶν) (4:10, 11), "a spring of water welling up to eternal life" (4:14). As we know

---

[34] For example, M.D. Hooker, "Traditions about the Temple in the Sayings of Jesus", *BJRL* 70 (1988) 7–19, at p. 15.

[35] So Thompson, "Reflections", 10–12.

from biblical texts (e.g. Isa 55:1; Zech 14:8; cf. Ezek 47:1–12) and from later in John's Gospel itself (7:37–39), water is a symbol of eschatological salvation generally and of the gift of the Spirit in particular.[36] But the woman has some way to go before Jesus can make this clear. First, there is a brief "to and fro" about her marital status. This allows Jesus to reveal that he knows that the woman has had five husbands and that her present relationship is adulterous (4:16–18). In turn, this leads the woman to acknowledge that Jesus is a "prophet" (4:19; cf. 9:17b). Curiously, she then proceeds directly to talk about Samaritan *worship*: "Our fathers worshipped [προσεκύνη-σεν] on this mountain; and you say that in Jerusalem is the place where men ought to worship [προσκυνεῖν]" (4:20). The link with the revelations about her marital status are quite opaque until we recognise that the "five husbands" along with her current adulterous relation are probably symbolic of idolatrous worship (cf. 2 Kings 17:13–34), having the biblical overtones of "going after" other gods as a kind of promiscuity (cf. Hos 2:2).[37] So the dialogue is not as incoherent as it at first appears. It is about *the true worship that comes from receiving from Jesus the gift of "living water" which is the Spirit.*

Jesus' climactic revelation, in which "worship" (προσκυνεῖν and cognates) occurs six times, makes this clear:

> Woman, believe me, the hour is coming when neither on this mountain nor in Jerusalem will you worship the Father. You worship what you do not know; we worship what we know, for salvation is from the Jews. But the hour is coming and now is, when the true worshippers will worship the Father *in Spirit* and truth, for such the Father seeks to worship him. God is Spirit, and those who worship him must worship *in Spirit* and truth (4:22–24).

Several comments are called for here. First, Jesus acknowledges the salvation-historical primacy of Israel: "salvation is from the Jews [ἐκ τῶν Ἰουδαίων]" (4:22b). So there is continuity with the life and worship of Israel as well as discontinuity. Second, Marianne Meye Thompson is right, I think, when she says that worship of the Father "in Spirit and truth" constitutes "neither a polemic against external ritual and forms of worship, nor an argument in favor of the interioriza-

---

[36] See M. Turner, *The Holy Spirit and Spiritual Gifts Then and Now* (Carlisle: Paternoster Press, 1996) 61.

[37] See on this, S.M. Schneiders, *The Revelatory Text* (San Francisco: HarperCollins, 1991) 190–1.

tion of worship, nor a criticism of the idea of 'sacred space' *per se*".[38]
The point at issue is primarily *pneumatological and eschatological*—"the
hour is coming *and now is*" (4:23a)—rather than sacerdotal. Third,
the reference to "true" worshippers and worship "in Spirit *and truth*"
is noteworthy. Implicit here is a recognition of the ever-present possibility of worship as communicative activity which is distorted and
therefore idolatrous—a failure to align the worship of God with the
character of God as Spirit (4:24a) and truth. Finally, there is the
extraordinary theological testimony that the Father "seeks" (ζητεῖ)
true worshippers to worship him truly (4:23b). This is testimony to
the reciprocity of divine love: God gives his Son in love (cf. 3:16)
so that his people might respond doxologically.

6. *Conclusion*

My concern in the preceding has not been to give a reconstruction
of "the Johannine community" according to the prevailing norms of
historical criticism. That is an exercise of the historical imagination
which others are engaged in, often with very interesting results: and
the present essay is indebted to that work in many ways. But I have
been attempting something different: not historical reconstruction but
theological interpretation historically informed. My goal has been to engage
in a reading of the Fourth Gospel as scripture with a view to discerning how it might speak today about the nature of Christian community, with the implications that might have for human sociality
in general.

My reading—and of course, it is a provisional, incomplete reading—has led me to three substantive conclusions. First, in so far as
the Gospel of John is shot through with motifs that can properly be
called "communicative", it seems legitimate to make the theological
inference that, seen in Johannine terms, Christian community is *constituted by communicative activity* of various kinds. The most important
communicative activity is between heaven and earth, and earth and
heaven. Christian community happens when heaven and earth meet.
Therefore, it is an eschatological and pneumatic reality which has
the nature of gift.

Second, Christian community is predicated on *the oneness of God*—

---

[38] Thompson, "Reflections", 13.

the oneness of the communicative activity of the Father and the Son in the Spirit who, by the same Spirit, brings into being a new oneness of the people of God on earth. Implicit in this oneness is a *critique of idolatry*, for idolatry, as the worship of that which is "not God", consists in communicative activity which is fundamentally distorted, confused or misdirected. If this is so, then the unity of the community depends upon confession of the truth that God is one— a unity (so Christians believe) of Father, Son and Holy Spirit whose love all humanity is invited to share.

Third, and related, Christian community has at its heart a particular form of communicative activity: that of true belief grounded in *worship of God "in Spirit and truth"*. Such belief and worship is what constitutes community—or, perhaps we should say, *communion*—with God and with our fellow creatures. It is also what forms and shapes us as individuals and in our common life. It does so because it has a *particular* locus: the "temple" of Jesus' body. It does so because it involves *particular* communicative acts: eating Jesus' flesh and drinking his blood (cf. 6:53–58). That creates identity and community. But it also creates division: "After this many of his disciples drew back and no longer went about with him" (6:66). The gift of love which is the way to eternal life is *not coercive*, it does not *force* people to belong: otherwise it would not be gift.

PREFORMED TRADITIONS AND THEIR IMPLICATIONS FOR PAULINE CHRISTOLOGY

E. Earle Ellis

My examination of preformed traditions in the New Testament began with an M.A. thesis,[1] followed by a doctoral dissertation on *Paul's Use of the Old Testament*.[2] This interest broadened, sparked by John Bowker's essay on the "Proem and Yelammedenu Form",[3] into studies of Old Testament expositions (midrashim) in Acts, the New Testament letters[4] and the Gospels.[5] In the mid-seventies initial work on a commentary on I Corinthians required an inquiry into various other kinds of preformed traditions in that letter[6] and in other Pauline literature.

The same period marked the beginnings of the study recently published, *The Making of the New Testament Documents*,[7] a full investigation of literary traditions and their implications for the authorship and dating of the Gospels and of the letters. The present essay can only briefly sketch the more comprehensive study with its new paradigm of the history of early Christianity. The chief purpose of the essay is to show the implications of certain preformed traditions in Paul's letters for the origins of the Apostle's Christology.

---

[1] E.E. Ellis, "The Nature and Significance of Old Testament Quotations in the Gospel of Mark", M.A. Thesis, Wheaton (IL) College Graduate School, 1953.

[2] E.E. Ellis, *Paul's Use of the Old Testament* (Edinburgh: Oliver and Boyd, 1957); cf. idem, "A Note on Pauline Hermeneutics", *NTS* 2 (1955–56) 127–33.

[3] J. Bowker, "Speeches in Acts: A Study in Proem and Yelammedenu Form", *NTS* 14 (1967–68) 96–111.

[4] E.E. Ellis, "Midrash, Targum and New Testament Quotations" (1969); "Midrashic Features in Acts" (1970); "Exegetical Patterns in 1 Corinthians and Romans" (1975); "How the New Testament Uses the Old" (1977); "Prophecy and Hermeneutic in Jude" (1978), *Prophecy and Hermeneutic in Early Christianity* (WUNT 18; Tübingen: Mohr-Siebeck, 1978) 147–72, 188–208, 213–36.

[5] E.E. Ellis, "New Directions in Form Criticism," *Jesus Christus in Historie und Theologie*. (FS H. Conzelmann; ed. G. Strecker; Tübingen: Mohr-Siebeck, 1975) 299–315 = Ellis, *Prophecy* (n. 4), 237–53.

[6] Given as a paper in an SNTS seminar led by Peter Stuhlmacher and myself, and published later as E.E. Ellis, "Traditions in 1 Corinthians", *NTS* 32 (1986) 481–502.

[7] E.E. Ellis, *The Making of the New Testament Documents* (Leiden: Brill, 1999).

The Making of the New Testament Documents

From Traditions to Gospels

For the Synoptic Gospels the study of expository forms discloses one clear dominical proem midrash[8] and numerous *yelammedenu rabbenu* type midrashim.[9] An examination of Gospel narratives reveals two stock patterns on which the large majority were constructed.[10] The first pattern, used mainly for healing episodes, has the following structure: Setting + Appeal to Jesus + Jesus' Response + Reactions.[11] It is highly christological and designed to serve as a teaching by narration as much as Jesus' parables (*meshalim*) were a teaching by illustrative story.[12] With a shift of emphasis the pattern can be structured as a narrative proper,[13] as a pronouncement story (apothegm),[14] or as a more extended saying, discourse or dialogue.[15]

The second pattern uses biblical quotations and allusions to frame the narrative, e.g. in the stories of Jesus and the Baptist,[16] of the Magi and Flight,[17] and of the Entry and the Cleansing of the Temple.[18] It may be termed a narrative midrash in that the story about Jesus is presented as an interpretation or fulfilment of the biblical texts

---

[8] Matt 21:33–44 T + Q. Cf. Ellis, *Prophecy* (n. 4), 251–3; in Strecker, *Jesus Christus* (n. 5), 313–5. So also, W.D. Davies and D.C. Allison, Jr., *The Gospel According to Saint Matthew* (3 vols., Edinburgh: T. & T. Clark, 1997) 3.174–5: "While . . . we have reservations about ascribing the pattern to Jesus himself, it does appear that Matthew's text in its current shape corresponds to an old form of synagogue address" (p. 175). But the pattern is present in parallel passages found in all three Synoptic Gospels (T) and apparently in a tradition used by Matthew and Luke that differs from Mark (Q).

[9] Matt 11:7–15 Q; 12:1–8 T + Q; 15:1–9 par; 19:3–9 par; 22:23–33 T + Q; 24:4–31 ? T + Q; Luke 10:25–37; cf. Matt 21:15–16. Cf. Ellis, *Making* (n. 7), 175n., 249n., 350; idem, *The Old Testament in Early Christianity* (Tübingen: Mohr-Siebeck, 1991) 97–8, 103n., 134–138 = Italian Translation (Brescia: Paideia, 1999): pp. 129–31, 138n., 174–9. Cf. also Matt 11:2–6, 7–15, where Jesus responds to biblical questions in the form of a (summarized) biblical commentary.

[10] Cf. Ellis, *Making* (n. 7), 333–56, 349–51.

[11] E.g. Exorcisms: Mark 1:21–28 par (unclean spirit); Matt 8:28–34 T (Gadarene); 12:22–32 T + Q (mute); healings: Matt 8:1–4 T + Q (leper); Mark 5:21–43 T + Q (Jairus' daughter).

[12] Cf. B. Gerhardsson, "Illuminating the Kingdom," in *Jesus and the Oral Gospel Tradition* (ed. H. Wansbrough; Sheffield: Sheffield Academic, 1991) 266–304.

[13] E.g. Leper (Matt 8:1–4 T + Q). Cf. Ellis, *Making* (n. 7), 341–3.

[14] E.g. Paralytic (Matt 9:1–8 T + Q).

[15] E.g. Jairus' daughter (Mark 5:21–43 T + Q).

[16] Matt 3:1–17 T + Q. Cf. Ellis, *Making* (n. 7), 345–8.

[17] Matt 2:1–17.

[18] Matt 21:1–17 T + Q + John.

that frame it. And it may be derived from the "text + exposition" midrashic patterns which Jesus, in my judgment, had taught his pupils to use to summarize his teaching.[19] Since the messianic understanding of the biblical texts is presupposed, the texts may have been detached from antecedent dominical expositions (midrashim) in which the christological meaning had been exegetically established,[20] just as certain clustered parables[21] or sayings of Jesus[22] were apparently detached expositions from similar expository episodes.

To communicate with and to persuade the Torah-centric Judaism of his day, Jesus of necessity had to justify his acts and teachings from the Scriptures.[23] In antithesis to the classical form criticism,[24] the Gospel traditions at root set forth a high Christology designed to present Jesus as the fulfilment of Old Testament promises. And, as J.W. Doeve, Birger Gerhardsson, Rainer Riesner and others have argued,[25] they were composed by apostles and transmitted in a carefully cultivated and controlled manner from their creation to their incorporation into the four Gospels.[26] As I understand the history, the Gospels are the products, respectively, of four apostolic missions,[27] whose leaders can be identified in Gal 2. The Jacobean mission, centered on Jerusalem, produced the Gospel of Matthew.[28] The Petrine mission, following Peter's departure from Jerusalem (Acts

---

[19] Cf. E.E. Ellis, *Christ and the Future in New Testament History* (Leiden: Brill, 2000) 25–31, 242–54.

[20] Cf. Ellis, *Prophecy* (n. 4), 252–3; idem, *Old Testament* (n. 9), 100–1, 130–8 = IT: 133–5, 163–80.

[21] E.g. Matt 13; Luke 15–16.

[22] Cf. Matt 5:31–2 with Matt 19:3–9; Matt 5:21–2 with Mark 9:41–8.

[23] Cf. J. Jeremias, *New Testament Theology I* (Göttingen: Vandenhoeck & Ruprecht, 1971), 205: "Jesus lived in the Old Testament"; Ellis, *Christ* (n. 19), 17–19.

[24] For a critique cf. Ellis, *Making* (n. 7), 19–27; idem, *Christ* (n. 19), 20–9, 246–54.

[25] J.W. Doeve, *Jewish Hermeneutics in the Synoptic Gospels and Acts* (Assen: Van Gorcum, 1954); B. Gerhardsson, *Memory and Manuscript* (Grand Rapids: Eerdmans, ²1998); R. Riesner, *Jesus als Lehrer* (Tübingen: Mohr-Siebeck, ³1988). Cf. also E. Güttgemanns, *Candid Questions Concerning Gospel Form Criticism* (Pittsburgh PA: Pickwick, 1979).

[26] Cf. Ellis, "From Traditions to the New Testament", "Traditions in John's Gospel", *Making* (n. 7), 1–47, 154–83; idem, *Christ* (n. 19), 14–16.

[27] Cf. Clement, *Stromata* 1.1.11: Clement's mentors whom he carefully sought out "preserved the true tradition (παράδοσιν) of the blessed teaching directly from Peter and James and John and Paul".

[28] Cf. Ellis, *Making* (n. 7), 251n, 290–1. Jesus traditions in James are closest in form and substance to the Gospel of Matthew. Peter is given more prominence in Matthew (esp. 10:7; 16:17–19; 17:24–7; cf. Davies, *Matthew* [n. 8], 2.647–52) than in Mark, reflective of James' desire to give Peter full credit for his important role in the church. Probably also, in Mark, the Gospel initially of the Petrine mission, Peter would not wish to have his own role overly emphasized.

12:17), was based for a time at Caesarea Palestine where Mark composed his Gospel.[29] The Johannine mission was located in Palestine until a few years before the Jewish revolt[30] where it produced and used traditions and perhaps an Aramaic proto-Gospel.[31] Afterward it was located at Ephesus where John composed our canonical Gospel.[32] The Pauline mission, for whom Luke wrote his Gospel, was based initially at Antioch. But it ranged across the breadth of the Roman world and was situated successively at Ephesus, Caesarea Palestine, Rome and Spain.[33]

Luke's Gospel[34] best explains the historical relationship between the four canonical Gospels.[35] It alone contains such a variety of sources, encompassing the Gospel of Mark (or proto-Mark), traditions in common with the Gospel of Matthew (Q), traditions in com-

---

[29] Cf. Ellis, "The Date and Provenance of Mark's Gospel", *Making* (n. 7), 357–76, 369–72. Irenaeus, commonly misread on this point, says only that Mark "delivered (παραδέδωκεν) his Gospel to Rome after Peter and Paul's departure" (ἔξοδον) to ministries elsewhere (pp. 360–1). The request by Roman Christians for a document of Jesus' word and work (Clement of Alexandria *apud* Eusebius *H.E.* 2.15.1) came during Peter's initial visit to Rome during Claudius' reign, probably in 53–4 CE (Hippolytus, *Ref.* 6.20 = 6.15; cf. Manson; Lietzmann). Mark returned to Caesarea and composed his Gospel in 55–58 CE from traditions then being used in congregations of the Petrine mission. Cf. Ellis, *Making* (n. 7), 265, 364–8; T.W. Manson, *Studies in the Gospels and Epistles* (Manchester: Manchester University, 1962) 39; H. Lietzmann, *A History of the Early Church* (4 vols; Cleveland OH: World, 1961; 1944) 1.111 (= German 1.110).

[30] Ellis, *Making* (n. 7), 152, 234–7, 402; cf. J.B. Lightfoot, "St. Paul and the Three", *St. Paul's Epistle to the Galatians* (Peabody MA: Hendrickson, 1993, [10]1892) 360; C.H. Dodd, *Historical Traditions in the Fourth Gospel* (Cambridge: CUP, 1965) 245; M. Hengel, *The Johannine Question* (London: SCM, 1989) 110–134 (= German 276–325).

[31] Cf. C.F. Burney, *The Aramaic Origin of the Fourth Gospel* (Oxford: Clarendon, 1922) 27; C.C. Torrey, *Our Translated Gospels* (New York: Harper, 1936), passim; W.H. Brownlee, "Whence the Gospel According to John?" in *John and Qumran* (ed. J.H. Charlesworth, London: Geoffrey Chapman, 1972) 185–7.

[32] John's Gospel was composed "at Ephesus in Asia" (Irenaeus), "last of all" (Clement), "in his old age" (Epiphanius); cf. Irenaeus, *A.H.* 3.1.1 = Eusebius *H.E.* 5.8.4; Clement Alex. *apud* Eusebius, *H.E.* 6.14.5ff.; Epiphanius, *Panarion* 51.12.2; 51.33.7–9. Cf. Ellis, *Making* (n. 7), 152, 213f., 234–7.

[33] Cf. Ellis, *Making* (n. 7), 256–63, 266–84, 391n, 422–5. Re Paul's mission to Spain cf. Rom 15:24, 28; Acts 1:8; 13:47 (ἐσχάτου τῆς γῆς); I Clem 5:7 (τὸ τέρμα τῆς δύσεως); Muratorian Canon *c*; Acts of Peter (*Vercelli*) 1–3, 40; Epiphanius, *Panarion* 26.6.5; E.E. Ellis, "'Das Ende der Erde' (Apg 1, 8)". *Der Treue Gottes trauen. . . .* FS. G. Schneider (ed. W. Radl et al.; Freiburg: Herder, 1991) 277–287 = English: *BBR* 1 (1991) 123–132.

[34] On the date and authorship cf. Ellis, *Making* (n. 7), 389–91, 397–405.

[35] Cf. Ellis, *Making* (n. 7), 251–2, 400–5; E.E. Ellis, *The Gospel of Luke* (Grand Rapids: Eerdmans, [7]1996) 21–9, 67, 271–2. On Luke's knowledge of Jerusalem cf. M. Hengel, *Between Jesus and Paul* (London: SCM, 1983) 101, 109, 126–8.

mon with the Gospel of John and traditions of the Jerusalem church.[36] Luke could have obtained access to these sources on one occasion, and probably only one, that is, during his time in Palestine at Paul's collection visit, arrest and subsequent detention in Caesarea for trial, 58–60 CE.[37]

At that time the three other missions were active in the area. The fact that Luke utilized Mark's Gospel, along with other evidence, datelines Mark at Caesarea between 55–58 CE.[38] In my judgment Luke employed only traditions from the Matthean and Johannine missions and not the Gospels of those missions; this dates the first and fourth Gospels later, at least in their Greek dress: Matthew in the early sixties[39] and John about 85–95 CE.[40] John's Gospel incorporates some ten oral or written traditions that are Synoptic-like[41] in substance or in form, but he probably did not use the Synoptic Gospels themselves[42] although he may have known them.

---

[36] Cf. Ellis, "Luke-Acts: A Key to the History of Earliest Christianity", *Making* (n. 7), 251–4; cf. 154–64, 181–3, 195–9, 389–91, 400–3.

[37] The "we" sections of Acts (16:10–7; 20:5—21:19; 27:1—28:16; cf. 1:1; Luke 1:2f.) in all probability refer to the author and thus place Luke with Paul at this time, whether or not he remained in Palestine during the whole two years. Cf. Ellis, *Making* (n. 7), 397–8; B. Witherington III, *The Acts of the Apostles* (Grand Rapids: Eerdmans, 1998) 53–4; C.J. Hemer, *The Book of Acts in the Setting of Hellenistic History* (Tübingen: Mohr-Siebeck, 1989) 312–34.

[38] See above, n. 29. Mark composed his gospel in Caesarea after his visit to Rome with Peter during the reign of the emperor Claudius (†13 October 54) but before Luke's use of the gospel between 58–60 CE.

[39] None of the Synoptic Gospels display any knowledge of the fulfilment of Jesus' prediction of the 70 CE destruction of Jerusalem and present it totally in terms of Old Testament judgments, especially that of 586 BCE (Dodd, Reicke). Equally, they know nothing of the Jerusalem Christians' flight to Pella about 66 CE. Cf. C.H. Dodd, "The Fall of Jerusalem and the 'Abomination of Desolation'", *More New Testament Studies*, (Manchester: Manchester University, 1968) 69–83; B. Reicke, "Synoptic Prophecies on the Destruction of Jerusalem", in *Studies in New Testament and Early Christian Literature* (FS A.P. Wingren; ed. D.E. Aune; Leiden: Brill, 1972) 125–6; Ellis, *Making* (n. 7), 288–92, 319, 375,389–91.; idem, *Christ* (n. 19), 227–33.

[40] See above, n. 32.

[41] I.e. John 1:19–34 (the Baptist); 2:13–22 (temple cleansing); 4:46–54 (healing official's son); 5:1–9 (healing at Bethesda); 6:1–15, 16:21 (feeding and walking on water); 9:1–7 (healing blind man); 12:1–8 (anointing); 12:12–9 (entry to Jerusalem); 18–20 (passion and resurrection narrative).

[42] So P. Gardner-Smith, *Saint John and the Synoptic Gospels* (Cambridge: CUP, 1938) 31 (from the perspective of the classical form criticism); P. Borgen, "The Independence of the Gospel of John," in *Early Christianity and Hellenistic Judaism* (Edinburgh: T. & T. Clark, 1996) 203–4 (from the perspective of current form criticism). Cf. also B. Lindars, *Essays on John* (Leuven: Leuven University & Peeters, 1992). 92–3; G. Beasley-Murray, *John* (Waco TX: Word, 1987) xxxvii; S.S. Smalley, "St. John's Gospel" *ET* 97 (1985–86) 103; D.M. Smith, *Johannine Christianity* (Columbia SC:

The Gospel titles (with authors) were probably attached only when more than one Gospel was being read in congregational worship, about the turn of the second century according to Bo Reicke.[43] Luke's name, however, would have been tagged to his work from the beginning when it was catalogued in the library of his patron, Theophilus.[44] In all probability the responsible authors are accurately identified by the titles. But in the composition of their Gospels all had secretarial help and, for Matthew and John at least, other co-worker assistants.[45] That no author's name was given in the Gospel text may point to the corporate nature of the authorship, or it may reflect only the Oriental custom of writing anonymously[46] and of giving priority to title over authorship.[47]

Traditions in the Letters

The New Testament letters were produced by the same four apostolic missions. But preformed pieces in them are less easy to recognize because, apart from Old Testament quotations, no antecedent forms or multiple uses of the same traditional pieces are extant.[48] However, following the pioneering work of Ernst Lohmeyer and

University, 1984) 170–1; E. Haenchen, *John* (2 vols., Philadelphia: Fortress, 1984) 1.75–6; L. Morris, *Studies in the Fourth Gospel* (Grand Rapids: Eerdmans, 1969) 15–63. Otherwise: C.K. Barrett, *The Gospel According to John* (London: SPCK, ²1978) 45; F. Neirynck, *Evangelica II* (Leuven: Peeters, 1991) 571.

[43] B. Reicke, *The Roots of the Synoptic Gospels* (Philadelphia: Fortress, 1986) 150–5. M. Hengel (*Studies in the Gospel of Mark* [London: SCM, 1985] 83–4; idem, *The Johannine Question* [London: SCM, 1989] 74–76, 193 n. 3) apparently places the titles at the Gospels' initial composition and use in worship.

[44] Ruth F. Strout ("The Development of the Catolog and Cataloging Codes", *The Library Quarterly* 26 [1956] 254–75, 257) points out that the Greeks introduced cataloging by author. The Oriental practice was to catalog by subject or title. Cf. Ellis, *Making* (n. 7), 379; idem, *Luke* (n. 35), 64–5. See below, n. 46.

[45] Cf. Matt 13:52 with 23:34; John 21:24 ("brothers"); Ellis, *Making* (n. 7), 36–9.

[46] Cf. M. Smith, "Pseudepigraphy in Ancient Israelite Tradition," in *Pseudepigrapha I* (ed. K. von Fritz, Geneve: Reverdin, 1972) 191–215 = idem, *The Cult of Yahweh* (2 vols., Leiden: Brill, 1996) 1.55–72: "Israelite literature was originally and customarily anonymous," including Ecclesiastes and the Wisdom of Solomon (p. 210 = p. 68), and later misattributed to a famous name. Only under Greek influence did pseudepigrapha appear, apparently as the product of related sectarian groups (p. 215 = pp. 71f.).

[47] See above, n. 44.

[48] The closest is the common use of a pre-existing tradition in the "rejected stone" theme in Rom 9:30–10:21 and in 1 Pet 2:4–10, expounding Isa 8:14; 28:16 (Ps 118:22). Cf. Ellis, *Making* (n. 7), 60, 136–8, 312–3; idem, *Paul's Use* (n. 2), 89–90; C.H. Dodd, *According to the Scriptures* (London: Nisbet, 1952) 35–6, 41–2.

Martin Dibelius,[49] many preformed pieces may be identified with a considerable degree of probability by the careful use of a number of criteria.

The task is to show that an episode or an underlying tradition was used in catechesis, sermons, liturgy and the like before it was incorporated into a New Testament letter. Significant criteria to do so are

1. the presence of formulas indicating that an antecedent tradition is being cited;[50]
2. the self-contained character of the passage vis-à-vis its context;[51]
3. the relative frequency of vocabulary, idiom, style or theological expression that differs both from the rest of the letter and from other letters of the same author;[52]
4. the presence of a highly similar piece in another contemporary writing by a different author with which no direct literary dependence is probable.[53]

Of course, not all criteria will be present in a given case, and different New Testament authors may reshape a tradition to their particular

---

[49] E. Lohmeyer, *Kurios Jesus* (Heidelburg: Winter, [2]1961, 1928); M. Dibelius in his various commentaries.

[50] A number have the same introductory formulas that elsewhere introduce Old Testament quotations; cf., e.g. 2 Cor 1:7b; Eph 5:5; Jas 1:3; 1 Pet 1:18; 2 Pet 1:20; 3:3 with Jude 5 and Acts 2:30 (1 Tim 1:9f.). Further, cf. Ellis, *Making* (n. 7), 64n, 99n, 119, 121, 135, 407–16; idem, *Prophecy* (n. 4), 222–4.

[51] E.g. 1 Cor 13; 2 Cor 6:14–7:1.

[52] A striking example is τὸ πνεῦμα τὸ ἐκ τοῦ θεοῦ in the pericope 1 Cor 2:6–16; cf. Ellis, *Prophecy* (n. 4), 25–6, 156, 213–6; idem, *Making* (n. 7), 78–9. Since the letters were composed in multiple copies—one retained by the author (Ellis) and probably one for the church from which the author wrote—and since transmission of the letters to other churches began almost immediately (Aland), theories of later interpolation (O'Neill, Walker) are without merit unless there is an extant manuscript lacking the passage in question. Cf. Ellis, *Making* (n. 7), 85–6, 430; K. Aland, "Neutestamentliche Textkritik und Exegese", in *Wissenschaft und Kirche* (FS E. Löhse; ed. K. Aland; Bielefeld: Luther, 1989) 142; cf. Col 4:16. Cf. W.O. Walker, Jr., "Romans 1.18–2.29: A Non-Pauline Interpolation?" *NTS* 45 (1999) 533–52, and the literature cited; J.C. O'Neill, *Paul's Letter to the Romans* (Baltimore MD: Penguin, 1975), passim.

[53] Cf., e.g. the arguments of Dodd, *Scriptures* (n. 48) regarding the midrash on the rejected stone at Rom 9:33 and 1 Pet 2:6ff.; admonitions on true and false wisdom in 1 Cor 2:6–16 and in Jas 3:13–18; cf. Ellis, *Making* (n. 7), 67; the commonality (40%–80% overlap) in vice lists in the Pauline, Petrine, Jacobean and Johannine missions; cf. Ellis, *Making* (n. 7), 59–69. See below, n. 66.

interests and emphasis. But the criteria provide guidelines that serve as a check on subjective judgments.

The percentage of probable or highly possible preformed traditions in New Testament letters range from zero in Philemon to 72% in Jude.[54] Interestingly, almost all letters considered pseudo-Pauline or pseudo-Petrine by scholars in the Baur tradition[55] evidence a large percentage of preformed material: Ephesians 54%; Colossians 42%; I Timothy 43%; Titus 46%; I Peter 39%; II Peter 33% or 55%.[56] Exceptions are II Thessalonians (24%) and II Timothy (16%). Of course, the percentages are approximate, and conclusions may differ in the analysis of other literary critics. But it is fair to say, I think, that most New Testament letters contain a substantial amount of preformed traditions, a number of them not composed by the letter's author.

Such traditions include Old Testament expositions (midrashim),[57] household[58] and congregational[59] regulations, paraenesis,[60] catechesis,[61] confessions,[62] hymns,[63] vice and virtue lists.[64] Ordinarily composed

---

[54] Cf. Ellis, *Making* (n. 7), 49–142, 139. Others are Romans, 27%; 1 Corinthians, 17%; 2 Corinthians, 11%; Galatians, 32%; Philippians, 7%; 1 Thessalonians, 37%; Hebrews, 37%; James, 12%. On 1–3 John cf. Ellis, *Making* (n. 7), 189–200.

[55] Cf. F.C. Baur, *Paul* (2 vols, London: Williams & Norgate, 1875–76) 2.35, 64–74, 101–5, passim = German: 1.276–9; 2.116–22; A. Hilgenfeld, *Historisch–Kritische Einleitung in das Neue Testament* (Leipzig: Fues, 1875) 246–7, 328–48. Baur found genuine only Romans, 1–2 Corinthians, Galatians and Revelation. His associate, Hilgenfeld, added Philippians, 1 Thessalonians and Philemon. For a critique cf. Ellis, "Ferdinand Christian Baur and his School," *Making* (n. 7), 440–5; idem, "Toward a History of Early Christianity," *Christ* (n. 19), 216–23.

[56] Depending on whether the two extensive midrashim, 2 Pet 1:20–2:22 and 2 Pet 3:3–13, are preformed pieces *en bloc* (= 55% of the letter) or whether they only made use of traditions, identifiable by formulas (= 33% of the letter), and were composed as a whole when the secretary prepared the epistle.

[57] E.g. Rom 4:1–25; 1 Cor 10:1–13; Gal 4:21c–31; cf. Ellis, *Making* (n. 7), 79–81, 96, 101–2; further, 117, 119, 120–30, 136–38.

[58] E.g. Eph 5:22—6:9; Col 3:18—4:1; 1 Pet 2:18f., 21b–25; 3:1–7.

[59] E.g. 1 Cor 11:3–16; 1 John 3:2b. Cf. 1 Thess 5:21 with 1 John 4:1; 1 Cor 14:34–5 with 1 Tim 2:9–12; 1 Pet 3:3–6; Ellis, *Making* (n. 7), 66–68, 82–3.

[60] E.g. Gal 5:25—6:10; Eph 4:25—5:14. Cf. 1 Pet 2:18—3:7. Further, cf. Jas 1:3–4 with Rom 5:3–5; I Pet 1:6–7; Ellis, *Making* (n. 7), 102–3, 119, 135.

[61] E.g. 1 Cor 8:6; Rom 5:12–21 (perhaps). Cf. Ellis, *Making* (n. 7), 96.

[62] E.g. 1 Cor 8:6; 12:4–11; 15:3–7; Eph 4:4a, 5–6; 1 Tim 2:5–6; 3:16. Confessions, hymns and catechesis overlap, and it is often uncertain just how a particular piece may have been used in the congregations.

[63] E.g. Phil 2:6–11; 3:20–1; Eph 1:3–14; Rev 4:8b; 5:9. Cf. 1 Tim 3:16 with 1 Pet 3:18, 22; Ellis, *Making* (n. 7), 68, 135–6.

[64] E.g. Gal 5:19–23; Col 3:5–15; Jas 3:14–18. For vice lists cf. Rom 1:29–31; 1

and originally utilized by and for the congregations of one mission (cf. Acts 13:1–3), they were, like Gospel traditions, shared at times with apostolic leaders of the other missions,[65] who (reworked and) used them and sometimes incorporated them or their motifs[66] into letters to their congregations. For example, judging from the incarnation/exaltation, descent/ascent theme reminiscent of the theology of the Johannine mission and from stylistic and other features pointing to an Aramaic or Semitic-Greek background,[67] the hymn to Christ in Phil 2:6–11 was probably created in Palestine. Paul founded no churches there, and the hymn is very likely non-Pauline.[68] It was obtained by Paul, probably in Caesarea, and later incorporated into his letter.

Implications of Preformed Traditions for the Authorships and Dates of the Letters

The Nature of Authorship

Numerous preformed traditions, many non-authorial,[69] raise doubts about the adequacy of internal literary criteria to test the authorship of New Testament letters. The influence of the secretary[70] and

---

Cor 6:9–10; 1 Tim 1:9–10; 1 Pet 4:3–4; Rev 9:20; 21:8; 22:15. Cf. Ellis, *Making* (n. 7), 61–64, 95, 106–9, 109–10, 232, 313, 407, 412.

[65] Cf. Ellis, *Making* (n. 7), 60–9, 310–14. See above nn. 53, 58, 59, 63.

[66] On a common response to antecedent motifs see above, n. 53. Further, on suffering and vindication (cf. Rom 5:3 with 1 Pet 1:6f.); on the support of Christian workers (cf. Matt 10:10 Q with 1 Pet 5:2; 1 Cor 9:9–14; Gal 6:6; 1 Tim 5:17).

[67] Cf. J.A. Fitzmyer, "The Aramaic Background of Phil 2:6–11", *CBQ* 50 (1988) 470–83; R.P. Martin, *Carmen Christi* (Cambridge: CUP, 1967) 38–41. Lohmeyer, *Kurios* (n. 49), 73, concludes that the origin of the hymn is to be sought "in circles of the oldest primitive Christian congregations", not excluding Jerusalem. For Johannine affinities cf. John 1:14; 3:13; 6:38, 42, 62; Rev 1:17f. Also favoring the preformed character of the hymn is the fact that it goes far beyond the needs of the present context, i.e. Christ's servant attitude as an example for Christian conduct and disposition, to include an incarnation/exaltation Christology. See below, 318–20.

[68] Cf. O. Hofius, *Die Christushymnus Philipper 2.6–11* (Tübingen: Mohr-Siebeck, [2]1991) 1; M. Silva, *Philippians* (Chicago: Moody, 1988) 105. Otherwise: M. Dibelius, *An die Thessalonischer I, II: An die Philipper* (Tübingen: Mohr-Siebeck, [3]1937) 73 (preformed, Pauline).

[69] E.g. 1 Cor 2:6–16; 2 Cor 6:14–7:1; Phil 2:6–11. Cf. Ellis, *Prophecy* (n. 4), 25–6; idem, *Making* (n. 7), 78–9, 99–100. See above, nn. 65 and 66.

[70] Quintilian (*Orat.* 10.3.19), who states that he rejects the "fashionable" use of a secretary, reveals what the common practice was. Indeed, the use of a secretary

sometimes of co-senders,[71] difficult matters to measure, make such
internal criteria more doubtful. These factors require the historian
to give more weight to the authorships stated in the letters and to
second-century external evidence. They are also significant for the
nature of authorship.

It has been traditionally assumed that the author penned the letter himself or dictated it verbatim. The literary and historical evidence shows, however, that authorship was more a corporate enterprise
in which the author employed co-worker secretaries and pieces composed by others in the letter that went out over his name.[72]

Dating the Documents

Preformed traditions, particularly the biblical expositions and the vice
lists, also have implications for the dating of the New Testament
documents. Biblical expositions, using patterns similar to the proem
and *yelammedenu rabbenu* forms found in the rabbis,[73] appear both in
Gospel traditions[74] and in the epistolary traditions of three apostolic
missions—Jacobean,[75] Pauline[76] and Petrine.[77] But in Christian documents that can be clearly dated after AD 70, e.g. the Epistle of
Barnabas,[78] the Old Testament expositions, while employing Jewish
techniques, do not appear to use such midrashic patterns.

---

was a virtual necessity in ancient letter writing, and his role could vary from taking dictation to being a co-author. Cf. E.R. Richards, *The Secretary in the Letters of
Paul* (Tübingen: Mohr-Siebeck, 1991) 23–67; O. Roller, *Das Formular der paulinischen
Briefe* (Stuttgart: Kohlhammer, 1933) 17–20, who estimates that, because of the poor
quality of writing materials—reed pen, poor ink, rough-surface papyrus, a skilled
secretary could compose less than one page per hour (13–14).

[71] Cf. 1 Cor 1:1; 2 Cor 1:1; Gal 1:1f.; Phil 1:1; Col 1:1; 1 Thess 1:1; 2 Thess
1:1; Phlm 1. Cf. E.E. Ellis, *History and Interpretation*, forthcoming.

[72] Cf. Ellis, *Making* (n. 7), 39–42.

[73] Cf. W.G. Braude, *Pesikta Rabbati* (2 vols., New Haven CT: Yale, 1968) 2.3–5.

[74] See above, nn. 8 and 9.

[75] Jas 2:20–26; cf. Jude 5b–19; Ellis, *Making* (n. 7), 119; idem, *Prophecy* (n. 4),
221–36.

[76] E.g. Rom 4:1–25; 1 Cor 2:6–16; 10:1–13; Gal 3:6–14; 4:21–5:1. Cf. Ellis,
Making (n. 7), 96, 78–81, 103, 101–2; idem, *Prophecy* (n. 4), 217–8; idem, *Old Testament*
(n. 9), 98–9.

[77] 2 Pet 1:20–2:22 and 3:3–13 are similar to the proem midrash in that they
open (2:1ff.; 3:3f.) and close (2:22; 3:13) with cited sacred texts and contain supporting biblical texts and commentary joined by catch-words. But the opening texts,
introduced by formulas, appear to be cited Christian prophecy. The Johannine letters and Revelation have "midrash pesher" formulas and other Jewish exegetical
terminology, but they do not use the proem or *yelammedenu rabbenu* patterns. Cf.
Ellis, *Making* (n. 7), 54–7, 120–33, 189–90, 193–5.

[78] The Epistle of Barnabas (16:3–4; c. 70–79 CE) clearly refers to the destruc-

Traditioned vice lists in all four missions,[79] based on the Ten Commandments and apparently with one root in a dominical teaching,[80] emphasize vices of sexual immorality and of idolatry, and they are sometimes directed against the teaching of opponents. They point to the broader question of the nature of the opposition or false teaching reflected in the letters of the four apostolic missions.

The New Testament letters do not picture the errors of the false teachers in precisely the same terms or as involving the same individuals. But they describe them with sufficient similarity to make probable that the same type of opposition is in view. The opponents can rightly be called gnosticizing Judaizers,[81] who were not isolated teachers but who formed a fifth mission,[82] also with claimed apostolic credentials,[83] in opposition to the allied missions of James, John, Paul and Peter. The common opposition reflected in the various New Testament letters strongly suggests that this literature was produced

---

tion of Jerusalem and cites the Old Testament frequently. He uses some Jewish techniques of quotation but does not employ the proem, *yelammedenu* or similar midrashic patterns, nor do other diaspora Christian writings such as the *Didache* (60–90 CE), *1 Clement* (68–70 CE) or the letters of Ignatius (c. 110 CE) or of Polycarp (c. 110 CE). A midrashic pattern was used by the Christian Persian sage, Aphraates (c. 300–350 CE), who was apparently trained to some degree in exegetical method by a Jewish sage. Cf. J. Neusner, *Aphrahat and Judaism* (Atlanta GA: Scholars, 1999, 1971) 6; P. Schaff et al., eds, *The Nicene and Post-Nicene Fathers. Second Series* (14 vols, Grand Rapids: Eerdmans, 1961 [1890–1900]) 13.345–412. Cf. Ellis, *Making* (n. 7), 182n.

[79] See above n. 64.

[80] Mark 7:20ff. = Matt 15:18ff. Similar lists are present at Qumran (1QS 10:21–26) and in Philo (*de sacrif. Abel.* §22, 27 = 77f., 88ff.; *de confus. ling.* §24 = 117f.). Cf. Ellis, *Making* (n. 7), 232–3.

[81] By gnosticizing I mean their claims and evident experience of extraordinary powers—visions, miracle working, ecstasies, that made them impressive promoters of their claim to have and to convey a divine gift of γνῶσις. Cf. 1 Cor 12:8: "word of knowledge;" 2 Cor 11:3–6, 12–15; 12:1, 11f.; 1 Tim 6:20: "knowledge falsely so called". By Judaizers I refer to that wing of the ritually strict Jewish Christians who insisted that Gentile Christians must follow the ritual law of Moses. Cf. Ellis, "The Circumcision Party and the Early Christian Mission," *Prophecy* (n. 4), 116–128. For similarities between the opponents of Paul and in 2 Peter; of Paul and of James; of Paul and of John cf. Ellis, *Making* (n. 7), 130–2, 316–8; 130, 258–9, 316–8; 202–8, 217–9, 315–8. On their character as an opposing mission and not isolated teachers cf. Ellis, *Making* (n. 7), 314–8; idem, *Prophecy* (n. 4), 101–15.

[82] See above, n. 81.

[83] In 2 Cor 10–13 Paul calls the opponents "pseudo-apostles" (11:13), but he does not deny that they had been commissioned by Jesus. They are "Hebraists" with roots in strict Palestinian Judaism (11:22). Probably they were apostles of Jesus Christ who, like Judas, perverted their calling. Cf. Ellis, "Paul and His Opponents", *Prophecy* (n. 4), 80–115, 89–95, 102–15.

in the same general chronological period. But for a more specific
dating of the documents, other evidence would have to be considered.[84]

Implications of Preformed Traditions for Pauline Christology

The Body of Christ and the Temple of God

Traditioned pieces used in the expression of Paul's Christology may
be classified as (1) those from the earthly Jesus and (2) other preformed christological concepts. An explicit reference to Jesus' christological teachings concerns the Last Supper. At that event Jesus
symbolically identified his body and his covenant blood with the
bread and wine that he directs his disciples to partake.[85] In I Cor
11:23–26, Paul both cites this tradition and defines it as a proclamation of "the Lord's death until he comes" (11:26). In I Cor
10:16–17 he explains theologically the actions of blessing the cup
and breaking the bread at the Lord's Supper (and the subsequent
common partaking) as a participation in the shed blood[86] and in the
crucified body of Christ. The Apostle later identifies a participation
in the Lord's Supper without discerning "the body" makes one liable
for the body and the blood, i.e. the death of the Lord.[87]

The body here refers to the "body of Christ" manifest in the congregation, in agreement with Paul's admonitions in the context and
with his teachings elsewhere that believers are "the body of Christ".[88]

---

[84] Cf. Ellis, *Making* (n. 7), 307–19. E.g. the stated authorships, supported by some
early patristic witnesses, and the absence of any references to the destruction of
Jerusalem in letters stressing divine judgment on ungodliness, e.g. Hebrews, 2 Peter,
Jude, suggest a pre-70 date for them.

[85] Cf. Matt 26:26–8; Mark 14:22–4; Luke 22:19–20. Paul and Luke are closer
to one another and may represent the independent use of the same traditional
piece. Cf. W. Schrage, *Die erste Brief an die Korinther* (4 vols, Neukirchen: Neukirchener,
1991–) 3.9; G.D. Fee, *The First Epistle to the Corinthians* (Grand Rapids: Eerdmans,
1987) 546–7; Ellis, *Luke* (n. 35), 249–252, 254–6; J. Jeremias, *The Eucharistic Words
of Jesus* (Philadelphia: Fortress, ⁴1977) 96–105, 111–114 = German: 90–9, 105–8.

[86] A.M. Stibbs in his *The Meaning of the Word "Blood" in Scripture* (London: Tyndale,
1962) 29–32 rightly argues that "blood" in this context is that which is poured out
in death and refers to the sacrifice of Christ that pays for sin and secures the forgiveness of God.

[87] 1 Cor 11:27–34, 27.

[88] 1 Cor 11:20–2, 12:27; Eph 1:22–3; 4:7–16, 12, 16; 5:29–32; Col 3:15; cf.
Rom 12:4–5; 1 Cor 6:15. Cf. Ellis, *Making* (n. 7), 72–4; idem, *Christ* (n. 19), 174–5;
Schrage, *Korinther* (n. 85), 3.5–107, 51; Fee, *Corinthians* (n. 85), 562–4 and the liter-
ature cited.

Paul's teaching on the church as the corporate body of Christ is an important theme in his letters, and it is once introduced as a tradition that he had taught the congregation previously.[89] It has its roots not only in the general Old Testament background of corporate personality[90] but more specifically in the traditioned teaching of Jesus at the Last Supper.[91]

A second christological theme that is rooted in the teaching of Jesus is Paul's temple typology. It is expressed in two somewhat different images. The first is Christ as the rejected temple stone, a conception found in a tradition underlying Rom 9:32–3 and I Pet 2:4–8[92] and derived to some degree from Jesus' exposition of Isa 5 in Mt 21:33–44 T + Q.[93] The second and more complex image identifies (the corporate) Christ and Christians as the eschatological temple of God.[94] Both themes are introduced with formulas that point to previously traditioned teaching.[95]

Jesus' identification of himself as God's temple, i.e. the locus of God's self-manifestation,[96] occurred during his teachings at Jerusalem with the enigmatic words, "Destroy this temple and in three days I will raise it up."[97] This saying, understood by all to refer to the Jerusalem temple, became the grounds for a charge against Jesus at his trial.[98] According to John 2:21–2, only after his resurrection did his disciples, his pupils, realize that he spoke of his body as God's

---

[89] Cf. 1 Cor 6:15f.: οὐκ οἴδατε ὅτι. Cf. Rom 11:2; Ellis, *Making* (n. 7), 73.

[90] Cf. S.W. Aaron Son, "Corporate Elements in Pauline Anthropology", Ph.D. Dissertation (Ft. Worth TX: Southwestern Seminary, 1999) 133–6, and the literature cited.

[91] Cf. Luke 22:19f. with 22:28: μετ' ἐμοῦ; Ellis, "Jesus' Use of the Old Testament and the Genesis of New Testament Theology"; "Eschatology in Luke Revisited"; "Present and Future Eschatology in Luke", *Christ* (n. 19), 29–31, 119n., 126n., 123n., 144n. See above, n. 90; cf. Ellis, *Making* (n. 7), 74–7.

[92] See above, n. 48; cf. Ellis, *Making* (n. 7), 74–7.

[93] Cf. Matt 21:42 (Ps 118:22–3), 44 (Dan 2:34–5, 44–5). See above, n. 8.

[94] E.g. 2 Cor 5:1: οἴδαμεν ὅτι; 1 Cor 3:16: οὐκ οἴδατε ὅτι. Cf. Ellis, "The Structure of Pauline Eschatology," *Christ* (n. 19), 147–164.

[95] See above, nn. 89, 94. Cf. Ellis, "Isaiah and the Eschatological Temple", *Christ* (n. 19), 52–61.

[96] Traditionally Judaism identified this locus as the holy of holies in the Jerusalem temple. Cf. Exod 25:22; Lev 16:2; A. Edersheim, *The Temple* (Grand Rapids: Eerdmans, 1950) 313f.

[97] John 2:19. Bultmann regarded this form of the saying as the relatively more original. Cf. R. Bultmann, *The Gospel of John* (Oxford: Blackwell, 1971) 126 (= German: 89).

[98] Mark 14:58 par. Cf. D. Catchpole, *The Trial of Jesus* (Leiden: Brill, 1971) 126–30; Ellis, "Deity Christology in Mark 14:58", *Christ* (n. 19), 56–61.

316 E. EARLE ELLIS

temple. It was apparently Stephen, the Hellenist prophet and forerunner of that mission, who first saw the broader implication of this
aspect of Jesus' teaching. He contrasts in Acts 7 the temple of the
old covenant with the new creation that is not made with hands in
which God dwells with the one who is "humble and contrite in
spirit".[99] Both Paul and Peter, and their respective missions, express
and elaborate this thought to affirm that the church is not only
Christ's corporate body but also the eschatological temple of God.

Several preformed christological traditions in Paul's letters appear
to have no antecedent, at least no direct antecedent, in Jesus' teachings. A number may be mentioned here: I Cor 8:6; 10:1–13; Phil
2:6–11; Col 1:15–20; I Tim 3:16. We shall look in more detail at
the first three.

1 Cor 8:6

Of three traditioned christological pieces in 1 Corinthians (8:6;
12:4–11;[100] 15:3–7)[101] 1 Cor 8:6 is notable for its *Deus/Christus Creator*
theme.[102] Introduced by a brief formulaic ἀλλά,[103] it has a balanced
parallelism that breaks the flow of Paul's argument and is similar
in form and idiom to traditioned pericopes elsewhere, e.g. Rom
11:36; Eph 4:4ff. and Col 1:15–20. It also goes beyond the theme
of the context to include *Deus/Christus Salvator*: "we for him"; "we
through him".

The formulation of 1 Cor 8:6 is similar to the Stoic affirmation
about the Logos or Cosmic Soul: "From (ἐξ) you are all things (τὰ
πάντα), in you are all things, for (εἰς) you are all things."[104] It is even
closer in Jewish writers. Philo apparently took over the phraseology
from the Stoics. And the Wisdom of Solomon (9:1f.) speaks of God,
"who made all things by your Word (τὰ πάντα ἐν λόγῳ) and by your

---

[99] Isa 66:1f.; Acts 7:46–50. Cf. Ellis, "Isaiah and the Eschatological Temple",
Christ (n. 19), 45–51.
[100] Cf. Ellis, *Making* (n. 7), 90; Schrage, *Korinther* (n. 85), 3.136f.
[101] Cf. Ellis, *Making* (n. 7), 90–1; P. Stuhlmacher, *Das paulinische Evangelium* (Göttingen:
Vandenhoeck & Ruprecht, 1968) 266–76; but see Fee, *Corinthians* (n. 88), 722–31.
[102] Cf. Ellis, *Making* (n. 7), 87–90.
[103] The term is also an introductory formula for Old Testament citations at Rom
9:7; 12:20; Gal 3:12, 16. Cf. Ellis, *Paul's Use* (n. 2), 160, 180, 182.
[104] Marcus Aurelius, *Meditations* 4.23; Chrysippos in Stobaeus, *Eklogai* 1.1.26, cited
in E. Norden, *Agnostos Theos* (Darmstadt: WBG, 1956, 1913), 240, 241–2.

wisdom (σοφία) formed man".[105] Paul's usage probably arises from
this Jewish background, from Jesus' teachings that associate or identify him with divine wisdom,[106] from Paul's and his co-workers' christological exegesis, and from the Apostle's Damascus experience.[107]

The wider use in Paul's letters of traditioned pieces with similar
expressions,[108] together with the background, literary form and context of the present passage, argue that 1 Cor 8:6 is a preformed
confession incorporated at this point in the epistle both to underscore the supremacy of God the Father and of the Lord Jesus Christ
over idols and over any demonic powers behind them and also to
assert that Christ is the mediator and thus the Lord over the present Genesis creation. This has been questioned in recent christological studies.[109] But the whole point of Paul's argument concerns
the present creation and its gifts. The "all things" that come from
the one God the Father are no different from the "all things" that
come through the one Lord Jesus Christ.

1 Cor 10:1–13

1 Cor 10:1–13 has a less clearly defined expository pattern than
some other Pauline midrashim. But its opening summary of Exodus
events (10:1–5) and its interpretive explanation of the one explicit
biblical quotation (10:7) reveal its commentary form. This, its self-
contained character, and its broadening of the question of food
offered to idols to the more general question of idolatry lend plausibility to Wayne Meeks' view that the passage is "a literary unit,
very carefully composed prior to its use in its present context".[110]

The christological question becomes explicit when the "spiritual"

---

[105] Cf. Philo, *quod deterius potiori insidiari soleat* §54; *de cherubim* §127; *de sacrificiis Abelis et Caini* §8 (III).

[106] Luke 7:35 Q; Matt 12:42 Q; S. Kim, *The 'Son of Man' as the Son of God* (Tübingen: Mohr-Siebeck, 1983) 90ff.; idem, *The Origin of Paul's Gospel* (Tübingen: Mohr-Siebeck, ²1984) 219–21, 245–6.

[107] Kim, *Origin* (n. 106), 223–233, 225: "this understanding [by Paul] of Jesus Christ really took place at the Damascus christophany (or shortly thereafter, but, in any case, in the light of it), ..."

[108] Rom 11:33–36.

[109] E.g. J.D.G. Dunn, *Christology in the Making* (Grand Rapids: Eerdmans, ³1996) 179–83.

[110] W.A. Meeks, "'And Rose up to Play': Midrash and Paraenesis in 1 Corinthians 10:1–22," *JSNT* 16 (1982) 65. Cf. Ellis, *Making* (n. 7), 79–81; idem, *Christ* (n. 19), 89–90.

following rock giving water to the Israelites in the wilderness is called Christ (10:4). By metonomy the miraculous work of God in the Old Testament can be called by the name God. But here the Rock is identified typically[111] and surprisingly not with God but with Christ, and it is related to the typological character of other Exodus events of redemption and judgment (10:6, 11). Paul goes on to warn the Corinthians, "Neither let us tempt Christ (Χριστόν, p[46] D) as some of [the Israelites] tempted him" (10:9). Thus, he places Christ both at the Exodus and in the present reality at Corinth. In a change of mind[112] I now agree with Anthony Hanson that "the real presence of the pre-existent Jesus" is Paul's meaning in 1 Cor 10:4.[113] If so, this preformed piece is a very early witness to the church's confession of the pre-existent Christ and, like 1 Cor 8:6 and Col 1:15–20, may be related to a wisdom Christology.[114]

Phil 2:6–11

Phil 2:6–11 has been explained christologically in two principal ways, as a purely Adam/Christ typology like that e.g. in Rom 5:12–21 and 1 Cor 15:22–55,[115] and as an incarnation/exaltation Christology that presupposes Christ's deity.[116] While there are some similarities to Paul's contrast between existence in Adam and in Christ, in the flesh and in the Spirit,[117] the major thrust of this hymn is quite different.

Even if J.B. Lightfoot's philosophical analogies may be questioned, his arguments and conclusion remain persuasive. The phrases, "in the form of God" (ἐν μορφῇ θεοῦ) and "the being equal with God (τὸ εἶναι ἴσα θεῷ), "must apply to the attributes of the Godhead" in the pre-incarnate Lord.[118]

The second half of the hymn (2:9–11) supports this view of the

---

[111] Cf. L. Goppelt, "τύπος," *TDNT* 8 (1972) 251f. According to Goppelt "type" is used "technically [as an] advanced presentation intimating eschatological events".

[112] Cf. Ellis, *Paul's Use* (n. 2), 131.

[113] A.T. Hanson, *Jesus Christ in the Old Testament* (London: SPCK, 1965) 6–7, 17–19, 172–8. Cf. E.E. Ellis, "ΧΡΙΣΤΟΣ in 1 Cor 10:4, 9," *Christ* (n. 19), 89–94.

[114] Cf. Ellis, *Christ* (n. 19), 92–3. Cf. also 2 Cor 8:9 (γινώσκετε γὰρ ὅτι).

[115] E.g. Dunn, *Christology* (n. 109), 114–21.

[116] For the literature, interpretive options and discussion cf. P.T. O'Brien, *The Epistle to the Philippians* (Grand Rapids: Eerdmans, 1991) 186–271.

[117] E.g. Rom 8:9–17; 12:2; 13:14; Eph 4:22–24; Col 3:1–3, 9–10, 12–4.

[118] J.B. Lightfoot, *Saint Paul's Epistle to the Philippians* (Peabody MA: Hendrickson, 1993 [[18]1913]) 127–33, 132.

matter. It ascribes to the exalted Christ "the name that is above every name" and applies to him the obeisance due only to Yahweh (Isa 45:23) and the confession, "Every knee shall bow . . . and every tongue confess that JESUS CHRIST IS YAHWEH to the glory of God the Father".[119] On an Adam/Christ typology this conclusion would yield only an adoptionist Christology, a man becoming God. The better reading, that fits both the structure and language as well as the theology of the hymn, is an incarnation/exaltation, descent/ ascent christological understanding. This understanding of Jesus as (also) a preexistent divine figure is, as Hengel has argued, the same Christology that Paul had preached in Philippi c. 50 CE, "and one is tempted to say that more happened [in Christology] in this period of less than two decades than in the whole of the next seven centuries" (p. 2).[120]

In 1 Cor 8:6 also Paul, using a preformed tradition, distinguishes, in binitarian fashion, deity from deity in terms of "God the Father" and "Lord".[121] In this respect he stands in the Jewish tradition of what Aubrey Johnson called *The One and the Many in the Israelite Conception of God* (Cardiff, 1961), i.e. the Old Testament teaching that God is a corporate and not a unitary being. The "oneness" (אֶחָד, Deut 6:4) of God was no more unitarian than the "oneness" of Adam and Eve (Gen 2:24).[122] Probably unitarian monotheism was a development in rabbinic Judaism, apparently in reaction to Christianity. In 1 Cor 8:6 and in other passages[123] the Apostle supplies us with the raw material that will later be refined and defined in the church's

---

[119] Cf. Phil 2:11 with Isa 45:23; D.B. Capes, *Old Testament Yahweh Texts in Paul's Christology* (Tübingen: Mohr-Siebeck, 1992) 164–5, 167–70. B.F. Westcott and F.J.A. Hort, *The New Testament in the Original Greek* (Cambridge: Macmillan, 1891) 440, and E. Nestle, *Novum Testamentum Graece* (Stuttgart: DBG, ²⁴1960), placed ΚΥΡΙΟΣ ΙΗΣΟΥΣ ΧΡΙΣΤΟΣ in capitals, indicating a conviction of the deity ascription of the phrase.

[120] M. Hengel, *The Son of God* (London: SCM, 1976) 1–2 (= German: 11).

[121] Elsewhere the contrast may be between God and Lord (1 Cor 12:5–6; 2 Cor 13:14) or between God the Father and Son (1 Cor 15:24–28).

[122] Cf. Ellis, "God: Unity in Plurality," *Old Testament* (n. 9), 112–16. For current discussion on the nature of first-century Jewish monotheism cf. R.J. Bauckham, *God Crucified* (Grand Rapids: Eerdmans, ²1999); C.A. Gieschen, *Angelomorphic Christology* (Leiden: Brill, 1998), and the literature cited.

[123] E.g. 1 Cor 12:4–6; 2 Cor 13:14; Eph 4:4a, 5–6. Cf. Ellis, *Making* (n. 7), 88, 90, 106; idem, *Christ* (n. 19), 3–94.

doctrine of the Trinity. This deity Christology is not a later development of early catholicism or even of a pagan-influenced early Christianity. Nor is it limited to the Pauline mission alone. It lies at the
beginnings of the church's confessions, even in the preformed traditions used by the Apostle Paul.

"NO LONGER JEW OR GREEK"
PAUL'S CORPORATE CHRISTOLOGY AND THE CONSTRUCTION OF CHRISTIAN COMMUNITY

David G. Horrell

In his careful study of the Apostolic Decree (Acts 15:20, 29), David Catchpole began by setting out briefly the "theological presupposi-tions of the Decree".[1] According to Catchpole, "the theology under-lying the Decree is one which sees the Christian gospel as doing nothing about the Jew/Gentile distinction. That is, Jews remain Jews, and Gentiles remain Gentiles." This theology "would have been re-pugnant to Paul. . . . For Paul, the Christian gospel does a very great deal to the Jew/Gentile distinction. Such a categorization . . . belongs to the first and obsolete era of human existence. In the second era now present, Christians are controlled by corporate participation 'in Christ Jesus' (Gal iii. 28). . . ."[2] Richard Bauckham has recently sug-gested that "Catchpole's claim" that the theology expressed in the Decree does nothing about the Jew/Gentile division "is mistaken": "The theology underlying the decree holds (as Paul does) that uncir-cumcised Gentiles belong fully to the eschatological people of God. The requirements of the decree are not understood as those which Jews in general held to apply to Gentiles, but as those which the Law of Moses prescribed for Gentile members of the eschatological people of God."[3]

However, leaving aside the questions concerning the theology of the Apostolic Decree and of Paul's attitude to it, questions which I shall not take up in this essay, it seems to me that Bauckham has perhaps failed to do justice to the difference between the position Catchpole presents as Paul's and that which Bauckham sees as shared by Paul and the Apostolic Decree. For Bauckham, it seems, Paul's

---

[1] D.R. Catchpole, "Paul, James and the Apostolic Decree", *NTS* 23 (1977) 428–44; here p. 429.

[2] Catchpole, "Paul, James and the Apostolic Decree", 430.

[3] R.J. Bauckham, "James and the Jerusalem Church", in *The Book of Acts in its Palestinian Setting* (ed. R.J. Bauckham; Grand Rapids: Eerdmans; Carlisle: Paternoster, 1995) 415–80; here p. 470 n. 164.

view (like that of the Decree) is that both Jews and Gentiles may
equally be saved through Christ and may both thus be members of
God's eschatological people, but in terms of their identity and conduct, Jews remain Jews and Gentiles remain Gentiles: Gentiles must
obey those precepts "which the Law of Moses prescribed *for Gentile
members* of the eschatological people of God". Catchpole, on the other
hand, suggests that for Paul, what God has done in Christ is to create a people among whom the distinction between Jew and Gentile
has been rendered obsolete, a distinction belonging to a former era
and now transcended by a new identity in Christ. While there is no
disagreement about the fact that Paul's gospel announces a route by
which Gentiles (as Gentiles) can be welcomed into the eschatological people of God, there is an important difference in terms of the
extent to which incorporation into Christ is seen as redefining the
identity and practice of both Jews and Gentiles. On this matter, contemporary scholarship is divided, and it is a point which has a
significant impact on the way we understand Paul's attitude to
Christian identity, to the Law, to ethics, and so on, not to mention
his attitude to James, Jerusalem, and the Apostolic Decree.

On the one hand, then, there are authors who in recent work
maintain—albeit in varied ways—that Paul has established groups
comprising both Jews and Gentiles who now share a distinct new
identity and for whom obedience to the Jewish Law is not fully and
literally required. Philip Esler, for example, argues that "Paul unambiguously asserts that the Christ-followers constituted a third group
set over against the Judaic and gentile worlds". Paul therefore dis-
cards the Law and regards it as irrelevant to the Christian congregations: it has "passed its use-by date", "had its day", and is now
replaced by the Spirit.[4] Daniel Boyarin emphasises Paul's desire to
create a unified humanity which is one in Christ. Thus he regards
Paul as having "given up his specific Jewish identity in order to merge
his essence into the essence of the gentile Christians and create the
new spiritual People of God".[5] John Barclay, while rejecting Boyarin's
notion that Jewish and Gentile identities are wholly erased or annulled

---

[4] P.F. Esler, *Galatians* (London and New York: Routledge, 1998) 89, 202–3; cf.
idem, "Group Boundaries and Intergroup Conflict in Galatians: A New Reading
of Galatians 5:13–6:10" in *Ethnicity and the Bible* (ed. M.G. Brett; Leiden: Brill, 1996)
215–40; see p. 233.
    [5] D. Boyarin, *A Radical Jew: Paul and the Politics of Identity* (Berkeley & Los Angeles,
CA; London: University of California Press, 1994) 155.

by Paul, preferring to speak of a relativising of former identities, sees Paul as an "anomalous" Diaspora Jew, associating intimately with Gentiles and creating distinct communities of Jews and Gentiles in which observance of the Law was relativised and in some respects abandoned altogether.[6]

On the other hand there are those who argue that, for all his insistence that *salvation* is through Christ alone, Paul clearly continues to view Jewish and Gentile believers as people with distinct identities and distinct obligations. Peter Tomson, for example, argues that Paul's view was that "Jews and gentiles should each stick to their respective ways of life" wherein "gentiles kept their minimum set of 'commandments of God' while Jewish Christians kept 'the whole law'".[7] Paul himself thus possessed a "double membership: of the group of those 'respecting the law', the Jews, and of the body of Christ".[8] Markus Bockmuehl presents a similar argument: "Paul himself in 1 Corinthians 7:17ff. makes clear that his 'rule for all the churches' is for Jews to keep the Torah (indeed Gal 5:3, too, may mean they are obliged to do so) and for Gentiles to keep what pertains to them."[9] Bockmuehl quotes Michael Wyschogrod with approval: "The distinction that needs to be made, therefore, is not between the law before Christ and after Christ, but the law for Jews and for Gentiles."[10] Karin Finsterbusch has likewise recently argued, "daß in Paulus' Augen die Thora universaler Maßstab für gerechtes Handeln ist, daß sie aber für Juden und Heiden nicht in gleichem Umfang gültig ist ... Die Rechtfertigung aus Glauben setzt die ethische Funktion der Thora also nicht außer Kraft."[11]

The debate is not so much about whether Paul sees Christ as the defining centre of the believer's identity—that much is clear—but

---

[6] J.M.G. Barclay, *Jews in the Mediterranean Diaspora From Alexander to Trajan (323 BCE–117 CE)* (Edinburgh: T. & T. Clark, 1996) 381–95; idem, "'Do We Undermine the Law?' A Study of Romans 14.1–15.6", in *Paul and the Mosaic Law* (ed. J.D.G. Dunn; Tübingen: Mohr Siebeck, 1996) 287–308.

[7] P.J. Tomson, "Paul's Jewish Background in View of His Law Teaching in 1 Corinthians 7", in *Paul and the Mosaic Law* (ed. Dunn), 251–70; here pp. 267, 269.

[8] P.J. Tomson, *Paul and the Jewish Law* (Assen/Maastricht: Van Gorcum; Minneapolis: Fortress, 1990) 281.

[9] M.N.A. Bockmuehl, "The Noachide Commandments and New Testament Ethics: With Special Reference to Acts 15 and Pauline Halakah", *RB* 102 (1995) 72–101; here p. 98.

[10] Bockmuehl, "The Noachide Commandments", 99.

[11] K. Finsterbusch, *Die Thora als Lebensweisung für Heidenchristen* (SUNT 20; Göttingen:

rather about the significance and the effect of this (re)definition. Is it essentially a soteriological affirmation or does it significantly affect social practice and interaction? In this essay I aim to approach this debate through an examination, informed by the social sciences, of Paul's corporate Christology and of the way in which this Christology constructs a community which is "one in Christ". I shall assess from Paul's own statements what concrete implications this has for the identity and practice of both Jewish and Gentile members of the Christian community.

Paul's Corporate Christology and Christian Identity

Paul's very frequent use of the phrase ἐν Χριστῷ (and near equivalents, such as ἐν κυρίῳ) has long been noted.[12] Albert Schweitzer famously saw this "being-in-Christ" as the key to Paul's theology, understanding it as a form of mysticism—Christ mysticism—in which the elect are united in one corporeity with Christ, having died and risen with him.[13] Schweitzer's basic emphasis, though differently nuanced and expressed, remains important to more recent attempts to capture the heart of Pauline thought, such as E.P. Sanders' "participationist eschatology" or Morna Hooker's "interchange".[14] Nevertheless, James Dunn considers that the theme of participation "in Christ" has been somewhat neglected in recent studies of Paul, compared with "the amazingly vigorous contemporary debate on justification by faith".[15]

It has proved difficult to express exactly what kind of "reality" Paul has in mind with the idea of Christians being "in Christ", together comprising the "body of Christ" (1 Cor 12:27). Adolf Deissmann famously found it nonsensical to speak of being "in" another person, and concluded that "Paul must have thought of Christ as a kind of an impersonal *continuum*, like the atmosphere".[16] Subsequent

Vandenhoeck & Ruprecht, 1996) 15, 83, *et passim*.

[12] G.A. Deissmann, *Paul: A Study in Social and Religious History* (2nd edn; London: Hodder & Stoughton, 1926) 140.

[13] A. Schweitzer, *The Mysticism of Paul the Apostle* (2nd edn; London: A. & C. Black, 1953) 10, 19, etc.

[14] E.P. Sanders, *Paul and Palestinian Judaism* (London: SCM, 1977) 549; M.D. Hooker, *From Adam to Christ: Essays on Paul* (Cambridge: CUP, 1990).

[15] J.D.G. Dunn, *The Theology of Paul the Apostle* (Edinburgh: T. & T. Clark, 1998) 395; cf. also A.J.M. Wedderburn, "Some Observations on Paul's Use of the Phrases 'In Christ' and 'With Christ'", *JSNT* 25 (1985) 83–97.

[16] Deissmann's view as summarised by C.F.D. Moule, *The Origin of Christology*

interpreters have rejected Deissmann's implausible suggestion, but have remained sympathetic to his perplexity concerning the meaning of the idiom.[17] But in terms of Paul's Christology this much at least is indisputable: Paul describes Jesus not solely in terms of what he as an individual is or has become—Messiah, Lord, Son of God, etc.—but as someone in and through whom believers live, both individually and *corporately*.[18]

More fruitful perhaps than a focus on what ontological status Paul implies with his "in Christ" language is an attempt to see what this corporate Christology-language *does* in terms of the construction of Christian identity, and here insights from the social sciences may be of considerable help. The sociology of knowledge approach known most widely through the work of Peter Berger and Thomas Luckmann explores the ways in which everything that passes for "knowledge"—expressed in language, symbols, ideas, etc.—forms a "symbolic universe", a body of tradition which shapes and orders human behaviour and relationships.[19] From this perspective, the separation all too evident in Pauline studies, between "doctrinal" subjects such as Paul's Christology or soteriology on the one hand, and his ethics and exhortations on the other, breaks down. Paul's statements about God, Christ, Spirit and so on, all serve to structure the identity and interaction of the Christian community. Recent studies informed by this perspective have examined the ways in which even such thoroughly theological symbols as Jesus' death on the cross serve to construct and shape the social praxis of the early Christian communities. In one such study, for example, Raymond Pickett, describing his project as an exercise in "sociological exegesis" and using Berger and

---

(Cambridge: CUP, 1977) 60; cf. Deissmann, *Paul*, 140.

[17] See Moule, *The Origin of Christology*, 47–96. On the various ways in which the phrases ἐν- and σὺν Χριστῷ may be understood grammatically, see Wedderburn, "Some Observations", who stresses that Paul's varied uses cannot be fitted into a single category, such as "locative", "instrumental" etc.

[18] It is not my concern here to investigate the background or origin of Paul's corporate Christology. Cautions have rightly been raised against too easily invoking a "Hebrew" idea of "corporate personality" (cf. J.W. Rogerson, "The Hebrew Conception of Corporate Personality: A Re-Examination", *JTS* 21 [1970] 1–16). Nevertheless, since a spatial or locative sense seems to be implied in at least some instances (Gal 3:27–28)—though this does not exclude an instrumental sense too (so Wedderburn, "Some Observations", 95–6 n. 37)—and since Paul unambiguously refers to Christians as the *body* of Christ, the description "*corporate* Christology" seems entirely and quite literally appropriate.

[19] P.L. Berger and T. Luckmann, *The Social Construction of Reality* (London: Penguin,

Luckmann's work as a theoretical resource, emphasises that his concern is to move beyond social and historical description to an analysis of the "social impact" that "a text, or symbol within the text, was designed to have in the realm of social interaction".[20]

Also important is the recent focus on the theme of *identity*, most developed from a social-scientific point of view in Philip Esler's use of social identity theory in a study of Galatians. Esler uses the work of social psychologist Henri Tajfel to shed light on the ways in which Paul seeks to construct and maintain "the distinctive identity of his congregations in relation to the Israelite and gentile outgroups".[21] In a situation of inter-group conflict, Paul is concerned to sustain the boundaries between the Christian community and both Israel on the one hand and the Gentiles on the other, and does so by creating a positive social identity for his converts. One of the benefits of Esler's focus on identity is that it links together both "theological" and "ethical" sections of Paul's letter(s) and highlights their "group-oriented" character: both serve "to maintain and enhance group identity".[22]

We may then valuably focus on Paul's corporate Christology, not out of a concern with his doctrine of Christ *per se*, nor with the category of "reality" which he has in mind in speaking of believers being in Christ, but rather with a focus on the ways in which this Christology serves to construct Christian identity and community, to shape and pattern relationships ἐν ἐκκλησίᾳ. This will hopefully enable us to consider afresh the question as to how, if at all, the identity and conduct of Jew and Gentile are redefined as a consequence of their being "in Christ".

In what must necessarily be a selective consideration, those texts which refer to baptism, the Christian ritual of initiation and entry for both Jews and Gentiles, are an obvious place at which to start. Baptism and Lord's Supper, the two most significant Christian rituals, serve not only to dramatise and recall the central doctrines of

1967) 113.
   [20] R. Pickett, *The Cross in Corinth: The Social Significance of the Death of Jesus* (JSNTSup 143; Sheffield: SAP, 1997) 34–5. A similar concern—but including more critical questions about the ideology and interests that a text reflects—underlies my approach in *The Social Ethos of the Corinthian Correspondence* (SNTW; Edinburgh: T. & T. Clark, 1996); see pp. 33–59.
   [21] Esler, *Galatians*, 42. See esp. H. Tajfel, *Human Groups and Social Categories: Studies in Social Psychology* (Cambridge: CUP, 1981); W.P. Robinson, ed., *Social Groups and Identities: Developing the Legacy of Henri Tajfel* (Oxford: Butterworth-Heinemann, 1996).

the early Christian groups, but also to construct their sense of identity and to structure their patterns of social interaction.[23] The most
important Pauline baptismal tradition in this regard is that which
appears in Gal 3:26–29, 1 Cor 12:13 and Col 3:9–11, where a connection with baptism is explicit in the first two passages and implicit
in the third (cf. Col 2:12).[24] While the form of the teaching varies
considerably in these three epistolary contexts, the multiple appearance of a similar tradition shows its basic importance for Paul and
for the Pauline churches. Common to all three passages is an emphasis on oneness or unity in Christ and an affirmation that this includes
both Jew and Gentile, slave and free (1 Cor 12:12–13; Gal 3:28;
Col 3:11). In both Galatians and Colossians the declaration is that
now "there is no longer Jew and Greek" (οὐκ ἔνι Ἰουδαῖος οὐδὲ
Ἕλλην/οὐκ ἔνι Ἕλλην καὶ Ἰουδαῖος . . .).

Commenting on the meaning of the other major Christian ritual,
the Lord's Supper, Paul similarly stresses that this is a celebration
of the unity and oneness of the body of believers who share κοινωνία
in the blood and body of Christ: "because there is one bread, we
many are one body, for we all partake of the one bread" (1 Cor
10:17). The fact that Paul presents this assertion concisely as an
apparently uncontroversial basis for his argument that the Corinthians
should avoid κοινωνία with demons (1 Cor 10:20–21) may indicate,
as Paul Gardner suggests, that this understanding of the Lord's Supper
was widely shared, at least between Paul and the Corinthians.[25] Paul's
conviction that the Lord's Supper should demonstrate the oneness
of the body of Christians also explains why he is so disturbed by
the divisions that currently appear when the Corinthians gather for
this meal (1 Cor 11:17–34), and why he considers that such a divided
celebration is no longer really the Lord's Supper at all (1 Cor 11:20).[26]

---

[22] See Esler, *Galatians*, 45, 229; also idem, "Group Boundaries", 215–40.

[23] See W.A. Meeks, *The First Urban Christians* (London & New Haven: Yale
University Press, 1983) 140–63; M.Y. MacDonald, *The Pauline Churches* (SNTSMS
60; Cambridge: CUP, 1988) 61–71, reprinted in *Social-Scientific Approaches to New
Testament Interpretation* (ed. D.G. Horrell; Edinburgh: T. & T. Clark, 1999) 233–47.

[24] On the similarities between the three passages see e.g. R. Scroggs, "Paul and
the Eschatological Woman", *JAAR* 40 (1972) 283–303; here p. 292. Colossians may
well not be by Paul himself, but nevertheless shows the influence of this baptismal
teaching within the Pauline tradition.

[25] P.D. Gardner, *The Gifts of God and the Authentication of a Christian: An Exegetical
Study of 1 Corinthians 8–11:1* (Lanham, New York, London: University Press of
America, 1994) 161–5.

[26] Cf. D.G. Horrell, "The Lord's Supper at Corinth and in the Church Today",

This oneness in Christ, which baptism initiates and the Lord's Supper celebrates, is most vividly and profoundly expressed in Paul's notion of the community as the body of Christ. The functioning human body perfectly illustrates the idea that a group of "members" can be diverse and different, with different functions to perform, yet also be essentially one (1 Cor 12:12–27). Paul, of course, goes beyond simply using the human body as an illustration of how a community of diverse people can be united, and actually describes the Christian congregation as "the body of Christ" (1 Cor 12:12, 27; cf. Rom 12:5). In terms of identity then, while a whole series of terms are used by Paul to describe the members of the Christian communities, a very basic description is that they are those who are ἐν Χριστῷ. Thus Paul can describe a person (himself, in this instance) as simply ἄνθρωπος ἐν Χριστῷ (2 Cor 12:2), where it seems to me to make most sense to see ἐν Χριστῷ as primarily a formulaic identity designation (though it may also serve to emphasise that it was in Christ's power that the visions and revelations Paul describes took place).[27]

From a social-scientific perspective, then, we would expect Paul's corporate Christology—the declaration that all converts are one body in Christ—both to function as a fundamental designation of distinctive group-identity and to structure social interaction within the congregations. However, that leaves open the question as to how, and in what ways, this defining identity affects other aspects of the believers' identity (social, cultural, religious, etc.) and social conduct. The answer to that question cannot be deduced from social-scientific theory but must be drawn from the evidence of Paul's letters. In what ways, we may ask, does this corporate Christology, and the fundamental "Christian" identity which it encapsulates, undergird a redefinition and restructuring of existing identities and practices? To what extent does Paul see his own and others' identities fundamentally redefined by their being in Christ, and is there any evidence that Paul's corporate Christology was controversial—perhaps precisely because of its implications for the social interaction and identity of the Christian congregations? I turn first to the question of controversy.

Theology 98 (1995) 196–202.

How Controversial was Paul's Corporate Christology?

The phrase ἐν Χριστῷ is unique to the Pauline letters in the New Testament, apart from three occurrences in 1 Peter (3:16; 5:10; 5:14; and cf. 1 John 5:20), which probably reflect the influence of Pauline language on the author of 1 Peter.[28] The notion of the congregation as the body of Christ is also unique to the Pauline tradition in the New Testament.[29] In view of the conflicts Paul faced in Antioch, Galatia and elsewhere, it may not be insignificant to note that the letter of James (connected with James, whether authentic or not) shows no trace of this corporate Christology. James and Paul evidently share the early Christian conviction that Jesus is Lord and Messiah/Christ (James 1:1; 2:1)—to this extent Paul's Christology is uncontroversial—but there is no evidence (though an argument from silence is always precarious) that they share the corporate christological notion of being (one) "in Christ". So "in Christ" language, and the corporate Christology which it reflects, is certainly *distinctive* to Paul, at least insofar as our literary evidence allows us to conclude; but is there any evidence to suggest that it was controversial?

First we may briefly consider the dispute at Antioch, reported by Paul in Gal 2:11–14, to which we shall have to refer later. Despite much continuing debate about the incident and its causes, certain things are clear: before the arrival of the people from James, both Jewish and Gentile Christians ate together (presumably in the common meals of the community, i.e. the Lord's Supper). This practice was regarded as unacceptable, at least in its current form, by the people from James, who convinced the Jewish Christians to separate themselves from this inclusive table-fellowship. What might have undergirded and legitimated this eating together which the people from James sought to bring to an end, or at least to suspend until further requirements had been met? The most obvious and plausible answer is: exactly the kind of corporate Christology which is expressed in the baptismal declaration Paul cites later in the letter (Gal 3:26–28) and which he sees embodied in the Lord's Supper

---

[27] Cf. R.P. Martin, *2 Corinthians* (WBC 40; Waco, TX: Word Books, 1986) 399.
[28] Though this does not imply that 1 Peter should be judged a "Pauline" letter. See, e.g., P.J. Achtemeier, *1 Peter* (Hermeneia; Minneapolis: Fortress, 1996) 18–19; O. Knoch *Der erste und zweite Petrusbrief. Der Judasbrief* (RNT; Regensburg: Friedrich Pustet, 1990) 17–18.

(1 Cor 10:17), "you are all one in Christ, in whom there is no longer Jew and Greek". The baptismal declaration of Gal 3:26–28 is often thought to represent a pre-Pauline tradition, originally from the Antioch community. Certainly there are firm indications that it is at least a pre-Galatians tradition, clearly distinct within its epistolary context, and if not strictly *pre*-Pauline then at least a product of the congregation's shared convictions rather than exclusively of Paul's.[29]

If the Antiochene/Pauline baptismal tradition did serve to under-pin theologically the community's practice in which Jews and Gentiles ate together without distinction—and it is much more plausible to assume that there *was* such a connection between theological decla-ration and community practice than that the declaration "one in Christ . . . no longer Jew or Gentile" had no direct meaning for social interaction within the congregations—then it seems reasonable to suggest that this corporate Christology itself, as well as the unification which it expressed and legitimated, was controversial. The "people from James" did not agree that "in Christ there is no longer Jew or Gentile", since they sought to reestablish the separation of the two groups, on the grounds either that the Gentile believers were failing to observe a minimum of Torah-observance regarding their food and drink, or that the Jewish believers could not be sure in such a con-text that they were not sinning in partaking of food and wine shared in common with Gentiles.[31] While the most obviously apparent issue of dispute in both Antioch and Galatia is that of the extent of Torah-observance required of Gentile converts, it seems highly likely that different christological convictions underpinned the conflicting posi-tions taken by Paul and his Jewish Christian opponents.[32]

---

[29] Though cf. also the corporate images found in John 15:1–4 and 17:20–23.

[30] See further H.D. Betz, *Galatians* (Hermeneia; Philadelphia: Fortress, 1979) 181–5; Horrell, *Social Ethos*, 84–5.

[31] Among the important discussions of the reasons for the criticism mounted by the people from James, see J.D.G. Dunn, "The Incident at Antioch (Gal 2.11–18)" in *Jesus, Paul and the Law* (London: SPCK, 1990) 129–82; E.P. Sanders, "Jewish Association with Gentiles and Galatians 2:11–14" in *The Conversation Continues: Studies in Paul and John in Honor of J. Louis Martyn* (ed. R.T. Fortna and B.R. Gaventa; Nashville: Abingdon, 1990) 170–88. Holmberg and Esler, however, argue for a greater degree of Jewish separatism in commensality than do Dunn and Sanders: see B. Holmberg, "Jewish *Versus* Christian Identity in the Early Church?", *RB* 105 (1998) 397–425; Esler, *Galatians*, 93–116.

[32] See further Holmberg, "Jewish *Versus* Christian Identity", who sees the Antioch incident as one where Paul demanded from Christian Jews the giving up of the marking of their Jewish identity for the sake of the church's unity: "Jewish identity

Further hints—though no more than hints—of Paul's distinctive and controversial Christology may be found in 2 Corinthians. In 2 Cor 11:4, in a strongly defensive and polemical context, Paul speaks of those who preach "another Jesus", and of the Corinthians receiving another Spirit, or another gospel. As Jerome Murphy-O'Connor has observed: "In 11:4 Paul makes a very clear distinction between his role and that of the Corinthians. He 'preached' Jesus, they 'received or accepted' the Spirit and the Gospel . . . The key element in 11:4, therefore, is 'Jesus'; the other two are dependent on it."[33] Although we can deduce very little from this reference about the contrasts between Paul's Christology and that of his opponents, who were connected (if not identical) with the so-called "super-apostles" (2 Cor 11:5) and stressed their Jewish (Jerusalem?) connections (2 Cor 11:22), it is at least a hint that their presentations of "Jesus" were different.

In what I judge to be a later section of 2 Corinthians,[34] certainly a less overtly polemical section, Paul refers to his changed perspective on "Christ" (2 Cor 5:16), in the context of a passage which expresses a thoroughly incorporative or participationist Christology (see vv. 14, 17, 21). Paul's conviction that Christ died and rose for all, and that all have therefore died and are summoned to live for Christ (5:14–15), leads him to two conclusions.[35] The first, a negative conclusion, is that no-one is any longer to be regarded from a worldly point of view (κατὰ σάρκα). Even though Paul once knew Christ from a perspective κατὰ σάρκα, he does so no longer (v. 16).[36] The second conclusion, positively stated, is that "if anyone is in Christ, there is a new creation; old things are gone, behold they

---

must cede to the common Christian identity" (p. 414). I am in substantial agreement with the argument of Holmberg's essay, though unfortunately Holmberg does not consider Paul's corporate Christology when he considers the *basis* from which Paul derives this sense of Christian identity (see pp. 416–25).

[33] J. Murphy-O'Connor, "Another Jesus (2 Cor 11:4)", *RB* 97 (1990) 238–51; here pp. 239–40.

[34] See Horrell, *Social Ethos*, 296–312.

[35] The two statements each introduced with ὥστε in vv. 16 and 17 are best taken as two conclusions each drawn from vv. 14–15 rather than as one conclusion (v. 16) from which another is then drawn; cf. C.K. Barrett, *The Second Epistle to the Corinthians* (BNTC; London: A. & C. Black, 1973) 173; P. Barnett *The Second Epistle to the Corinthians* (NICNT; Grand Rapids: Eerdmans, 1997) 296 n. 41.

[36] This verse is notoriously difficult and its interpretation much discussed. The various opinions are reviewed in M.E. Thrall, *A Critical and Exegetical Commentary on the Second Epistle to the Corinthians* (vol. 1; ICC; Edinburgh: T. & T. Clark, 1994)

have become new" (v. 17). In stating that he no longer regards Christ κατὰ σάρκα, Paul may be expressing a veiled polemic against his opponents, though the immediacy and intensity of the conflict is less than in 2 Cor 10–13 (cf. 2 Cor 2:17–3:1; 4:2). Is it possible that here again we glimpse a significant difference in Christology between Paul and his Jewish-Christian opponents?[37] They proclaim "another Jesus", a Jesus who, from Paul's point of view, is a Christ regarded κατὰ σάρκα (note Rom 9:5). It is difficult to be sure exactly what Paul means by that—it seems unlikely that he is primarily meaning to disavow any interest in the historical Jesus[38]—but it certainly stands in contrast with the perspective on Christ which Paul himself now holds and which is spelt out in the surrounding context. For Paul, as the context of 2 Cor 5:16 makes clear, the event of Christ's death and resurrection marks the disjunction between the old age and the new, between an old way of knowing and a new epistemology, one which is "thoroughly and without remainder christological".[39] As Graham Stanton concludes: "The main point of 2 Cor. 5:16 is clear: as a consequence of the death and resurrection of Jesus, Christians have a new perspective on all things and all people and no longer 'know' κατὰ σάρκα. Any attempt to evaluate others, even Christ, as though the death and resurrection of Jesus had not brought about a totally new situation is to be rejected most firmly."[40] Christ is the one in whose death all have participated, the one "in" whom all believers are no longer to be regarded κατὰ σάρκα; no longer, we may suggest, regarded as Jew and Gentile, but as together καινὴ κτίσις ἐν Χριστῷ.

There is some evidence, then, to support the hypothesis that Paul's corporate Christology was not only distinctive but also to some degree controversial. It appears to represent one point of contrast between Paul (together with the Antioch community, at least prior to the "incident" there) and the varied forms of Jewish Christianity associ-

---

412–20.

[37] Cf. Barnett, *The Second Epistle to the Corinthians*, 296.

[38] Rudolf Bultmann famously argued that the history and preaching of Jesus are unimportant for Paul; see e.g. *Theology of the New Testament vol. 1* (London: SCM, 1952) 188–9; "The Historical Jesus and the Theology of Paul", in *Faith and Understanding I* (London: SCM, 1969) 220–46. See discussion in G.N. Stanton, *Jesus of Nazareth in New Testament Preaching* (SNTSMS 27; Cambridge: CUP, 1974) 87–93.

[39] J.L. Martyn, "Epistemology at the Turn of the Ages", in *Theological Issues in the Letters of Paul* (SNTW; Edinburgh: T. & T. Clark, 1997) 89–110; here p. 110.

ated with James and the Jerusalem church. Specifically, Paul's corporate Christology seems likely to have underpinned his controversial conviction that, because Jews and Gentiles are together one body in Christ, a new creation, they can and must share unbounded fellowship at the Lord's table.

"No Longer Jew or Greek": But What Does That Mean in Practice?

It is explicit in the baptismal declarations examined above that Paul regards the Christian community as a body of people which is one in Christ, in whom "there is no longer Jew or Greek". But what exactly does that phrase mean? To what extent does it imply a redefinion of former identities and a restructuring of former practices? That is not immediately apparent and a range of interpretations are possible. It might be taken as essentially a *soteriological* declaration: that Jews and Gentiles are equally and without distinction saved in Christ, but that their identities and accompanying ethical imperatives remain distinct. Or, at the other end of the spectrum, it might be taken to mean that the identity distinction between Jewish and Gentile Christians has essentially been dissolved, that a new identity "in Christ" has displaced the former labels (or rather that the identity labels of Israel now apply without distinction to all who are ἐν Χριστῷ—see below) and that whatever ethical obligations there are apply to the whole people of God in Christ. From a perspective informed by the sociology of knowledge, one would expect both the positive declaration ("you are one in Christ") and its negative counterpart ("there is no longer Jew and Gentile") to reflect not merely some theoretical standpoint "in the sight of God" (can any statement "merely" do that?) but to define the identity of the Christian congregations and to structure their social interaction. In what ways does this appear to be evident?

We may first consider some of the statements Paul makes about himself. His continuing sense of his Jewish identity is clear from Rom 9:3 and 2 Cor 11:22, though in the first case it is notable that he specifies that the Jews are his kindred κατὰ σάρκα (precisely the perspective from which he no longer views those who are in Christ, according to 2 Cor 5:16) and in the second his statements are presented as a piece of foolish boasting, necessitated by the Corinthians' acceptance of rival missionaries who make much of their Jewish

credentials. As in 2 Cor 11:22, in Phil 3:4–8 Paul lists his Jewish
credentials in a polemical context, describing them as a basis for
confidence ἐν σαρκί, but as "loss" and "rubbish" compared with
knowing Christ, though whom Paul, according to his own testimony,
has indeed lost everything (δι' ὃν τὰ πάντα ἐζημιώθην—3:8). Christ
has become the all-defining centre of Paul's identity. Further relevant evidence is found in 1 Corinthians, where Paul strikingly states
that he became to the Jews ὡς Ἰουδαῖος and that he himself is not
ὑπὸ νόμον (1 Cor 9:20; cf. Rom 7:6; Gal 4:12).[41] In Galatians Paul
speaks of his "former life in Judaism" (Gal 1:13–14) and describes
himself and Peter as φύσει Ἰουδαῖοι but as now living in a way that
is not Jewish (2:15; see further below). In Gal 2:18–20, in a passage
to which we shall return, Paul describes himself as having died to
the Law, as having "torn down" his previous basis for righteousness,
as someone who has been crucified with Christ and now lives only
insofar as Christ lives in him. It would seem accurate to conclude
that Paul remains conscious of his identity as Jew but that this identity is no longer defining—or at least is radically redefined—in the
light of his new identity as ἄνθρωπος ἐν Χριστῷ.

But if Paul sees his own identity transformed in Christ, what is
his view of other Jewish Christians? Crucial here is the much discussed and difficult passage in Gal 2:14–21. Paul reports that his
challenge to Peter began with the words: Εἰ σὺ Ἰουδαῖος ὑπάρχων
ἐθνικῶς καὶ οὐχὶ Ἰουδαϊκῶς ζῇς, πῶς τὰ ἔθνη ἀναγκάζεις Ἰουδαΐζειν;
(v. 14).[42] Distinguishing here the different identities of Gentile and
Jewish believers (εἰ σὺ Ἰουδαῖος ὑπάρχων; cf. v. 15 ἡμεῖς . . .) is an
essential starting point for addressing the issue of conflict at Antioch

---

[40] Stanton, *Jesus of Nazareth in New Testament Preaching*, 93.

[41] These statements do not fit with Peter Tomson's view of Paul as a law-abiding Jew whose letters represent *halakah* for Gentiles and who urges law-observance
for Jewish Christians, so he accepts the rather weak textual evidence for omitting
the ὡς and the phrase μὴ ὢν αὐτὸς ὑπὸ νόμον (Tomson, *Paul and the Jewish Law*,
276–79). The latter phrase is most likely to have been omitted through homoeotele-
ton and most commentators accept the ὡς (omitted only in F, G*, 6*, 326, 1729
pc) as original (see G.D. Fee, *The First Epistle to the Corinthians* [NICNT; Grand
Rapids: Eerdmans, 1987] 422 nn. 2–3; B.M. Metzger, *TCGNT* [2nd edn] 493).

[42] This statement is again difficult for Tomson to fit into his picture of Paul, and
he accepts the less than compelling textual evidence for the omission of the words
καὶ Ἰουδαϊκῶς ζῇς following P[46]) and paraphrases the sentence thus: "Before, you
agreed to live and eat as a Jew together with the gentiles, and although some call
that 'living like a gentile', why do you now separate and wish to eat with them
only if they become Jews?" (Tomson, *Paul and the Jewish Law*, 229–30). This seems

and Galatia: who or what should change when these two groups are integrated as εἰς ἐν Χριστῷ? The "conditional clause evidently refers . . . to an admitted fact":[43] Peter (and the other Jewish Christians) have been living ἐθνικῶς. It hardly seems likely, as some have suggested, that this assessment is merely Paul's reporting of the accusation of the people from James.[44] The logic of Paul's argument requires that both he and Peter (as well as the people from James) *agree* that what they have been doing is living ἐθνικῶς, and that *therefore*, since they have abandoned in some way their Jewish way of life (οὐχὶ Ἰουδαϊκῶς ζῇς) it makes no sense now to alter that policy and compel the Gentiles to judaise[45]—which is what the Jewish Christians' separation implies as the requirement for restored unity. Despite the fact the Peter and Paul are "by nature Jews and not Gentile sinners" (Paul's use of a Jewish stereotypical distinction between Jews and Gentiles)[46] they have believed in Christ for righteousness rather than seek that righteousness ἐξ ἔργων νόμου (vv. 15–16). In other words, the basis of their membership of God's covenant people comes not on the basis of being Jewish and living by the Law (which would distinguish them from "Gentile sinners") but ἐκ πίστεως Χριστοῦ, an identical basis for both Jew and Gentile.[47] Verse 17 seems to acknowledge that by finding the basis of their righteousness, their covenant belonging, ἐν Χριστῷ, and not ἐξ ἔργων

---

to me quite clearly to alter the sense of what Paul actually writes.

[43] Burton, *Galatians*, 112.

[44] So Dunn, *The Epistle to the Galatians* (BNTC; London: A. & C. Black, 1993) 128; Tomson, *Paul and the Jewish Law*, 230.

[45] "[T]o adopt Jewish customs or live like a Jew" (Barclay, *Obeying the Truth*, 36 n. 1; cf. BAGD, 379; Dunn, *Jesus, Paul and the Law*, 149–50). Richard Longenecker's "to become a Jew" is too strong (R.N. Longenecker, *Galatians* [WBC 41; Waco: Word Books, 1990] 78). That the verb itself does not necessarily imply full conversion to Judaism is implied by Josephus' report of Metilius' promise καὶ μέχρι περιτομῆς ἰουδαΐσειν (*J.W.* 2.454; cf. 2.463). Cf. also Esth 8:17 (LXX) καὶ πολλοὶ τῶν ἐθνῶν περιετέμοντο καὶ ἰουδάιζον διὰ τὸν φόβον τῶν Ἰουδαίων; Ign. *Magn.* 10:3; Plutarch *Cicero* 7.5.

[46] ". . . stereotypical depictions of insiders and outsiders to the covenant—stereotypes common in much of Jewish literature of the time but soon to be disqualified by Paul." B.W. Longenecker, "Defining the Faithful Character of the Covenant Community: Galatians 2.15–21 and Beyond", in *Paul and the Mosaic Law* (ed. Dunn), 75–97; here p. 81. Also Barclay, *Obeying the Truth*, 77 n. 7, citing, *inter alia*, Ps 9:18 (LXX); *Pss. Sol.* 2:1–2; 17:25; *Jub.* 23:23–24; 24:28 (and cf. 22:16); 4 Ezra 3:28–36; Matt 5:47 with Luke 6:32; Matt 26:45 with Luke 18:32. Note also Tob 13:8 (LXX).

[47] See further Longenecker, "Defining the Faithful Character"; idem, *The Triumph of Abraham's God*, 89–115. By leaving πίστις Χριστοῦ untranslated, I am of course avoiding the debate over its interpretation, but that is not strictly relevant to my

νόμου, Paul, Peter and other Jewish Christians ("we . . .")—like the Gentile "sinners" from whom their Jewish identity previously distinguished them (v. 15)—are themselves found to be "sinners" (εὑρέθημεν καὶ αὐτοὶ ἁμαρτωλοί). Paul does not by this mean that they are actually guilty of sin before God, but rather that from the perspective of Torah-observance, by their unbounded fellowship with Gentile believers, they have become "sinners", stepping outside the boundaries of covenant-loyalty centred on Torah.[48] Hence the need for a response to the question, "Is Christ then a minister of sin?", an understandable and logical objection to which Paul had more than once to respond (cf. Rom 3:8; 6:1; Acts 21:21) and which here as elsewhere receives his characteristic and emphatic negation: μὴ γένοιτο (cf. Rom 6:2, 15; 7:7, 13 etc.). The real sin would be for Paul to rebuild what he had already torn down (namely a righteous identity based on Torah); in that case he would show himself to be a "transgressor".[49] He has died to the Law and lives to God, and to return to the Law would be to annul the significance of Christ's death (v. 21). It is therefore highly unlikely that Gal 5:3 means that Paul regards every Jewish Christian as obligated to obey the whole Torah, as Bockmuehl tentatively suggests.[50] In context it serves as a reason why the Gentile Christians should not submit themselves to circumcision (5:1–6). Jewish Christians, if they follow Paul's interpretation of the gospel, have died to the Law (2:19; cf. Rom 7:1–6) and now are righteoused in Christ and not by the Law (2:16; cf. 5:4). Thus, for both groups, circumcision and uncircumcision now achieve nothing (5:6). As Paul makes clear later in the letter (5:13–25), however, living ἐν Χριστῷ and not ὑπὸ νόμον does not mean living lawlessly; it involves living in the Spirit's power and *thus* fulfilling the

---

argument.

[48] Cf. Barclay, *Obeying the Truth*, 79; Holmberg, "Jewish *Versus* Christian Identity", 415.

[49] Either of the Law, based on his current practice, or (rather more attractive, in my view) of the will of God, which now summons people to live ἐν Χριστῷ and not ὑπὸ νόμον. This latter view probably makes better sense of the verse, and of v. 19 which follows (esp. its contrast between dying to the Law and living to God); cf. J. Lambrecht, "Paul's Reasoning in Galatians 2:11–21", in *Paul and the Mosaic Law* (ed. Dunn), 53–74; here pp. 65–6; idem, "Transgressor by Nullifying God's Grace: A Study of Gal 2, 18–21", *Bib* 72 (1991) 217–36; Longenecker, "Defining the Faithful Character", 84.

Law—though precisely what this means is yet another conundrum in Pauline interpretation.[51]

Paul's understanding of the implications of the Antioch incident may therefore be summarised. For Jews and Gentiles to share unbounded table-fellowship requires one of two things: for Jews to live ἐθνικῶς or for Gentiles ἰουδαΐζειν. Since the former has already taken place, on the theological grounds that being righteoused comes through Christ and not Torah, it makes no sense now to require the latter; indeed, to do so would be to deny the heart of the gospel as Paul sees it, namely that no one, Jew or Gentile, is righteoused other than in Christ. In this case it is clear that identity is redefined and social relationships restructured by a new defining identity ἐν Χριστῷ. This shared identity—and this identity alone—defines the boundary between insider and outsider, and establishes the basis for intimacy and commensality.[52]

Another important passage is found in 1 Cor 7:18–20:

περιτετμημένος τις ἐκλήθη, μὴ ἐπισπάσθω· ἐν ἀκροβυστίᾳ κέκληταί τις, μὴ περιτεμνέσθω. ἡ περιτομὴ οὐδέν ἐστιν καὶ ἡ ἀκροβυστία οὐδέν ἐστιν, ἀλλὰ τήρησις ἐντολῶν θεοῦ. ἕκαστος ἐν τῇ κλήσει ᾗ ἐκλήθη, ἐν ταύτῃ μενέτω.

According to Markus Bockmuehl (quoted above) Paul here "makes clear that his 'rule for all the churches' is for Jews to keep the Torah . . . and for Gentiles to keep what pertains to them".[53] Similarly, Peter Tomson maintains that this passage reveals that *"the observance of distinct sets of commandments by Jewish and gentile Christians was the basic principle of Paul's missionary work"*.[54]

However, it may be questioned whether this makes the best sense of what Paul writes here, and in the strikingly similar formulations in Gal 5:6 and 6:15. This section of 1 Corinthians 7 (vv. 17–24) is widely agreed to provide illustrations of the wider principle Paul invokes during his answers to the Corinthians' questions about marriage and sexual relationships (7:1–40): on the whole, though with

---

[50] Bockmuehl, "The Noachide Commandments", 98, quoted above.
[51] See e.g. S. Westerholm, "On Fulfilling the Whole Law (Gal 5:14)", *SEÅ* 51–52 (1986–87) 229–37.
[52] Cf. Holmberg, "Jewish *Versus* Christian Identity", 416: "when it happens, as it did in the Antioch incident, that Jewish identity conflicts with Christian identity, the former must be abandoned" (see also p. 414).
[53] Bockmuehl, "The Noachide Commandments", 98.

exceptions countenanced throughout, people should remain as they
are. In this connection Paul thus states that Jewish Christians should
not seek to *remove* (μὴ ἐπισπάσθω) the marks of their circumcision (i.e.
of their Jewish identity),[55] nor should Gentile Christians become circumcised. The reason given, however, is that circumcision and uncircumcision are *nothing* (οὐδέν). Paul follows this with the assertion that
what *does* count is "keeping the commandments of God" (v. 19). His
Jewish-Christian opponents in Galatia would no doubt have perceived a sharp oxymoron in Paul's juxtaposition of the statements
"circumcision is nothing" and "but keeping the commandments of
God", since Gen 17:9–14 clearly states that circumcision is a permanent obligation for all who would be descendants of Abraham (as
all "in Christ" clearly are, in Paul's view: Gal 3:6–4:6).[56] However,
as the distinction between dying νόμῳ and living θεῷ shows (Gal
2:19), keeping the commandments of God does not necessarily mean
for Paul upholding literally "the whole Law". (It is also noteworthy
that the commands, instructions, and advice Paul gives in 1 Corinthians
7 are based explicitly either on the teaching of Jesus or on his own
instruction [vv. 10, 17, 25; cf. 1 Cor 14:37].) Paul does not wish his
converts to alter or eradicate the marks of their identity as Jew or
Gentile, but insists that these distinctions are now "nothing". A similar insistence appears twice in Galatians, where Paul specifies what
matters as "faith working through love" (5:6) and as "a new creation" (6:15). In all three cases, the marks of identity and practice
which previously *distinguished* Jew and Gentile (circumcision/uncir-
cumcision) are transcended by an exhortation or declaration which
applies to all "in Christ" without distinction: "keeping the commandments of God"; "faith working through love"; "a new creation".
This would appear then to support an interpretation which took
Paul's meaning in 1 Corinthians 7 to be that the Christian communities of Jews and Gentiles, now united as a new creation, obey
God's commands as they together live in holiness and love, *but that
the identity-distinction between them has now become* οὐδέν, "*nothing*". Paul's
commentary on the Antioch incident shows that for him this may

---

[54] P.J. Tomson, "Paul's Jewish Background", 268, emphasis his.
[55] On the reasons why this might have been done, see B.W. Winter, *Seek the
Welfare of the City: Christians as Benefactors and Citizens* (Grand Rapids: Eerdmans, 1994)
147–52.
[56] Cf. Boyarin, *A Radical Jew*, 96: "*keeping the Law while being uncircumcised is simply
an oxymoron from the perspective of rabbinic Judaism, because being circumcised is part of the*

entail an abandonment of customs which are part of what it means to live Ἰουδαϊκῶς, when the unity and identity of the Christian congregation is at stake.[57] Phil 3:8 expresses a similar conviction: it is not merely that Paul *considers* his Jewish identity and righteousness as loss, compared with Christ (3:7), but that Christ is the one δι' ὃν τὰ πάντα ἐζημιώθην (3:8).

One final passage remains to be considered, where Paul is clearly writing to a mixed congregation, or group of congregations: Romans 14:1–15:13.[58] It is interesting to contrast Paul's strategy here with that which he adopted in Antioch and Galatia, and to consider how the different contexts determine that strategy. Moreover, in view of tendency to make Romans the dominant lens through which Paul's theology is viewed, the particularity of the letter should be remembered: Paul is writing to a church (or churches) he has neither founded nor previously visited, writing to commend (or defend) himself and his gospel (Rom 1:16; 3:8 etc.). In Antioch and Galatia the danger, as Paul saw it, was that "Judaisers" were insisting that for the community to be united it was necessary for Gentile converts to judaise. In such a case of conflict between Jewish practice and identity and the unity of the new creation "in Christ" Paul is clear: rather than effectively compel Gentiles to judaise, Jewish practice and identity must be compromised.[59] However, in Rome the situation is different: those believers who do not observe Jewish Law with regard to food regulations, sabbath observance etc., are inclined to despise the sensibilities of their Law-observant Christian ἀδελφοί.[60]

Law!"

[57] Cf. Boyarin, *A Radical Jew*, 112–4; Holmberg, "Jewish *Versus* Christian Identity".

[58] Stanley Stowers' argument that Romans is addressed to Gentiles only has been effectively refuted by Richard Hays. See S.K. Stowers, *A Rereading of Romans: Justice, Jews, and Gentiles* (New Haven: Yale University Press, 1994); R.B. Hays "'The Gospel is the Power of God for Salvation to Gentiles Only'? A Critique of Stanley Stowers' *A Rereading of Romans*", *CR* 9 (1996) 27–44.

[59] So Holmberg, "Jewish *Versus* Christian Identity", 414–6.

[60] It is not necessarily the case that the "strong" and the "weak" are exclusively Gentiles and Jews respectively (after all, Paul counts himself among "the strong": 15:1). But it does seem most compelling to regard the distinction as between those who follow Jewish customs regarding foods etc., and those who do not; so Barclay, "Do We Undermine the Law?", 289–93. In his recent monograph, Mark Reasoner attempts to show that the issues dividing the strong and the weak are not exclusively those of Jewish custom: the abstinence of the weak may be motivated by a range of influences. However, the evidence he adduces to connect the situation Paul addresses with Jewish concerns is much stronger than that by which he attempts to connect the practice of the weak with other traditions of vegetarianism and asceticism in Rome. See M. Reasoner, *The Strong and the Weak: Romans 14.1–15.13 in Context*

The two groups are apparently in a situation where there is some antagonism and division between them, and Paul's aim is to unite them (15:7). Yet in this very different context—where the pressures seem to emanate more from Gentile-Christian arrogance (cf. 11:13–24) than from judaising pressure—he does so not by insisting that Jewish demands be ignored, but by seeking to establish a situation in which the different customs and practices of Jewish and Gentile believers are accepted side-by-side, as long as they do not prevent the unity and fellowship of both groups within the community which is one body in Christ (Rom 12:5).[61] However, Paul makes it clear that he, a Jew, stands firmly on the "Gentile" side of the division here, insofar as his own ethical convictions "in the Lord Jesus" are concerned: "nothing is unclean (κοινόν) in itself" (Rom 14:14a; cf. 15:1). His view of food is that πάντα καθαρά (14:20). In view of the extensive instructions as to what is unclean in the Torah, Paul's convictions seem hardly to be those of a Torah-observant Jew,[62] nor of one who urged that "Jews and gentiles should each stick to their respective ways of life".[63] Nevertheless, in this situation, Paul's concern is to defend the position of the "weak", and, as in 1 Cor 8:1–11:1, he urges that the strong accommodate their practice to that of the weak (Rom 14:15, 21; 15:2–3). Here then we see a context in which the maintenance of Jewish identity is defended (though not urged, or "ruled") within the overall context of a unity in Christ: it is because all are servants of the same κύριος that judgment of one another is inappropriate (Rom 14:4–13). Yet, as Boyarin and Barclay argue, this reduction of Jewish legal observance to what Boyarin terms "a matter of taste", a purely personal decision, ultimately undermines the cultural and social integrity of Law-observant Jewish Christians:[64] identity, social practice and community boundaries are no longer to be marked by a distinctive stance with regard to eating, drinking, and celebrating special days, but rather by common commitment to Christ (Rom 15:5–7).

(SNTSMS 103; Cambridge: CUP, 1999).

[61] Cf. Boyarin, *A Radical Jew*, 112.

[62] John Barclay puts the point more forcefully: "This constitutes nothing less than a fundamental rejection of the Jewish law in one of its most sensitive dimensions" ("Do We Undermine the Law?", 300). Cf. e.g. Lev 11:1–47; Deut 14:3–21; *m. Hul.* esp. 7–10. Contrast Tomson, *Paul and the Jewish Law*, 247–54. On κοινός as unclean, cf. Matt 15:11–20; Mark 7:15–23; Acts 10:14–15, 28; 11:8–9.

[63] Tomson, "Paul's Jewish Background", 267.

[64] See Boyarin, *A Radical Jew*, 32, cf. 9–10, *et passim*; Barclay, "Do We Undermine

Christian Identity as (Redefined) Jewish Identity

Having focused primarily on Paul's corporate Christology as the foundation for the common identity which both Jewish and Gentile believers share, one might gain the impression that Paul perceived this body of people "in Christ" as a new entity, a "third race", as some later writers would express it.[65] Paul does indeed *de facto* seem to be involved in constructing the identity and social practice of a *new* social grouping, one in which there is "no longer Jew or Gentile" but which is something distinct called the ἐκκλησία τοῦ θεοῦ (1 Cor 10:32).[66] However, he did not himself see it in those terms. Rather, Paul claims for those in Christ the privileged identity descriptions which traditionally belong to what Paul calls τὸν Ἰσραὴλ κατὰ σάρκα (1 Cor 10:18; cf. Rom 9:3). Although he never explicitly formulates the parallel designation, Ἰσραηλ κατὰ πνεῦμα, to describe the Church, it may be argued to be implicit in 1 Corinthians 10, and virtually explicit in Gal 4:29 (cf. also Rom 9:6–8).[67] Most explicit of all of course is the unique and much disputed phrase in Gal 6:16—τὸν Ἰσραὴλ τοῦ θεοῦ—which seems most likely to refer to the Christian community.[68] All who are in Christ are equally and without distinction descendants of Abraham (Gal 3:6–4:6, 21–31; cf. Rom 9:8; 2 Cor 11:22), inheritors of God's promise (Gal 3:29; 4:28), children of the Jerusalem above (Gal 4:26), ἀδελφοί (cf. e.g. Deut 15:2–3, 7, 12 etc.), and υἱοὶ θεοῦ (Rom 8:14; Gal 3:26, etc.). They are the 'people of God' (cf. Rom 9:24–25; 2 Cor 6:16); the scriptures were written for their instruction (Rom 15:4; 1 Cor 10:11); the patriarchs are their fathers (1 Cor 10:1; cf. Rom 4:1). And despite Paul's polemic against physical circumcision, he describes Christians as 'the circumcision' (Phil 3:3; cf. Rom 2:28–29). In view of all this, it must be said that Gentile converts who are "in Christ" are, for Paul, as much a part of (a redefined) Israel as are Christian Jews, and both belong by virtue of their being in Christ (and by this means alone!),

the Law?", 305–8.
[65] See e.g. Aristides, *Apol. 2*; Tertullian, *Ad Nat.* 8; *Scorp.* 10; A. Harnack, *The Expansion of Christianity in the First Three Centuries I* (London: Williams and Norgate, 1904) 336–52; M. Simon, *Verus Israel* (Oxford: OUP, 1986) 107–11.
[66] See further E.P. Sanders, *Paul, the Law and the Jewish People* (London: SCM, 1983) 171–9; Esler, *Galatians*, 88–92.
[67] Cf. N.A. Dahl, "Der Name Israel: Zur Auslegung von Gal 6,16", *Judaica* 6 (1950) 161–70; here p. 163.
[68] For arguments in favour of this interpretation, see e.g. Dahl, "Zur Auslegung

who is the (singular) seed of Abraham (Gal 3:16). They are all equally part of the Israel of God, but an Israel whose identity and practice are redefined, reconfigured around Christ and not Torah.[69]

In tension with all this, however, is Paul's continuing awareness of ethnic Israel, to whom the promises of God still intrinsically belong and whose "failure" to believe is a cause of considerable anguish and theological wrestling for Paul (Rom 9–11). Unlike most later generations of Christians, Paul held onto this conviction in spite of its tension with his belief that God had recreated Israel as the body of people in Christ.[70] Of course, Paul believed that in the providential purposes of God this tension would be resolved—and soon!—when Israel's time of hardening was ended and she finally came to be saved (Rom 11:26).

Conclusions: Identity and Community "In Christ"

What then can we conclude about the implications of Paul's corporate Christology for the construction of Christian community and for the redefinition and restructuring of converts' identity and practice? The implications of the sociology of knowledge have been influential throughout this investigation, informing the conviction that (theological) symbols and ideas serve to construct identity and to shape social interaction, though the specific ways in which they do this can only be ascertained by exegesis of the relevant texts. This perspective, however, raises questions over the plausibility of a sharp separation between soteriology and ethics, as is required for the thesis that, while Paul's soteriology was based solely on faith in Christ, his ethical teaching was for Jews and Gentiles to "stick to their respective ways of life".[71] On the basis both of a sociological appreciation of the close relationship between "symbolic orders" and social practice, and of the exegesis of Pauline texts, this proposal appears mistaken.

---

von Gal 6,16"; Barclay, *Obeying the Truth*, 98; Longenecker, *Galatians*, 298–9.

[69] Cf. the argument of T.L. Donaldson, *Paul and the Gentiles: Remapping the Apostle's Convictional World* (Minneapolis: Fortress, 1997), who proposes that Paul conceived of Gentile admission on the model of Jewish proselytism, but that Paul's Judaism was reconfigured around Christ and not Torah.

[70] See further Donaldson, *Paul and the Gentiles*, 239–48, 297–9, 305–7.

[71] Tomson, "Paul's Jewish Background", 267; cf. 266 ("the soteriological equal-

Paul's emphatic and repeated declaration that in Christ there is no longer Jew and Gentile reflects not just a soteriological conviction, but a profound statement about the identity and unity of the new community which God has created, a statement which shapes and structures social interaction in the congregations in real and sometimes controversial ways. Both the positive christological declaration— "you are all one in Christ"—and its negative corollary—"there is no longer Jew or Greek"—do indeed fundamentally (re)define identity and social practice, in ways which, at least in certain circumstances, compromise or even abrogate previous patterns of identity-forming conduct.

The evidence from Paul's letters indicates that for Paul himself a new and defining identity ἐν Χριστῷ implies a radical transformation of his Jewish identity and practice (1 Cor 9:20; Gal 2:15–20; 4:12; Phil 3:8 etc.). Similarly, Paul is clear that the identity distinction between Jewish and Gentile Christians, the circumcised and the uncircumcised, is now "nothing" (οὐδέν) since both are part of God's new creation in Christ (1 Cor 7:19; Gal 5:6; 6:15)—on this point the writer to the Ephesians seems to me a good interpreter of Pauline theology (Eph 2:14–18). Jew and Gentile have become one in Christ, equally and without distinction descendants of Abraham and members of the Israel of God. Hence what defines the "ingroup" as opposed to the "outgroup" is quite simply being ἐν Χριστῷ. *The distinction to be drawn in terms of moral obligation and social interaction is not between Jew and Gentile but between those who are in Christ and those who are not.* It is this latter distinction which determines the boundaries in such crucial spheres of social interaction as commensality (1 Cor 5:11) and marriage (1 Cor 7:39—μόνον ἐν κυρίῳ).[72] Indeed, the change in focus is epitomised in Paul's insistence that he is not ὑπὸ νόμον but ἔννομος Χριστοῦ; "in-lawed"[73] in a way which is commensurate with his new identity ἐν Χριστῷ (1 Cor 9:21; Gal 6:2).[74] While Paul's understanding of (Christian!) identity and ethical responsibility

---

ity of Jewish and gentile Christians" *bis*); also Finsterbusch, *Die Thora als Lebensweisung*, 61, 63–4, 82–3; M.N.A. Bockmuehl, "Review of Finsterbusch, *Die Thora als Lebensweisung*", *JTS* 49 (1998) 787.

[72] Cf. Barclay, *Jews in the Mediterranean Diaspora*, 385–6.

[73] As E.P. Sanders points out, the phrase ἔννομος Χριστοῦ is "virtually untranslatable" (*Paul, the Law and the Jewish People*, 100). The phrase in Gal 6:2, ὁ νόμος τοῦ Χριστοῦ, is of course more straightforward—in translation if not in interpretation.

[74] See further R.B. Hays, "Christology and Ethics in Galatians: The Law of

remains profoundly Jewish—and this point should not be underemphasised—that understanding is reconfigured and recentred around Christ.[75]

It seems to me, therefore, that David Catchpole was entirely correct to insist that for Paul, "the Christian gospel does a very great deal to the Jew/Gentile distinction". Paul's corporate Christology provides the basis for his conviction that all who are in Christ have died to the old era and now live (corporately) as "one", a new creation, the body of Christ, in the power of the Spirit: former distinctions signify nothing. Paul's corporate Christology thus underpins a (controversial) model of community in which Jew and Gentile enjoy unbounded table-fellowship, sharing one bread and one cup, demonstrating in concrete social interaction that they are "one body in Christ".[76]

Christ", *CBQ* 49 (1987) 268–90; Barclay, *Obeying the Truth*, 126–35.

[75] Cf. Donaldson, *Paul and the Gentiles*.

[76] I am extremely grateful to John Barclay, Bruce Longenecker and Christopher Tuckett for their comments on a draft of this essay. Needless to say, they should not be held in any way responsible for the opinions, or any errors, herein.

OPENLY PORTRAYED AS CRUCIFIED: SOME OBSERVATIONS ON GAL 3:1–14

Peder Borgen

It is a privilege and a pleasure for me to contribute an essay to the *Festschrift* in honour of my treasured colleague and good friend David Catchpole. I got to know him at the annual meetings of the *Studiorum Novi Testamenti Societas*, especially during the period when he was its Secretary. Catchpole demonstrated that it is possible to combine outstanding and firm leadership with a gracious and caring attitude towards colleagues. When SNTS accepted the invitation to have one of its General Meetings at our University in Trondheim, it was a great experience to work together with him in the planning and carrying out of the conference. Later he arranged a guest lecture tour for me to several universities in the United Kingdom and Ireland. The tour was a very memorable experience for my wife and myself. When we visited the University of Exeter, we had the pleasure of staying in his home, meeting the family and experiencing their generous and warm hospitality. Both then and at conferences it has been good to talk and share both as colleagues and as friends.

When Paul in 1 Cor 15:3ff. quoted a Christological tradition that he had received, the death of Jesus was referred to in the following words: "that Christ died for our sins in accordance with the Scriptures" (v. 3).

In a recent essay I discussed the wording "in accordance with the Scriptures".[1] I argued that the meaning was broader and more general than that of the Scriptures providing one or more proof texts. In support for this understanding I mentioned the parallel phrase "in accordance with the Law". The preposition used, κατά, introduces the norm according to which something takes place. In connection with the death of Jesus, John 18:31 offers a good parallel.

---

[1] P. Borgen, "'In accordance with the Scriptures'", in J.M.G. Barclay and J.P.M. Sweet, eds, *Early Christian Thought in Its Jewish Context* FS Morna Hooker (Cambridge: CUP, 1996) 193–206.

Pilate said to the Jewish leaders "judge him 'in accordance with your law'".

Moreover, I maintained that "since it was known that the trial (whether performed formally or informally) and execution of Jesus was a legal action and not a murder, then the words 'died for our sins in accordance with the Scriptures' with necessity presupposed the opposite view, that he, 'in accordance with the Scriptures', died as a lawbreaker for his own sins."[2] Both those who maintained that Jesus died "for his own sins" and those who thought he died "for our sins" would claim that their different understandings were "in accordance with the Scriptures".

The section Gal 3:1–14 is of particular interest in this connection. Here the death of Christ Jesus is a central feature, as already seen in v. 1, where Paul in an emphatic way refers to the crucifixion: "You foolish Galatians! Who has bewitched you—you before whose eyes Jesus Christ was openly portrayed as crucified?"[3]

Another central characteristic of Gal 3:1–14 is that the passage contains extensive quotations and allusions to words from the Scriptures, such as Gen 15:6; 12:3; 18:18; Deut 27:26; Hab 2:4; Lev 18:5; Deut 21:23. In this essay observations will be made on some of these references to the Scriptures in Gal 3:1–14. In the opening verses, Gal 3:1ff., the theme of crucifixion and the theme of faith stand out, and the focus will be mainly set on the development of the theme of crucifixion.

As a background for the examination of the theme of crucifixion, a brief comment might be given on the use of this form of execution in New Testament times. The use of this cruel form of death penalty was widespread in the ancient world, even among Greeks.[4] Crucifixion represented the uttermost humiliation of the victim. Often the victim was refused burial and the corpse served as food for wild beasts. In general those who were crucified would be suffering the death penalty for their own crimes, as lawbreakers, rebels, etc. This would at least normally be the claim of those who sentenced them

---

[2] Ibid., 198.

[3] In the present essay the translation given in J.D.G. Dunn, *The Epistle to the Galatians* (London: Black, 1993) is followed.

[4] See M. Hengel, *Crucifixion* (London: SCM, 1977), translated by J. Bowden from "'Mors turpissima crucis': Die Kreuzigung in der antiken Welt und die 'Torheit' des 'Wortes vom Kreuz'", in J. Friedrich, W. Pöhlmann and P. Stuhlmacher, eds, *Rechtfertigung*. FS Ernst Käsemann (Tübingen: Mohr-Siebeck, 1976).

to death and others after them. Against this background it is obvious that when Paul and others preached the message of Jesus Christ
as crucified, it would cause offence both among Jews and non-Jews,
as stated in 1 Cor 1:23, "... we preach Christ crucified, a stum-
bling-block to Jews and folly to Gentiles ...". In his book on crucifixion
M. Hengel writes:

> When Paul spoke in his mission preaching about the "crucified Christ"
> (1 Corinthians 1:23; 2:2; Galatians 3:1) every hearer in the Greek-
> speaking East between Jerusalem and Illyricum (Romans 15:19) knew
> that this "Christ"—for Paul the title was already a proper name—had
> suffered a particularly cruel and shameful death, which as a rule was
> reserved for hardened criminals, rebellious slaves and rebels against
> the Roman state.[5]

In Gal 3:1–14 Paul did not refer in a direct way to this Graeco-
Roman background, but interpreted the crucifixion primarily within
the context of the Sinaitic law.

As already stated, Paul refers in an explicit way to the crucifixion
of Jesus Christ in Gal 3:1. Without the word itself being used,
crucifixion is also mentioned in 3:13, where Deut 21:23 is quoted.
Paul's rendering of Deut 21:23 reads: "Cursed is every one who has
been hanged on a tree." Against the background of Gal 3:1 it is
obvious that crucifixion is meant. Important parallels have been found
in the Dead Sea Scrolls, especially in an exposition of Deut 21:22–23
in 11QTemple 64:6–13. Here the practice of executing the death
penalty by means of crucifixion seems to have influenced the exposition. 11QTemple 64:6–12 reads:

> If a man informs against his people, and delivers his people up to a
> foreign nation, and does harm to his people, you shall hang (תלה) him
> on the tree, and he shall die. . . . And if a man has committed a crime
> punishable by death, and had defected into the midst of the nations,
> and has cursed his people and the children of Israel, you shall hang
> him on the tree, and he shall die. And their body shall not remain
> upon the tree all night, but you shall bury them the same day, for
> those hanged on the tree are accursed by God and men . . .[6]

For comparison Deut 21:22–23 is cited:

---

[5] Ibid., 83.
[6] Translation by Y. Yadin, *The Temple Scroll: Vol 2: Text and Commentary* (Jerusalem:
The Israel Exploration Society, 1983) 288–91.

> And if a man has committed a crime punishable by death and he is put to death, and you hang (תלה) him on a tree, his body shall not remain all night upon the tree, but you shall bury him on the same day, for a hanged man is accursed by God . . .

The Temple Scroll has a different sequence for the verbs "to hang" (תלה) and "to die" from that formulated in Deut 21:22–23. Deut 21:22–23 as such may mean that the person is hanged on a tree after having been executed by other means, such as by stoning or strangulation.[7] According to the Temple Scroll the hanging itself causes the person to die.[8] Thus the person is executed by means of hanging on the tree, probably by a form of crucifixion.[9] Philo adds support to the understanding that crucifixion is meant. In *Spec.* 3:151–52 he defines the hanging in Deut 21:22–23 as "to fix on a pole, impale" (ἀνασκολοπίζω). When Philo uses this verb in *Somn.* 2:213 he explicitly says that the fixing is done by nailing (προσηλόω). The crucified person concerned suffers capital punishment for his own sins. Moreover, it is important that the Temple Scroll witnesses to the fact that crucifixion was understood to be a form of punishment prescribed in and sanctioned by the Torah.

In Gal 3:13 Paul applied Deut 21:23 to the death of Christ Jesus: he became a curse. As seen from the interpretation in 11QTemple 64:6–10 the use of this scriptural reference in Gal 3:13 presupposed that some would understand Jesus to be a criminal who was cursed and executed by crucifixion for his own sins.[10]

In Gal 3:13 Paul turned such an interpretation around in three ways. First, Christ Jesus became a curse for us, and not for his own sins. Second, Paul transferred the characterization of Jesus as a cursed person to serve as a characterization of "us" who are under the curse of the law. Third, as a curse for "us", Christ redeemed us

---

[7] See Palestinian Targum, ad loc.; *m. Sanh.* 6:4; *b. Sanh.* 46b.

[8] Among the several studies which deal with 11QTemple 64:6–10 (and 4QpNah 1:7–8), see for example O. Betz, "Jesus and the Temple Scroll," in J.H. Charlesworth, ed., *Jesus and the Dead Sea Scrolls* (New York: Doubleday, 1992) 75–103, and J. Zias and J.H. Charlesworth, "CRUCIFIXION: Archaeology, Jesus, and the Dead Sea Scrolls," in ibid., 277–9.

[9] See the different views in Y. Yadin, "Pesher Nahum (4QpNahum) Reconsidered", *IEJ* 21 (1971) 1–12; idem, *The Temple Scroll, Vol. 1: Introduction*, 373–9, and J.M. Baumgarten, "Does TLH in the Temple Scroll Refer to Crucifixion?", *JBL* 91 (1972) 472–81.

[10] Cf. Justin, *Dial.* 89:1–90. See further G. Jeremias, *Der Lehrer der Gerechtigkeit* (Göttingen: Vandenhoeck & Ruprecht, 1963) 134–5.

from the curse of the law. In this way Paul moved from Christology to anthropology and to soteriology.

On this basis one might ask: Are there other formulations in Gal 3:1–14 which elaborate upon the theme of crucifixion? With this question in mind, let us look at the quotations of Deut 27:26 in Gal 3:10 and Lev 18:5 in Gal 3:12, and then turn to the phrase "works of the law" in Gal 3:2, 5 and 10.

Gal 3:10 reads: "For all who rely on works of the law are under a curse; for it is written, 'Cursed is every one who does not abide by all that has been written in the book of the law to do it'." Paul's logic is difficult to unravel. One would think that "all who rely on works of the law" would be "every one who does . . . abide by all that has been written in the book of the law to do it". If so, those who relied on the works of the law would not be under the curse, but under the blessing.

Understandably enough, what exactly Paul meant by the citation of Deut 27:26 in Gal 3:10 is controversial. Consequently, exegetes have suggested various interpretations.[11] Some scholars have taken an anthropological point of departure and assume that Paul quotes Deut 27:26 in order to show the impossibility of fulfilling the whole law for a human being. This interpretation is hardly correct, since Paul in Phil 3:6 claims that he as a Pharisee was blameless with regard to the law. Others suggest that Paul rejects the law because its claim to give life is incompatible with the gospel, according to which Christ had died in order to give life. It may be objected here that in citing Deut 27:26 in Gal 3:10 Paul is hardly just thinking of two competing and mutually exclusive claims between the law and the gospel, since he places emphasis on death by means of crucifixion.

A more viable approach is to understand Gal 3:10 on the basis of the reference to crucifixion in v. 1 and in v. 13. Gal 3:10 has several similarities with 3:13, although only the latter verse is followed by ἵνα-clauses (v. 14). In both cases scriptural words about a curse are cited. And in both places the quotations give scriptural basis for a proposition formulated by Paul. In the following quotations words from the scriptures are in italics.

---

[11] See the survey of interpretations in J.M. Scott, "'For as many are of the works of the law are under a curse' (Galatians 3:10)", in C.A. Evans and J.A. Sanders, eds, *Paul and the Scriptures of Israel* (Sheffield: Sheffield Academic Press, 1993) 187–94.

3:13:
Proposition:
Christ redeemed us from *the curse* of the law, having become *a curse* for us
Scriptural basis:
　For it is written,
　Cursed be every one who hangs on a tree.

3:10:
Proposition:
　For all who rely on "the works of *the law*" are under *a curse*;
Scriptural basis:
　For it is written,
　Cursed be every one who does not abide by all things written in the book of the law to do them.

Furthermore, Paul's formulation of the curse of Deut 21:23 in Gal 3:13 has a form different from that in the MT and LXX, but shows close similarity to that of Deut 27:26 as cited in Gal 3:10:

Deut 27:26 as cited in Gal 3:10: ἐπικατάρατος πᾶς ὅς . . .
Deut 21:23 as cited in Gal 3:13: ἐπικατάρατος πᾶς ὁ . . .
Deut 21:23 LXX: κεκατηραμένος ὑπὸ θεοῦ πᾶς . . .

It is also important that the word ἐπικατάρατος occurs both in Deut 27:26 as cited in Gal 3:10 and in Deut 21:23 as cited in Gal 3:13. A word for curse is also present in the LXX: κεκατηραμένος and in the MT: . . . קללה. Thus the hermeneutical rule of *gezerah shavah* seems to be at work, which means that because the two passages of Scripture have a term in common the interpretation of each is illuminated by the other.[12]

　When Deut 21:23 ("Cursed be every one who hangs on a tree") is applied in Gal 3:13 to Christ Jesus, this means that at the outset he is seen as a criminal and lawbreaker. Also when Jesus Christ, according to 3:1 has been portrayed to the Galatians as crucified, he is likewise presented as one who suffered the punishment of a

---

[12] See M. Jastrow, *A Dictionary of the Targumim, the Talmud Babli and Yerushalmi, and the Midrashic Literature*, (reprint in Israel, no date; 1st ed. 1903) גזרה 2: "*G'zerah shavah*, an equal or identic category, i.e. an analogy between two laws established on the basis of verbal congruities in the texts . . ."

criminal and a lawbreaker. And when the curse (Deut 21:23) in
Gal 3:13 implied that Jesus was brought to death as a criminal and
lawbreaker, this agrees with what is stated as a general rule about
a lawbreaker in Deut 27:26, cited in Gal 3:10: the person is cursed.
Against this background Deut 27:26 in Gal 3:10 should be applied to Christ Jesus in the following paraphrase: "Cursed be Christ
Jesus who (according to those who executed him and others after
them) did not abide by all things written in the book of the law to
do them."

According to Paul the problem was the malfunctioning of the law,
as made evident in the execution of Christ Jesus. Thus, Jesus' death
as a lawbreaker made evident that "those who rely on the law are
under a curse" (Gal 3:10a). Likewise, when Paul stated in Gal 3:12
that Lev 18:5 formulates the principle of the law, that "He who does
them shall live by them", then again the failure of the law in the
case of Jesus was evident: he was executed and died like a person
who did not do the law.

Paul's main point is this: the fact that Christ Jesus was crucified
as a cursed criminal made it evident that those who relied upon this
Sinaitic law were themselves under a curse. Thus Christ's death
marked the end of the Sinaitic law and the beginning of the new
era when the blessing of Abraham would come to the Gentiles and
"we" could receive the promise of the Spirit (Gal 3:14).

Against this background some comments should be made on the
phrase "works of the law" used in Gal 3:2, 5, 10. Verse 2 may illustrate Paul's use: ". . . was it by works of the law that you received
the Spirit, or by hearing with faith?" Verse 5 reads: "Does he who
supplies the Spirit to you and works miracles among you do so by
works of the law, or by hearing with faith?" There is a strong exegetical tradition in which the phrase "works of the law" is understood
to mean human self-achievement over against God's gift of grace.
Scholars such as K. Stendahl, E.P. Sanders, and J.D.G. Dunn hold
a different view. They maintain that the use of the expression "works
of the law" in Galatians has its context in the relationship between
Jews and Gentiles.[13] Sanders states that Paul's phrase "works of the
law" does not refer to "how many good deeds an individual must

---

[13] See the brief survey in P. Borgen, "Jesus Christ, the Reception of the Spirit,
and a Cross-National Community", in J.B. Green and M. Turner, eds, *Jesus of
Nazareth: Lord and Christ* (Grand Rapids, MI: Eerdmans, 1994) 223–9.

present before God to be declared righteous at the judgment, but . . .
whether or not Paul's Gentile converts must accept the Jewish law
in order to enter the people of God or to be counted truly members."[14]

In general the views of Stendahl, Sanders and Dunn indicate the
proper context within which the concept of "works of the law" is
to be understood: it is to be understood within the relationship
between the Jewish nation and the Gentiles. More can be said, however, about the dynamic which brought about the cleavage between
"works of the law" and the hearing which expressed itself in faith.[15]

Paul's opponents, the "intruders" into the Galatian congregations,
might have claimed that many points in Paul's preaching were in
agreement with the Jewish law, and rightly so. Such points would
be the call for the Gentile Galatians to turn away from the many
gods to God (Gal 4:8–9), and to turn away from pagan idolatry and
immorality (Gal 5:19–21) to a life in accordance with the commandment of neighbourly love (Lev 19:18) as a fulfillment of the
whole law (Gal 5:14).

One important part of Paul's response is that he preached Christ
Jesus as crucified, that is, one who, from the perspective of the law,
was executed as a criminal and law-breaker. Since Paul in Gal 3:1
emphasizes that Christ Jesus had been openly portrayed as crucified
before the eyes of the Galatians, this crucifixion of Christ Jesus was
part of Paul's gospel which the Galatians heard. They had heard—
and accepted in faith—this message about Christ Jesus as a criminal,
although re-interpreted positively in Paul's preaching. The crucifixion
of Jesus meant to Paul that within the jurisdiction of the law Christ
Jesus had been sentenced to death as a criminal and a lawbreaker.
To Paul this sentence made clear that those who relied on the works
of the law were under a curse (Gal 3:10), and that Christ's death
meant the end of the era of the Sinaitic law. Thus the hearing with
faith took place outside of the jurisdiction of the law and works on
that basis. There was a sharp contrast between works of the law and
faith. Therefore the Galatian converts belonged to God's people without belonging to this jurisdiction of the law. Thus they were not
obliged to join this jurisdiction and on that basis do works of the
law, such as taking on circumcision (Gal 5:2, etc.), in order to remain

---

[14] E.P. Sanders, *Paul, the Law, and the Jewish People* (Philadelphia: Fortress, 1983) 20.
[15] Concerning the meaning of the phrase ἐξ ἀκοῆς πίστεως, see Dunn, *The Epistle
to the Galatians*, 154–5.

in the people of God. In this way Paul rejected the attempt of the "intruders" to harmonize the gospel and the Sinaitic law, and to integrate the Galatian converts into the nation of the law as regular proselytes.

Paul's view is given a pointed formulation in Gal 2:21: ". . . if justification were through the law, then Christ died to no purpose." Then Christ's death had just been the death of a criminal who was sentenced to death on the basis of this law. Paul interpreted Christ's crucifixion differently, as he also stated in 2 Cor 5:21: "For our sake he [God] made him to be sin who knew no sin. . . ."

.

CHRISTOLOGY, CONTROVERSY AND APOCALYPSE: NEW TESTAMENT EXEGESIS IN THE LIGHT OF THE WORK OF WILLIAM BLAKE[1]

Christopher Rowland

A fundamental part of critical exegesis has been the invocation of parallel material to illuminate, and to offer a standpoint from which one may be able to judge, the biblical text. That exercise is essentially an exercise in comparative literary study, though the parallels which tend to dominate the pages of the monographs and commentaries on the New Testament come from the world of antiquity. A moment's reflection would indicate the precarious nature of this enterprise which can often be based on the assumption that contemporaneity means relevance. But why should a text be given priority merely because it is contemporary with a biblical text when its subject-matter may have little or no resonance with it? It seems to me that affinity of subject-matter, even if the text dates from centuries later, may in certain circumstances afford us that critical perspective we seek. It is for this reason that I think that the extraordinary careers of Abulafia in the thirteenth century or Sabbatai Sevi in the seventeenth century, precisely because both of them claimed to be messiah, may shed light on the earlier, Christian, messianism in a way which few other texts or movements can.[2] The same is true of the work of William Blake which is more likely to enable an understanding of Revelation or apocalyptic hermeneutics than many Jewish texts like the majority of the Dead Sea Scrolls or the Mishnah (contemporary as they are with the New Testament but of a rather different provenance and genre). My hope is that the keen critic of the New Testament to whom this volume is dedicated will accept

---

[1] This is in large part the material used in the Ethel M. Wood Lecture, University of London, March 1997. References to Blake's writings are taken from *William Blake. The Complete Writings* (ed. G. Keynes; Oxford: OUP, 1972) (= K).

[2] M. Idel, *Messianic Mystics* (New Haven: Yale University, 1998); G. Scholem, *Sabbatai Sevi* (London: Routledge, Kegan & Paul, 1973), and the perceptive comments of W.D. Davies in "From Schweitzer to Scholem", in *Jewish and Pauline Studies* (London: SPCK, 1984).

this, rather different, perspective on texts to which he has devoted
so much fruitful labour in recent decades.

This essay has two parts. In the first I shall examine Blake's use
of particular biblical themes and their significance for biblical interpretation. I start with Blake's prophecy and in particular focus on
the vision of God enthroned in glory, a subject which has been of
ongoing interest to me down the years in my study of apocalyptic
texts and the origins of *merkabah* mysticism. I shall suggest that Blake's
caricature of the enthroned divinity in his *Europe A Prophecy* was part
of his challenge to dominant conceptions of God in a way which
parallels John's vision of the Lamb and the throne in the book of
Revelation. Both John's and Blake's apocalyptic prophecies offer a
transformed perspective on divine monarchy. I shall move on to
explore Blake's approach to the two testaments and the way in which
he sets up a dialectic between old and new revelations in ways similar to that found in the Pauline corpus. I conclude the first part of
this essay with a look at the significance of Blake's relationship with
Milton's writing, and the way Blake explores the redemptive possibilities which take place through creative re-reading of an earlier
author. In the second part of the essay I shall offer some reflections
on the hermeneutical opportunities and challenges of Blake's reading of Scripture. In the conclusion I will consider briefly the character of Blake's biblical exegesis and try to connect with the theme
of the volume as a whole: Christology and controversy, both of which
themes Blake, in his peculiar way, illuminates greatly.

I

"Would to God That All the Lord's People Were Prophets"

William Blake was a visionary. He communed with angels and even
his dead brother regularly. Early biographers report that he saw his
first vision when he saw on Peckham Rye a tree filled with angels.
In his *Descriptive Catalogue* he speaks of the way in which the eye of vision
enhances what appears to the senses: "he who does not imagine in
stronger and better lineaments, and in stronger and better light than
his perishing and mortal eye can see, does not imagine at all." Blake
was suspicious of memory, by which he meant the mere repetition
of that which was received without that enhancement of that which
has been received through the creativity of the visionary imagina-

tion. He reports that some of his words and ideas came as the result of inspiration. Indeed, in some of his words and ideas versions of *Europe* there is an additional plate in which he describes his meeting with a fairy who dictated the poem to him. At the opening of *Jerusalem* he writes of the moment "when this Verse was first dictated to me", and wants to emphasize that "We who dwell on earth can do nothing of ourselves, every thing is conducted by Spirits, no less than Digestion or Sleep." This is not just rhetoric, the product of poetic licence. The remarkable technological researches of Joseph Viscomi have shown that Blake evolved a technique for engraving which allowed him to give full rein to his visionary creativity as he wrote.[3] Form and meaning evolve from the continual interactive relationship between mind and language on the one hand and the medium of expression on the other. Material execution is a part not a consequence of the creative process for the visionary. Writing is a creative process and not the mere transfer into another medium of that which had been conjured up elsewhere. Viscomi's work gives a new slant on the way in which writing itself can offer the space for creativity. So, when in a vision John the seer was commanded to write, we may, in the light of what we can know of Blake's inspiration and its translation into another medium, be able to glimpse how a mind saturated in the scriptures could be impelled in new directions by the motor of the scriptural imagery and the very act of writing itself. The command "write what you see" (Rev 1:10) provides the catalyst for the expression of the vision and the ready recourse to the scriptural images and words with which the visionary mind was saturated.

Although the last book of the Bible opens with the words "Apocalypse of Jesus Christ", elsewhere the book is described by John as prophecy. Blake thought of himself as standing in a tradition of prophets like John. In Copies A & B of Milton, the Preface quotes Num 11:29 "Would to God that all the Lord's people were prophets". The sense of prophetic vocation and insight equips Blake to offer the meaning of contemporary events, like the biblical prophecies against the nations, or the visions of the beast and Babylon in the book of Revelation. Indeed, he recognises the prophets of the Bible as kindred spirits (after all in *The Marriage of Heaven and Hell* he dines with Isaiah and Ezekiel). The major hero of his own idiosyncratic

---

[3] J. Viscomi, *Blake and the Idea of the Book* (Princeton: Princeton University Press, 1993), especially pp. 42–3.

myth is Los, a figure whose prophetic role is thoroughly explored. Blake can write in their style and use their images imitating the abrupt and rapid transitions between heaven and earth, and difficulties of interpretation, in both biblical and Blake's prophetic texts. These are characteristics outlined by Robert Lowth, Blake's contemporary, as typical of the "prophetic impulse" . . . . "which bears away the mind with irresistible violence, ... in rapid transitions from near to remote objects, from human to divine".[4]

Blake's prophecies were not intended to predict exactly what would happen, for they were written after the events that are described, as he puts it succinctly in a marginal note he wrote in 1798:

> Prophets in the modern sense of the word have never existed. Jonah was no prophet, in the modern sense, for his prophecy of Nineveh failed. Every honest man is a Prophet; he utters his opinion both of private & public matters. Thus: If you go on So, the result is So. He never says, such a thing shall happen let you do what you will. A Prophet is a Seer, not an Arbitrary Dictator (*Annotations to Watson*, K 392).

The prophecies lay bare the inner dynamic, of history and revolution, the potential for positive change that exists and the corruption of those impulses. It is no romantic dreaming, Blake's insight into social change is not that of the utopian. In *Europe A Prophecy* there is no naive expectation of the inevitable success of revolution, none of the optimism about revolution expressed in Coleridge's early "Religious Musings" written roughly contemporary with Blake's prophecies.[5] Indeed, quite the reverse. Throughout *Europe* there is recognition of the profound subversion of revolution and the multi-faceted forms of resistance to change, avoidance of reality, and temptation to delusion. Any revolutionary optimism that Blake may have harboured in the last decade of the eighteenth century is tempered by a need to plumb the complexities of the human personality and its succumbing to the "dark delusions" of the world in which religion and theology have all too often played their part. Europe, a continent which was to be briefly lit with the flame of revolution, is seen as sleepy and immune to this spirit of change. Milton in "On

---

[4] R. Lowth, *Lectures on the Sacred Poetry of the Hebrews* II (London, 1816) 85–6 (reprinted London: Routledge/Thoemmes Press, 1995).

[5] See J. Mee, *Dangerous Enthusiasm* (Oxford: OUP, 1991) 35ff., and Morton D. Paley, *The Apocalypse and the Romantic Imagination* (Oxford: OUP, 1999).

the Morning of Christ's Nativity" saw the incarnation as the moment when old errors were dispersed and the way of truth triumphed (a text probably alluded to in Blake's *Europe*).[6] Blake, in less sanguine vein, sees the coming of Christ as a moment which in reaction increased rather than diminished the power of the pagan deities and the false religion and culture they encouraged.[7] Europe is entangled in a religion and an ethic which made it impervious to revolutionary change, a dreamy world cut off from reality. Revolution would only produce "the strife of blood" not the bliss of Paradise. The coming of Christ heralds not only the blissful salvation of the Lamb but the wrath of the "Tyger", to use Blake's contrasting images in *Songs of Innocence and Experience*. This parallels the awesome consequences of the exaltation of the Lamb in Rev 5–8 which results in the cataclysmic apocalypse described in the following chapters.

There is a similar juxtaposition in the opening of Paul's letter to the Romans (1:17–18) where gospel and judgement go hand in hand. The righteousness of God in the gospel provokes wrath from heaven, just as in Rev 6 the taking of the sealed book by the Lamb provokes not eschatological bliss but the Four Horsemen of the Apocalypse. Blake wrestles with an issue which runs like a thread through early Christian literature: the delay of, and resistance to, the messianic kingdom.[8] Resistance to the gospel pervades the New Testament, epitomised by the repeated use of Isa 6:9. Only a few dimly perceive what is going on as the cares and priorities of the world choke the growth of the Kingdom of God. For the majority, things which might provoke a change of perspective are just enigmatic parables (Mark 4:12). Those who perceive the mystery of the kingdom of God have need of patient endurance in face of the tribulation. Indeed, those who are called to be the prophets may have to wash their robes and "make them white in the blood of the Lamb" (Rev 7:14), or, in the closing words of Blake's *Europe* endure "the strife of blood" in the face of persistent delusion and reaction (plate 15). The prophet must speak, but it is no privileged role, for, as Blake's Isaiah puts it in *The Marriage of Heaven and Hell* 12, "the voice of honest indig-

---

[6] See L. Tannenbaum, *Biblical Tradition in Blake's Early Prophecies: The Great Code of Art* (Princeton, 1982) 168, and M.J. Tolley, "Europe to those ychaind in sleep", in D. Erdman and J. Grant, *Blake's Visionary Forms Dramatic* (Princeton, 1970).

[7] Tannenbaum, *Biblical Tradition*, 168–9.

[8] Tannenbaum, *Biblical Tradition*, 153.

nation" [which] is the voice of God, who cares "not for consequences but wrote", echoing Jeremiah's words in Jer 20:9.

The Vision of God

In *Europe*, in particular, Blake explores the extent of human delusion and the forgetfulness of the practice of love and the forgiveness of sins among a populace bound by the "mind forg'd manacles", to quote the highly suggestive word of "London" (from *Songs of Experience*). A similar pessimism with regard to human society is evident in an ancient Jewish text, a translation of which was published in English towards the end of Blake's life. The *Apocalypse of Enoch*, brought back from Ethiopia where it had been preserved by the Ethiopian Church, was first published at the beginning of the nineteenth century. It is a book which has fascinated and tantalised biblical scholars ever since because of the many similarities with passages in the gospels, particularly the references to the Son of man, and many commentators have suggested that Jesus and the earliest Christians may have drawn on it. Blake left illustrations for it incomplete at his death in 1827 (though he may have been aware of the book and had access to excerpts of translations from it years before).[9] One can understand why this enigmatic work should have fascinated Blake. It is a visionary work full of the mythological approach to the world, which characterizes much of Blake's poetry. Its doctrine of the origin of human sin, in contrast with that in Genesis, ascribes the primal sin to the illicit communication of wisdom which corrupts humanity (*1 Enoch* 6–18 parallel to Gen 6).[10] Angels teach humanity charms and spells and the art of warfare. The result is, as *1 Enoch* puts it, that "the world was profoundly changed". In consequence judgement comes on those who had revealed illicit wisdom and on those who had colluded with them. Enoch, who is considered a prophet in the NT Letter of Jude, is commissioned to intercede between God and the angels (*1 Enoch* 12:1). He appears as a mysterious figure standing on the boundary between angels and humans with access to divine secrets, a "steward of the mysteries of God" (1 Cor 4:1), a situation not unlike that in which Blake found himself.

---

[9] J. Beer "Blake's Changing View of History: the Impact of the Book of Enoch", in S. Clark and D. Worrall, *Historicizing Blake* (Basingstoke: Macmillan, 1994) 159ff. On the importance of 4 Ezra or 2 Esdras also for the exponents of radical Christianity, see A. Hamilton, *Apocryphal Apocalypse* (Oxford: OUP, 1999).

[10] M. Barker, *The Older Testament* (London: SPCK, 1987).

Among the unfinished sketches there is one of *1 Enoch* 14:8ff., a chapter which has exercised the minds of students of Second Temple Judaism, because it offers an extended description of the vision of God, the Great Glory, enthroned in the inmost recesses of the heavenly Temple. *1 Enoch* 14 is full of imagery borrowed from Ezek 1, itself a chapter which became the basis for later visionaries to glimpse again the awesome vision which had appeared to the prophet by the waters of Babylon.

In Rev 5 the conventional imagery of the divine throne and its environs, familiar to us from contemporary Jewish texts, is extended to include the presentation of a Lamb which then shares the divine throne and becomes the agent of the opening of eschatological mysteries. In the light of the overwhelming vision of Rev 1 where John sees Christ as an angelic figure, one like a son of man, we might have expected that divine figure also in ch. 5 to have appeared as the suppliant before the divine throne. Instead, Christ is represented as a Lamb. And it is this symbol which is used throughout the apocalypse. It is "a Lamb standing as if it had been slaughtered" who comes to share the divine throne and opens the seals which led to the descent of the new Jerusalem in Rev 21. Until then the divine throne is set in heaven. In Rev 4 the vision of God is of a transcendent deity far removed behind the firmament in heaven accessible only to angels and seers like John. When at last the New Jerusalem comes, the remote God descends to earth with the Lamb, and the boundary between God and humanity is removed; God becomes all in all, and wipes tears from every eye; then sorrow and sighing shall be no more. The Lamb's sharing of the divine throne changes the relationship between heaven and earth, God and humanity. Apocalyptic conventions are shattered as the understanding of the course of history and God's relationship with it are re-described.

The first chapter of Ezekiel exercised Blake's imagination and was the inspiration of his poem *The Four Zoas* or *Vala*. In addition he captures the vision in visual form in his picture "Ezekiel's Wheels". What is striking about this picture is the prominence of the human figure among the four creatures (man, lion, ox and eagle) which surround the divine throne-chariot. In Jewish midrashim (e.g. *B*ᵉ*reshith Rabbah* 47.6; 69.3; 82.6; Targumim on Gen. 28:12; and *The Prayer of Joseph*) the figure of a man was linked with ancestors like Jacob or Abraham, and in early Christian use of this passage the human figure was linked with Christ (John 12:41; Justin, *Dialogue* 126). Ezek 1 lies at the basis of John's vision in Rev 4–5 also. Blake painted this in his "Four and Twenty Elders" in which we have an evocation of both Rev 4 & 5.

The narrative of the transformation of divine monarchy begun in Rev 5 and completed with the vision of the new Jerusalem come down from heaven in some ways anticipates Blake's caricature of the monarchical law-giver and the need for an understanding of God which is less abstract and remote. Blake ruthlessly parodies the remote deity found in Plate 11 from *Europe*, with his "brazen Book That Kings and Priests had copied on Earth, Expanded from North to South". Here the grim law-giver appears with his forbidding book of brass. It is that kind of theology which Blake repeatedly challenges, nowhere better demonstrated than in the paintings and engravings of his "Job" sequence.[11] The one enthroned is the power which holds humanity in thrall through a religion of law. It is the stern words "Thou shalt not" which determine life rather than mutual forgiveness. This is characteristic of the religion of Europe, dominated by a remote deity, too exalted to wipe tears from eyes. For Blake the worship of God involves a recognition of God not as remote divinity, such as he captured so tellingly in his "Ancient of Days" which forms part of the preface to *Europe A Prophecy*, but in the person of other men and women who embody the divine image: "The worship of God is: Honouring his gifts in other men each according to his genius" . . . (*The Marriage of Heaven and Hell* 22).

It is clear that John's apocalyptic vision is a central component of many aspects of Blake's visionary world and also informs his understanding of his own political situation. As he put it in 1798 in his annotations to his copy of Bishop Watson's "Apology for the Bible", "To defend the Bible in this year 1798 would cost a man his life. The Beast and the Whore rule without control" (K 383). Indeed, Blake explicitly traces a continuity between his own mythical world and the vision seen by John, as he makes clear at the conclusion of the Eighth Night of *The Four Zoas*: "Rahab triumphs over all; she took Jerusalem Captive, a Willing Captive, by delusive arts impell'd To worship Urizen's Dragon form, to offer her own Children Upon the bloody Altar. John saw these things Reveal'd in Heaven

---

[11] William Blake, *Blake's Illustrations for the Book of Job* (New York: Dover, 1995), cf. Book of Urizen 4 where the book of brass concerns "one King, one God one Law".

On Patmos Isle, and heard the souls cry out to be deliver'd. He saw
the Harlot of the Kings of Earth, and saw her Cup Of fornication,
food of Orc & Satan, pressd from the fruit of Mystery" (*Four Zoas*
8.597ff.). Nevertheless, as is evident from the previous quotation,
Blake's use of the Apocalypse represents a visionary continuity with
the text rather than a commentary or analysis of it. He stands in
the prophetic tradition of which John of Patmos also is a part, whose
honest indignation might enable humans to see that "every kindness
to another is a little death In the Divine Image, nor can Man exist
but by Brotherhood" (*Jerusalem* 96.28).

The Old and New Testaments

Blake described "the Old and New Testaments as "the great code
of art" (Laocoön K 775). Yet in his work he offers a radical critique of aspects of Old Testament religion, particularly of law and
sacrifice. His is an ambivalent relationship with the Old Testament.
At first sight his portrayal of the law-giving deity, called in his peculiar mythology Urizen (or Your-Reason) seems to be the Old Testament
deity in Satanic guise (as is particularly evident in his illustration to
Job 7:14), a throw-back to some second century gnostic theology.
Blake, however, uses his stark contrasts between the religion of the
Old and New Testament as a heuristic device to illuminate the antin-
omies in the human personality and the way society exploits a religion of law to deny imagination and mutual forgiveness. With this
aim, Blake probes the fissures in the depiction of God within the
narrative of Genesis,[12] partly to challenge dominant readings of the
Bible of his day, in which appeal to an authoritative book was used
to inculcate a particular form of moral virtue. Blake, heir to Protestant
radical writing in England of an antinomian kind,[13] considered a
religion based on rules, contrary to the religion of Jesus. In *The
Marriage of Heaven and Hell* Jesus exemplifies the protest against the
religion of rules:

---

[12] Blake exploited the Yahweh/Elohim distinctions long before the source-critical
solutions of the Pentateuch became fashionable and was probably indebted to the
source criticism of Alexander Geddes; see Mee, *Dangerous Enthusiam*, 165ff.

[13] E.P. Thompson, *Witness against the Beast. William Blake and the Moral Law*
(Cambridge: CUP, 1993); C. Hill, *The World Turned Upside Down* (London: Penguin,
1972); J.F. McGregor and B. Reay, *Radical Religion in the English Revolution* (Oxford:
OUP, 1984).

.... did he not mock at the sabbath, and so mock the sabbath's God? .... turn away the law from the woman taken in adultery? steal the labour of others to support him? bear false witness when he omitted making a defence before Pilate? covet when he pray'd for his disciples, and when he bid them shake off the dust from their feet against such as refused to lodge them? I tell you, no virtue can exist without breaking these ten commandments. Jesus was all virtue, and acted from impulse, not from rules (*Marriage of Heaven and Hell* 24).

Blake explores in his own myth-making the disjunctions and inconsistencies of the biblical text, much as Marcion, in a negative way, or even Origen in a much more positive way, did centuries before. In addition to his prophecies, Blake wrote books which parody the Pentateuch, particularly the account of creation. *The Book of Urizen* is the best example. Existing as it does in different versions, Blake wants to deny readers recourse to one authoritative text and, in a manner which has a very post-modern ring to it, challenges the notion of a hegemonic text. Blake subverts the elevation of scripture into a text which, in a transparent manner, could transmit a list of moral rules demanded of the believer.[14]

The critique of a religion of law, and the pre-eminence of the prophetic and the visionary, both contribute to Blake's remarkable exegesis of the book of Job, a project he completed only shortly before his death. We are assisted in understanding the theological significance of Blake's images of Job by virtue of the fact that, in addition to the watercolours, we have the later engravings in which he comments on what he has portrayed by reference to biblical passages.[15] For Blake, Job is like the "Lutheran Paul" who converts from book religion to the immediacy of vision. The religion of law and

---

[14] J.L. McGann quoted in J. Mee, *Dangerous Enthusiasm*, 16. See further David Parker, *The Living Text of the Gospels* (Cambridge: CUP, 1997).

[15] Passages portrayed in the Job sequence: **1:1** (Matt 6:9; 2 Cor 3:6); **1:6** (Dan 7:9; מלאך יהוה "angel of the presence"; Job 19:26; Ps 89:26; "we shall wake up in thy likeness"); **1:15–19** (Job 2:2); **1:13** (Job 1:12); **2:7** (Satan going forth from presence of Lord, Job 2:6; 30:25; Ps 104:4); **2:7** (Satan smiting Job, Job 1:21); **2:12** (James 5:11); **3:3** (Job 2:12; 3:7); **4:15** (Job 4:17–18); **7:14** (Job 19:22ff.; 20:5; 30:17; 30:30; 2 Cor 11:14; 2 Thess 2:4); **19:21** (Job 14:1; 12:4; 13:15; 23:10); **32:6** (Job 33:14f.; 33:23, 24; 34:21; 35:5,6); **38:1f.** (Job 38:28; Ps 104:3); **38:7** (38:31; Gen 1); **40:15f.** (Job 36:29; 37:11; 41:34); **the Fall of Satan** (Job 36:17; 11:8; 26:6; 11:7; Rev 12:10; John 12:31; Luke 10:17–18; 1 Cor 1:26); **the Vision of Christ** (Job 42:5; 1 Sam 2:6; 1 John 3:2; Ps 8:3f; John 10:30; 14:7, 9, 10, 16, 17, 21, 23); **42:8, 10** (Matt 5:44ff.); **42:11** (1 Sam 2:7; Job 38:41; Ps 136:23); **42:12ff.** (Rev 15:3; Ps. 51:16); **42:15** (Ps 139:8, 17; *Testament of Job* 46ff.).

sacrifice is diabolical (we may note the contrast between Job sacrificing and praying in 1:5 and 42:8). The remote god of that kind of religion needs to be dethroned thereby enabling the annihilation of "the selfhood of deceit and false forgiveness" (Blake, *Milton*, 15). Job's conversion comes about as the result of visionary insight. Elihu bears witness to the importance of the visionary as a means of true understanding of God, anticipating the vision of God to Job, and the function of the Elihu sequence is seen as a precursor of the dramatic revelation to Job. The vision of God in the whirlwind is interpreted christologically as a vision of Jesus Christ (similarly also in the New Testament in John 14:8, the latter passage actually being quoted in Blake's engraving). Blake not only reads in his own interpretative agenda into the text of Job but brilliantly exploits the space offered by a text which is "not too explicit" to read the book of Job as an account of a conversion not, as most modern commentators have done, as a profound disquisition about the problem of evil, a reading which has to ignore significant parts of this enigmatic text.[16] Blake's concern throughout the illustrations is to challenge the monarchical transcendent god of church and state and to stress the prominence which is to be given to the visionary element in religion. Job starts as an adherent of a religion of the letter who is overwhelmed by apocalypse and converted to a religion of the spirit.

The tensions between Old Testament and New, the Law and Christ, and between the authoritative moral code and the inward promptings of the spirit within are an important part of Pauline theology also. Indeed, Blake's views on the Law parallel many of Paul's more polemical utterances, particularly those in the letter to the Galatians, where the antagonism to the Law of Moses is at its height. But Romans and 1 Corinthians also exhibit the fault-line between the novelty of the new revelation and internal spiritual freedom on the one hand and the pressure for an external code of moral virtue to enforce communal conformity on the other.

Paul's language about his own and human existence reflects a

---

[16] William Blake, *Blake's Illustrations for the Book of Job*; M. Butlin, *The Paintings and Drawings of William Blake* (New Haven: Yale University, 1981); K. Raine, *The Human Face of God: Blake and the Book of Job* (London: Thames and Hudson, 1982); K. Raine, *Golgonooza City of Imagination: Last Studies in William Blake* (Ipswich: Golgonooza, 1991), especially pp. 121ff. on Job; H. Fisch, *The Biblical Presence in Shakespeare, Milton and Blake* (Oxford: OUP, 1999).

sense of fragmentation of human identity and a longing for the overcoming of divisions in the human person. The tension between
different parts of the human person comes to the fore most obviously in Rom 7, where the body of death, from which he longs for
release, is the site of a struggle between the law of God and another,
demonic, law. The Paul of Romans cannot bring himself to deny
the importance of law (Rom 7:16) and yet he sees the emergence
of another law which is at odds with the law of God. Paul cries out
at the end of Rom 7 "who will rescue me from the body of death?"
The spectre of the other law standing over against what the "inner
person" most desires is the object of Paul's critique, just as the
Urizenic religion of repression and moral virtue is for Blake. In *Milton*
Blake writes of the annihilation of selfhood (*Jerusalem* 45.13; *Milton*
17.3) which encourages a perverted religion of "laws of chastity and
sacrifice for sin" (*Jerusalem* 49.24).[17] In plate 15 of *Milton* the ancient
code is finally fractured[18] as the Urizenic figure is confronted by a
man to be redeemed under the caption "to annihilate the selfhood
of deceit and false forgiveness". It is surrounded with minstrels suggesting rejoicing: "there is joy among the angels in heaven over one
sinner who repents" (Luke 15:25 and Exod 15:20).

Blake's depiction of Milton in *Milton*, belatedly redeemed, presupposes a doctrine reminiscent of that in the letter to the Colossians.
Here we have one of the best examples of the way in which redemption from the religion of law is tied up with "putting off the body
of flesh". In Col 2:11f. (cf. Rom 6:1ff.) the putting off of the body of
flesh is closely linked with a new perspective on, and new way of,
life.[19] This was a doctrine which was taken further in gnostic texts
like the *Epistle to Rheginos on the Resurrection* ("do not live in conformity with the flesh, for the sake of unanimity, but flee from the division and the fetters and you already have resurrection"). In the
soteriology worked out Blake rejects sacrificial religion, which involves
the denial of prophetic inspiration and the bondage of ceremonial

---

[17] *Milton a Poem* (Blake's Illuminated Books 5; ed. R.N. Essick and J. Viscomi;
London: Blake Society/Tate Gallery, 1993) 12.
[18] The Hebrew letters on the tablets of stone make no sense, apart from תוהו
suggesting chaos. Elsewhere blots and smudges are found in the picture of *Book of
Urizen* 4, indicating that this book of brass really made no sense.
[19] Cf. T. Gorringe, *Redeeming the Time. Atonement through Education* (London: Darton,
Longman and Todd, 1986); C. Elliott, *Memory and Salvation* (London: Darton Longman,
and Todd, 1995), esp. pp. 175ff.

law (*Book of Ahania* 4; K 252).[20] A religion of sacrifice and law, is, in Blake's view, a throwback to Canaanite theology which contaminated Israel when it entered the promised land. It is sacrificial religion which Blake, by his own inspired re-reading of Milton, seeks to expunge from the writing of his predecessor, much as New Testament writers sought to reclaim and redeem their literary ancestors in their formulation of their new redemptive vision.

Blake and the Protestant radicals would have echoed the extraordinary language of 1 Cor 2:11ff. Here Paul claims that life in the Spirit enables the truly spiritual person to have the mind of Christ and to understand the things of God. There is no need for an external code. And yet in the second half of 1 Corinthians that is precisely what Paul seems to offer in the apostolic counsel. The contrast which exists say in Romans and 1 Corinthians between the life of those guided by the Spirit within and the lists of instructions is striking. While Blake would have understood the sentiments of 1 Cor 2, the second half of 1 Corinthians suggests the spectre of the return of what Blake calls the "web of religion", the authoritarian religion of rules and memory, which has enslaved humanity, and so graphically evoked in these words from *Europe*, "over the doors Thou shalt not; and over the chimneys fear is written" (*Europe*, 12). Just as the relationship between Law and Gospel is a refrain in Paul's major letters, so throughout Blake's writing there is a probing of the relationship between the law-giver and the divine mercy, as well as the rational and the imaginative. While *The Marriage of Heaven and Hell* suggests that by temperament Blake sided with the prophetic, the hope expressed in Blake's *Jerusalem* is for an eschatological integration of imagination and reason when true prophetic religion would be linked with the philosophical and scientific rationalism of Newton, Bacon and Locke, that trinity whose baleful influence, in Blake's view, epitomised the triumph of reason over imagination in the society of his day.

Milton and Blake

Blake was a creative, imaginative interpreter not a detailed exegete. He took earlier texts, whether biblical or otherwise, and allowed them to become part of his mental furniture and imaginative world.

---

[20] Tannenbaum, *Biblical Tradition*, pp. 233ff.

For him any re-reading of an authoritative text is a creative process.[21] This is exemplified in Blake's *Milton*. In this poem the living poet (Blake) takes up and reformulates the work of a deceased predecessor,[22] thereby through this second act of creativity to redeem the inadequacies of Milton's writing and life. *Milton* is in part a critique by Blake of the turn taken by the seventeenth century poet to a religion of rules. But it is also a moment of inspired recapitulation in which the later poet redeems the earlier's work, initiated when Blake sees Milton's spirit enter into his left foot (*Milton* 14.49f.).[23]

In *Milton*, there is confusion of identity between the writer and the ancient poet. The way in which the latter's artistic and personal redemption is effected has overlaps with themes in biblical texts where successors take up, take further, refine or even alter the work of a predecessor. Blake's relationship with Milton is a "tandem relationship" similar to those scattered throughout the Bible, whereby the persona or charisma of one is carried on and transformed in new situations. One thinks of Elijah and Elisha, of John the Baptist and Jesus, and of Jesus and the Spirit-Paraclete. Elisha asks Elijah to give him a double portion of his spirit (2 Kings 2:9). In the case of Blake and Milton, however, the successor is more important than the predecessor and corrects the work of the earlier poet.

One wonders whether the phenomenon of pseudepigraphy may be explained in some such way? We find several written ancient Jewish and early Christian texts written in the name of, and in the light of the experiences of, biblical figures like Enoch, Ezra, Abraham or Isaiah. This phenomenon has been the subject of much debate. We do not know whether it was a deliberate attempt to deceive readers, or whether it reflects beliefs among late Second Temple writers that they were in some sense writing in the spirit of, or even correcting, the ideas of, their ancestors in the faith. That this last may have been the case has been suggested by a modern writer on

---

[21] P. Ricoeur, "Preface to Bultmann", in *Essays on Biblical Interpretation* (London: SCM, 1981) 51.

[22] *Milton a Poem* (n. 17 above) 12: "It is an existence Blake wished to overcome and replace with a more fluid and open concept of being where the gulf between self and other is bridged—indeed, annihilated."

[23] There is a parallel depiction of Blake's deceased brother Robert's moment of prophetic inspiration. Robert does not appear in the text but his role as an inspired prophet poet alongside William is clearly important. Robert died in 1787 but William said that he conversed with him daily, "saw him in his imagination and wrote at his dictate" (K 797).

early Jewish mysticism. David Halperin has written of the ancient Jewish apocalyptists and mystics in their appropriation of the book of Ezekiel as those who "see something. . . . as it really was, as (the prophet) should have seen it, had he been inspired wholly and not in part".[24] This is similar to what we find Blake doing with Milton.

There is possibly something similar going on in Paul's relationship with Jesus. As an apostle of Jesus Christ Paul was not merely an agent but also an embodiment of Christ as the result of the indwelling Spirit: "it is no longer I who live but Christ who lives in me" (Gal 2:20). His person is not found solely in his corporeal presence, for, as 1 Cor 5:4 indicates, Paul is able "in spirit" to be with a community assembled "in the name of the Lord Jesus". Of course, unlike Blake, Paul did not think of his apostolic vocation as a correction of the ministry of Christ (though one wonders whether the kind of freedom Paul feels able to manifest in 1 Cor 9:14f. to ignore the command of Jesus may be coming close to this). There is, however, continuation of identity, a reproduction in new circumstances of the dying Jesus, even a completion of the vicarious effects of his sufferings: "in my flesh I am completing what is lacking in Christ's afflictions for the sake of his body, that is the church" (Col 1:24).

II

What I have attempted in the first part of this essay is to take themes which I hope illustrate aspects of Blake's distinctive use of the Bible and suggest places where the juxtaposition of Blake's work and the Bible might be mutually illuminating. In my final section I want to look at the way in which Blake continues to offer readers a means whereby the imagination may itself be stimulated and assumptions challenged.

The World of Imagination

For Blake the visionary and imaginative is all important. Allowing reason to triumph over imagination denies a wisdom "Permanent in the Imagination", through which one could be "open [to] the Eternal

---

[24] D. Halperin, *Faces of the Chariot* (Tübingen: Mohr, 1988) 71.

Worlds". Such access would be "to open the immortal Eyes Of Man inwards into the Worlds of Thought, into Eternity Ever expanding in the Bosom of God, the Human Imagination" (*Jerusalem* 5.18). A "mental fight" is required to gain access to that other perspective on existence, particularly given the dominant ideology which militates against at it. This perspective can at once be a refuge and a resource for thinking and doing things differently. It is imperative that this is done, for, as Blake's prophetic hero Los at the beginning of *Jerusalem* asserts, "I must Create a System or be enslav'd by another Man's. I will not Reason and Compare: my Business is to Create" (*Jerusalem* 10.20). It is only by the suspension of what counts for normality that humanity may glimpse how "the dark Religions are departed and sweet Science reign" (*Four Zoas* End of Night the Ninth).[25]

So Blake invokes the exercise of the imagination. The vocation of readers of the Bible is to become participants in mental agony which may confound and entices from habit and convention,[26] which stand like a closed door preventing access to that which is eternal. There is need for a hermeneutical conversion reminiscent of Paul's suggestion that what is required is not a preoccupation with the letter which kills (2 Cor 3:6) but the Spirit who offers freedom and life (3:16). Readers are called like John in Rev 4 to "come up here, to go through an open door, and I will show you what must take place". Indeed, the use of the door as an image of insight or incomprehension in several prints e.g. *Jerusalem* frontispiece, *America Songs of Experience* "London", and *Jerusalem* 84. In "London" and *Jerusalem* the old man (a symbol, perhaps, of the ancient deity and a tired culture) is led by a child. Blake's use of the child leading the old man, reminiscent of the use made by Jesus in Matt 18 and 19, suggests that innate wisdom may need to guide the wisdom of experience and mere rote learning, to new and more wonderful insights. In a letter (Trusler K 793f.), Blake suggests that "a great majority of [children] are on the side of imagination or spiritual sensation" and "take a greater delight in contemplating my pictures than I ever hoped".[27]

---

[25] Cf. the suggestive words of Theodor Adorno, "Perspectives" are "fashioned that displace and estrange the world, reveal it to be, with its rifts and crevices, as indigent and distorted as it will appear one day in the messianic light", *Minima Moralia* (London: Verso, 1985) 247.

[26] On this see N. Frye, *Fearful Symmetry* (Princeton: Princeton University, 1947) 3ff.

[27] Children also appear in the two "Holy Thursday" poems in *Songs of Innocence and Experience*, where Blake uses the images of the Apocalypse as a way of viewing

Reading some of Blake's poems presents formidable problems for interpreters, particularly so with the illuminated books where the process of reading is complicated by the engagement with the visual images (the opening of *Europe A Prophecy* is a good example where text and illustration seem to have nothing to do with one another). Readings of the text must be set in the context of the illuminations. Here the problems start, for text and illumination seem to have little contact. We tend to link what we see with what we read. An early commentator (A. Swinburne, *William Blake: A Critical Essay*) wrote with regard to the opening page of *Europe* "the amount of connection between the texts and the designs. . . . [is]. . . . in effect about as small as possible". As the poem goes on in both writing and illumination there is oscillation between the historical and the mythological with the boundaries between the two remaining constantly vague as Blake exemplifies the abrupt transitions from heaven to earth which Lowth said were so typical of prophetic writings. The readers/beholders of Blake's illuminated text find themselves disconcerted, without a stable means of interpreting.[28] The indeterminate relationship between writing and illustration demands that readers engage with the text, and their own imagination contributes to making sense of the two.[29] There is no escape for the reader who is throughout encouraged to "rouze the faculties to act" in order to find meaning in what is very deliberately "not too explicit" (K 793). Blake wishes to do all he can to resist the idea that there is an authoritative interpretation offered by authoritative interpreters. His texts are there for all to use and to have their own imaginations stimulated.

What is striking about some Blake criticism that I have read is the intensive investigation of the popular culture of the late eighteenth century[30] which has enabled one to see that Blake was not totally isolated and idiosyncratic. We can chart some of the background to his prophecy.[31] What is of interest to students of the Bible with fewer

---

contrasting scenes in contemporary London: see C. Rowland, "'Rouzing the faculties to act': Apocalypse and the 'Holy Thursday' Poems", in S. Brent Plate, ed., *The Apocalyptic Imagination: Aesthetics and Ethics at the End of the World* (Glasgow: Trinity St Mungo, 1999) 26–36.

[28] *The Continental Prophecies* (Blake's Illuminated Books 4; ed. D.W. Dörrbecker; London: Blake Society/Tate Gallery, 1995) 153.

[29] H. Glen, *Vision and Disenchantment* (Cambridge: CUP, 1983), esp. 71.

[30] E.g. J. Mee, *Dangerous Enthusiasm*, and also on the prophetic context S. Goldsmith, *Unbuilding Jerusalem* (Ithaca: Cornell University, 1993).

[31] See D.V. Erdman, *Blake. Prophet against Empire* (Princeton: Princeton University, 1977).

historical resources at their disposal is that, with the range of materials available to the interpreter of Blake, we can gain some insight
into the way in which the prophet wove the myth out of the social
and political conditions of the day. Nevertheless, in the fascinating
quest for historical referents in the poetry and pictures, there lurks
a danger that interpretation will become the elucidation of elaborate ciphers, comprehensible only to those who know the peculiari-
ties of a fearful late eighteenth and early nineteenth century England.
Blake's works demand the use of the language of imagination as a
gateway, a hermeneutical device which opens up eternity and is not
to be reduced or translated, so that its peculiar hermeneutical properties are to be made ineffective. The same is true of the elaborate
historical reconstructions of the social and religious life behind the
biblical texts.[32] In Blake's works and in the Apocalypse also biblical
texts have become part of, and transmuted into, the prophet's visionary world. In Revelation, for example, recollections of events have
infused the visionary's imagination and become part of the apparatus of the symbolic world. Their original historical and contextual
significance is transcended and ceases to determine the import they
have within the framework of the prophecy as a whole. The Blakean
myth, drawing on an array of contemporary ideas, demands of the
reader not some explanatory key so much as the imaginative participation, to explore the tensions and problems that the text poses,
for "to the eyes of the man of imagination, nature [can be] imagination itself" (K 794). With eyes attuned we may perceive "visions
of eternity . . . [but] we only see as it were the hem of their garments when with our vegetable eyes we view these wondrous visions"
(*Milton* 26.10). So "The Old and New Testaments as the Great Code
of Art" (Laocoön K 777), are just the most symptomatic form of
art which can, with proper use, open up the way to the eternal and
thereby link the divine and humanity, pervaded as it is with divine
imagination, however dulled the sense of it might be. Why, writes
Blake, "is the Bible more Entertaining & Instructive than any other
book? Is it not because they [sic] are addressed as to the Imagination,
which is Spiritual Sensation and but mediately to the understanding
or reason" (Letter to Trusler K 794).

---

[32] Recognised by Mee, *Dangerous Enthusiasm*, 2, who employs a historical exegetical approach to Blake.

An essay on Blake may at first sight seem out of place in a collection of this kind, intended for the New Testament exegete. Indeed, the study of Blake's writing has been more the preserve of literary critics than theologians. But should this remain so, particularly for those interested in the apocalyptic tradition? In the Blake corpus, by common consent, we have a visionary, saturated in the Bible and inventive in the way in which he seeks to release the Bible from the hegemonic discourses of his day. His work presents peculiar, and at times formidable, problems of interpretation and epitomises the difficulty of assessing the interplay between tradition and innovation which has been such a central feature of much New Testament theology. Blake's later works seem to represent a retreat from politics, mirroring in some ways the process which is said to have been at work in early Christianity as the initial messianism became more spiritual and was routinised into something which was more permanent. Blake's strategy of retreat into concentration on individual renewal in the last years of his life, dominated as they were by conservative politics in church and state, may be seen as the only way to talk about politics in perilous times. They were the necessary means by which he could illuminate the complexities of life and the demands and insight that discipleship brought. It is no accident that Blake prefaced his most complicated text, *The Four Zoas*, with a quotation from Eph 6:10, reflecting a dominant strand of early Christian experience where warfare is focused on the life of the spirit, albeit with the expectation that one would have to resist the earthly principalities and powers.

If we turn to a comparison of Blake's work with the themes of this book: Christology and controversy in the New Testament, we find that Blake continues a major strand of the New Testament and its history: the prophetic and the challenge to convention and above all the letter of the text. If Paul's letters have become part of the foundation of Christian theology, they have done so because they contain elements which encourage the conventional as well as supporting the validity of the prophetic and innovatively apostolic. In the last resort in the Pauline Corpus if utterances from prophetic personae differ from the authoritative apostle, they are to be questioned, an expedient with which Blake would not have been in agreement. We have seen, particularly in Blake's "Job" sequence, the way in which Blake takes up the Pauline questioning of the preoccupation with the "letter that killeth" and suggests a way of being religious which is focused on divine immediacy rather than acceptance of the ancestral tradition. This echoes in particular the Paul of Galatians who emphasises experience in contrast with the Paul of the Pastoral Epistles who evinces a more typically rabbinic approach. The Paul of 1 Corinthians possibly takes a mediating position between these two poles.

In his Christology Blake is not greatly interested in the Christ of history. Like his radical English forbear, Gerrard Winstanley, what is important is the present Christ, the divine image which empowers the Christ-like prophetic voice and is latent within "heathen turk and jew" ("The Divine Image", *Songs of Innocence*). It is the present, indwelling, Christ of prophecy and imagination that is all-important. That kind of "actualisation" of christological language in which the narrative paradigms of the past beckon the reader to "act them out" now in the present is one that is familiar to Paul and exemplifies his distinctive apostolic consciousness. Indeed, on rare occasions Paul could describe himself (Gal 2:20; cf. Gal 1:16) and Christians (Rom 8:10) as being indwelt by Christ.[33] The divine messiah/Son of God now permeates the being of his apostle and informs his life and words. Paul sees himself as so closely identified with the crucified Christ, that he can write of bearing his death in his body (2 Cor 4:10; cf. Gal 6:14) or the tribulations of Christ which are something which the apostle shares and fills up what is lacking (Col 1:24). There is a particularly close relationship between the Christ and his apostle. Whether in the person of the apostle, one of his co-workers, or through letter, the Christ confronts congregations (Rom 15:14–29; 1 Cor 4:14–21; 1 Cor 5:3–5; Phil 2:12). So Paul is not just the imitator of Christ (1 Cor 11:1), therefore, looking back and seeking to emulate. He is more than that; he is an embodiment of the messiah (Gal 2:20), and his coming to the churches will be with power (1 Cor 4:19) and will bring blessing (Rom 15:29).[34] Like the Risen Christ who stands in the midst of his churches in Rev 1:13–17, the apostle of Christ comes as a threat and a promise: a threat to those who have lost their first love or exclude the messiah and his apostle; a promise of blessing at his coming for those who conquer.

This notion of the continuing embodiment of the person and sav-

---

[33] See C.F.D. Moule, *The Origin of Christology* (Cambridge: CUP, 1977) 56–69, where the contrast between Pauline and Johannine indwelling language is explored.
[34] R. Funk, "The Apostolic Parousia", in W.R. Farmer, C.F.D. Moule and R. Niebuhr, eds, *Christian History and Interpretation* (FS J. Knox; Cambridge: CUP, 1967).

ing work of the messiah is a particular feature of mystical religion
and is a feature of radical movements in Christian history. Here the
barrier between divine and human is broken down, as an individual or group becomes the bearer of the divine nature. The mediation of knowledge of the divine is not dependent on those with the
knowledge of the Scriptures or those who have been appointed to
be a religion's functionaries by their apprenticeship in the religious
traditions or their institutional power. It becomes available through
supernatural insight and the immediacy of revelation. God speaks
directly, and Scripture and tradition provide a secondary support for
insight obtained by other means. The important thing is to respond
to the prompting of the Spirit and to subordinate the letter to the
Spirit, a view expressed most clearly by Paul in 1 Cor 2:10–16 and
2 Cor 3. Perhaps the Corinthians whose views are castigated by a
more sober Paul glimpsed something of that transgression of the
bounds of normality in Paul and his workers and took him at his
word that they too could share in this privilege and did not need
an apostle to teach them wisdom. Typical of this radical approach
is a use of the tradition which refuses to be content with the letter
but pierces to the real meaning of the text. At times this attitude
may manifest itself as a rejection of the priority of Scripture and a
subordination of it to the inner understanding which comes through
the Spirit. Blake is an inheritor of these currents in Christianity, not
just from the seventeenth century Christian radicalism but from the
Bible itself. What emerges in Blake's work is a theological critique
of the hegemonic theology of his day which stressed the transcen-
dence of God and the subservience of ordinary believers to the dic-
tates of authoritative ecclesial exponents. Instead there is the underlining
of the words which he quotes immediately after the stanzas commonly known as "Jerusalem" which stand at the beginning of one
version of his *Milton*. Here the desire of Moses that all God's people should be prophets (in Num 11:29) is used in support of a protest
against a religion of excessive rationality and one which excludes
ordinary people from being open to the divine spirit of imagination
at work within them. Such elements concerning divine presence
abound in the New Testament but they are complemented with
an emphasis on future fulfilment which contributes to the New Testament's eschatological distinctiveness. Blake may exemplify the kind
of problems that emerged when individuals believed, as apparently
those at Corinth did, that they had already reached the messianic

CHRISTOPHER ROWLAND

kingdom and were reigning in it (if this is what is being hinted at in 1 Cor 4:8).

Blake would, I think, have frowned on an exegetical enterprise which meant that imagination was excluded and the way to eternity closed off as a result. He could, like his older contemporary Hermann Samuel Reimarus, the pioneer of the quest for the historical Jesus,[35] see Jesus as the leader of a revolution that seemed to fail (*Everlasting Gospel*). But in staying at the level of history one misses the significance of Jesus as an icon of human brotherhood, a trigger for the imagination. The Bible is not to be regarded solely as a history of past events, for "the Hebrew Bible and the Gospel of Jesus are . . . Eternal Vision or Imagination of all that exists" (*A Vision of the Last Judgement* K 604). We may be curious about the origin or meaning of symbols, perplexed by historical reference, and desirous of elucidation. Nevertheless the exegetical task involves reading, hearing, appropriating, in whatever way our faculties allow, and with whatever aids we need to break the "mind forg'd manacles", that discourse in which the conventions and wisdom of the age are passed on without question. Exegesis of the Bible needs must involve a variety of essays whose aim is to provide ways of "rousing the faculties", to offer ever new moments of unveiling, through images, metaphors, additional words or myths. If I look for analogies to Blake's exegesis, I turn to the enigmatic appropriations of Ezekiel's vision or the journeys through the heavenly palaces to the divine *merkabah* in those writings which come from those shadowy figures who stand at the beginning of the Jewish mystical tradition. Or in *The Spiritual Exercises of Ignatius of Loyola*, in which the reader is asked to place herself within the narrative, thereby in effect creating another story through the act of imaginative identification which has been set in train. Or in the typological and contextual appropriations of the basic ecclesial communities meeting in shanty towns in Brazil and other parts of the Third World.[36] All these seem to parallel in different ways Blake's use of the Bible.

The neglect of Blake by biblical exegetes and theologians is to the impoverishment of biblical study and theology. Not only is he a

---

[35] H.S. Reimarus, *Fragments* (Philadelphia: Fortress, 1970).
[36] See C. Rowland, *The Cambridge Companion to Liberation Theology* (Cambridge: CUP, 1999), especially pp. 109–152.

significant epitome of trends in religion at the beginning of the nine-teenth century, and is an example of the characteristics of radical Christianity,[37] but he also offers a well-documented source for an understanding of the confluence of the visionary and antinomian cur-rents and the distinctive hermeneutical perspective they offer. His myth-making and creative use of Scripture, filtered through personal experience and social upheaval, represents a unique opportunity for the interpreter to see how the visionary mind appropriates and trans-forms received traditions within a particular, and well-documented, social context. Blake was a visionary, saturated in the Bible and inventive in the way in which he seeks to liberate the Bible from the dominant patterns of interpretation of his day. His exegesis rep-resents a distinctive reformulation of the text, woven as it is into his own mythical world. His work presents peculiar, and at times for-midable, problems of exposition and epitomises the difficulty of assess-ing the interplay between tradition and innovation which has always been such a central feature of New Testament exegesis. He is one of the most biblically based, and prophetic, poets yet his poems are often only loosely related to the Bible, and reformulate the Bible in new ways leaving behind the determining character of their original context.[38] Mere repetition or even derivative exegesis of what was in the Bible was unable to wrest the Bible from the hands of those who misunderstood it and forged it into a system which supported the political and economic interests of the rulers of empire. A different perspective was needed to tell the story in language which might subvert a Bible in thraldom to dominant ways of interpreting. Blake's hermeneutical radicalism is, in a sense, already suggested by the Apocalypse itself, which is not a biblical interpretation but itself a reformulation of prophetic predecessors. Blake and John of Revelation

---

[37] I can see now that a section on Blake would have added weight to my thesis in *Radical Christianity* (Oxford: Polity, 1988). Many of the patterns of religion I dis-covered in radicals like Muentzer and Winstanley are apparent also in Blake's work.

[38] In this respect Blake's work represents a strong challenge to the work of writ-ers like Richard Hays (*Echoes of Scripture in the Letters of Paul* [New Haven, 1989], cf. S.P. Moyise *The Old Testament in the Book of Revelation* [Sheffield, 1995]) who argues that biblical context is carried over into the use of the Old Testament in the New Testament. Blake, I believe, like Paul uses the biblical language but as a vehicle for a new understanding of the divine message which may at times be at odds with the letter of the text (see further Rowland, "Revelation", *New Interpreter's Bible* 12 (Abingdon: Nashville, 1999).

present the symbols and myths of Scripture in a new visionary guise, much as Blake accomplished in his mythic writings which seek to revive their message and challenge the domestication that overcomes metaphorical texts. Blake's resort to Scripture and myth in his illuminated books are a means by which the complexities of life, and the insight into, and response to, the divine mystery could be expounded. They are, to paraphrase Blake's own words, examples of a "Poetry Unfetter'd" (*Jerusalem* 3); the purpose of both is, for Blake, above all, "to rouze [our] Faculties to act" (Letter to Trusler K 793).

INDEX OF BIBLICAL REFERENCES

INDEX OF MODERN AUTHORS CITED

SUPPLEMENTS TO NOVUM TESTAMENTUM

ISSN 0167-9732

2. Strobel, A. *Untersuchungen zum eschatologischen Verzögerungsproblem auf Grund der spätjüdische-urchristlichen Geschichte von Habakuk 2,2 ff.* 1961. ISBN 90 04 01582 5

16. Pfitzner, V.C. *Paul and the Agon Motif.* 1967. ISBN 90 04 01596 5

27. Mussies, G. *The Morphology of Koine Greek As Used in the Apocalypse of St. John.* A Study in Bilingualism. 1971. ISBN 90 04 02656 8

28. Aune, D.E. *The Cultic Setting of Realized Eschatology in Early Christianity.* 1972. ISBN 90 04 03341 6

29. Unnik, W.C. van. *Sparsa Collecta.* The Collected Essays of W.C. van Unnik Part 1. Evangelia, Paulina, Acta. 1973. ISBN 90 04 03660 1

31. Unnik, W.C. van. *Sparsa Collecta.* The Collected Essays of W.C. van Unnik Part 3. Patristica, Gnostica, Liturgica. 1983. ISBN 90 04 06262 9

34. Hagner, D.A. *The Use of the Old and New Testaments in Clement of Rome.* 1973. ISBN 90 04 03636 9

37. Reiling, J. *Hermas and Christian Prophecy.* A Study of The Eleventh Mandate. 1973. ISBN 90 04 03771 3

43. Clavier, H. *Les variétés de la pensée biblique et le problème de son unité.* Esquisse d'une théologie de la Bible sur les textes originaux et dans leur contexte historique. 1976. ISBN 90 04 04465 5

47. Baarda, T., A.F.J. Klijn & W.C. van Unnik (eds.) *Miscellanea Neotestamentica.* I. Studia ad Novum Testamentum Praesertim Pertinentia a Sociis Sodalicii Batavi c.n. Studiosorum Novi Testamenti Conventus Anno MCMLXXVI Quintum Lustrum Feliciter Complentis Suscepta. 1978. ISBN 90 04 05685 8

48. Baarda, T., A.F.J. Klijn & W.C. van Unnik (eds.) *Miscellanea Neotestamentica.* II. 1978. ISBN 90 04 05686 6

50. Bousset, D.W. *Religionsgeschichtliche Studien.* Aufsätze zur Religionsgeschichte des hellenistischen Zeitalters. Hrsg. von A.F. Verheule. 1979. ISBN 90 04 05845 1

52. Garland, D.E. *The Intention of Matthew 23.* 1979. ISBN 90 04 05912 1

53. Moxnes, H. *Theology in Conflict.* Studies in Paul's Understanding of God in Romans. 1980. ISBN 90 04 06140 1

56. Skarsaune, O. *The Proof From Prophecy.* A Study in Justin Martyr's Proof-Text Tradition: Text-type, Provenance, Theological Profile. 1987. ISBN 90 04 07468 6

59. Wilkins, M.J. *The Concept of Disciple in Matthew's Gospel, as Reflected in the Use of the Term 'Mathetes'.* 1988. ISBN 90 04 08689 7

64. Sterling, G.E. *Historiography and Self-Definition.* Josephos, Luke-Acts and Apologetic Historiography. 1992. ISBN 90 04 09501 2

65. Botha, J.E. *Jesus and the Samaritan Woman.* A Speech Act Reading of John 4:1-42. 1991. ISBN 90 04 09505 5

66. Kuck, D.W. *Judgment and Community Conflict.* Paul's Use of Apologetic Judgment Language in 1 Corinthians 3:5-4:5. 1992. ISBN 90 04 09510 1

67. Schneider, G. *Jesusüberlieferung und Christologie.* Neutestamentliche Aufsätze 1970-1990. 1992. ISBN 90 04 09555 1

68. Seifrid, M.A. *Justification by Faith.* The Origin and Development of a Central Pauline Theme. 1992. ISBN 90 04 09521 7

69. Newman, C.C. *Paul's Glory-Christology*. Tradition and Rhetoric. 1992.
ISBN 90 04 09463 6
70. Ireland, D.J. *Stewardship and the Kingdom of God*. An Historical, Exegetical, and Contextual Study of the Parable of the Unjust Steward in Luke 16: 1-13. 1992.
ISBN 90 04 09600 0
71. Elliott, J.K. *The Language and Style of the Gospel of Mark*. An Edition of C.H. Turner's "Notes on Marcan Usage" together with other comparable studies. 1993.
ISBN 90 04 09767 8
72. Chilton, B. *A Feast of Meanings*. Eucharistic Theologies from Jesus through Johannine Circles. 1994. ISBN 90 04 09949 2
73. Guthrie, G.H. *The Structure of Hebrews*. A Text-Linguistic Analysis. 1994.
ISBN 90 04 09866 6
74. Bormann, L., K. Del Tredici & A. Standhartinger (eds.) *Religious Propaganda and Missionary Competition in the New Testament World*. Essays Honoring Dieter Georgi.1994. ISBN 90 04 10049 0
75. Piper, R.A. (ed.) *The Gospel Behind the Gospels*. Current Studies on Q. 1995.
ISBN 90 04 09737 6
76. Pedersen, S. (ed.) *New Directions in Biblical Theology*. Papers of the Aarhus Conference, 16-19 September 1992. 1994. ISBN 90 04 10120 9
77. Jefford, C.N. (ed.) *The* Didache *in Context*. Essays on Its Text, History and Transmission. 1995. ISBN 90 04 10045 8
78. Bormann, L. *Philippi – Stadt und Christengemeinde zur Zeit des Paulus*. 1995.
ISBN 90 04 10232 9
79. Peterlin, D. *Paul's Letter to the Philippians in the Light of Disunity in the Church*. 1995.
ISBN 90 04 10305 8
80. Jones, I.H. *The Matthean Parables*. A Literary and Historical Commentary. 1995.
ISBN 90 04 10181 0
81. Glad, C.E. *Paul and Philodemus*. Adaptability in Epicurean and Early Christian Psychagogy. 1995 ISBN 90 04 10067 9
82. Fitzgerald, J.T. (ed.) *Friendship, Flattery, and Frankness of Speech*. Studies on Friendship in the New Testament World. 1996. ISBN 90 04 10454 2
83. Tilborg, S. van. *Reading John in Ephesus*. 1996. 90 04 10530 1
84. Holleman, J. *Resurrection and Parousia*. A Traditio-Historical Study of Paul's Eschatology in 1 Corinthians 15. 1996. ISBN 90 04 10597 2
85. Moritz, T. *A Profound Mystery*. The Use of the Old Testament in Ephesians. 1996.
ISBN 90 04 10556 5
86. Borgen, P. *Philo of Alexandria - An Exegete for His Time*. 1997. ISBN 90 04 10388 0
87. Zwiep, A.W. *The Ascension of the Messiah in Lukan Christology*. 1997.
ISBN 90 04 10897 1
88. Wilson, W.T. *The Hope of Glory*. Education and Exhortation in the Epistle to the Colossians. 1997. ISBN 90 04 10937 4
89. Peterson, W.L., J.S. Vos & H.J. de Jonge (eds.). *Sayings of Jesus: Canonical and Non-Canonical*. Essays in Honour of Tjitze Baarda. 1997. ISBN 90 04 10380 5
90. Malherbe, A.J., F.W. Norris & J.W. Thompson (eds.). *The Early Church in Its Context*. Essays in Honor of Everett Ferguson. 1998. ISBN 90 04 10832 7
91. Kirk, A. *The Composition of the Sayings Source*. Genre, Synchrony, and Wisdom Redaction in Q. 1998. ISBN 90 04 11085 2
92. Vorster, W.S. *Speaking of Jesus*. Essays on Biblical Language, Gospel Narrative and the Historical Jesus. Edited by J. E. Botha. 1999. ISBN 90 04 10779 7
93. Bauckham, R. *The Fate of Dead*. Studies on the Jewish and Christian Apocalypses. 1998. ISBN 90 04 11203 0

94. Standhartinger, A. *Studien zur Entstehungsgeschichte und Intention des Kolosserbriefs.* ISBN 90 04 11286 3 *(In preparation)*
95. Oegema, G.S. *Für Israel und die Völker.* Studien zum alttestamentlich-jüdischen Hintergrund der paulinischen Theologie. 1999. ISBN 90 04 11297 9
96. Albl, M.C. *"And Scripture Cannot Be Broken".* The Form and Function of the Early Christian *Testimonia* Collections. 1999. ISBN 90 04 11417 3
97. Ellis, E.E. *Christ and the Future in New Testament History.* 1999. ISBN 90 04 11533 1
98. Chilton, B. & C.A. Evans, (eds.) *James the Just and Christian Origins.* 1999. ISBN 90 04 11550 1
99. Horrell, D.G. & C.M. Tuckett (eds.) *Christology, Controversy and Community.* New Testament Essays in Honour of David R. Catchpole. 2000. ISBN 90 04 11679 6
100. Jackson-McCabe, M.A. *Logos and Law in the Letter of James.* The Law of Nature, the Law of Moses and the Law of Freedom. 2000. ISBN 90 04 11994 9 *(In preparation.)*